THE BOOK OF ANGELS
Dreams – Signs – Meditation

The Traditional Study of Angels

The Hidden Secrets

Kaya
Christiane Muller

universe/city Mikaël
NON-PROFIT ORGANIZATION

universe/city mikaël (ucm)
Non-profit organization
Publishing House
51-53, Saint-Antoine Street
Sainte-Agathe-des-Monts, QC
Canada J8C 2C4

Administrator: Jean Morissette, lawyer

Telephone: 514-351-7272
Business and Administration: 819-321-0072
Fax: 514-352-5272
Email: publishing@ucm.ca
Website: www.ucm.ca

English translation: Blànaid Rensch
Revision: Micheline Marcotte, Nicole Beaulieu, Joëlle Dussiaume, Josée Landry,
Josée Disario and Joanie Boux
Proofreading: Zozita Translations
Transcription, structuring and revision of original French version: Andrée Hamelin
Cover and illustrations by Gabriell, "The Book of Angels" Exposition Angelica
Photographer: M'Dean Mazboudi
Graphic designer: Ozalid Graphik

Legal deposit: 1st term 2008
National Library of Québec
National Library of Canada
ISBN-13: 978-2-923097-11-4
Printed in Canada

Printed on Rolland Enviro100, which contains 100% recycled post-consumer fibre, is EcoLogo,
Processed Chlorine Free and FSC Recycled certified and manufactured using biogas energy.

The reader will better understand the language
used in this volume if he bears in mind that,
apart from the introductory chapters,
this is an oral teaching.

Kaya

This book has been produced from excerpts
of lectures that my husband and I prepared
and that I presented to the public in several countries.
The love that unites us is the very breath of my words.

I invite you to discover our everyday life
as well as that of other people who are inspired
by this Ancient Path of Knowledge.

Christiane Muller

Note: To facilitate the reading, we have used the masculine
when referring to both males and females.

PREFACE

Preface by Blánaid Rensch

In this day and age of individualism, consumerism, materialism and fundamentalism, how wonderful it is to have been guided towards a practical philosophy that leads to spiritual autonomy, self-responsibility and the development of qualities, virtues and powers in their purest form.

For those of you who, like me, have been seeking a workable and easily-applicable spirituality, The Traditional Study of Angels is for you.

I rejected the rather rigid faith of my childhood. I read book after book and attended lecture after lecture. I thought I'd found what I was looking for only to feel disappointed after a while because the apparently perfect recipe hadn't made me a better person, nor had it brought me long-lasting happiness. I had the feeling I was going around in circles until I came across The Traditional Study of Angels and I went to one of Christiane's inspiring lectures.

There, I learned that repeating the name of an Angel (no, not a little winged cherub but a symbol of Divine, uplifting Energy and a Divine State of Conscience) would set off dreams. Those dreams would then guide my conscience and give deep meaning to my life. Eventually, they would set me on the long journey towards Enlightenment.

I decided to give it a try. Indeed, not only did I experience striking coincidences, but I also started dreaming frequently. The more I repeated the name of an Angel during the day, the more dreams I received at night. Noting down my dreams and studying them, while applying the logical and accessible language of symbols, I began to slowly see the sense of some of my dreams. I began to understand their message (some immediately, some after long meditation, while others still remain a mystery to me.) I finally began to see hitherto hidden and repressed parts of myself.

It's not always easy. It requires perseverance, self-discipline, effort and even courage, but it is clearly so instructive and enlightening that ever since that first encounter, I have been repeating the Names of the 72 Angels in order to gain access to information about myself, to help make the right decisions, to see my faults, flaws and distortions, to cleanse the distorted aspects that are revealed and to reinforce the qualitative aspect of that same distortion. The hope is that I shall one day truly transcend these distortions of mine and go on to develop pure qualities.

Oh! The happiness that comes from a better understanding of the Universe and our purpose here on Earth (the perfect school for us) is so fulfilling that the slightest task can become a source of joy because it is part of our Divine Work and a way of improving our soul, provided we make that our intention.

Our personal soul computer can be totally reprogrammed from our conscious reality, right down to our deepest unconsciousness, which is revealed to us through dreams, symbols, synchronicities and signs in our everyday lives.

At last, life makes sense and the progress I make along this spiritual path depends entirely on my efforts, my Work and whatever Up Above has planned for me.

I cannot recommend The Traditional Study of Angels highly enough. Never before have I encountered such a practical and uplifting method. It leads us from one discovery to the next according to our own personal rhythm and capacity for understanding.

Kaya and Christiane's devotion to passing on this Knowledge is a gift beyond measure. The resulting spiritual autonomy provides us with an eternal key to the Divine Knowledge and Truth that lies locked within us.

When I reached 40, I thought I had already achieved all my dreams. I had a family, a home, a job I enjoyed. It allowed me to combine motherhood and a profession. I wondered what could possibly inspire me now. Well, I encountered the Angels and life has become a challenging, wonder-filled adventure where the bad moments, the nightmares, the falls from pride, the often shameful awakenings along with the surprising synchronicities, the awe-inspiring dreams and visions and unexpected gifts turning up out of the blue lead to the knowledge that I am now empowered to cleanse my faults, purify my flaws, pay off some of my debts, transcend my distortions and develop pure qualities to rediscover my Divine self and to fulfill my purpose here on Earth. Detoxifying is not always very pleasant, but the benefits gained lead us to dreams beyond our imagination. As I approach 50, I can laugh at my 40 year-old self for I have so many dreams now, it'll last me all this life (and God knows how many more) to be fulfilled!

To Kaya, Christiane and Kasara, the UCM team and all the volunteers, my sincerest and most heartfelt gratitude for your selfless devotion, inspiring generosity and pure love for the Divine.

To all of you who decide to start working on yourselves with The Traditional Study of Angels, and for those of you who start studying at the *Universe/City Mikaël*, rest assured, you are about to embark on the most marvelous journey of discovery: discovery of yourself and discovery of the Divine Laws that govern the Universe and Knowledge of that perfect Cosmic Intelligence, the Divine Hierarchy and God Himself.

INTRODUCTION

We will all recognize ourselves within the pages of this book. The true stories and the dreams that you will read about come from people who attended the lectures of Universe/City Mikaël and, from other people we know.

In particular, people who are consciously committed to following a spiritual path will find this to be a precious guide that will not only help them to analyze their dreams and the situations they encounter in their daily lives but also to acquire an overall view of their initiatory journey. The numerous interpretations of dreams and signs are told in a very simple manner and allow us to become familiar with symbolic language. The fundamental theories of The Traditional Study of Angels are also explained in a very accessible way with a view to practical use.

Contrary to what we commonly imagine, an Angel is not a winged being that flies about in the air above. The Angels are a part of us and of our Divine nature. In fact, an Angel is a state of greater Consciousness that represents Qualities and Virtues in their essence and their original conception. Our mission as human beings is to rediscover these States of Consciousness and to use them to reprogram our thoughts, feelings, and actions. If initiatory science has always used the metaphor of winged beings to express what happens within us when these powerful energies are reactivated, it is because the rediscovery of Knowledge, Peace, Freedom and Love gives us wings.

When a human being manages to integrate and become these Angelic Energies, the door to true Knowledge opens up to him. His subconsciousness and various levels of his unconsciousness become accessible to him. He acquires constant guidance through his dreams and signs in his everyday life and discovers parallel worlds and the mysteries of the Universe.

In the first chapters of this book, you will find the basic theories and the historical origins of The Traditional Study of Angels and the methods involved in the Work to be done with the Angels, the tables that serve to identify your personal Angels, also called Guardian Angels, and a description of the Tree of Life and of Its Sephiroth. Then follows the description of the 72 Angels in the form of the qualities and virtues They represent. These are accompanied by a list of their associated distortions.

The core of the book is the transcript of 8 lectures on the Angels that we gave in several countries. It is truly a journey into the heart of The Traditional Study of Angels. These lectures represent hundreds of testimonials by people who study their dreams and the events they experience. These dreams and situations are analyzed and viewed from the perspective of the initiation process.

THE TRADITIONAL STUDY OF ANGELS

The Traditional Study of Angels comes from the Ancient times of the Judeo-Christian tradition, from a very old secret teaching received by Jesus and all the great initiates, which is known by the name of Kabbalah. The Traditional Study of Angels and the Kabbalah together constitute an extraordinary Knowledge and heritage. It is a legacy of the evolutionary research undertaken by great initiates to rediscover their Origins. The ultimate goal of this Ancestral Tradition is to guide us through the numerous initiations that will allow us to rediscover our Celestial Origin and our full spiritual powers and capacities. The Traditional Study of Angels can also be referred as The Traditional Angelology.

THE KABBALAH

The Kabbalah means Hidden Wisdom and Word Received. It is a teaching that is transmitted by word of mouth. This initiatory science allows everyone to reach the highest spiritual levels through an in-depth study of his own consciousness. Considered in its essence, this teaching, or philosophy, brings us the knowledge of physical and metaphysical experimentation. The study of its founding principles plunges the human being into intense introspection. This reaches its heights the moment he discovers the profound nature of man, of woman, of an Angel and of Divine Workmanship and its Creator through the perfect union of Spirit and matter.

The Kabbalah brings together a set of methods that allows us to truly understand the Creation of the Universe. It consists of 1) the study of the Great Principles and the Laws of the Universe, 2) the Work to be done with the Angels, which is the most important part and which comes from what we might call the initiatory psychology, and 3) the study of symbolism, and the interpretation of dreams and signs occurring in our daily lives.

It is difficult to trace with precision the historical origin of The Traditional Study of Angels and the Kabbalah because it goes back to the oldest antiquity. According to the available sources, it would have originated in Egyptian, Phoenician and Babylonian civilizations and would have been recorded by the Israelite scribes held in captivity in Babylon around the year 450 BC.

The Kabbalah has been, and still is, the greatest and most esoteric hidden mystery of Judaism and, therefore, of Christianity. In the "Zohar" or "Book of Splendor," a visionary commentary of the books written by Moses and inspired by Divine Powers, we read: "When Adam was in the Garden of Eden, the Holy One had the Archangel RAZIEL bring him down a book about Hochmah, the mysteries of Supreme Wisdom. This book contained the holiest, most exalted secrets, the Holy Wisdom of the 72 types of Knowledge, Virtues and Powers." (Zohar, 155B).

Among the teachings of the Kabbalah, those that constitute the practical and psychological aspects, that is to say The Traditional Study of Angels, are the ones that were kept secret the longest. The States of Consciousness brought about by the study of Angelic Energies gives people so much force and power that there was a tendency to occult this science, even among the initiates themselves. Traditional Kabbalah tells us that several great beings such as Abraham, Moses, Joseph, and Jesus received this teaching of Highest Knowledge that was only transmitted orally to those predestined to receive it.

The philosophical study of the Kabbalah, or the intellectual study of the great Principles of the Universe, is useful, but it will never replace the groundwork that each individual must carry out in order to rediscover his Origin and to acquire Knowledge, that is, the key to peace and happiness. In fact, the most important aspect of this approach consists in discovering these secrets directly, within oneself, through the in-depth study of the Angelic States of Consciousness. This is commonly called The Traditional Study of Angels or the Practical Kabbalah.

PRACTICAL KABBALAH

The first known school of Practical Kabbalah, known as the Kahal, was founded in 1160 AD, in Gerona, a little Catalonian town in North-Eastern Spain at Isaac el Cec's instigation. The students of this school worked out a way to apply Knowledge to everyday life. The Kahal flourished from 1200 to 1475, during which time the detailed structure of the Tree of Life and the list of the Angels' Qualities and their associated distortions were drawn up for the first time.

In 1492, under the Inquisition, the Jews of Gerona were forced to choose between conversion to Catholicism or exile. In the case of exile, they could take nothing but their personal belongings with them. The Kahal was closed by order of the Inquisitors, and the entire old Jewish quarter of Gerona was walled up. But the descendants of the Jews who had converted to Catholicism and who had stayed close to their ancestral quarters in Gerona continued to transmit their oral tradition in secret. Then, in 1975, some of them reopened the walled-up district and discovered the Angel texts that their ancestors had hidden and sealed in a building that today has become a historical site.

WHAT IS AN ANGEL?

An Angel represents Qualities, Virtues and Powers of the Creator in their purest form. In the Ancient texts of the Kabbalah, the Angels are the 72 Facets of the Creator. When we manage to rediscover Them and to reintegrate Them in their Essence, we then attain great states of Consciousness, happiness and bliss. This constitutes a long journey but it is our only reason for being here on Earth.

The Angel is pure Energy. But as humans, we are rather ignorant and we don't have a proper understanding of the Energy of God and we use it badly. We distort the Essential Aspects of the Creator. This gives rise to our faults and weaknesses, in other words, the distortions associated with each Angel. The fact remains, however, that these Essences reside within everyone, whether or not we know the Names of the Angels.

As recorded in The Traditional Study of Angels, each Essence has a Hebrew name and a vibration. When we pronounce this sacred Name aloud or in silence, it sets off a vibratory echo that acts directly on our cellular memory. Thus, we connect with the immense Field of Consciousness designated by the Sacred Name. Over time, the high levels of Consciousness that we attain give us wings. A number is also attributed to each Angel, positioning It in the Celestial Hierarchy.

THE ADVANTAGES OF THE TRADITIONAL STUDY OF ANGELS

We might wonder why we should pray to the Angels rather than to the Creator directly. The reason is that the Work we do with the Angels gives us guidelines and a structure of God's Consciousness. God is so vast and so abstract when we set out on our path.

The work with the Angels is distinctive in that it allows us to identify precisely what it is that we need to rectify. It gives us the means to carry out this transformation work. It also allows us to measure the extent of the changes that take place in our unconsciousness as our consciousness gradually opens up.

When we work with one Angel in particular, the other Angels continue to exist within us, but we focus on one specific ray of the Great Cosmic Intelligence. In fact, all the Angelic Energies are interconnected.

WORKING WITH THE ANGELS

Working with the Angels consists in reprogramming our unconscious memories. The expression we commonly use for this is *Angel Work*. It involves work that leads to purification. The memories that have been tainted with distortions are rectified one by one by the Power of the Angel and by our own intention. By invoking States of Angelic Consciousness, we activate our intention to purify ourselves. Thus, we learn to be centered and to become very intense. The Kabbalists call this important step Kawana, which means the intensity of the intention. It occurs in each person who discovers that spirituality is not a hobby, but actually an intense transformation process that leads him through many stages. These often become steps on the path to the detoxification of his consciousness.

During our apprenticeship on Earth and throughout our various incarnations, all of our experiences are recorded onto our soul, in the same way that a computer records its data. All of our fears, sufferings, limitations, qualities and potential are recorded in our subconsciousness and in the various layers of our unconsciousness. Figure 1 (cf. page 5) shows the Consciousness Diagram. It represents our soul and its different strata. The double line on the top part of the diagram represents the veil that hides almost all of our memories from our consciousness. It is called the veil of unconsciousness.

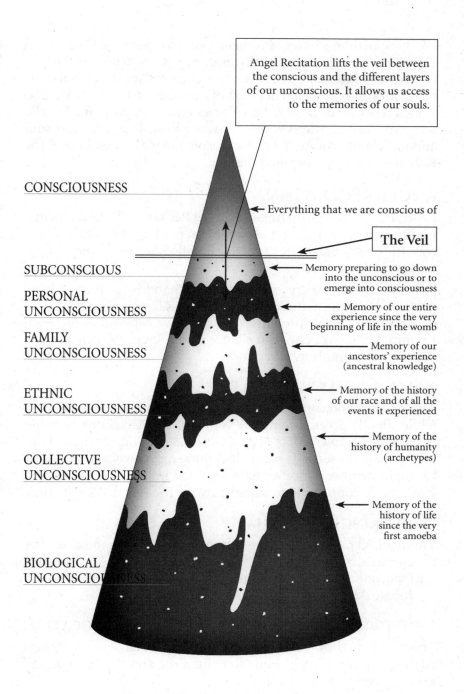

Angel Recitation lifts the veil between the conscious and the different layers of our unconscious. It allows us access to the memories of our souls.

CONSCIOUSNESS

← Everything that we are conscious of

The Veil

SUBCONSCIOUS

Memory preparing to go down into the unconscious or to emerge into consciousness

PERSONAL UNCONSCIOUSNESS

Memory of our entire experience since the very beginning of life in the womb

FAMILY UNCONSCIOUSNESS

Memory of our ancestors' experience (ancestral knowledge)

ETHNIC UNCONSCIOUSNESS

Memory of the history of our race and of all the events it experienced

COLLECTIVE UNCONSCIOUSNESS

Memory of the history of humanity (archetypes)

Memory of the history of life since the very first amoeba

BIOLOGICAL UNCONSCIOUSNESS

Figure 1: The Consciousness Diagram

Working with the States of Angelic Consciousness makes this veil disappear. In other words, through our Work with the Angels, we create a passageway between our consciousness, our subconsciousness and the different layers of our unconsciousness. We also gain access to our distorted memories and we reprogram Angelic States of Consciousness within. This work aims to purify our soul and to help us acquire full consciousness so we can rediscover the Knowledge that is inscribed therein.

ANGEL RECITATION

Central to Working with Angels is Angel Recitation. Several Oriental traditions advocate the repetition of sacred formulas called mantras. In the Kabbalah, this practice is called *Schem Hamephorash*, or Angel Recitation.

Angel Recitation is very easy to practice. Standing, sitting, or lying down, we breathe naturally while continually repeating the Name of an Angel. We continue for as long as we can and at our own rhythm. We invoke either in silence or out loud. We can also use one of the methods listed below.

1) INVOKING AS WE INHALE

This first method consists in taking a deep breath through the nose while silently pronouncing the Name of the Angel one or more times. For example: "*MIKAEL, MIKAEL, MIKAEL...*" We then hold our breath for a few seconds before breathing out slowly and gradually through the nose. Once we have regained inner calm, we breathe freely while continuing to silently invoke the Angel as we inhale.

2) INVOKING AS WE EXHALE

This method consists in taking a deep breath through the nose after which we exhale while pronouncing the Name of the Angel quietly, out loud, or in silence. For example: "*VEHUIAH, VEHUIAH, VEHUIAH...*" We inhale deeply once again and we repeat the process.

3) DEEP BREATHING DURING CONTINUOUS INVOCATION

This third method consists in repeating the Name of the Angel continually and silently while fully inhaling and then completely exhaling the air from the lungs.

For those unaccustomed to deep breathing, this may cause dizziness. If so, the breathing rhythm can be slowed down or altered with another method of invoking. It is important to respect personal rhythm.

4) INVOKING WITH AN INTENTION IN MIND

This method consists in repeating the Name of the Angel quietly or silently, according to one of the methods above, while adding to it a message to the Angel. This message shares with Him our intention to develop a quality or a particular faculty, or even to rectify or transcend a distortion. For example: "*Angel HARIEL, purify my soul and guide me towards purity. HARIEL, HARIEL, HARIEL. Help me become pure and help me integrate Wisdom within me. HARIEL, HARIEL, HARIEL. Purify me and teach me what I need to understand. HARIEL, HARIEL, HARIEL. Purify my soul. HARIEL, HARIEL, HARIEL…*"

5) INVOKING WITH A QUESTION IN MIND

This method consists of helping us find the answer to a question. First of all, we formulate a clear question, then we invoke according to one of the first three methods, all the while incorporating the question and the request so as to be enlightened and guided towards the answer. For example: "*Angel JELIEL, is it right for me to marry this person? JELIEL, JELIEL, JELIEL. Help me sense whether this is the right person for my evolution. JELIEL, JELIEL, JELIEL. Enlighten me. JELIEL, JELIEL, JELIEL. I wish to follow the Will of God. JELIEL, JELIEL, JELIEL. Is it right for me to marry this person? JELIEL, JELIEL, JELIEL…*"

When we do our Angel Recitation with a question, we must call upon the same Angel for at least five days or until we receive an answer. By focusing on the question, we gain access to the program that Cosmic Intelligence has prepared for us. This will activate dreams and signs that will answer our question. When we do our Angel Recitation with a request, we must in the same manner call upon the same Angel for at least five days so that the desired transformation may manifest itself.

Whichever method we choose, Angel Recitation remains a simple exercise that can be practiced in any context and in any of life's situations. It can be done while walking, driving, meditating, relaxing, practicing sports and doing house work. It can be done before falling asleep or upon wakening. It can be done during difficult times as well as in moments of happiness. We must, however, remember that it is important to respect our own rhythm and to invoke with a sense of sacredness.

The intensified energy that occurs while working with an Angel manifests itself through intuition, dreams, signs and coincidences encountered in our daily lives. It is fascinating to see the relevance between the Quality of the Angel and what is shown to us in dreams and in everyday life, as much in their pure form as in their distorted form. Angel Recitation sets in motion or intensifies the initiatory process. In that sense, the Name of the Angel serves as a magic formula. Working with Angels is an initiatory adventure that immerses a person in the contemplation of multiple realities.

A wonderful way of optimizing the benefits of Angel Recitation is to practice it while doing Angelica yoga exercises. These exercises are the subject of other publications under the designation *Angelica yoga*, also published by Universe/City Mikaël.

CHOOSING AN ANGEL

In choosing the Angel to be invoked, it is suggested that a person follow Angel Calendar no.1 (see pages 14 and 15). This is also called the Annual Angel Calendar. The use of this Calendar has the advantage of allowing us to familiarize ourselves throughout the year with the 72 States of Angelic Consciousness. Inherently, it provides us with a work structure and allows Cosmic Intelligence to plan the many steps of our apprenticeship in advance and with precision.

Although the use of Angel Calendar no.1 allows for an extraordinary method of working, the choice of Angel remains a personal one and can very well be determined according to a particular situation. In fact, any Angel can be chosen because of Its affinity to a situation that has come up and that we wish to understand or resolve. For this purpose, you will find at the end of this volume a list of situations and common problems associated with the Angel to invoke.

It is suggested that we only use one Angelic Energy at a time and for a period of at least five days in order to truly activate Its Field of Consciousness. Needless to say, five days are not enough to integrate all of the Qualities and Virtues of an Angel, but throughout the work we do with the many Angels over the years we eventually come to a point where we have visited all the rays of our consciousness. We advance methodically on the road that leads to Illumination.

We can work more than five days with the same Angel if we wish to go further into this particular Field of Consciousness. It is, however, preferable to change regularly as our consciousness needs to visit all parts of the Essences of the Creator so that one day we can fully manifest Them.

SHORT-TERM EFFECTS

When we do housework in real life, we can naturally expect to find things we've lost, but also a lot of dust. If, for example, we do our Angel Recitation with Angel 7 ACHAIAH, whose principal Quality is patience, we may suddenly become much more impatient than usual. This is because the Angel opens the door to our consciousness and liberates the memories connected to impatience. Liberating them may take several minutes, several hours, or even several days. If we have no expectations, and as if by magic, we suddenly feel good again because certain memories of our consciousness corresponding to Angel ACHAIAH have been cleansed. During this period of adjustment, we will also tend to come across impatient people and go through situations that try our patience. This bears witness to the fact that we are directly linked to the ray of the Angel chosen. So we should use these situations as sacred opportunities to get to know ourselves better.

Imagine that all of a sudden you discover a new room in your house, a room that you have never visited. Upon opening the door, you notice that it is full of dust, rats, etc. Simply opening the door lets so much dust into the other rooms that a full, top-to-bottom cleaning of the house has to be done. When you work with the Angels it is as if you choose not to close the door but to extend your house. You continue to clean until the entire house is completely clean. While doing the housework, you discover treasures and books in the new room. These represent knowledge and you decide to include them in your library.

During this period of intense cleansing, we alternate from one extreme frame of mind to another. When we have an important dream or a nightmare, or when a particular event activates in us a new state of open-mindedness, our entire being is perturbed. This is why we need to be aware and warn those close to us that we may display unusual behavior. In truth, we are getting a taste of the Qualities of the Angelic Energy and this causes us to experience states of real bliss. But shortly afterwards, because we have to cleanse our distorted memories, we plunge into difficult states of mind and great anxieties resurface. When we understand the process, we get used to it. Eventually, great stability is established. We find our wings once again and we feel good all the time. This, however, may require years of inner work.

All the while we are led to dream and to notice signs that are present in our environment. This occurs with irregular frequency. The symbolic study of dreams and of signs is complementary to the Work we do with the Angels since symbols are the vocabulary of the language of unconsciousness and of the soul. Thus, we learn to read everyday signs and we realize that coincidence does not exist.

THE EFFECTS OF WORKING WITH THE ANGELS

When carried out on a daily basis, the Work we do with the Angels creates a gradual opening of our subconsciousness and of our unconsciousness that manifests itself in several ways. These are:

⊙ As mentioned above, a first occurrence may be that we experience extreme mood swings. For example, we may go from a profound state of well-being to deep anxiety;

⊙ The sharpness of our five senses (sight, hearing, smell, taste and touch) is considerably increased and this leads us to develop clairvoyance, clairaudience and clairsentience;

⊙ The frequency and intensity of our dreams are gradually increased and we can better interpret them;

⊙ The interpretation of dreams and the reading of everyday signs will bring about a deeply mystical experience;

⊙ We acquire great spiritual autonomy, because the study of signs and dreams allows us to gradually learn the various steps of our initiatory journey;

⊙ Our soul acquires the capacity to leave its body and to visit the different dimensions of time and space, thereby discovering the secrets of the Universe.

Working with Angelic Energies takes us well beyond time and space. The Angels enable us to travel through the numerous dimensions of the Universe.

GUARDIAN ANGELS

At birth, a person receives three Guardian Angels. Their qualities and associated distortions show us the strengths and weaknesses that we are to transcend in this life.

1. The first Guardian Angel corresponds to our physical body. It guides the world of actions. We can identify it in Angel Calendar no. 1, according to our date of birth.

2. The second Guardian Angel corresponds to our emotions and our feelings. It shows us the potential and virtues that we need to work on from an emotional point of view. We can find its Name in Angel Calendar no. 2, according to the day we were born.

3. The third Guardian Angel corresponds to our intellect and concerns the world of thoughts. We can identify it in Angel Calendar no. 3, according to our time of birth.

As with astrology, we use the time of birth as a simple indicator and starting point that also depends on our country of birth. It is important to note that these calendars were inspired by the ancient astrology of the Kabbalah. However, their meaning goes much deeper in that they correspond to the symbolic aspect of daily life. For example, children normally go to school at 8 o'clock in the morning, eat at noon and go to bed early at night. In whatever country we were born in, we find a symbolic way of living that is similar. It is the same with our time of birth. According to this universal way of behaving, we take into account the local time to find our third Guardian Angel. This is the One that corresponds to our intellect. The Angel calendars are universal and can be applied in every country.

The goal of Working with the States of Angelic Consciousness consists in integrating not only our three Guardian Angels, but also the entire Knowledge that the 72 Angels of this Tradition represent.

ANGEL
CALENDARS

ANGEL CALENDAR No. 1
Physical Aspect

March 21	to	March 25	1	VEHUIAH
March 26	to	March 30	2	JELIEL
March 31	to	April 04	3	SITAEL
April 05	to	April 09	4	ELEMIAH
April 10	to	April 14	5	MAHASIAH
April 15	to	April 20	6	LELAHEL
April 21	to	April 25	7	ACHAIAH
April 26	to	April 30	8	CAHETEL
May 01	to	May 05	9	HAZIEL
May 06	to	May 10	10	ALADIAH
May 11	to	May 15	11	LAUVIAH
May 16	to	May 20	12	HAHAIAH
May 21	to	May 25	13	IEZALEL
May 26	to	May 31	14	MEBAHEL
June 01	to	June 05	15	HARIEL
June 06	to	June 10	16	HEKAMIAH
June 11	to	June 15	17	LAUVIAH
June 16	to	June 21	18	CALIEL
June 22	to	June 26	19	LEUVIAH
June 27	to	July 01	20	PAHALIAH
July 02	to	July 06	21	NELKHAEL
July 07	to	July 11	22	YEIAYEL
July 12	to	July 16	23	MELAHEL
July 17	to	July 22	24	HAHEUIAH
July 23	to	July 27	25	NITH-HAIAH
July 28	to	August 01	26	HAAIAH
August 02	to	August 06	27	YERATHEL
August 07	to	August 12	28	SEHEIAH
August 13	to	August 17	29	REIYEL
August 18	to	August 22	30	OMAEL
August 23	to	August 28	31	LECABEL
August 29	to	September 02	32	VASARIAH
September 03	to	September 07	33	YEHUIAH
September 08	to	September 12	34	LEHAHIAH
September 13	to	September 17	35	CHAVAKHIAH
September 18	to	September 23	36	MENADEL

ANGEL CALENDAR No. 1 (con't)
Physical Aspect

September 24	to	September 28	37	ANIEL
September 29	to	October 03	38	HAAMIAH
October 04	to	October 08	39	REHAEL
October 09	to	October 13	40	IEIAZEL
October 14	to	October 18	41	HAHAHEL
October 19	to	October 23	42	MIKAEL
October 24	to	October 28	43	VEULIAH
October 29	to	November 02	44	YELAHIAH
November 03	to	November 07	45	SEALIAH
November 08	to	November 12	46	ARIEL
November 13	to	November 17	47	ASALIAH
November 18	to	November 22	48	MIHAEL
November 23	to	November 27	49	VEHUEL
November 28	to	December 02	50	DANIEL
December 03	to	December 07	51	HAHASIAH
December 08	to	December 12	52	IMAMIAH
December 13	to	December 16	53	NANAEL
December 17	to	December 21	54	NITHAEL
December 22	to	December 26	55	MEBAHIAH
December 27	to	December 31	56	POYEL
January 01	to	January 05	57	NEMAMIAH
January 06	to	January 10	58	YEIALEL
January 11	to	January 15	59	HARAHEL
January 16	to	January 20	60	MITZRAEL
January 21	to	January 25	61	UMABEL
January 26	to	January 30	62	IAHHEL
January 31	to	February 04	63	ANAUEL
February 05	to	February 09	64	MEHIEL
February 10	to	February 14	65	DAMABIAH
February 15	to	February 19	66	MANAKEL
February 20	to	February 24	67	EYAEL
February 25	to	February 29	68	HABUHIAH
March 01	to	March 05	69	ROCHEL
March 06	to	March 10	70	JABAMIAH
March 11	to	March 15	71	HAIAIEL
March 16	to	March 20	72	MUMIAH

ANGEL CALENDAR No. 2
Emotional Aspect

JANUARY	FEBRUARY	MARCH
1: #65 DAMABIAH	1: #25 NITH-HAIAH	1: #53 NANAEL
2: #66 MANAKEL	2: #26 HAAIAH	2: #54 NITHAEL
3: #67 EYAEL	3: #27 YERATHEL	3: #55 MEBAHIAH
4: #68 HABUHIAH	4: #28 SEHEIAH	4: #56 POYEL
5: #69 ROCHEL	5: #29 REIYEL	5: #57 NEMAMIAH
6: #70 JABAMIAH	6: #30 OMAEL	6: #58 YEIALEL
7: #71 HAIAIEL	7: #31 LECABEL	7: #59 HARAHEL
8: #72 MUMIAH	8: #32 VASARIAH	8: #60 MITZRAEL
9: #1 VEHUIAH	9: #33 YEHUIAH	9: #61 UMABEL
10: #2 JELIEL	10: #34 LEHAHIAH	10: #62 IAHHEL
11: #3 SITAEL	11: #35 CHAVAKHIAH	11: #63 ANAUEL
12: #4 ELEMIAH	12: #36 MENADEL	12: #64 MEHIEL
13: #5 MAHASIAH	13: #37 ANIEL	13: #65 DAMABIAH
14: #6 LELAHEL	14: #38 HAAMIAH	14: #66 MANAKEL
15: #7 ACHAIAH	15: #39 REHAEL	15: #67 EYAEL
16: #8 CAHETEL	16: #40 IEIAZEL	16: #68 HABUHIAH
17: #9 HAZIEL	17: #41 HAHAHEL	17: #69 ROCHEL
18: #10 ALADIAH	18: #42 MIKAEL	18: #70 JABAMIAH
19: #11 LAUVIAH	19: #43 VEULIAH	19: #71 HAIAIEL
20: #12 HAHAIAH	20: #44 YELAHIAH	20: #72 MUMIAH
21: #13 IEZALEL	21: #45 SEALIAH	21: #1 VEHUIAH
22: #14 MEBAHEL	22: #46 ARIEL	22: #2 JELIEL
23: #15 HARIEL	23: #47 ASALIAH	23: #3 SITAEL
24: #16 HEKAMIAH #17 LAUVIAH	24: #48 MIHAEL	24: #4 ELEMIAH
	25: #49 VEHUEL	25: #5 MAHASIAH
25: #18 CALIEL	26: #50 DANIEL	26: #6 LELAHEL
26: #19 LEUVIAH	27: #51 HAHASIAH	27: #7 ACHAIAH
27: #20 PAHALIAH	28: #52 IMAMIAH	28: #8 CAHETEL
28: #21 NELKHAEL	29: #52 IMAMIAH	29: #9 HAZIEL
29: #22 YEIAYEL		30: #10 ALADIAH
30: #23 MELAHEL		31: #11 LAUVIAH
31: #24 HAHEUIAH		

How to find the Guardian Angel that governs your emotions

It is very easy to find this Guardian Angel. In Calendar no. 2, shown above, the first figure corresponds to your date of birth. The second figure corresponds to the number of your Angel. For example, the Angel that governs May 5 at the emotional level is Angel 45 SEALIAH. **Particularities: 1)** The asterisk (*) included with seven of the dates means that from midnight to midday of that day the Angel of the preceding day presides, while the

ANGEL CALENDAR No. 2 (con't)
Emotional Aspect

APRIL	MAY	JUNE
1: #12 Hahaiah	1: #41 Hahahel	1: #71 Haiaiel
2: #13 Iezalel	2: #42 Mikael	2: #72 Mumiah
3: #14 Mebahel	3: #43 Veuliah	3: #1 Vehuiah
4: #15 Hariel	4: #44 Yelahiah	4: #2 Jeliel
5: #16 Hekamiah	5: #45 Sealiah	5: #3 Sitael
6: #17 Lauviah	6: #46 Ariel	6: #4 Elemiah
7: #18 Caliel	7: #47 Asaliah	7: #5 Mahasiah
8: #19 Leuviah	8: #48 Mihael	8: #6 Lelahel
9: #20 Pahaliah	9: #49 Vehuel	9: #7 Achaiah
10: #21 Nelkhael	10: #50 Daniel	10: #8 Cahetel
11: #22 Yeiayel	11: #51 Hahasiah	11: #9 Haziel
12: #23 Melahel	12: #52 Imamiah	12: #10 Aladiah
13: #24 Haheuiah	13: #53 Nanael	13: *
14: #25 Nith-Haiah	14: #54 Nithael	14: #11 Lauviah
15: #26 Haaiah	15: #55 Mebahiah	15: #12 Hahaiah
16: #27 Yerathel	16: #56 Poyel	16: #13 Iezalel
17: *	17: #57 Nemamiah	17: #14 Mebahel
18: #28 Seheiah	18: #58 Yeialel	18: #15 Hariel
19: #29 Reiyel	19: #59 Harahel	19: #16 Hekamiah
20: #30 Omael	20: *	20: #17 Lauviah
21: #31 Lecabel	21: #60 Mitzrael	21: #18 Caliel
22: #32 Vasariah	22: #61 Umabel	22: #19 Leuviah
23: #33 Yehuiah	23: #62 Iahhel	23: #20 Pahaliah
24: #34 Lehahiah	24: #63 Anauel	24: #21 Nelkhael
25: #35 Chavakhiah	25: #64 Mehiel	25: #22 Yeiayel
26: #36 Menadel	26: #65 Damabiah	26: #23 Melahel
27: #37 Aniel	27: #66 Manakel	27: #24 Haheuiah
28: #38 Haamiah	28: #67 Eyael	28: #25 Nith-Haiah
29: #39 Rehael	29: #68 Habuhiah	29: #26 Haaiah
30: #40 Ieiazel	30: #69 Rochel	30: #27 Yerathel
	31: #70 Jabamiah	

Angel of the following day presides from midday to midnight. For example, Angel no. 27 presides all day on April 16 and until midday on April 17, while Angel no. 28 presides on April 17 from midday until midnight and all day on April 18. 2) Where dates refer to two numbers, as is the case for January 24 and December 27, the first Angel governs from midnight to midday, while the second governs from midday to midnight.

ANGEL CALENDAR No. 2 (con't)
Emotional Aspect

JULY	AUGUST	SEPTEMBER
1: #28 Seheiah	1: #57 Nemamiah	1: #15 Hariel
2: #29 Reiyel	2: #58 Yeialel	2: #16 Hekamiah
3: #30 Omael	3: #59 Harahel	3: #17 Lauviah
4: #31 Lecabel	4: #60 Mitzrael	4: #18 Caliel
5: *	5: #61 Umabel	5: #19 Leuviah
6: #32 Vasariah	6: #62 Iahhel	6: #20 Pahaliah
7: #33 Yehuiah	7: #63 Anauel	7: #21 Nelkhael
8: #34 Lehahiah	8: #64 Mehiel	8: #22 Yeiayel
9: #35 Chavakhiah	9: #65 Damabiah	9: #23 Melahel
10: #36 Menadel	10: #66 Manakel	10: #24 Haheuiah
11: #37 Aniel	11: #67 Eyael	11: #25 Nith-Haiah
12: #38 Haamiah	12: #68 Habuhiah	12: #26 Haaiah
13: #39 Rehael	13: #69 Rochel	13: #27 Yerathel
14: #40 Ieiazel	14: #70 Jabamiah	14: #28 Seheiah
15: #41 Hahahel	15: #71 Haiaiel	15: #29 Reiyel
16: #42 Mikael	16: #72 Mumiah	16: #30 Omael
17: #43 Veuliah	17: #1 Vehuiah	17: #31 Lecabel
18: #44 Yelahiah	18: #2 Jeliel	18: #32 Vasariah
19: #45 Sealiah	19: *	19: #33 Yehuiah
20: #46 Ariel	20: #3 Sitael	20: #34 Lehahiah
21: #47 Asaliah	21: #4 Elemiah	21: *
22: #48 Mihael	22: #5 Mahasiah	22: #35 Chavakhiah
23: #49 Vehuel	23: #6 Lelahel	23: #36 Menadel
24: #50 Daniel	24: #7 Achaiah	24: #37 Aniel
25: #51 Hahasiah	25: #8 Cahetel	25: #38 Haamiah
26: *	26: #9 Haziel	26: #39 Rehael
27: #52 Imamiah	27: #10 Aladiah	27: #40 Ieiazel
28: #53 Nanael	28: #11 Lauviah	28: #41 Hahahel
29: #54 Nithael	29: #12 Hahaiah	29: #42 Mikael
30: #55 Mebahiah	30: #13 Iezalel	30: #43 Veuliah
31: #56 Poyel	31: #14 Mebahel	

How to find the Guardian Angel that governs your emotions
It is very easy to find this Guardian Angel. In Calendar no. 2, shown above, the first figure corresponds to your date of birth. The second figure corresponds to the number of your Angel. For example, the Angel that governs May 5 at the emotional level is Angel 45 Sealiah. **Particularities: 1)** The asterisk (*) included with seven of the dates means that from midnight to midday of that day the Angel of the preceding day presides, while the

ANGEL CALENDAR No. 2 (con't)
Emotional Aspect

OCTOBER	NOVEMBER	DECEMBER
1: #44 Yelahiah	1: #3 Sitael	1: #33 Yehuiah
2: #45 Sealiah	2: #4 Elemiah	2: #34 Lehahiah
3: #46 Ariel	3: #5 Mahasiah	3: #35 Chavakhiah
4: #47 Asaliah	4: #6 Lelahel	4: #36 Menadel
5: #48 Mihael	5: #7 Achaiah	5: #37 Aniel
6: #49 Vehuel	6: #8 Cahetel	6: #38 Haamiah
7: #50 Daniel	7: #9 Haziel	7: #39 Rehael
8: #51 Hahasiah	8: #10 Aladiah	8: #40 Ieiazel
9: #52 Imamiah	9: #11 Lauviah	9: #41 Hahahel
10: #53 Nanael	10: #12 Hahaiah	10: #42 Mikael
11: #54 Nithael	11: #13 Iezalel	11: #43 Veuliah
12: #55 Mebahiah	12: #14 Mebahel	12: #44 Yelahiah
13: #56 Poyel	13: #15 Hariel	13: #45 Sealiah
14: #57 Nemamiah	14: #16 Hekamiah	14: #46 Ariel
15: #58 Yeialel	15: #17 Lauviah	15: #47 Asaliah
16: #59 Harahel	16: #18 Caliel	16: #48 Mihael
17: #60 Mitzrael	17: #19 Leuviah	17: #49 Vehuel
18: #61 Umabel	18: #20 Pahaliah	18: #50 Daniel
19: #62 Iahhel	19: #21 Nelkhael	19: #51 Hahasiah
20: #63 Anauel	20: #22 Yeiayel	20: #52 Imamiah
21: #64 Mehiel	21: #23 Melahel	21: #53 Nanael
22: #65 Damabiah	22: #24 Haheuiah	22: #54 Nithael
23: #66 Manakel	23: #25 Nith-Haiah	23: #55 Mebahiah
24: #67 Eyael	24: #26 Haaiah	24: #56 Poyel
25: #68 Habuhiah	25: #27 Yerathel	25: #57 Nemamiah
26: #69 Rochel	26: #28 Seheiah	26: #58 Yeialel
27: #70 Jabamiah	27: #29 Reiyel	27: #59 Harahel
28: #71 Haiaiel	28: #30 Omael	#60 Mitzrael
29: #72 Mumiah	29: #31 Lecabel	28: #61 Umabel
30: #1 Vehuiah	30: #32 Vasariah	29: #62 Iahhel
31: #2 Jeliel		30: #63 Anauel
		31: #64 Mehiel

Angel of the following day presides from midday to midnight. For example, Angel no. 27 presides all day on April 16 and until midday on April 17, while Angel no. 28 presides on April 17 from midday until midnight and all day on April 18. 2) Where dates refer to two numbers, as is the case for January 24 and December 27, the first Angel governs from midnight to midday, while the second governs from midday to midnight.

ANGEL CALENDAR No. 3
Intellectual Aspect

0:00 A.M.	to	0:19 A.M.	1	VEHUIAH
0:20 A.M.	to	0:39 A.M.	2	JELIEL
0:40 A.M.	to	0:59 A.M.	3	SITAEL
1:00 A.M.	to	1:19 A.M.	4	ELEMIAH
1:20 A.M.	to	1:39 A.M.	5	MAHASIAH
1:40 A.M.	to	1:59 A.M.	6	LELAHEL
2:00 A.M.	to	2:19 A.M.	7	ACHAIAH
2:20 A.M.	to	2:39 A.M.	8	CAHETEL
2:40 A.M.	to	2:59 A.M.	9	HAZIEL
3:00 A.M.	to	3:19 A.M.	10	ALADIAH
3:20 A.M.	to	3:39 A.M.	11	LAUVIAH
3:40 A.M.	to	3:59 A.M.	12	HAHAIAH
4:00 A.M.	to	4:19 A.M.	13	IEZALEL
4:20 A.M.	to	4:39 A.M.	14	MEBAHEL
4:40 A.M.	to	4:59 A.M.	15	HARIEL
5:00 A.M.	to	5:19 A.M.	16	HEKAMIAH
5:20 A.M.	to	5:39 A.M.	17	LAUVIAH
5:40 A.M.	to	5:59 A.M.	18	CALIEL
6:00 A.M.	to	6:19 A.M.	19	LEUVIAH
6:20 A.M.	to	6:39 A.M.	20	PAHALIAH
6:40 A.M.	to	6:59 A.M.	21	NELKHAEL
7:00 A.M.	to	7:19 A.M.	22	YEIAYEL
7:20 A.M.	to	7:39 A.M.	23	MELAHEL
7:40 A.M.	to	7:59 A.M.	24	HAHEUIAH
8:00 A.M.	to	8:19 A.M.	25	NITH-HAIAH
8:20 A.M.	to	8:39 A.M.	26	HAAIAH
8:40 A.M.	to	8:59 A.M.	27	YERATHEL
9:00 A.M.	to	9:19 A.M.	28	SEHEIAH
9:20 A.M.	to	9:39 A.M.	29	REIYEL
9:40 A.M.	to	9:59 A.M.	30	OMAEL
10:00 A.M.	to	10:19 A.M.	31	LECABEL
10:20 A.M.	to	10:39 A.M.	32	VASARIAH
10:40 A.M.	to	10:59 A.M.	33	YEHUIAH
11:00 A.M.	to	11:19 A.M.	34	LEHAHIAH
11:20 A.M.	to	11:39 A.M.	35	CHAVAKHIAH
11:40 A.M.	to	11:59 A.M.	36	MENADEL

ANGEL CALENDAR No. 3 (con't)
Intellectual Aspect

12:00 P.M.	to	12:19 P.M.	37	Aniel
12:20 P.M.	to	12:39 P.M.	38	Haamiah
12:40 P.M.	to	12:59 P.M.	39	Rehael
13:00 P.M.	to	13:19 P.M.	40	Ieiazel
13:20 P.M.	to	13:39 P.M.	41	Hahahel
13:40 P.M.	to	13:59 P.M.	42	Mikael
14:00 P.M.	to	14:19 P.M.	43	Veuliah
14:20 P.M.	to	14:39 P.M.	44	Yelahiah
14:40 P.M.	to	14:59 P.M.	45	Sealiah
15:00 P.M.	to	15:19 P.M.	46	Ariel
15:20 P.M.	to	15:39 P.M.	47	Asaliah
15:40 P.M.	to	15:59 P.M.	48	Mihael
16:00 P.M.	to	16:19 P.M.	49	Vehuel
16:20 P.M.	to	16:39 P.M.	50	Daniel
16:40 P.M.	to	16:59 P.M.	51	Hahasiah
17:00 P.M.	to	17:19 P.M.	52	Imamiah
17:20 P.M.	to	17:39 P.M.	53	Nanael
17:40 P.M.	to	17:59 P.M.	54	Nithael
18:00 P.M.	to	18:19 P.M.	55	Mebahiah
18:20 P.M.	to	18:39 P.M.	56	Poyel
18:40 P.M.	to	18:59 P.M.	57	Nemamiah
19:00 P.M.	to	19:19 P.M.	58	Yeialel
19:20 P.M.	to	19:39 P.M.	59	Harahel
19:40 P.M.	to	19:59 P.M.	60	Mitzrael
20:00 P.M.	to	20:19 P.M.	61	Umabel
20:20 P.M.	to	20:39 P.M.	62	Iahhel
20:40 P.M.	to	20:59 P.M.	63	Anauel
21:00 P.M.	to	21:19 P.M.	64	Mehiel
21:20 P.M.	to	21:39 P.M.	65	Damabiah
21:40 P.M.	to	21:59 P.M.	66	Manakel
22:00 P.M.	to	22:19 P.M.	67	Eyael
22:20 P.M.	to	22:39 P.M.	68	Habuhiah
22:40 P.M.	to	22:59 P.M.	69	Rochel
23:00 P.M.	to	23:19 P.M.	70	Jabamiah
23:20 P.M.	to	23:39 P.M.	71	Haiaiel
23:40 P.M.	to	23:59 P.M.	72	Mumiah

THE TREE OF LIFE

God is like an immense computer that contains Love, Perfection, Supreme Wisdom, and Absolute Power over all of creation. It is actually possible for us to understand the functioning of this Cosmic Computer in which we live. The Tree of Life (cf. page 25) is a central figure in the Kabbalah and illustrates the configuration of Consciousness and of the human body. Thus, it is a key that allows us to decipher the Mysteries of Creation. The Tree of Life represents the causal spheres and, as we descend along the Tree, the energies condense to give rise to materialization.

The Kabbalistic Tradition portrays the Universe as ten distinct and interconnected regions corresponding to the first ten numbers. All numerical combinations are possible. These regions are represented in the Tree of Life by circles called Sephirah, or Sephiroth in plural form. The term Sephirah means numeration. There is an eleventh, hidden Sephirah, located just below Sephirah Kether, between Binah and Hochmah. It is called Daath and it represents the Great Universal Library in which all the information of the Universe is hidden and recorded.

In The Traditional Study of Angels, each Sephirah is identified by an Archangel as well as by a corresponding planet. Sephiroth are interlinked by paths of communication corresponding to the 22 letters of the Hebraic alphabet.

The Sephiroth can also be considered Cosmic Memories ruled by God. He uses these to communicate with us.

The ancients used the image of the tree to express the link, or the unity, between Heaven and Earth. The roots buried deep in the ground, the trunk, the branches, the leaves and the fruit are all interlinked and form a whole. By adding to this symbol the notion that God is like a Living Computer, we can better comprehend the immensity and power of Cosmic Organization. A region named AIN SOPH AOUR, or Everlasting Light, exists above the Sephirah Kether. It is the Kabbalists' place in the Tree of Life, or Computer of Life, that expresses realities beyond human understanding.

The Sephiroth are positioned in three columns. The one on the right represents Clemency and masculine power. It includes the Sephiroth Hochmah, Hesed and Netzach. The column on the left symbolizes Rigor and feminine power. It includes the Sephiroth Binah, Guebourah and Hod. The central column represents Perfect Balance. It includes the Sephiroth Kether, (Daath), Tiphereth, Yesod and Malkouth.

The harmonization of the left and right columns, represented by the central column, signifies the balance between the masculine and feminine poles. It is a balance that all human beings must one day attain.

THE ANGELIC CONFIGURATION OF THE TREE OF LIFE

Apart from the Sephirah Malkouth, each Sephirah of the Tree of Life is home to a group of eight Angels governed by an Archangel. Figure 2 (cf. page 25) lists each Sephirah and its respective Archangel as well as the meaning of their Names.

There are nine Sephiroth and each shelters eight Angels. This gives us 72 Angelic Energies. Figure 3 (cf. pages 29-30) shows how the Angels are distributed in the Sephiroth and what their Names signify.

The fact that God is represented by a Tree of Life is the subject of permanent meditation. The same goes for the concept of a Cosmic Computer. In terms of Knowledge, the content of these images is inexhaustible.

MEANINGS OF THE NAMES OF THE SEPHIROTH AND OF THE ARCHANGELS

Figure 2

Sephirah	Meaning	Archangel	Meaning
1 Kether	Crown	METATRON	Who shares the Throne
2 Hochmah	Wisdom	RAZIEL	God's Secret
(Daath)	The Universal Library		
3 Binah	Laws	TSAPHKIEL	God's Laws
4 Hesed	Clemency	TSADKIEL	God's Wealth
5 Guebourah	Rigor	KAMAEL	God's Force
6 Tiphereth	Consciousness	MIKAEL	In God's Likeness
7 Netzach	Beauty	HANIEL	God's Grace
8 Hod	Intelligence	RAPHAEL	God's Healing
9 Yesod	The Foundation	GABRIEL	God's Purity
10 Malkouth	The Kingdom	SANDALFON	God is my Light (the force that unifies Spirit and matter)

TREE OF LIFE OR COSMIC COMPUTER

The Tree of Life is a diagram representing the structure of the Universe from a macrocosmic point of view and of the human being from a microcosmic point of view.

The Angelic Hierarchy consists of groups of eight Angels. The eight Angels in each of the groups are represented by an Archangel. There are nine groups of eight Angels for a total of 72 Angels. The 10th Sephirah, called Malkouth, represents Earth.

1. Angels 1 to 8 inhabit Kether,
   Archangel METATRON

2. Angels 9 to 16 inhabit Hochmah,
   Archangel RAZIEL

   Daath, the Great Universal Library

3. Angels 17 to 24 inhabit Binah,
   Archangel TSAPHKIEL

4. Angels 25 to 32 inhabit Hesed,
   Archangel TSADKIEL

5. Angels 33 to 40 inhabit Guebourah,
   Archangel KAMAEL

6. Angels 41 to 48 inhabit Tiphereth,
   Archangel MIKAEL

7. Angels 49 to 56 inhabit Netzach,
   Archangel HANIEL

8. Angels 57 to 64 inhabit Hod,
   Archangel RAPHAEL

9. Angels 65 to 72 inhabit Yesod,
   Archangel GABRIEL

10. Malkouth,
    Archangel SANDALFON

AIN SOPH AOUR

Everlasting light

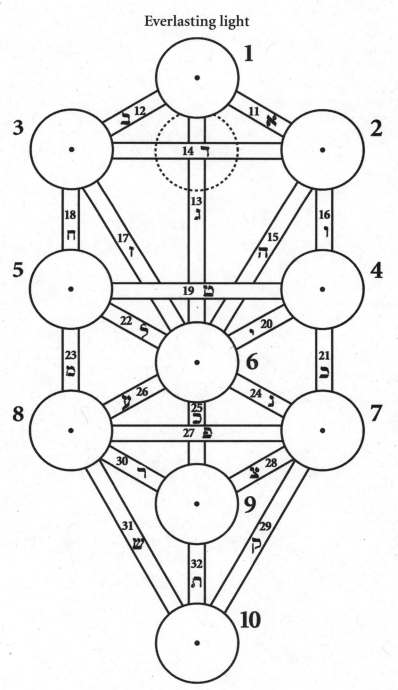

MEANINGS OF THE NAMES OF THE ANGELS

Figure 3

Sephirah	Archangel	Angel	Meaning of the Names of the Angels
1 Kether	METATRON	1 VEHUIAH	God Raised and Exalted Above All Things
		2 JELIEL	God the Conciliator
		3 SITAEL	God Builder of the Universe
		4 ELEMIAH	Hidden God
		5 MAHASIAH	God the Savior
		6 LELAHEL	God of Beauty
		7 ACHAIAH	God, Good and Patient
		8 CAHETEL	God of Blessings
2 Hochmah	RAZIEL	9 HAZIEL	God of Mercy
		10 ALADIAH	God of Divine Grace
		11 LAUVIAH	God Praised and Exalted
		12 HAHAIAH	God of Shelter
		13 IEZALEL	Faithful God
		14 MEBAHEL	God Who Keeps His Promises
		15 HARIEL	God the Purifier
		16 HEKAMIAH	Loyal God
3 Binah	TSAPHKIEL	17 LAUVIAH	God the Revealer
		18 CALIEL	God of Justice
		19 LEUVIAH	God Who Remembers
		20 PAHALIAH	God the Savior
		21 NELKHAEL	God of Knowledge
		22 YEIAYEL	God's Right Hand
		23 MELAHEL	God Who Delivers from all evil
		24 HAHEUIAH	God the Protector
4 Hesed	TSADKIEL	25 NITH-HAIAH	God Who Bestows Wisdom
		26 HAAIAH	God Who Harmonizes
		27 YERATHEL	God of Confidence
		28 SEHEIAH	God of Eternal Life
		29 REIYEL	God the Liberator
		30 OMAEL	God Who Multiplies
		31 LECABEL	God Who Inspires
		32 VASARIAH	God the Merciful

Sephirah	Archangel	Angel	Meaning of the Names of the Angels
5 Guebourah	KAMAEL	33 YEHUIAH	God the Initiator
		34 LEHAHIAH	God of Obedience
		35 CHAVAKHIAH	God the Conciliator
		36 MENADEL	God of Work
		37 ANIEL	God of Changes
		38 HAAMIAH	Offering to God
		39 REHAEL	Receptivity to God
		40 IEIAZEL	God of Consolation
6 Thipereth	MIKAEL	41 HAHAHEL	God, Shepherd of Souls
		42 MIKAEL	Like God
		43 VEULIAH	God of Abundance
		44 YELAHIAH	Servant of God
		45 SEALIAH	Motivating Force Behind All Things
		46 ARIEL	God Who Perceives
		47 ASALIAH	God Who Indicates the Truth
		48 MIHAEL	God of Fertility
7 Netzach	HANIEL	49 VEHUEL	God, Great and Elevated
		50 DANIEL	God's Word
		51 HAHASIAH	God of Medicine
		52 IMAMIAH	God of Deliverance
		53 NANAEL	Communication with God
		54 NITHAEL	God of Eternal Youth
		55 MEBAHIAH	God Who Sees All
		56 POYEL	God Who Supports the Universe.
8 Hod	RAPHAEL	57 NEMAMIAH	God of Discernment
		58 YEIALEL	God of Creative Thinking
		59 HARAHEL	God Who Knows All Things
		60 MITZRAEL	God Who Relieves the Oppressed
		61 UMABEL	Meeting with God
		62 IAHHEL	Supreme Being
		63 ANAUEL	Universal God
		64 MEHIEL	God Who Animates All Things
9 Yesod	GABRIEL	65 DAMABIAH	God, Fountain of Wisdom
		66 MANAKEL	God Above Good and evil
		67 EYAEL	Sublime God
		68 HABUHIAH	God the Healer
		69 ROCHEL	God Who Restores
		70 JABAMIAH	God Who Accompanies
		71 HAIAIEL	God, Master of the Universe
		72 MUMIAH	God of Rebirth

DESCRIPTION OF THE SEPHIROTH

A Sephirah is a Center of Life and a transformer of the Creator's Energy. In this section, we will examine each Sephirah's specific characteristics and its symbolic association with a planet.

1. SEPHIRAH KETHER

Sephirah Kether represents the Breath of God that creates our Universe. It represents the Creative Will and the source of will as a whole. It symbolizes Original Fire. This Center of Life is symbolically manifested by the planet Neptune, which represents the inspiration of the Divine Plan.

2. SEPHIRAH HOCHMAH

Fountain of Light is a pouring forth of Cosmic Energy in its purest form and the home of Supreme Love and Wisdom. The Sephirah Hochmah is symbolically manifested by the planet Uranus. Since Goodness, a characteristic of Uranian energy, is a stranger to evil, it will dissolve it. The planet Uranus also represents fraternity, altruism and evolution.

3. SEPHIRAH BINAH

Sephirah Binah is the one that determines form. It is responsible for all the crystallizations that allow the Spirit to make use of a physical vehicle to carry out its experiments. It represents the feminine power of the Universe, or the Original Womb. In a way, Sephirah Binah contains the Handbook of the Cosmic Rules and Laws. It is symbolically manifested by the planet Saturn, which represents the sense of duty, perseverance, concentration and stability, among other things.

4. SEPHIRAH HESED

This Center of Life is the bearer of organization, realization, abundance, power and autonomy. Sephirah Hesed has a heavenly aspect. It is symbolically associated with the planet Jupiter, which represents the application of Laws, sociability, optimism and general expansion, among other things.

5. SEPHIRAH GUEBOURAH

This Center of Life is home to the Celestial Surgeon who operates in cases where Cosmic Laws have not been respected. Sephirah Guebourah procures strength and vigor and concerns work. It is symbolically associated with the planet Mars, which represents frankness, activity, dynamism and courage, among other things.

6. SEPHIRAH TIPHERETH

This Center of Life is the one that establishes consciousness in a human being. It acts as a place of transmission between the dimensions of the Spirit and those of form. Sephirah Tiphereth constitutes the synthesis of all the Sephiroth. It is symbolically associated with the Sun, which represents creativity, authority, synthesis and emanation, among other things.

7. SEPHIRAH NETZACH

This Center of Life inspires beauty. It is the aspect of our inner Divinity that offers us gifts and happy solutions. It is the materialization of love. Sephirah Netzach bestows happiness. As an oasis and a zone of tranquility and well-being, it is symbolically manifested by the planet Venus, which represents happy events, gentleness, refinement, and love of beauty, among other things.

8. SEPHIRAH HOD

The final stage in the elaboration of the plan of life, Sephirah Hod applies the Laws of Sephirah Binah at a level of materialization relatively close to the physical world. In the material universe, this Sephirah is symbolically manifested by the planet Mercury, which represents practical intelligence, the faculty of analysis, the science of analogies, and the capacity of the human intellect to discern true from false, among other things.

9. SEPHIRAH YESOD

An image producing Center, this Sephirah, represented by Sephirah Tiphereth, projects Superior Consciousness towards the lower regions and gives rise to the physical act. In so doing, it houses the synthesis of the commands of the other Sephiroth granting them the power of materialization. Conversely, it channels upwards the information coming from Sephirah Malkouth, that is to say, the entire knowledge acquired by our actions on the physical level, and transmits it to Superior Consciousness. On the physical level, this Sephirah is symbolically manifested by the moon, which represents receptivity, the feminine pole, imagination, and fertility, among other things. Its neutral quality allows it to transmit, to condense, and to crystallize the energy received without altering it.

10. SEPHIRAH MALKOUTH

This Center of Life represents the Physical Self and it is associated with the planet Earth. It therefore concerns materiality.

OUTWARD AND HOMEWARD-BOUND PATHS

We have seen that the Angels are divided into nine groups of eight Angels that share the particular coloration of the Sephirah in which They reside. However, among the eight Angels of the same group, each one expresses Itself in a Sephirah other than Its home, with the exception of one in each group, which expresses Itself in Its home Sephirah. Each Angel is therefore distinguished from the others in Its group by the way It expresses Itself. We refer to this as Its specificity.

To understand this idea, we shall use an analogy and compare the Sephiroth to countries with their own culture. If someone called A was born in Germany and he emigrated to Italy, he would keep his original culture but he'd have to adapt to the mentality of his adopted country and speak its language. This movement describes what we call a path from Germany to Italy. The opposite path, from Italy to Germany, can be defined by someone called B who was born in Italy and, having emigrated to Germany, will have to adapt to the culture and express himself in the language of his foster country, Germany. In this example, A and B are complementary.

Bearing this in mind, we shall consider the example of two complementary Angels. Angel 22 YEIAYEL resides in the sphere of Binah and finds its specificity or its expression in the sphere of Netzach. Conversely, Angel 50 DANIEL resides in Sephirah Netzach and finds its expression in the sphere of Binah. These two Angels are said to be complementary because they describe the paths that connect the same Sephiroth, but each in the opposite direction. Of course, the Angels that express themselves in their home Sephirah are comparable to people who stay in their native country their entire lives.

In the Tree of Life, if we take into account the numeric order of the Sephiroth, Sephirah Binah is above Sephirah Netzach. Because of this, Angel 22 YEIALEL describes what we call an outward-bound path. Conversely, Angel 50 DANIEL describes a homeward-bound path because its movement is an ascendant and subtle one. Thus, the Angels are classified in pairs of complementary Angels. In the Tree of Life, they define the outward-bound and homeward-bound paths. Figure 4 (cf. page 34) illustrates this concept. In this table we find under the name of every Angel the name of its complement. The outward-paths are indicated with an O and the homeward paths with an H.

OUTWARD AND HOMEWARD-BOUND PATHS

Figure 4

1 KETHER			2 HOCHMAH			3 BINAH		
1 VEHUIAH	Hochmah	O	9 HAZIEL	Hochmah	D	17 LAUVIAH	Hochmah	H
						10		O
2 JELIEL	Binah	O	10 ALADIAH	Binah	O	18 CALIEL	Binah	D
			17		H			
3 SITAEL	Hesed	O	11 LAUVIAH	Hesed	O	19 LEUVIAH	Hesed	O
			25		H	26		H
4 ELEMIAH	Guebourah	O	12 HAHAIAH	Guebourah	O	20 PAHALIAH	Guebourah	O
			33		H	34		H
5 MAHASIAH	Tiphereth	O	13 IEZALEL	Tiphereth	O	21 NELKHAEL	Tiphereth	O
			41		H	42		H
6 LELAHEL	Netzach	O	14 MEBAHEL	Netzach	O	22 YEIAYEL	Netzach	O
			49		H	50		H
7 ACHAIAH	Hod	O	15 HARIEL	Hod	O	23 MELAHEL	Hod	O
			57		H	58		H
8 CAHETEL	Yesod	O	16 HEKAMIAH	Yesod	O	24 HAHEUIAH	Yesod	O
			65		H	66		H

4 HESED			5 GUEBOURAH			6 TIPHERETH		
25 NITH-HAIAH	Hochmah	H	33 YEHUIAH	Hochmah	H	41 HAHAHEL	Hochmah	H
11		O	12		O	13		O
26 HAAIAH	Binah	H	34 LEHAHIAH	Binah	H	42 MIKAEL	Binah	H
19		O	20		O	21		O
27 YERATHEL	Hesed	D	35 CHAVAKHIAH	Hesed	H	43 VEULIAH	Hesed	H
			28		O	29		O
28 SEHEIAH	Guebourah	O	36 MENADEL	Guebourah	D	44 YELAHIAH	Guebourah	H
35		H				37		O
29 REIYEL	Tiphereth	O	37 ANIEL	Tiphereth	O	45 SEALIAH	Tiphereth	D
43		H	44		H			
30 OMAEL	Netzach	O	38 HAAMIAH	Netzach	O	46 ARIEL	Netzach	O
51		H	52		H	53		H
31 LECABEL	Hod	O	39 REHAEL	Hod	O	47 ASALIAH	Hod	O
59		H	60		H	61		H
32 VASARIAH	Yesod	O	40 IEIAZEL	Yesod	O	48 MIHAEL	Yesod	O
67		H	68		H	69		H

7 NETZACH			8 HOD			9 YESOD		
49 VEHUEL	Hochmah	H	57 NEMAMIAH	Hochmah	H	65 DAMABIAH	Hochmah	H
14		O	15		O	16		O
50 DANIEL	Binah	H	58 YEIALEL	Binah	H	66 MANAKEL	Binah	H
22		O	23		O	24		O
51 HAHASIAH	Hesed	H	59 HARAHEL	Hesed	H	67 EYAEL	Hesed	H
30		O	31		O	32		O
52 IMAMIAH	Guebourah	H	60 MITZRAEL	Guebourah	H	68 HABUHIAH	Guebourah	H
38		O	39		O	40		O
53 NANAEL	Tiphereth	H	61 UMABEL	Tiphereth	H	69 ROCHEL	Tiphereth	H
46		O	47		O	48		O
54 NITHAEL	Netzach	D	62 IAHHEL	Netzach	H	70 JABAMIAH	Netzach	H
			55		O	56		O
55 MEBAHIAH	Hod	O	63 ANAUEL	Hod	D	71 HAIAIEL	Hod	H
62		H				64		O
56 POYEL	Yesod	O	64 MEHIEL	Yesod	O	72 MUMIAH	Yesod	D
70		H	71		H			

Angels who find their expression or specificity in their home Sephirah, that is, Angels 9 Haziel, 18 Caliel, 27 Yerathel, 36 Menadel, 45 Sealiah, 54 Nithael, 63 Anauel and 72 Mumiah are said to be Double Angels because their place of arrival is the same as their place of departure. The letter D indicates Double Angels.

There is no homeward-bound path to Sephirah Kether. This is explained by the fact that this Sephirah symbolizes Divine Will.

THE 72 ANGELS
THE TRADITIONAL STUDY
OF ANGELS

When we travel within an unknown country, geographical maps are very useful, if not indispensable. The same applies when we explore our consciousness. The latter is so vast that when we wish to work on it, we need markers so as not to get lost. Each ray of our consciousness is specific, and the Work we do with the Angels provides us with a list of the Qualities of each Angel as well as the associated distortions so we can understand better the structure of our consciousness and visit the memories that constitute who we are. This is what you will find in this chapter. Regular consultation of these lists familiarizes us with each of the 72 Angels and structures our Work.

These very ancient lists are the product of centuries of rigorous research and work on consciousness. As presented here, they have been adapted to our contemporary era with a view to universal use.

How do we use these lists? If we invoke an Angel for at least five days, we focus on this Angel. In other words, we focus on this specific ray or aspect of our consciousness. It is then possible to observe the manifestation of the Angel. Depending on the contents of the memories lodged within the chosen ray, the Angel manifests Itself in all Its Purity or It activates our distortions. One thing is for sure, It does manifest Itself. Thus, and this is what is extraordinary, in our dreams and in everyday life, we encounter the exact characteristics of the Angel invoked. By paying attention to our dreams and to the situations we experience, we can recognize in them the contents of the lists presented here. This allows us to consciously participate in the work the Angel is doing.

NB: It is important to interpret the qualities and distortions first and foremost in terms of consciousness. In other words, they are not to be taken literally.

1 VEHUIAH

* **Divine Will**
* **Brings the Primordial Creative Fire**
* **Capacity to initiate, to begin**
* **Success for all new creations**
* **Guides toward innovative work in an avant-garde field**
* **Sets the example, serves as a model and a leader**
* **Allows us to get out of an impasse and confusion**
* **Renewed energy that heals depression**
* **Abundance of energy, courage, audacity, bravery**
* **Loves as if it were for the first time**

Distortions

* *Lack of dynamism and willpower*
* *Stubborn, relentless, authoritarian, imposing*
* *Triggers anger, turbulence*
* *Intervenes in affairs that will end badly*
* *Rushes into things without thinking, dangerous passion*
* *Violent situation, impetuosity, destruction of entourage, excessive reactions*
* *Incapable of deciding on which direction to take*
* *Imposes one's will, forces Destiny*

Physical: **March 21 to March 25**
Emotional: **March 21, June 3, August 17, October 30, January 9**
Intellectual: **Midnight to 12:19 A.M.**
Residence: **Kether** / Specificity: **Hochmah**

2 JELIEL

* **Love, Wisdom**
* **Capacity to materialize and consolidate any reality whatsoever**
* **Providential association**
* **Grants reliability, tranquility and fertility**
* **Grants the fidelity of one's spouse**
* **Settles any dispute or conflict**
* **Altruistic, seeks to manifest love everywhere**
* **Mediator, conciliator**
* **Unifies masculine and feminine principles**
* **Conviviality, harmonious life**
* **Powerful use of words that inspire calm**
* **Allows us to calm our inner turmoil**
* **Capacity to persuade, insight into theoretical analysis**

Distortions

* *Lack of love, absence of wisdom*
* *Perverse behavior, corruption*
* *Bad associations*
* *Tyranny, oppression, quarrels, perpetual conflict*
* *Divorce, separation, disagreement*
* *Selfish celibacy, refuses children out of egoism*
* *Difficulty in meeting a spouse*

Physical: **March 26 to March 30**
Emotional: **March 22, June 4, August 18, August 19 in the morning, October 31, January 10**
Intellectual: **12:20 A.M. to 12:39 A.M.**
Residence: **Kether** / Specificity: **Binah**

3 SITAEL

* Construction
* Master builder on the inside as well as on the outside
* Planner, great strategist, gifted with a practical mind
* Honest, upright administrator
* Allows us to overcome all difficulties and adversities
* Grants us the power to expand, makes everything fructify
* Allows us to become aware of our errors and thus eliminate our karmic debts
* Nobility, magnanimity, generosity, clemency
* Faithful to one's word, peacemaker
* Work with important responsibilities
* Architect and engineer in the service of the Divine
* Gift for negotiating, enthusiasm
* Social and political renown

Distortions

• Destruction, collapse of structures, unfavorable period
• Greed, excess, diabolic strategy
• Error in preparing, planning, and evaluating
• Aggression, ungratefulness, boastfulness
• Hypocrisy, emphasis placed on the façade, lack of authenticity
• A person who does not keep his word or his promises

Physical: **March 31 to April 4**
Emotional: **March 23, June 5, August 19 in the afternoon, August 20, November 1, January 11**
Intellectual: **12:40 A.M. to 12:59 A.M.**
Residence: **Kether** / Specificity: **Hesed**

4 ELEMIAH

* **Divine Power**
* **Fair and impartial authority**
* **Rectification, discovery of a new path**
* **Capacity to make decisions, force that helps us act**
* **Participation in the creation of Destiny**
* **Study and revelation of life-plans**
* **Discovery of professional orientation**
* **Initiative, enterprise, commitment**
* **Optimism, end of a difficult period**
* **Disappearance of agitation and torment**
* **Allows us to identify those who have betrayed us so we can make peace with them**

Distortions

* *Diabolic power directed towards the satisfaction of personal needs*
* *Inertia, destructive tendencies*
* *Professional failure, bankruptcy, setbacks, period of destruction*
* *Pessimism, turmoil, dangerous discoveries*
* *Betrayal, existence of inner traitors*
* *Avidity and abuse of power*
* *Domination by others*
* *Exhaustion, stretched to the limit*
* *Feeling of superiority or inferiority*

Physical: **April 5 to April 9**
Emotional: **March 24, June 6, August 21, November 2, January 12**
Intellectual: **1:00 A.M. to 1:19 A.M.**
Residence: **Kether** / Specificity: **Guebourah**

5 MAHASIAH

* **Rectification of errors**
* **Reforms, re-establishes Divine Order**
* **Rectifies what is growing crooked before it materializes**
* **Facilitates learning**
* **Capacity to live in peace and enjoy simple, natural things**
* **Successful exams**
* **Admittance into a school of initiation**
* **Dream analysis, study of symbolic language**
* **Decoding everyday signs**
* **Aptitude for initiatory science**
* **Improvement of one's character, a beautiful and happy existence**
* **Aptitude for languages**

Distortions
- *Resentment, prejudice, arrogance, tendency to want revenge*
- *Wicked, pernicious*
- *Ignorance*
- *Debauchery, sexual abuse*
- *Denial of one's errors, poor character, difficult to live with*
- *Difficulty with learning, poor choices, authoritarianism*
- *Joining a spiritual movement to escape reality*
- *Precarious health*

Physical: **April 10 to April 14**
Emotional: **March 25, June 7, August 22, November 3, January 13**
Intellectual: **1:20 A.M. to 1:39 A.M.**
Residence: **Kether** / Specificity: **Tiphereth**

6 LELAHEL

* **Divine Light that heals everything (Light of Love)**
* **Insight, clear understanding**
* **Renown, happiness, fortune**
* **Embellishment, natural beauty**
* **Mirror of the soul**
* **Art of expression in society**
* **Celebrity through talent and achievement**
* **Artist**

Distortions

- *Ambition*
- *Masks, multiple personalities*
- *Exterior beauty only*
- *Thinking oneself indispensable*
- *Feeling of superiority or inferiority*
- *Useless spending, wasting, squandering*
- *Tendency to take everything for granted*
- *Illicitly acquired wealth (dirty money)*
- *Ambitiousness, pride*
- *Caring only for the material aspect of things and people*
- *Uses charm for selfish purposes*
- *Lives beyond one's means*
- *Unstable situation*

Physical: **April 15 to April 20**
Emotional: **March 26, June 8, August 23, November 4, January 14**
Intellectual: **1:40 A.M. to 1:59 A.M.**
Residence: **Kether** / Specificity: **Netzach**

7 ACHAIAH

* Patience
* Discovery of the role of patience in the Creation of the Universe
* Exploration, helps to discover truth
* Good use of waiting periods
* Ease of execution of difficult work
* Beneficial force in the use of computers and programming
* Capacity to discern and discover that which has been occulted
* Insight and discovery of hidden aspects
* Propagator of Light (Knowledge)
* Facilitates media coverage through computers, television, radio, the press and publishing
* Helps to pass examinations and solve difficult problems, gives us the patience for learning
* Discovers hidden secrets, finds original solutions

Distortions
• *Impatience, rebellion, resignation*
• *Laziness, negligence, heedlessness, ignorance*
• *Has no desire to learn, does not study*
• *Failed exams*
• *Paralysis in the face of adversity*
• *Excluded from positions of authority*
• *Media manipulation, seeks personal glory*
• *Incomprehension*
• *Does not keep promises*

Physical: **April 21 to April 25**
Emotional: **March 27, June 9, August 24, November 5, January 15**
Intellectual: **2:00 A.M. to 2:19 A.M.**
Residence: **Kether** / Specificity: **Hod**

8 CAHETEL

* **Divine Blessing**
* **Gratitude**
* **Materializes God's Will**
* **Conceiving, giving birth**
* **Easy success, progress, helps to change one's lifestyle**
* **Great capacity for work, active life**
* **Material wealth**
* **Fertile lands, abundant harvests, food for the soul**
* **In harmony with the Cosmic Laws**
* **Patron of the four elements: fire, air, water and earth**
* **Sets us free from evil spirits**

Distortions

- *Self-interest, self-centered, predator*
- *Material failure, ruin*
- *Useless, sterile activities*
- *Excessive willfulness, rigidity*
- *Tyranny, bad temper, blasphemy*
- *Wealth used solely for material purposes, pride*
- *Torrential rains, floods, polluted waters*
- *Catastrophic climate, fires*
- *Confused feelings, aggression, transgression*
- *Corruption, defies the law, crushes others*

Physical: **April 26 to April 30**
Emotional: **March 28, June 10, August 25, November 6, January 16**
Intellectual: **2:20 A.M. to 2:39 A.M.**
Residence: **Kether** / Specificity: **Yesod**

9 HAZIEL

* Universal Love
* Divine Mercy
* Gift of forgiveness, reconciliation
* Good faith
* Trust, sincerity
* Goodness that absolves all evil
* Powerful energy that transforms all negativity
* Support, encouragement, friendship, grace, favors from those in power
* Promises, commitment
* Altruism, unselfishness, impartiality
* Childlike purity

Distortions

• *Absence of love, possessiveness, jealousy, passion, fear of loving and being loved*
• *Hatred, war, non-reconciliation*
• *Hypocritical, deceives others*
• *Manipulates to obtain the favors of those in power*
• *Resentment, malevolence, hostility*

Physical: **May 1 to May 5**
Emotional: **March 29, June 11, August 26, November 7, January 17**
Intellectual: **2:40 A.M. to 2:59 A.M.**
Residence: **Hochmah** / Specificity: **Hochmah**

10 ALADIAH

* **Divine Grace that absolves and pardons all faults**
* **Dissolves all karma**
* **Spiritual and material abundance**
* **Innocence**
* **Reinsertion into society**
* **Great healing power**
* **Regeneration, flourishing health**
* **Helps the underprivileged**
* **New beginnings, a second chance**

Distortions
* *Dangerous spirituality, false guru*
* *Squandering*
* *Broken promises*
* *Hidden crimes*
* *Moral decadence*
* *Negligence*
* *Nonchalance, indifference, laxness*
* *Poor health, difficult karma*
* *Bulimia, sexual excess, lust*
* *Prisoner, lawbreaker*

Physical: **May 6 to May 10**.
Emotional: **March 30, June 12 and June 13 in the morning, August 27, November 8, January 18**
Intellectual: **3:00 A.M. to 3:19 A.M.**
Residence: **Hochmah** / Specificity: **Binah**

11 LAUVIAH

* * Victory
* * Renown, celebrity, success
* * Expertise
* * Life of devotion
* * Altruism, kindness
* * Receives the Light of God
* * Confidence, enthusiasm, joy
* * Successful initiations
* * Exalted love for Divine Work
* * Businesses that are useful and profitable for humanity
* * Can obtain anything from the great people of this world
* * Cosmic Organization

Distortions

• *Failure, envy, jealousy, pride, slander*
• *Extravagance, ambition, greed for power*
• *Refuses notoriety*
• *Mediocre life*
• *Wants only to enjoy physical resources*
• *Uses trickery to succeed, perverse work*
• *Aims too high or too low*
• *Destruction by lightning, reprimand from Cosmic Intelligence*
• *Excesses*

Physical: **May 11 to May 15**
Emotional: **March 31, June 13 in the afternoon, June 14, August 28, November 9, January 19**
Intellectual: **3:20 A.M. to 3:39 A.M.**
Residence: **Hochmah** / Specificity: **Hesed**

12 HAHAIAH

* **Refuge, meditation, interiorization**
* **Likes solitude**
* **Inner harmony through self-evaluation**
* **Transforms destructive attitudes**
* **Isolates negative tendencies in a circle of energy**
* **Examination of one's personal life**
* **Dissolves aggression**
* **Facilitates the interpretation of dreams, grants access to occult mysteries**
* **Grants peace and protection**
* **Increases psychic abilities**
* **Positive attitude, discretion**

Distortions

- *Isolation, alienation*
- *Impulsiveness, aggression*
- *Addictions*
- *Negativity, indiscretion*
- *Lies, betrayal, breach of trust*
- *Hallucinations*
- *Deceitful practice and wild imaginings of an unbalanced medium*
- *Confusion between dreams and reality*
- *Phobias: agoraphobia, claustrophobia, etc*

Physical: **May 16 to May 20**
Emotional: **April 1, June 15, August 29, November 10, *January 20**
Intellectual: **3:40 A.M. to 3:59 A.M.**
Residence: **Hochmah /** Specificity: **Guebourah**

13 IEZALEL

* **Fidelity**
* **Reconciliation, affinity**
* **Facilitates learning**
* **Good memory**
* **Friendship, get-togethers**
* **Faithful servant**
* **Preparation for meetings**
* **Faithful to Divine Principles**
* **Gives life to unity and to union**
* **Complementarity and balance of the masculine and the feminine**
* **Order, harmony**

Distortions

• *Infidelity*
• *Enslavement, passion*
• *Marital difficulties, separation*
• *Ignorance, error*
• *Limited mind*
• *Tendency not to learn from the lessons of experience*
• *Distanced from loved ones*
• *Lies, cheating*
• *Does not want to learn*
• *Negative influence on others or on situations*

Physical: **May 21 to May 25**
Emotional: **April 2, June 16, August 30, November 11, January 21**
Intellectual: **4:00 A.M. to 4:19 A.M.**
Residence: **Hochmah** / Specificity: **Tiphereth**

14 MEBAHEL

* Commitment
* Humanitarian aid, altruism
* Motto: Truth, Liberty and Justice
* Unconditional love
* Inspiration from Higher Worlds
* Liberates the oppressed and the prisoners
* Helps those who have lost hope
* Equity, likes accuracy, re-establishes natural order
* Respectful conduct towards the environment
* Exorcist
* Mediator, arbitrator
* Wealth, elevates the senses

Distortions
- Lack of commitment
- Does not keep promises
- Feeling of being disliked or rejected
- Diabolical forces, inner struggle
- Lies, false testimony
- Lawsuits, accusations, captivity, oppression, slander
- Usurpation, adversity, lawbreaker, criminal
- Tyrant and victim
- Identifies with social laws
- Goes against the tide

Physical: **May 26 to May 31**
Emotional: **April 3, June 17, August 31, November 12, January 22**
Intellectual: **4:20 A.M. to 4:39 A.M.**
Residence: **Hochmah** / Specificity: **Netzach**

15 HARIEL

* **Purification**
* **Moral purity, innocence**
* **Spiritual sentiments**
* **Discovery of new methods, useful inventions**
* **Inspiration for scientists and artists**
* **Absolves the conscience by simultaneously instilling Law and Knowledge**
* **Procures great insight, awakens discernment**
* **Re-establishes communication between individuality and personality**
* **Liberates from paralysis, from anything that prevents action**
* **Liberates from all forms of addictions**

Distortions
* *Puritanism*
* *Becomes an accomplice to the forces of darkness*
* *Willing to die to impose or defend an unnatural truth*
* *Terrorist, extremist*
* *Sectarian mind*
* *Failure, collapse*
* *Fights against natural order*
* *Dry, hardened attitude, over-analytical mind, tendency toward excessive dissection*
* *Mistaken judgment, inverted principles*
* *Separatism*

Physical: **June 1 to June 5**
Emotional: **April 4, June 18, September 1, November 13, January 23**
Intellectual: **4:40 A.M. to 4:59 A.M.**
Residence: **Hochmah /** Specificity: **Hod**

16 HEKAMIAH

* **Loyalty to Divine Principles**
* **Royal attitude**
* **Respects commitment**
* **Coordinator, pacifier**
* **Candor, nobility**
* **Granted responsibilities**
* **Liberator**
* **Universal Love**
* **Becomes a leader, a boss, a president**
* **Political and social organization**

Distortions

• *Treachery, betrayal, war, rebellion*
• *Agonizing struggle, torn by remorse or indecision*
• *Obstructs the realization of our superior nature*
• *Selfish love, passion*
• *Plotting, scheming*
• *Gives rise to dissension in a group*
• *Feeling of being diminished, servility*
• *Irresponsible*
• *Idolatrous, self-serving, megalomaniac*
• *Disagreement*

Physical: **June 6 to June 10**
Emotional: **April 5, June 19, September 2, November 14, January 24 jointly
with Angel no.17**
Intellectual: **5:00 A.M. to 5:19 A.M.**
Residence: **Hochmah** / Specificity: **Yesod**

17 LAUVIAH

* Revelations
* Telepathy, knows how the psyche works, intuitive understanding without analyzing or studying
* Acts against torment and sadness
* Permanent state of joy, spiritual ascension
* Gift for music, poetry, literature and transcendental philosophy
* High science
* Revelations in dreams and in daydreams, allows us to perceive the great mysteries of the Universe (Cosmic Laws) during the night
* Penetrates the unconscious

Distortions

• Ignorance, false perceptions, erroneous behavior, atheism, does not keep one's promises
• Torment, depression, sadness
• Insomnia, hyperactivity
• Existential anguish, anxiety, dropout, marginality
• Prophet of misfortune, unhealthy and misleading spirit
• Stubbornness, poor perception, material problems
• Lacking faith, enthusiasm, self-confidence and trust in others
• Discrepancy between body and spirit, gets lost in abstraction
• Science without conscience
• Difficulty expressing Knowledge

Physical: **June 11 to June 15**
Emotional: **April 6, June 20, September 3, November 15, January 24 jointly with Angel no. 16**
Intellectual: **5:20 A.M. to 5:39 A.M.**
Residence: **Binah** / Specificity: **Hochmah**

18 CALIEL

* **Absolute Truth**
* **Eliminates all doubt, proves innocent**
* **Divine Justice, karmic vision**
* **Court of jurisdiction for our conscience**
* **Discerns what is right**
* **Understanding of the interaction between good and evil**
* **Respects Divine Laws**
* **Perfect judgment, honesty**
* **Judge, lawyer, notary, magistrate**
* **Integrity, love of justice**
* **Discovers Truth from Up Above, rediscovers the source of elevation**
* **Capacity to see through intentions**

Distortions

* *Condemnation*
* *Uses justice for the sole purpose of material gain*
* *Seeks to win, rivals others*
* *False witness, false evidence, flattery*
* *Unfair trial, adversity*
* *Scandal, baseness, corruption, dishonesty, falseness*
* *Confused, entangled situation*
* *Moves away from the Truth, dark period*

Physical: **June 16 to June 21**
Emotional: **April 7, June 21, September 4, November 16, January 25**
Intellectual: **5:40 A.M. to 5:59 A.M.**
Residence: **Binah** / Specificity: **Binah**

19 LEUVIAH

* **Expansive intelligence**
* **Memory of past lives, Cosmic Memory**
* **Prodigious capacity for memorization**
* **Gateway to Memory, guardian of the DAATH Archives (the Universal Library)**
* **Mastery of feelings through reason, great patience**
* **Communicative temperament, modesty, generous mentality**
* **Allows us to bear adversity with patience and acceptance**
* **Ready to help those in need**

Distortions

* *Loss of one's intellectual faculties*
* *Useless memories, amnesia, memory lapses*
* *Atrocities committed in past lives*
* *Grief, mortification, sterility, mistrust, narrow-mindedness*
* *Sadness, despondency, despair, doleful attitude*
* *Subject to losses, induced bitterness, complicated person*
* *Accuses and makes others feel guilty*
* *Manipulates by using desire, tries to impress*
* *Absence of human kindness, inability to express one's feelings*
* *Uses one's intelligence to serve the forces of evil*

Physical: **June 22 to June 26**
Emotional: **April 8, June 22, September 5, November 17, January 26**
Intellectual: **6:00 A.M. to 6:19 A.M.**
Residence: **Binah** / Specificity: **Hesed**

20 ĐAHALIAH

* Deliverance
* Transcendence of sexuality
* Awakening of the Kundalini, of one's vital energy
* Subjects concerning spirituality and morality
* Knowledge of good and evil
* Purity, consents to sacrifice in order to evolve
* Rectification of errors committed because of exalted desires
* Establishes rules in one's instinctual behavior, rigor
* Undergoes ordeals with courage and dynamism
* Great initiate, irreproachable moral behavior
* Redemption, encounter with one's divinity
* Harmonious spiritual life

Distortions
* Sexual abuse and squandering
* Debauchery, short-lived affairs, prostitution
* Abuse of power, fanaticism, extreme violence
* Relentless struggle, difficult destiny, rigidity
* Despondency, discouragement, fear, illness
* Does not believe in a Higher Power, transgresses Divine Laws
* Seeks material possessions
* Dogmatically religious, seeks to convert

Physical: **June 27 to July 1**
Emotional: **April 9, June 23, September 6, November 18, January 27**
Intellectual: **6:20 A.M. to 6:39 A.M.**
Residence: **Binah** / Specificity: **Guebourah**

21 NELKHAEL

* **Facilitates learning**
* **Loves studying, successful exams**
* **Omniscience**
* **Goes from the concrete to the abstract, from reality to ideas**
* **Gifted for science, technology and poetry**
* **Understanding of geometry, astronomy, astrology and mathematics**
* **Inspires scientists and philosophers**
* **Conscience of Cosmic Organization**
* **Good concentration, development of knowledge**
* **Anticipation**
* **Protects against calumny, spells and trickery**
* **Exorcism through Knowledge**
* **Teacher, excellent pedagogue**

Distortions
* *Ignorance, learns without understanding*
* *Seeks and uses Knowledge for one's own ends*
* *Rejects learning, weak mentality, gets lost in abstraction*
* *Prejudiced, vindictive*
* *Erroneous mental structures*
* *Incapable of applying Knowledge*
* *Bewitchment through lack of Knowledge*

Physical: **July 2 to July 6**
Emotional: **April 10, June 24, September 7, November 19, January 28**
Intellectual: **6:40 A.M. to 6:59 A.M.**
Residence: Binah / Specificity: **Tiphereth**

22 YEIAYEL

* **Renown, celebrity**
* **Patronage, philanthropy**
* **Political, artistic and scientific activities**
* **Great generosity**
* **Encourages goodness**
* **Leader**
* **Diplomacy, leadership**
* **Fortune, wealth, business, altruism**
* **Allows us to make surprising discoveries**
* **Travel**

Distortions

• *Megalomaniac, tyrant, profiteer*
• *Slavery, repression*
• *Manipulation, relentlessness, competition*
• *Unacknowledged, wants to be rich and famous*
• *Difficulty recognizing oneself*
• *Greedy, grasping, insatiable, proud*
• *Loss, contradictory feelings*
• *Unbalanced life, opposition to progress*

Physical: **July 7 to July 11**
Emotional: **April 11, June 25, September 8, November 20, January 29**
Intellectual: **7:00 A.M. to 7:19 A.M.**
Residence: **Binah** / Specificity: **Netzach**

23 MELAHEL

* Capacity for healing
* Doctor, pharmacologist, healer, scientist
* Knows the properties and virtues of medicinal plants
* Healthy food and cultivation
* Naturopathy, herbalist, natural sciences
* The self becomes a medicinal plant
* Pacifying and soothing
* Masters one's emotions, adapts to every situation
* Faith that anticipates Knowledge
* Protection of the environment, respect for nature
* Initiated into the secrets of the Forces of nature

Distortions
• Illness, disease
• Medicine without conscience
• Uses medicine solely for material gain
• Pollution that is harmful to vegetation and the environment
• Corrupt feelings and undertakings
• Difficulty improvising and expressing feelings
• Artificial agriculture and food
• Unhealthy thoughts, destructive and polluting mind

Physical: **July 12 to July 16**
Emotional: **April 12, June 26, September 9, November 21, January 30**
Intellectual: **7:20 A.M. to 7:39 A.M.**
Residence: **Binah** / Specificity: **Hod**

24 HAHEUIAH

* **Protection**
* **Warning in the wake of danger**
* **Honesty, incorruptibility**
* **Blocks evil, renders justice**
* **Protects immigrants and those in exile**
* **Protects against thieves and murderers**
* **Protects against diabolical forces**
* **Protects against harmful animals**
* **Protects against bewitchment, magic and evil spells**
* **Allows us to return to our country of origin**
* **Sincerity, likes the truth**
* **End of a difficult period**

Distortions

• *Does not understand the sense behind an ordeal*
• *Instability, inconsistency, going astray*
• *Feeling of revenge, persecution, punishment*
• *Flees responsibility*
• *Indifference and emotional coldness*
• *Evil forces*
• *Lives by illicit means, acts illegally*
• *Delinquent, criminal, reaps the benefits of violence*
• *Corruption, fraud, theft, imprisonment*
• *Victim of judicial rigidity*

Physical: **July 17 to July 22**
Emotional: **April 13, June 27, September 10, November 22, January 31**
Intellectual: **7:40 A.M. to 7:59 A.M.**
Residence: **Binah** / Specificity: **Yesod**

25 NITH-HAIAH

* **Bearer of Supreme Love and Wisdom**
* **Mastery of Spiritual Forces**
* **Study of metaphysics and the Kabbalah**
* **Understanding of the notion of time**
* **Hears the music coming from High Spheres**
* **Like an Angel**
* **Can obtain everything**
* **Discovery of the hidden mysteries of Creation**
* **Facilitates visions, revelations in meditation and dreams**
* **Helps find a place or house in which to meditate**
* **Loves peace, solitude and silence, a calm person**
* **White magic, wishes the well-being of others**
* **Spiritual charisma**

Distortions

* *Black magic, satanic pact*
* *Renounces God, atheism*
* *Possession, bewitchment*
* *Misfortune, despair*
* *Material interests, self-centeredness*
* *Agitated, incoherent, impatient*
* *Goes against destiny and the Universal Laws*

Physical: **July 23 to July 27**
Emotional: **April 14, June 28, September 11, November 23, February 1**
Intellectual: **8:00 A.M. to 8:19 A.M.**
Residence: **Hesed** / Specificity: **Hochmah**

26 HAAIAH

* **Discretion**
* **Sense of organization and family**
* **Contemplation of Divine Structures**
* **Political Science, harmonizes social life**
* **Peaceful cohabitation, Divine Order**
* **Ability to adapt to any situation**
* **Scientific and political attitudes in accordance with Divine Science**
* **Political and social leader, administrator, decision-maker, diplomat, ambassador, dispenser of justice**
* **Allows us to know how to behave in ambiguous situations**
* **Seeks truth through reason**
* **Creator of positive atmosphere, the driving force behind teamwork**

Distortions

- *Indiscretion, self-centeredness, family problems*
- *Proud, vain, jealous, motivated by ambition and covetousness, flees one's responsibilities, one's life-plan*
- *Desire for earthly power and glory, abuse of authority and power, competitive spirit, passion, abides by the law of the jungle*
- *Anarchy, conspiracy, treachery, social disorder*
- *Imposes one's point of view, does not listen to others*
- *Inferiority or superiority complex*
- *Negative consequences from disorderly action*

Physical: **July 28 to August 1**
Emotional: **April 15, June 29, September 12, November 24, February 2**
Intellectual: **8:20 A.M. to 8:39 A.M.**
Residence: **Hesed** / Specificity: **Binah**

27 YERATHEL

* **Confidence**
* **Inexhaustible source of energy**
* **Propagates the Light**
* **Creator of positive atmosphere, optimism**
* **Teachings through the spoken and written word**
* **Civilizes, brings sociability**
* **Liberates from slanderers, from evil intentions**
* **Liberates in the case of possession**
* **Likes justice, science, art and literature**
* **Liberates from those who are opposed to our development**
* **Dissipates confusion, leads to success**

Distortions

• *Hyperactivity*
• *Possession, slavery*
• *Squandering*
• *Addictions, perverted habits, fanaticism*
• *Compulsive desire to please, provocation*
• *Compulsive gambler*
• *Egoism, flattery, emphasis on appearances*
• *Law of the jungle, meanness, ignorance, intolerance, slander*
• *Destructive science, art, literature and music*

Physical: **August 2 to August 6**
Emotional: **April 16, April 17 in the morning, June 30,**
September 13, November 25, February 3
Intellectual: **8:40 A.M. to 8:59 A.M.**
Residence: **Hesed** / Specificity: **Hesed**

28 SEHEIAH

* **Foresight**
* **Happy longevity**
* **Protection against falls, accidents, fire, lightning and illness**
* **Miraculous healing, rehabilitation, health**
* **Providential protection, Celestial insurance**
* **Grants wisdom through the examination of past experiences**
* **Premonition, protective inspiration**
* **Caution, ability to foresee events**
* **Complete calm**

Distortions

* *Lack of foresight, carelessness, deep worry*
* *Incoherence*
* *Falls, illness, accidents*
* *Destruction, turmoil, turbulence*
* *Sets off catastrophes, scatterbrained*
* *Anxiety, fear of the future*
* *Impetuous action, absent-mindedness*
* *Whirling, swirling energy*
* *Excessive willpower, angry temperament*
* *Inner and outer paralysis*

Physical: **August 7 to August 12**
Emotional: **April 17 in the afternoon, April 18, July 1, September 14, November 26, February 4**
Intellectual: **9:00 A.M. to 9:19 A.M.**
Residence: **Hesed** / Specificity: **Guebourah**

29 REIYEL

* Liberation
* Leads to High Summits
* Sets us free from evil, spells and bewitchment
* Not linked to any particular credo, does not belong to a particular sect or religious group
* Improvement of life through meditation and study of oneself
* Confidence, spreads the Truth
* Free citizen of the Universe, global vision
* Behavioral Science
* Search for truth, material detachment
* Conception, achievement, production
* Discovers the mysteries of God's Work through meditation
* Divine Work with High Inspirations
* Establishes a connection with the guides

Distortions

• Limiting situation, impasse
• Mistrust, fanaticism, hypocrisy
• Propagation of false and dangerous ideas
• Bewitchment, keeps bad company
• Sectarianism, bigotry, religious struggle
• Indoctrination, nationalism
• Prisoner
• Opposition to altruistic actions
• Materialistic philosophy, worldly pleasures

Physical: **August 13 to August 17**
Emotional: **April 19, July 2, September 15, November 27, February 5**
Intellectual: **9:20 A.M. to 9:39 A.M.**
Residence: **Hesed** / Specificity: **Tiphereth**

30 OMAEL

* **Multiplication**
* **Materialization, development, expansion**
* **Production, achievement, application, planning**
* **Patience, sense of responsibility**
* **Re-establishes health, leads to healing, relates to the medical profession**
* **Fertility, birth, concerns pregnant women**
* **Fulfillment, joy, living antidepressant**
* **Tonic, energizer**
* **Patron of the vegetable and animal kingdoms**
* **Favors plantation and harvest**
* **Rediscovery of the inner child**

Distortions

* Sterility, lack of success, repeated failure
* Corrupt materialization, lack of planning and organization, materialistic philosophy
* Poverty, impatience
* Vivisection (dissection on the living)
* Euthanasia, suicide, bearer of death
* Genocide, extermination, monstrous experiments, devastating fury
* Sadness, depression, despair
* Bad for harvests

Physical: **August 18 to August 22**
Emotional: **April 20, July 3, September 16, November 28, February 6**
Intellectual: **9:40 A.M. to 9:59 A.M.**
Residence: **Hesed** / Specificity: **Netzach**

31 LECABEL

* Talent for solving life's enigmas
* Lucidity, powerful intellect, finds practical solutions
* Masters emotion through reason
* Strategist, administrator, engineer, architect, agronomist
* Decision maker, designer, planner of the future
* Study of exact sciences, business management
* Luminous ideas generating abundance
* Love of exactitude and precision
* Revelation of Cosmic processes through the observation of the infinitely small
* Excellence, seeks material order
* Respects stages and cycles, plans for the long-term

Distortions
* *Manipulates and exploits others*
* *Illicit means, shady deals, drug-trafficking*
* *Opportunist, dishonest, greedy*
* *Dissatisfied perfectionist, manages in an over-analytical manner*
* *Squandering, permissiveness, sloppiness*
* *Bankruptcy, loss in business, insoluble problems, acts too hastily, poor use of capital and resources*
* *Possessive, forces Destiny, places importance on results*

Physical: **August 23 to August 28**
Emotional: **April 21, July 4, July 5 in the morning, September 17, November 29, February 7**
Intellectual: **10:00 A.M. to 10:19 A.M.**
Residence: **Hesed** / Specificity: **Hod**

32 VASARIAH

* Clemency
* Uprightness, benevolence, magnanimity
* Allows us to set ourselves free from guilt
* Nobility, elevated sense of justice
* Understands the meaning of ordeals
* Natural pardon
* Judge, magistrate, lawyer
* Gifted speaker
* Modesty, kindness
* Memory, Knowledge of good and evil
* Goodness, generous mentality

Distortions

• Revenge
• Unfair, disgraceful, resentful
• Guilt, accusation, condemnation
• Flees when faced with responsibilities, difficulty discerning good and evil
• Does not want to evolve, nourishes harmful intentions towards others
• Puritan, moralist, harmful influence
• Illness that can worsen
• Focuses on bad memories
• Presumptuous, impolite, ill-mannered
• Proud, materialistic

Physical: **August 29 to September 2**
Emotional: **April 22, July 5 in the afternoon, July 6, September 18, November 30, February 8**
Intellectual: **10:20 A.M. to 10:39 A.M.**
Residence: **Hesed** / Specificity: **Yesod**

33 YEHUIAH

* **Subordination**
* **Capable of withstanding high tension, advanced initiation**
* **Letting go, averts confrontation**
* **Honest, faithful to what is superior**
* **Capable of recognizing true hierarchy**
* **Conscious of one's place in the Cosmic Order**
* **Allows us to unmask traitors and to uncover schemes and plotting**
* **Supports altruistic initiatives, brings a sense of duty**
* **Gives rise to scientific discoveries**
* **A trustworthy person**
* **Contract, alliance, commitment, philanthropic association**

Distortions

* *Insubordination, rebellion, aggression*
* *Cannot deal with hierarchy, pushed aside or dismissed from positions of command*
* *Confronts orders from Up Above*
* *Perversity, multiple desires, lack of moral strength*
* *Dropout, abandonment, quest for the useless*
* *Conflict, betrayal inscribed in one's genetic code, in the unconsciousness*
* *Contempt*
* *Feeling of superiority or inferiority*
* *Worldly pleasures*

Physical: **September 3 to September 7**
Emotional: **April 23, July 7, September 19, December 1, February 9**
Intellectual: **10:40 A.M. to 10:59 A.M.**
Residence: **Guebourah** / Specificity: **Hochmah**

34 LEHAHIAH

* Obedience
* Faithful servant
* Trust and favor from superiors
* Discipline, sense of order
* Loyalty, devotion, altruistic acts
* Obeys Divine Laws and the authority that represents them
* Life of devotion to the service of an established order
  (minister, president, director, government leader)
* Peace, harmony, intelligence, at ease with ambiguity
* Obedience without necessarily understanding
* Understanding of Divine Justice
* Upright, responsible, incorruptible
* Accepts the rigors of one's destiny without protest

Distortions

• Disobedience
• Unfair laws, authoritarianism, dictatorship
• Lack of authority, incomprehension
• Competitive spirit, opposition, contradicts for the sake of
  being right
• Violence, treachery, dangerous anger, triggers destruction
• Rebellion, frustration, conflict with one's superiors
• War, rigidity, discord
• Emotional nature, tendency to rebel against laws
• Rejection, impulsiveness, absence of receptivity

Physical: **September 8 to September 12**
Emotional: **April 24, July 8, September 20, September 21 in the morning,
December 2, February 10**
Intellectual: **11:00 A.M. to 11:19 A.M.**
Residence: **Guebourah /** Specificity: **Binah**

35 CHAVAKHIAH

* **Reconciliation**
* **Harmonious family relationships**
* **Loyalty rewarded, services appreciated**
* **Ability to bring out ancestral Wisdom**
* **Humanities and Social Sciences**
* **Mediator, peacemaker**
* **Return to lost paradise**
* **Inheritance, donations, sharing of possessions**
* **Brings people closer, re-establishes links**
* **Loves peace**

Distortions

* *Family problems*
* *Dissension*
* *Unfair trial*
* *Offence*
* *Ruin*
* *Holding onto the past*
* *Bigoted, racist, nationalist, narrow-minded*
* *Egoism*
* *Social disorganization and disorder*
* *Hereditary illness*

Physical: **September 13 to September 17**
Emotional: **April 25, July 9, September 21 in the afternoon, September 22, December 3**
Intellectual: **11:20 A.M. to 11:39 A.M.**
Residence: **Guebourah** / Specificity: **Hesed**

36 MENADEL

* Work
* Altruism, vocation, cooperation
* Foreman in the Divine factory
* Help finding work
* Provides the resources to live a balanced life
* Truth and freedom found through work
* Inner work, facilitates adaptation
* Liberates prisoners and outcasts
* Understands the meaning of work
* Procures the willpower to set to work
* Recuperation of one's potential
* Dedication

Distortions

• *Materialistic philosophy*
• *Slavery*
• *Loss of employment, difficulty finding work*
• *Exile, flight, laziness, avoidance of responsibilities*
• *Lack of goals and intensity, scarcity of ideas*
• *Person too preoccupied with matter*
• *Exhaustion, coldness, isolation*
• *Incomprehension of work*
• *Forces Destiny, seeks success at any cost*
• *Seeks personal glory*

Physical: **September 18 to September 23**
Emotional: **April 26, July 10, September 30, December 4, February 12**
Intellectual: **11:40 A.M. to 11:59 A.M.**
Residence: **Guebourah** / Specificity: **Guebourah**

37 ANIEL

* **Breaks old patterns**
* **Change of mentality, new ideas**
* **Develops an independent will**
* **Breaks the circle of addictions**
* **Mastery when faced with intellectual and emotional impulses**
* **Spiritual autonomy**
* **Liberates negative forces**
* **Breaks the circle of emotions that isolate us from Cosmic Thought**
* **Bearer of new sciences and new conceptions of the Universe**
* **Encourages novelty**

Distortions

* *Resistance to new currents*
* *Attachment to old structures, to what is old*
* *Subjection to matter*
* *Goes round in circles rehashing the same old thoughts*
* *Relentless struggle to maintain the status quo*
* *Charlatan, perverted and misleading spirit*
* *Fierce and unshakeable traditionalist*
* *Emotional and material addictions*
* *Talks about what one does not know*

Physical: **September 24 to September 28**
Emotional: **April 27, July 11, September 24, December 5, *February 13**
Intellectual: **Noon to 12:19 P.M.**
Residence: **Guebourah** / Specificity: **Tiphereth**

38 HAAMIAH

* Sense of ritual and preparation
* Leads to the utmost human realizations
* Transposes ritual into daily life
* Science of behavior and conduct
* Beauty, peace, harmony
* Politeness, friendliness, good manners
* High place of transcendence
* Exorcism
* Dissolves inner and outer violence
* Helps find the perfect complement
* Extraordinary love story
* Rituals, ceremonies, initiation
* Adores the Divine

Distortions

• Black magic cults, rituals and ceremonies
• Lack of preparation
• Lies, errors, refusal to respect the rules
• Absence of spirituality
• Contrary to the truth
• Worshipper of monuments
• Demon, evil spirit, possession, aggression, violence
• Lacks manners
• Guided by one's material interests, absence of love

Physical: **September 29 to October 3**
Emotional: **April 28, July 12, September 25, December 6, February 14**
Intellectual: **12:20 P.M. to 12:39 P.M.**
Residence: **Guebourah** / Specificity: **Netzach**

39 REHAEL

* Submission, receptivity
* Perfect submission to fair parents and to the right authority
* Paternal love
* Obedience and respect
* Healing of anxiety, depression and mental illness
* Regeneration
* Respect for hierarchy

Distortions

- Insubordination, rebellion
- Absence of respect for hierarchy
- Does not listen, lacks receptivity
- Crime against parents and children
- Parents projecting onto their children what they didn't succeed in doing
- Violence, hatred, cruelty
- Authoritarianism
- Imposes obedience with cruel severity
- Mental illnesses
- Emotional problems
- Anxiety, anguish, depression, suicide

Physical: **October 4 to October 8**
Emotional: **April 29, July 13, September 26, December 7, February 15**
Intellectual: **12:40 P.M. to 12:59 P.M.**
Residence: **Guebourah** / Specificity: **Hod**

40 IEIAZEL

* Consolation, comfort
* Sets us free from emotional conditioning and addictions (alcohol, drugs, etc.)
* Consolation following effort
* Restores and revitalizes the body
* Prevents emotions from boiling over
* End of a period of ordeal or difficult situations, sets the beginning of an easier period
* Beginning of a new creation
* Rejoicing
* Sets prisoners free
* Concerns reading, writing, printing, editors
* Concerns the arts: music, painting, etc.

Distortions

• *Pessimistic thoughts, sadness*
• *Unhappy, sad writing*
• *Discouragement, lack of confidence*
• *Illness that could lead to death*
• *Tendency to flee social life, reclusion*
• *Music and other forms of destructive art*
• *Addictions, passion, tumultuous emotions*
• *Difficult period, ordeals*

Physical: **October 9 to October 13**
Emotional: **April 30, July 14, September 27, December 8, February 16**
Intellectual: **1:00 P.M. to 1:19 P.M.**
Residence: **Guebourah** / Specificity: **Yesod**

41 HAHAHEL

* **Mission**
* **Faithful servant**
* **Gives unconditionally**
* **Shepherd of souls, missionary**
* **Vocation in relation to spirituality**
* **Heightens faith**
* **Spiritual riches**
* **Non-attachment to worldly things**
* **Acts in an impersonal, detached manner on the invisible plane**
* **Wards off enemies of spirituality**
* **Reveals the Universal God**
* **Capacity to sacrifice oneself, nobility of soul**

Distortions

• *Seeks to convince*
• *Identifies with martyrs, feels persecuted*
• *Fights what one cannot be*
• *Scandalous behavior*
• *Fails in one's projects*
• *False virtue, based on appearances only*
• *Denies one's Divinity*
• *Enemy of spirituality*
• *Mockery, scorn, hatred*
• *Inquisition, religious fanaticism*

Physical: **October 14 to October 18**
Emotional: **May 1, July 15, September 28, December 9, February 17**
Intellectual: **1:20 P.M. to 1:39 P.M.**
Residence: **Tiphereth** / Specificity: **Hochmah**

42 MIKAEL

* **Political order**
* **Establishes the Laws of Heaven on Earth**
* **Procures lucidity**
* **Unmasks traitors**
* **Allows us to discover secrets, mysteries**
* **Natural authority, obedience, loyalty**
* **President, leader, minister, ambassador, consul, person in charge**
* **Teacher**
* **Security and protection while traveling**
* **Protects against accidents**
* **Success in external relations**
* **Instructs and teaches during the night**
* **Establishes absolute Power of the Spirit**

Distortions

* *Democratic system that legalizes the expression of our base instincts*
* *Double dealings, corrupt government*
* *Utters words that do not correspond to Divine Thought*
* *Betrayal of ideals, propagator of false news*
* *Lies, slander, treachery, conspiracy, defamation*
* *Accident*
* *Political and social disorder*

Physical: **October 19 to October 23**
Emotional: **May 2, July 16, September 29, December 10, February 18**
Intellectual: **1:40 P.M. to 1:59 P.M.**
Residence: **Tiphereth** / Specificity: **Binah**

43 VEULIAH

* **Prosperity**
* **Wealth, abundance, joy, enriches our consciousness**
* **Abundance of noble feelings**
* **Astute strategist, capable of overcoming inner and outer enemies**
* **Altruistic use of one's personal possessions**
* **Makes everything fructify, helps others**
* **Natural authority, trusted by superiors**
* **Opening of one's conscience to liberate it from obscure motives (vicious and pernicious habits)**
* **Peace, completeness**
* **Prepares future employers**
* **Gives unconditionally**

Distortions

• *Artificial and illusory prosperity, materialistic philosophy*
• *Discord, poverty, profound insecurity*
• *Waste of money and energy, search for artificial paradise*
• *Theft, greed, abuse of power, existential struggle*
• *War, division, separatism, revolution, destruction*
• *Wealth sought and obtained through illicit means*
• *Worry about the future*

Physical: **October 24 to October 28**
Emotional: **May 3, July 17, September 30, December 11, February 19**
Intellectual: **2:00 P.M. to 2:19 P.M.**
Residence: **Tiphereth** / Specificity: **Hesed**

44 YELAHIAH

* Warrior of the Light
* Universal Protector
* Application of Divine Justice
* Ability to resolve conflicts created by our behavior
* Helps with initiations
* Military talent in the service of just causes
* Life oriented towards liquidation of karmic debts
* Leads to victory and establishes peace
* Frank, loyal, brave, courageous
* Success in difficult situations
* Acquired Wisdom

Distortions
• Fanatic, terrorist
• War, scourge
• Brutal, aggressive, vindictive
• Diabolical forces
• Massacre and merciless treatment of prisoners
• Criminal, evildoer, lawbreaker
• Serves time in prison
• Injustice
• Tendency to overwork

Physical: **October 29 to November 2**
Emotional: **May 4, July 18, October 1, December 12, February 20**
Intellectual: **2:20 P.M. to 2:39 P.M.**
Residence: **Tiphereth** / Specificity: **Guebourah**

45 SEALIAH

* Motivation
* Rediscovered willpower, concentration
* Hope, fervor, enthusiasm
* Awakening, motor of the Universe that awakens those who are asleep
* Restarts what is stuck
* Gives back hope to the humiliated and deprived
* Confounds the proud and vain
* Exalts our consciousness
* Return to a balanced vital energy
* Bearer of health and healing
* Patron of the four elements: fire, air, water, earth

Distortions

• Lacks motivation and enthusiasm
• Proud, conceited, excessive
• Full of oneself, despotic, difficult to live with
• Imbalance and excess of natural elements (earthquakes, floods, tornadoes,
• droughts, natural catastrophes, volcanic eruptions) and their inner correspondence
• Difficulty with life, ordeals
• Forces Destiny, lacks self-control

Physical: **November 3 to November 7**
Emotional: **May 5, July 19, October 2, December 13, February 21**
Intellectual: **2:40 P.M. to 2:59 P.M.**
Residence: **Tiphereth** / Specificity: **Tiphereth**

46 ARIEL

* Revelatory perception
* Psychic abilities
* Discovery of hidden treasures
* Discovery of nature's secrets
* Acknowledgment, gratitude
* Subtlety, discretion
* Bearer of new ideas, inventor
* Revelatory dreams and meditations
* Clairvoyance, clairaudience, clairsentience
* Discovery of philosophical secrets that
* lead to the reorientation of one's life

Distortions
• *Mediumship without purity*
• *False perception*
• *Weak mentality*
• *Incoherence, indecision, tribulation, senseless behavior*
• *Timidity*
• *Insoluble problems*
• *Useless activity*

Physical: **November 8 to November 12**
Emotional: **May 6, July 20, October 3, December 14, February 22**
Intellectual: **3:00 P.M. to 3:19 P.M.**
Residence: **Tiphereth** / Specificity: **Netzach**

47 ASALIAH

* Contemplation
* Glorification of the Divine, mystical experience
* Global perspective, overall view
* Contemplates from an elevated viewpoint
* Synthesizes information easily
* Initiate, supra-normal faculties
* Pedagogue, instructor, professor
* Psychologist
* Finds Truth in little everyday things
* Revelation of Cosmic Processes
* Strategist, creative genius, talent for planning
* Intuitive, balanced, radiates from discernment and integrity
* Great interest in the esoteric

Distortions

• *Immoral and scandalous action*
• *Inverted truth, dishonesty, charlatan, fake teacher*
• *False beliefs, blind admiration, teaching of erroneous and dangerous systems*
• *Excessive dissecting and analyzing*
• *Lies, error of evaluation, ignorance*
• *Attributes the reincarnation of famous people to oneself*
• *Sexual abuse and waste*

Physical: **November 13 to November 17**
Emotional: **May 7, July 21, October 4, December 15, February 23**
Intellectual: **3:20 P.M. to 3:39 P.M.**
Residence: **Tiphereth** / Specificity: **Hod**

48 MIHAEL

* **Fertility**
* **Marital peace and harmony**
* **Marriage, marital fidelity**
* **Reconciliation, fusion of masculine and feminine poles**
* **Reproduction, growth**
* **Helps engender a noble soul**
* **Ease in associations and partnerships**
* **Gift of clairvoyance, improved perception**
* **Inner and outer peace**
* **Helps materialize Divine Intentions**
* **Providential protection**

Distortions

- *Jealousy and discordance between spouses*
- *Sterility*
- *Infidelity, inconsistency, disagreement*
- *Subservience, machismo, possessiveness, fear of losing the other*
- *Lust, passion, seeks sensual pleasures to compensate for the absence of a spiritual life*
- *Unproductive business*
- *Claims the place of another, competition*
- *Feelings of attraction and repulsion*
- *Lewdness, prostitution, multiple relationships*

Physical: **November 18 to November 22**
Emotional: **May 8, July 22, October 5, December 16, February 24**
Intellectual: **3:40 P.M. to 3:59 P.M.**
Residence: **Tiphereth** / Specificity: **Yesod**

49 VEHUEL

* Elevation towards greatness and wisdom
* Serves to exalt and glorify the Divine
* Enlightenment
* Detachment from matter
* Elevation through service
* Concerns great people
* Elaborates the seed of human thought
* Sensitive and generous mentality
* Source of inspiration
* Altruism, diplomacy
* Distances one from the hold of instinctive desires
* Feelings of fraternity, humanitarian aid
* Aspiration to what is elevated
* Great writer
* Great devotion to others

Distortions

• Self-abasement, enslavement to material impulses
• Egoism, hypocrisy, absence of principles
• Opposes feelings of fraternity
• Critical writer, person of negative influence
• Passion, hatred
• Escape
• Fear of matter

Physical: **November 23 to November 27**
Emotional: **May 9, July 23, October 6, December 17, February 25**
Intellectual: **4:00 P.M. to 4:19 P.M.**
Residence: **Tiphereth** / Specificity: **Hochmah**

50 DANIEL

* Eloquence
* Expresses things beautifully and pleasantly
* Speaks well so as to hurt no one
* Speech that attenuates the Power of a Truth
* Beauty, harmony, goodness
* Helps to see clearly
* Helps to see events as they are and to make the most appropriate decisions
* Allows detachment from matter so as to perceive essential truth
* Capacity to materialize thoughts through deeds
* Speeches, singing

Distortions

- Eloquence for personal gain
- Flatterer, deceiver
- Speaks artfully to fool the gullible, the naïve
- Elocution difficulties
- Deterioration of language
- Egoism
- Shady deals, trickery
- Lives from illicit means
- Manipulates by ensuring the support of influential people

Physical: **November 28 to December 2**
Emotional: **May 10, July 24, October 7, December 18, February 26**
Intellectual: **4:20 P.M. to 4:39 P.M.**
Residence: **Netzach** / Specificity: **Binah**

51 HAHASIAH

* Universal Medicine
* Infinite goodness, unconditional service
* Capacity to understand
* Leads to lasting healing through understanding
* Allows us to detect and identify the cause of illnesses
* Great healer, bearer of universal remedies
* Bestows the philosopher's stone
* Patron of High Science
* Gives the essential truth leading to the understanding of the dynamics of the Universe
* Expert in esoteric knowledge: the Kabbalah, alchemy, metaphysics, etc.
* A truly wise person, an elevated soul

Distortions

• *Uses medicine solely for material gain*
• *Charlatan, doesn't keep promises*
• *Flatterer*
• *Abuses the good faith of others*
• *Deceiver, manipulator*
• *Victim of fraud*
• *Illusion*
• *Science without conscience*
• *Seeks power, ambition*

Physical: **December 3 to December 7**
Emotional: **May 11, July 25, July 26 in the morning, October 8, *December 19, February 27**
Intellectual: **4:40 P.M. to 4:59 P.M.**
Residence: **Netzach** / Specificity: **Hesed**

52 IMAMIAH

* Ease in recognizing one's errors
* Allows us to expiate, pay for and repair our errors (karmas)
* Easy execution of difficult work
* Support during difficult moments
* Harmonious social life
* Ardor, strength, great vigor
* Makes peace with one's enemies
* Sets us free from prisons within
* Faithful servant
* Patience, courage
* Humility, simplicity

Distortions

- *Unstable, tumultuous emotional life*
- *Competitive love*
- *Passionate relationship, perverted desires*
- *Aversions, fights, quarrels, vulgarity*
- *Overly emotional, excessive willpower*
- *Spitefulness due to lack of recognition of one's errors, offences and misdeeds*
- *Worsens one's karma, difficult destiny*
- *Conflicting, rebellious spirit*
- *Pride, blasphemy, rivalry, animosity*

Physical: **December 8 to December 12**
Emotional: **May 12, July 26 in the afternoon, July 27, October 9,**
*December 20, February 28, February 29
Intellectual: **5:00 P.M. to 5:19 P.M.**
Residence: **Netzach** / Specificity: **Guebourah**

53 NANAEL

* Spiritual communication
* Inspires meditation
* Knowledge of abstract science and of philosophy
* Interested in spiritual life and teaching
* Fascinated by the contemplation of Higher Worlds
* Mysticism
* Loves solitude and meditative states
* Facilitates communication with the Divine

Distortions

• Refuses spiritual Knowledge and communications
• Ignorance
• Often makes mistakes
• Finds it hard to learn
• May enter a religious order through fear of facing life
• Difficulty achieving one's aims
• Fear in facing daily tasks
• Feeling of failure
• Teaches spirituality without having acquired Knowledge
• Seeks spiritual power
• Isolation, melancholic temperament
• Selfish, egotistical celibacy
• Difficulty living as a couple

Physical: **December 13 to December 16**
Emotional: **May 13, July 28, October 10, December 21, March 1**
Intellectual: **5:20 P.M. to 5:39 P.M.**
Residence: **Netzach** / Specificity: **Tiphereth**

54 NITHAEL

* **Eternal youth**
* **Beauty, grace, refinement**
* **Hospitality, warm welcome**
* **Artistic and aesthetic talents**
* **Celebrity, prestige**
* **Freshness, candor of childhood**
* **Healing**
* **Legitimate successor**
* **Synchronicity, stability**

Distortions
- *Seduction for personal gain*
- *Focused on external beauty and on appearances*
- *Lust, ambition, blind admiration*
- *Illegitimacy*
- *Reversal, permanent conspiracy*
- *Attitude that does not correspond to one's words*
- *Illness, accident, ruin*
- *Unstable situation*
- *Takes for granted*
- *Fear of growing old*
- *Bulimia, anorexia*
- *Feelings of inferiority or superiority*

Physical: **December 17 to December 21**
Emotional: **May 14, July 29, October 11, December 22, March 2**
Intellectual: **5:40 P.M. to 5:59 P.M.**
Residence: **Netzach** / Specificity: **Netzach**

55 MEBAHIAH

* **Intellectual lucidity**
* **Clarity of ideas allowing goodness and kindness**
* **Understanding through the senses**
* **Adjusts and regulates desires**
* **Harmonization of behavior**
* **Sense of duty and responsibility**
* **Opens the heart with discernment**
* **Consolation born through understanding**
* **Communicates the mystery of Morality to the intellect**
* **Profound, mystical and spiritual experience**
* **Example of Morality, exemplary behavior, commitment**

Distortions

* *Excessive logic, dry, analytical mind*
* *Lack of lucidity, mental opacity*
* *Lies*
* *Destroys spirituality*
* *Against the principles of Morality*
* *Only interested in material things*
* *Failure*
* *Negation of feelings*
* *Mistrust, fights positive ideas*
* *Dissatisfied perfectionist*
* *Capricious person*

Physical: **December 22 to December 26**
Emotional: **May 15, July 30, October 12, December 23, March 3**
Intellectual: **6:00 P.M. to 6:19 P.M.**
Residence: **Netzach** / Specificity: **Hod**

56 ꝕOYEL

* **Fortune, support**
* **Modesty, simplicity, altruism**
* **Brings gifts from Providence**
* **Fortune on all levels**
* **Creator of ideas and atmosphere**
* **Renown and celebrity in complete humility**
* **Health, talents**
* **Esteemed by all**
* **Ease of elocution, expresses oneself clearly and simply**
* **Agreeable disposition**
* **Hope, optimism**
* **Humor**

Distortions

• *Poverty*
• *Pride, ambition, bad mood*
• *Elocution problems*
• *Wants to rise above others*
• *Feelings of inferiority or superiority*
• *Squandering, worldly pleasures, excessive person*
• *Poor use of resources*
• *Illness*
• *Boasting, display of material wealth*
• *Criticism, controversy, inhibition, mediocrity, puts down others*

Physical: **December 27 to December 31**
Emotional: **May 16, July 31, October 13, December 24, March 4**
Intellectual: **6:20 P.M. to 6:39 P.M.**
Residence: **Netzach** / Specificity: **Yesod**

57 NEMAMIAH

* Discernment
* Procures a sense of action
* Reveals the cause of problems
* Liberates prisoners
* Renounces material privileges to devote oneself to a Mission
* Strategic genius, decisiveness
* Participates in building a new world
* Magnanimity
* Devotion to great causes through one's ideas
* Comprehension of life-plans
* Gifted intellect, power of anticipation

Distortions

• *Dark mentality, devoid of principles*
• *Complicated, obscure life*
• *Relationship problems*
• *Disagreement*
• *Betrayal, cowardice*
• *Indecisive, irresolute*
• *Bogged down in routine*
• *Does not commit oneself to action*
• *Prisoner of the psyche*
• *Flees experimentation and the concrete world*
• *Chronic illness and fatigue*

Physical: **January 1 to January 5**
Emotional: **May 17, August 1, October 14, December 25, March 5**
Intellectual: **6:40 P.M. to 6:59 P.M.**
Residence: **Hod** / Specificity: **Hochmah**

58 YEIALEL

* **Mental power**
* **Disciplined thinking**
* **Develops mental faculties**
* **Awareness, demonstration of logic and patience**
* **Ability to concentrate, seeks precision**
* **Force beneficial to the use of computers and programming**
* **Competent, clear-sighted person**
* **Masters passions and emotional impulses**
* **Frankness, bravery**
* **Sense of order, justice, thoroughness and unconditional loyalty**

Distortions
* *Cunning, imposes one's ideas*
* *Obstinacy, stubbornness*
* *Moroseness, sadness, pessimism*
* *Crime*
* *Anger, abuse of power*
* *Rigidity*
* *Inconsistency*
* *Lies, betrayal*
* *Harsh, vengeful, vindictive*
* *Bad intentions*
* *Manipulator*

Physical: **January 6 to January 10**
Emotional: **May 18, August 2, October 15, December 26, March 6**
Intellectual: **7:00 P.M. to 7:19 P.M.**
Residence: **Hod** / Specificity: **Binah**

59 HARAHEL

* Intellectual abundance
* Emanates goodness, beauty, truth
* Well-balanced intelligence in business and in all fields
* Likes learning
* Intellectual fecundity
* Children obedient and respectful towards parents
* Learns easily
* Practical intelligence
* Can make a fortune with intellectual qualities
* Writing, journalism, publishing and printing

Distortions

• *Intellectual aberration*
• *Destructive writings, broadcastings and influences that are negative to humanity*
• *Mental opacity, incomprehension*
• *Sterility*
• *Rebellious, disrespectful children*
• *Fire, burns everything on its path*
• *Enemy of the Light*
• *Projects doomed to failure*
• *Manipulation of the media for personal gains*
• *Fraud*

Physical: **January 11 to January 15**
Emotional: **May 19, May 20 in the morning, August 3, October 16, December 27 jointly with Angel no. 60 in the evening, March 7**
Intellectual: **7:20 P.M. to 7:39 P.M.**
Residence: **Hod** / Specificity: **Hesed**

60 MITZRAEL

* **Reparation**
* **Understanding of obedience and authority**
* **Rectification**
* **Facilitates the practice of psychology and psychiatry**
* **Healing of mental illnesses**
* **Reparation through awareness**
* **Intellectual work and harmonization**
* **Simplicity**

Distortions
- *Insubordination, disobedience*
- *Persecution*
- *Everyone for himself*
- *Rebellion*
- *Mental illnesses: madness, schizophrenia, paranoia, etc.*
- *Vindictive, critical, complicated*
- *Chronic fatigue and migraines*

Physical: **January 16 to January 20**
Emotional: **May 20 in the afternoon, May 21, August 4, October 17, December 27 jointly with Angel no. 59 during the day, March 8**
Intellectual: **7:40 P.M. to 7:59 P.M.**
Residence: **Hod** / Specificity: **Guebourah**

61 UMABEL

* Friendship, affinity
* The study and understanding of the Law of Resonance
* Helps penetrate the subconscious to reveal true motives
* Physics, astronomy, astrology
* Helps us understand the analogies between the Universe and the Earth
* Reveals the secrets of the mineral, vegetable and animal kingdoms
* Helps develop a conscience
* Capacity to teach what has been learned
* Instructor, teacher
* Learning the unknown through the known

Distortions

• Solitary heart, difficulty to find friends
• Problems with one's mother
• Return to the past, nostalgia, solitude
• Narcissism
• On the fringe, acts against the natural order
• Drug problems, lewdness
• Science without conscience
• Fake teacher

Physical: **January 21 to January 25**
Emotional: **May 22, August 5, October 18, December 28, March 9**
Intellectual: **8:00 P.M. to 8:19 P.M.**
Residence: **Hod** / Specificity: **Tiphereth**

62 IAHHEL

* **Knowledge rediscovered**
* **Philosopher, mystic**
* **Enlightenment**
* **Procures Wisdom and a sense of responsibility**
* **Beneficial for retreats, facilitates the internalization process**
* **Modesty, gentleness**
* **Solitude, tranquility**
* **Favors the meeting of a man and a woman**
* **Payment of karmic debts**
* **Pacifism**
* **Refinement of the senses: clairvoyance, clairaudience, clairsentience**

Distortions

- *Appropriates knowledge for oneself*
- *Swindler, pseudo-learned person*
- *Scandal, luxury, ambition*
- *Need for pleasure*
- *Fickleness*
- *Divorce, division*
- *Use of knowledge only for material purposes*
- *Vanity*
- *Restlessness, aggression*
- *Need for approval*
- *Isolation*

Physical: **January 26 to January 30**
Emotional: **May 23, August 6, October 19, December 29, March 10**
Intellectual: **8:20 P.M. to 8:39 P.M.**
Residence: **Hod** / Specificity: **Netzach**

63 ANAUEL

* Perception of unity
* Success in human relationships
* Initiator of projects and enterprises dedicated to the service of the Divine
* Mastery of emotions
* Sense of organization and altruism
* Administrator, coordinator, planner
* Merchant, banker, businessman at the service of the Divine
* Visionary, industrialist, manufacturer
* Logic, practical intelligence, ease of communication
* Global vision of events
* Citizen of the Universe

Distortions

• *Does not believe in a superior power*
• *Lacks common sense and vision*
• *Extravagance, spends more than one has*
• *Ruin, waste*
• *False reasoning, manipulated by desires*
• *Exclusively rational mind*
• *Cold appreciation*
• *Critical and limited mind*

Physical: **January 31 to February 4**
Emotional: **May 24, August 7, October 20, *December 30, March 11**
Intellectual: **8:40 P.M. to 8:59 P.M.**
Residence: **Hod** / Specificity: **Hod**

64 MEHIEL

* **Vitalization, inspiration**
* **Intense, productive life**
* **Antidote against the forces of darkness**
* **Concerns writing, printing, publishing, distribution, bookshops, orators**
* **Beneficial force for intellectual activity, for computers and programming**
* **Technological development**
* **Concerns television and radio programs**
* **Develops mental faculties in harmony with the imagination**
* **Helps understand and reflect upon personal experience**

Distortions
* *Lacks inspiration*
* *Contradiction, criticism, controversy*
* *Distortion of reality, compliance to illusion*
* *Tyranny, oppression, falseness*
* *Destructive, forces Destiny*
* *Does not understand one's own life scenario*
* *Megalomania*
* *Excess of rationality*
* *Plays a role, lacks authenticity*
* *Personality problem*

Physical: **February 5 to February 9**
Emotional: **May 25, August 8, October 21, December 31, March 12**
Intellectual: **9:00 P.M. to 9:19 P.M.**
Residence: **Hod** / Specificity: **Yesod**

65 DAMABIAH

* Fountain of Wisdom
* Purity, gentleness, goodness
* Radiates great spiritual values such as altruism, devotion, generosity,
* detachment and unconditional love
* Helps us advance the easy way
* Success in business that is useful for the community
* Linked to water, sea, river, spring, emotions and feelings
* Providential person capable of solving compromising situations

Distortions

- Storm, shipwreck
- Tumultuous emotions
- Anger, aggression
- Unstable feelings, Puritanism
- Leads to fatality
- Lacks generosity
- Excessive behavior, compulsions

Physical: **February 10 to February 14**
Emotional: **May 26, August 9, October 22, January 1, March 13**
Intellectual: **9:20 P.M. to 9:39 P.M.**
Residence: **Yesod** / Specificity: **Hochmah**

66 MANAKEL

* Knowledge of Good and Evil
* Stability, confidence
* High morality
* Calms, heals illness
* Kindness, goodness
* Liberates the potential buried deep inside of us
* Dreams, daydreams, High Initiation
* Reunification of the qualities of the body and the soul

Distortions

• *Machiavellian, dangerous manipulator*
• *Physical and moral disturbances*
• *Seeks only material pleasure and social prestige*
• *Without principles or altruistic values*
• *In women: late development of personality*
• *In men: belated meeting with a woman*
• *Anger towards God, rebellion*
• *Refuses to apply Knowledge*
• *Destructive spirit, impulsiveness*
• *Does not keep promises*
• *Dangerous friendships*

Physical: **February 15 to February 19**
Emotional: **May 27, August 10, October 23, January 2, March 14**
Intellectual: **9:40 P.M. to 9:59 P.M.**
Residence: **Yesod** /Specificity: **Binah**

67 EYAEL

* **Sublimation**
* **Science of mixtures and exchanges**
* **Transubstantiation (changing one substance into another)**
* **Universal History**
* **Change, mutation, metamorphosis, transfiguration, transfer**
* **Culinary art, painting, music**
* **Capacity to detect origin and genesis**
* **Visionary, able to read signs**
* **Abstract truth transformed into concrete truth**
* **Study of High Science**
* **Joy**
* **Likes solitude**

Distortions

• *Fear of change*
• *Error, prejudice, worry, sadness, isolation*
• *Propagates erroneous systems, fake teacher*
• *Lack of clarity, without morals or principles*
• *Goes from one experience to another without understanding*
• *Heaviness, absorption in matter, does not meditate*
• *Artificial food*

Physical: **February 20 to February 24**
Emotional: **May 28, August 11, October 24, January 3, March 15**
Intellectual: **10:00 P.M. to 10:19 P.M.**
Residence: **Yesod** / Specificity: **Hesod**

68 HABUHIAH

* **Healing**
* **Adjusts and regulates desires**
* **Adjustment to Divine Standards**
* **Restoration of balance following phase discrepancies**
* **Reharmonizes when we are feeling out of synchronism**
* **Love of nature, country life, open spaces**
* **Agriculture, harvest, agricultural expertise**
* **Fertile nature, creative power**

Distortions

• *Arid soil, famine*
• *Anti-life attitude*
• *Misery, pollution, plagues of insects*
• *Epidemics, contagious diseases*
• *Double life, discrepancy between thoughts and emotions*
• *Not in the right place*
• *Reluctance to abandon old privileges*
• *Discrepancy between what one wants to be and do and what one is and does*
• *In women: tendency to dominate*
• *In men: tendency to let themselves be dominated by women*

Physical: **February 25 to February 29**
Emotional: **May 29, August 12, October 25, January 4, March 16**
Intellectual: **10:20 P.M. to 10:39 P.M.**
Residence: **Yesod** / Specificity: **Guebourah**

69 ROCHEL

* Restitution, grants each person what he is entitled to
* Finds lost or stolen objects, thoughts and sentiments
* Succession, inheritance
* Notary, magistrate
* Intuition
* Study of Law and Justice
* Study of History
* Archives and the Universal Library (DAATH)
* Practical and theoretical science
* Giving and taking
* Administration, accounting, secretarial work
* Rediscovery of the Divine Self, of the original androgyny
* Clearing of karmic content, elimination of karma

Distortions

• *Taking what does not belong to us*
• *Jealousy, possessiveness, spousal relationship based solely on sexuality and materialism*
• *Sexual abuse, lewdness and multiple relationships*
• *Theft, cunning, usurpation of goods*
• *Ruin*
• *Flagrant injustice, unending lawsuit or trial*
• *Vampirism, takes the energy of others*
• *Existential fear, insecurity*
• *Family problems*
• *Lack of receptivity or emissivity*

Physical: **March 1 to March 5**
Emotional: **May 30, August 13, October 26, January 5, March 17**
Intellectual: **10:40 P.M. to 10:59 P.M.**
Residence: **Yesod** /Specificity: **Tiphereth**

70 JABAMIAH

* **Alchemy**
* **Transforms evil into good**
* **Healing**
* **Regenerates, revitalizes, re-establishes harmony**
* **Transforms, transmutes into spiritual gold**
* **Masters instincts**
* **Guides the first steps of the deceased into the other world**
* **Transforms society with enlightened ideas**
* **Helps accompany the dying**

Distortions

- *Blockage, retention*
- *Tendency to get bogged down*
- *Problems of obesity*
- *Incomprehension of good and evil*
- *Atheism, disbelief*
- *Conflict, confrontation*
- *Incurable disease*
- *Fear of change and death*
- *Outbursts, excessive reactions*
- *Heaviness, overflow*
- *Incapable of setting objectives*

Physical: **March 6 to March 10**
Emotional: **May 31, August 14, October 27, January 6, March 18**
Intellectual: **11:00 P.M. to 11:19 P.M.**
Residence: **Yesod** / Specificity: **Netzach**

71 HAIAIEL

* **Divine Arms**
* **Discernment (symbol of the sword)**
* **Luminous aura (symbol of the shield)**
* **Divine Protection to make the right decision**
* **Freedom from those who oppress us**
* **Overcomes adversity**
* **Protects and leads to victory, bravery and courage**
* **Develops great energy**
* **Leadership**

Distortions

- *Terrorist, activist*
- *Vindictive, dictator, tyrant*
- *Discord, betrayal*
- *Provides weapons for killing*
- *Bearer of internal contradictions*
- *Rupture (divorce, broken contracts, etc.)*
- *Criminal ideas, extremist*
- *Excessive rationality*
- *No respect for commitments*
- *War, continual conflicts*
- *Corrupt government*

Physical: **March 11 to March 15**
Emotional: **June 1, August 15, October 28, January 7, March 19**
Intellectual: **11:20 P.M. to 11:39 P.M.**
Residence: **Yesod** / Specificity: **Hod**

72 MUMIAH

* **Rebirth**
* **Sows the seed of a new life**
* **Understanding of the law of reincarnation**
* **Announces the end of one cycle and the beginning of a new one**
* **Brings to an end, helps terminate what has been started**
* **Concrete realizations, materialization**
* **Concerns medicine and health**
* **Terminal phase in which the seed of renewal is found**
* **Accompanying the dying**
* **Great experience of life**
* **Opening of consciousness**

Distortions

* *Suicide, unconscious death*
* *Despair, dead end, depression, blocked horizon*
* *Repudiates one's own existence, negative influence*
* *Bad health, handicap*
* *Collapse, ruin, loss of employment, of spouse, of friends, etc.*
* *Goes from one experience to the next without understanding*
* *Seeks to convince*
* *Goes against the natural order*
* *Forces materialization*
* *Lacks openness*

Physical: **March 16 to March 20**
Emotional: **June 2, August 16, October 29, January 8, March 20**
Intellectual: **11:40 P.M. to 11:59 P.M.**
Residence: **Yesod** / Specificity: **Yesod**

Angel 24 Haheuiah
Divine Protection

Are we always protected? This is the theme this evening. The lecture that follows was put together by Cosmic Intelligence to help us change our concept of protection and to lead us to the realization that the invisible world is always present and ready to help us, but not necessarily in the way we may have imagined.

If we stop and think about the destiny of the two people that I will be talking to you about and we remain in ordinary conscience, we could end up thinking that they weren't protected because they were assassinated. But if we go deeper, we realize that nothing was left to chance. By the amazing number of coincidences linking these two lives, you'll see that in the Universe, everything is calculated with great precision right down to the tiniest detail. It's a question of the most advanced mathematics: Universal Mathematics.

How are our destinies and our life-plans established? They are determined by our experiments in our past lives. The main lines of each person's life have been pre-ordained. A certain number of inter-signs linking the lives of the two people I'm going to talk to you about were noted by a journalist. An inter-sign is a mysterious link that exists between two apparently totally independent facts. It is what is commonly referred to as coincidence, except the term "inter-sign" emphasizes the fact that the link is full of significance.

The series of inter-signs that follows compares the facts of the lives of two very famous presidents of the United States of America. The first is Abraham Lincoln, who lived in the 19th century, and the second is John F. Kennedy, who lived in the 20th century. Lincoln was elected to Congress in 1846 and Kennedy one hundred years later, in 1946. Lincoln was elected president in 1860. Kennedy was elected in 1960, also one hundred years later. Each man's wife lost a child while she was living in the White House. Lincoln's secretary was called Kennedy, and Kennedy's secretary was called Lincoln. Both presidents were killed by a bullet to the head. Both were shot by a man from the South. Lincoln's murderer was born in 1839, Kennedy's in 1939, also one hundred years later. Each President's successor was a man named Johnson. Lincoln's successor was born in 1808, Kennedy's in 1908, one hundred years later. Both murderers were killed before appearing in court. Finally, a week before being assassinated, Lincoln was in Monroe, Maryland, and Kennedy was in the company of Marilyn Monroe. Isn't that impressive?

When we pay attention to inter-signs we learn to read history differently. And we realize that everything is remote-controlled. Everything is orchestrated by a great number of guides who work in parallel worlds.

Abraham Lincoln marked the history of the United States for many reasons, including the abolition of slavery. This man left us the account of a dream he had 13 days before being assassinated. This dream bears witness to the existence of Destiny. He told the dream to his wife and a few friends three days before his death. You can easily find this narration online in his biographical documentation.

Here's the account of that dream: *"I found myself in a place and I could hear someone sobbing. I felt great distress, an atmosphere of death, but I couldn't see anyone. I went down the stairs. At the bottom, I went from room to room, and everything there was familiar to me. At one moment, I opened a door and I got a shock. Soldiers were guarding a body covered with a sheet and ready for burial. Addressing one of the soldiers, I asked, 'So who's dead in the White House?' He replied, 'It's the President. He's been assassinated.' Then, I saw a huge crowd sobbing, weeping, overcome with distress."*

You can easily imagine that he was impressed with this dream and obsessed over it during the thirteen days he had left to live. Through this dream, he had learnt what was going to happen to him. Abraham Lincoln and John F. Kennedy were chosen to share so many inter-signs because they were important, powerful, public figures. They marked the social history of Earth. Through these inter-signs and this dream, Cosmic Intelligence wanted to tell whoever wants to hear, "Look, everything has been decreed. God exists."

Through inter-signs, we learn to change our concepts and to read history differently. We learn that if we develop the powers and capacities of our spirit, Cosmic Intelligence will one day give us daily guidance through our dreams and daily signs, and it will be possible to anticipate Destiny and to consciously participate in its Creation.

Other great beings like Jesus were also warned through their dreams. Jesus knew all that was going to happen to him. Scripture is very clear on this subject. We only need to remember what he prophesied to Peter. *"When the cock crows three times,"* he said. *"You will have denied me three times."* Both the event and his own death had been announced to him in a dream. Initiates and great prophets have left numerous accounts of this phenomenon during their passage on Earth. But for Up Above to give us our future and to allow us to anticipate it, we must be ready. We must have acquired great wisdom because we cannot change certain aspects, such as those written for individual or collective karmic purposes and those special missions intended to help humanity evolve, like the missions given to certain great initiates.

Gradually, as we purify and gain increasing access to Knowledge, we manage to understand the dynamics of the Universe. One day, these States of Consciousness will be openly revealed to us. Our purification process consists of cleansing all the limitations that prevent the free circulation of information. All our fears, including the fear of material loss, the fear of not being loved along with all the behavior and attitudes that are derived from them must be rectified. Then, one day, we are no longer afraid of death. We have transcended this fear and will always feel protected. Fear is a mechanism of the mind that holds a person back and limits him in his spiritual development.

Finally, one day, by meditating and visiting the parallel worlds in dreams, physical reality will no longer be more important or more tangible than other realities. From that moment on, the passage that is death ceases to cause us fear. That's how, one day, we succeed in understanding the concept of Divine Protection. But, of course, a long period of work on ourselves is necessary to succeed in always feeling protected, no matter what happens.

There is an Angel who can help us understand the true concept of Protection. This is a new concept for some of you. It is Angel number 24 HAHEUIAH. As we have already seen, an Angel is an Essence of the Creator and represents Qualities, Virtues and Powers in their purest form. Protection is an essential quality that we need to develop in order to understand that evil is educational and a limitation of our own spirit. Through the interpretation of some experiences and dreams, we shall see that we don't need to protect ourselves from evil in the usual sense. Evil, which is seen as an educational force in the Traditional Study of Angels, exists. It is part of us and we have to transcend it so as to truly be protected. In reality, evil has no real power in the Universe. It is subject to Cosmic Intelligence and directed by It with the one and only aim of helping our consciousness evolve. The Traditional Study of Angels helps us discover that, in reality, God commands Good and evil.

⊙

Knowledge Comes From Within

We always receive Knowledge from within. How? We receive Knowledge through our dreams, through daily signs and by voluntarily elevating our consciousness. An evolved consciousness is a consciousness that knows evil and decides, with its own free will, not to do evil.

How can we elevate our consciousness while the huge task of cleansing our interior remains undone? We aren't perfect, are we? We raise our conscience through the practice of Angel Recitation, that is, by invoking the Angel by reciting Its name. For at least five days, we invoke the same Angel. For example, we repeat "HAHEUHIAH, HAHEUIAH, HAHEUIAH." We must also carefully read the Qualities of the Angels and the human distortions to detect the gradual modification of our consciousness. The understanding of the Angels' Qualities and human distortions, which are well integrated through the Angel Recitation, constitutes a map of the consciousness that allows us to recognize (mainly through our dreams) the work going on. At any moment, as if by magic, what we detect in our dreams and daily signs can be identified with the Angel Qualities and human distortions we are working with.

Angel Work sets off a great opening of our consciousness. But, before getting down to the heart of the matter, let's have a look at the *Consciousness Diagram*. (Figure 1, page 5). When we do Angel Recitations and our purification work, slowly but surely, the veil that conceals the subconscious and the unconscious is lifted and disappears. Thus, we become conscious of ourselves. For example, how do we explain that suddenly, without any change in our physical environment, we suddenly feel anxiety or fear when, up until then, we felt absolutely fine? Where does this anxiety or this fear come from? It comes from within. Of course, we tend to justify this anxiety or fear and we try to dress it up by attributing it to some exterior event. In Angel Work, we use these moments because they reveal to us memories of past situations that we have recorded in our soul, a little like a computer that stores information.

Rather than attributing it to an exterior reason, each time a fear rises to the surface we use this opportunity to identify what is emerging from ourselves and creating discomfort, sadness or any other feeling or emotion. We do our Angel Recitations and, one by one, the memories are gradually cleansed. Eventually, our conscience expands, becomes clear, enlightened and, one day, we are totally connected with the other dimensions. Dreams become reality. There no longer exists any separation between the earthly dimension and the parallel worlds. But before reaching this supra-consciousness, we have to do major cleansing, which involves profound work on ourselves.

When we begin Angel Work, we are led to experience contrasting moods, like the movements of a pendulum. We feel great well-being and, suddenly, a few hours later or the following morning, we find ourselves dealing with existential anxieties and fears plunging us into various uncomfortable moods. This is normal. We are calling on Energy in its purest form. Up Above, They answer, "You want to find this Energy again? Okay. That's good. We are very happy. But you have to go within and cleanse your old memories." The contents of those old memories of which we are often totally unaware (because many come from past lives) re-emerge in our conscience.

Reading daily signs and interpreting dreams play a key role in Angel Work. We learn to read in depth and one day this leads us to experience mystical events on a daily basis and to live differently. We realize that coincidence does not exist and that God is an immense Living Computer in which we live. Great precision is established in our understanding of things and in everything we do, in order to allow us to reach the goal of our life-plan.

⊙

Types of Dreams

With Angel Work, dreams become more frequent and, above all, we can interpret them better. To simplify, we can say there are two types of dreams. The first type is very frequent, especially at the beginning of our spiritual path. This type of dreams allows us to cleanse our personal file, what we call the *personal unconscious*. In these dreams, we may meet all sorts of people, known or unknown, who help us become aware of certain aspects of our personality. Each person in a dream reveals a certain psychological profile and shows us, in a subtle way, which realities we need to modify or correct in ourselves. Often, these are aspects that we didn't even suspect existed in us. But if we reflect a little, we recognize them very well. What occurs in the subtle dimension is preparation for what is about to materialize.

One day, we can move out of our personal file to visit the *collective file*. Then, we find ourselves in the second type of dream, where we visit the souls of others. These dreams allow us to continue our evolution while helping others, directly in the parallel worlds. These are participative dreams because we act in the dimension of destiny programming, continually supervised by Cosmic Intelligence. We shall see an example of this type of dream this evening.

⊙

The Law of Resonance

One concept we must be sure to understand well when we work with the Angels is the Law of Resonance. This Law is based on the principle that we attract exactly what we are. Naturally, at the beginning we only know a tiny part of ourselves (the conscious part) because the major part remains hidden from us.

By observing little daily events, it is possible to become conscious of what is inside us. In fact, a great number of unconscious memories emerge in the form of events so that we may become aware of their existence. If we are attracted to what's beautiful, pure and divine, it is because we have these qualities within. If we are attracted to distorted aspects or situations, that means we have these within us, too. The same goes for each time we are put out by something, someone or a situation. Regardless of the degree of frustration, it is because we have memories in our unconscious that resonate with whatever is bothering us. This is an absolute fact. Even if we apparently have nothing to do with what we are shown, it remains that there's resonance in the dimension of our memories. This is called the Law of Disturbance and is a corollary of the Law of Resonance.

By observing our inner states and by establishing connections with what happens on the outside, we have enough information to identify what needs to be modified within ourselves. We understand the Law of Resonance and decide to observe its application in our daily lives. Above all, when we use it, our soul starts to evolve very quickly and we stop going around in circles. We cleanse all our karma and poor actions because we stop being aggressive or critical towards others. We come back to ourselves and do our Angel Recitation first, before saying anything to them, even if they act unfairly or what they do is awful. This requires a lot of humility but it is the route to finding those very high levels of Consciousness once again. We will see many examples of the application of this Law.

Invoking an Angel leads us to participate directly in the Law of Resonance. We often hear of the mirror effect. Reality is said to be a mirror. In other words, others and all our experiences are the reflection of who we are. Working with Angels and, especially, the conscious use of the Law of Resonance, leads us much further. We really participate in the mirror process and we intervene in it. Subtly, on the energetic level, we enter the inter-relationship that exists between the various dimensions because we consciously enter the dynamics of the mechanism that links unconscious memory and its materialization. The Law of Resonance is one of the fundamental concepts of the Kabbalah.

We will go over the list of Qualities and distortions related to Angel number 24 HAHEUIAH, but first here are a few comments on the number 24. It is an important symbol. Twenty-four hours form the complete cycle of a day and a night. We also talk of the 24 Old Men in the Bible and the 24 Lords of Karma in certain Oriental traditions. Therefore, this number symbolizes the completion of the cycle of life as well as judgment and justice. What links these three concepts? Reincarnation. It is a fundamental principle of Divine Justice based on the outcome of a life according to a person's acts in other incarnations. Thus, the figure 24 represents an energy which leads us to once again find Divine Justice within ourselves and to respect the Divine Laws because when we don't respect them everything is rendered much more difficult for us.

When we read through the Qualities of Angel 24 HAHEUIAH, we notice that one of those qualities *blocks* evil. We could interpret this according to the old concept that when something hurts or frightens us, we have to block it out. We will see that, on the contrary, we must neither confront evil nor pretend it doesn't exist. With the Angel HAHEUIAH, we acquire a growing capacity to bear great tension, that is, situations where there's conflict and negative or aggressive people in our environment, while still remaining receptive. It's a principle of Wisdom.

We often hear "I have to protect myself from that person's negativity." However, closing up doesn't protect us from anything. It is through Knowledge and understanding that we protect ourselves. We remain receptive, we let the information penetrate us and we analyze it. Eventually, we manage to send another type of energy automatically, a positive one, to the other person. We send back compassion and understanding, sometimes without having to say a single word. This attitude can be very disarming to a lot of people because they are not used to positive feedback. When we behave like this, the other person doesn't feel judged or unloved. However, if we respond aggressively, whether it is explicit or on a subtle level, we nourish and amplify the negative energy. This can create conflict with the person. Otherwise, we'll have to go through a similar situation later where someone will respond aggressively towards us.

We can also put on armor or hunch up because we cannot bear the negativity of the person or the situation. It hurts too much. By closing up, we fall into the distortion related to the Angel HAHEUIAH, that is, *indifference* and *emotional coldness*. It's the shell principle. But emotional indifference and coldness are the antithesis of love. To attain Universal Love, we must aspire to being completely open and to fusing with others.

Of course, when we resonate with what is presented to us, it is difficult. We aren't immediately receptive. But we can begin a process based on a new understanding of evil. Consciously, we make an effort not to close up or to defrost all our unconscious memories tinged with coldness. Some people show more emotional indifference and coldness than others. However, people who have an exuberant, overflowing temperament, even if they don't give the impression of coldness, also have frozen, unconscious memories concealing emotional coldness. How can we know this? Any unbounded exuberance or excess at the other end of the scale indicates a lack. When we learn to be totally receptive and understand distortions and evil, we become capable of managing all the information that reaches us, and we send back messages of hope to others.

When we read the qualities *protect immigrants and those in exile,* and *allows us to return to our country of origin,* we might think, "Well, that doesn't concern me. I am not an immigrant or in exile." When we interpret these Qualities, we must always do it in terms of degrees of consciousness because what occurs on the outside reflects what exists within. All of our memories tinged with injustice exile us in terms of consciousness. These memories have become unconscious. We all have a country of origin. High levels of Consciousness is what we must find one day, that is, the 72 Angels representing the essential Qualities, well-being and total happiness. The work we do with the Angel HAHEUIAH provides us with the inner strength and protection we need to retrieve these exiled, fugitive parts which are delinquents of our conscience.

Among the distortions related to this Angelic Energy, we can see *delinquent, criminal.* Delinquents are our inner rebels along with all our memories that were recorded on the occasions we rebelled. in a given situation. What is rebellion? It is being dissatisfied with what we have. It is a refusal of the life-plan that was conceived for us by Cosmic Intelligence in accordance with our personal apprenticeship and for the good of our spiritual development. The minute we are discontent with something, whether to an infinitesimal or to a great degree, it's rebellion, or delinquency, towards Destiny.

In order to stabilize the high levels of Consciousness of our Celestial Homeland while we are here, with our two feet on Earth, we have to repatriate all those wild, fugitive, rebel parts. We have to bring them to the surface of our consciousness and re-educate them, one by one. It is a job that is done on a daily basis. That's what work with The Traditional Study of Angels provides. If we don't do an inner repair job, sooner or later the negative parts will take on a physical form and come and destroy our life.

We can, of course, confine ourselves to a small space, limiting ourselves while no longer walking the spiritual path. Here, we find that things aren't going too badly. We experience all sorts of situations and we have a certain energetic potential as well as physical resources. There is a reason and a meaning to all of this. Certain degrees of apprenticeship are necessary. A person cannot develop spiritual powers if he doesn't wish it ardently with his whole soul and conscience. In any case, if spirituality is not inscribed in his program, his will to develop spirituality will only be superficial and will fail at the slightest difficulty. If we wish to expand our consciousness, we absolutely must respect the rhythm of apprenticeship of our brothers and sisters, because every step is spiritual. Every single step on the staircase is essential to allow us to reach the upper floors.

If we fervently wish to regain our spirituality, Cosmic Intelligence will, at the right moment, open up all those sleeping, anaesthetized and unconscious spaces that limit us. In The Traditional Study of Angels this opening depends on the intensity of our Angel Recitation. One day, we can fuse with God and attain Enlightenment. But as long as we have inner divisions, memories tinged with distortions, we cannot sustain an Angelic Consciousness. Of course we attain certain relatively high levels from time to time. But then we relapse.

The Angel HAHEUIAH *protects against thieves.* This evening, through examples and their symbolic interpretation, we shall try to understand the meaning of theft, or why we get robbed in the concrete world. Energetic theft is another manifestation of theft that is more difficult to detect and more pernicious. With this Angel, we'll see the attitudes with which we steal other people's energy and the attitudes with which others steal ours. We'll also study the reasons that push us to steal the energy of others.

It is important for our development and well-being to understand this question because each time we get robbed, we become poorer. This results in energetic deficiencies and sentimental poverty. Even if we benefit from lots of material resources, we can still experience sentimental and energetic poverty. When we are poor on the inside, we automatically take energy on the outside, seeking compensation. Thus the Angel HAHEUIAH leads us to the most interesting levels of Understanding and It procures better health for us. All dimensions are affected.

I would like to talk to you about a famous person who has the Angel HAHEUIAH as his physical Guardian Angel so as to illustrate some of the qualities and some of the distorted aspects related to this Angel. It is Nelson Mandela. Born on July 18th, this person worked to liberate South Africa. He always worked against the oppression of the Blacks by the Whites, but also against that of the Blacks over their own people. His ideal was a homeland. His aim for this homeland was in the physical dimension but it was based on beautiful values. In his youth, Nelson Mandela was a *victim of judicial rigidity*, one of the distortions related to the Angel HAHEUIAH. Considered a terrorist by the authorities, he was condemned for treason and conspiracy against the State. He was sentenced to life imprisonment. We know that this person spent 27 years in prison.

Using our ordinary consciousness, we might say, "That person wasn't protected, was he?" In fact, we shall see just how well he was protected and what his life-plan was. This person was molded and shaped to become a great symbol of freedom. Cosmic Intelligence had planned the broad outlines of his destiny, including the date and time of his birth, and the great events surrounding his arrival on Earth. When we really understand what protection is, we realize that it is always there with us. But we don't always recognize its presence because of the form it may take.

Nelson Mandela experienced riots and other violent situations, and he spent a lot of time in exile. These are distortions related to the Angel HAHEUIAH. He comes from an African royal family, and the following anecdote is told in a film about his life.

A young boy said to him, "You were lucky to live in a royal family. You must have had lots of servants to help you."

With his great simplicity, Nelson Mandela answered, "We had people to help us but I was also a servant. At a very young age, I went to help my uncle who was king and I was his servant. One of the tasks I had to do was to iron his trousers for the ceremonies. He was very demanding. If there was the slightest crease, the trousers were sent back to me. Just through this ironing task that I carried out for years, I had to learn concentration, patience, perseverance, discipline and the sense of duty."

We realize that this person, while receiving great recognition towards the end of his life, had to do lots of little tasks at the beginning of his journey in order to learn great qualities. What we often find so hard to accept is that we must learn by carrying out little tasks that don't bring us any recognition and seem thankless to us.

See all you can learn by ironing trousers? Maybe the next time you do your ironing, you'll think about Nelson Mandela. This person was incarcerated for 27 years because he defended social equality. That's very different from the little inconveniences we sometimes complain about.

Nelson Mandela liked boxing. This tells us he had some aggression in his spirit. People don't choose a particular sport by chance, and the choice of boxing reveals a need to channel aggression. Later, this person transformed this aggression. He used the limits imposed on him, including exile and imprisonment, to develop exemplary qualities. And, like other great human beings, he learned to love his enemies. He had a remarkable attitude towards his prison officers and the politicians who hounded him. It was a wise attitude.

On our own spiritual path we can allow ourselves to be inspired by this person because great limits may be imposed on us. At first, a person is overburdened so he can see his weaknesses and limitations. Gradually, through sustained ordeals, he develops the best of himself and finally liberty is established within him. We can draw an analogy with personal conscience on the one hand and the example of Nelson Mandela and South Africa on the other. We can view our entire unconscious memories as countries, some of which still have areas where slavery and domination reign. These are the areas which prevent peace, justice and truth from reigning completely in a person because the Divine Self has been impoverished.

Riots and numerous battles take place within us. They are manifested in our dreams, as in a film. When we get used to studying them, we become aware of the anarchy that is rife in our spirit. For example we might see ourselves in dreams, in the worst years of South Africa's oppression, or in another country that is affected by civil war, and this represents memories and aspects of our personality.

Every country that exists on Earth lives in us, in terms of consciousness. For example, the present-day phenomenon of globalization is creating shockwaves and adjustments that will continue to increase because a country cannot prosper indefinitely when based on distorted concepts. One day it will have to suffer the consequences of its behavior. The same goes for our consciousness. Every thought, whether positive or negative, materializes one day or another.

Sustained work with the Angel HAHEUIAH allows us to reeducate and to reunify ourselves. This Angel helps us to block the evil within us. First, It halts evil so the havoc may cease. Next, It allows us to begin to repair and, finally, to be enriched, to grow and to find our qualities.

When we become aware of the amazing number of inter-signs and coincidences, as we did in the introduction, we are filled with wonder at God's Power. To devote oneself to inner work and to the observance of signs that are present in daily life is essential. Otherwise, a person will finish reading this book and, a few days later or even the next day, old memories will settle back in. We forget everything. As soon as there is aggression or misunderstanding, we forget our Celestial Homeland and we continue to write difficult scenarios that will eventually have to be repaired.

Making a habit of reading signs and studying our dreams allows us to build up within ourselves an ever-richer library of symbols and experiences. With this practice our faith becomes unshakable. We know we are always guided by the invisible world. We no longer forget that parallel worlds exist and that there are thousands of beings to help us carry out our life plan. All that becomes real.

That's what Angel Recitation helps us to do. It helps us retain a certain level of consciousness. Because of the many distorted memories that we have recorded, we go through experiences that make us lose our clarity of thought. We no longer hear anything and we no longer see anything. We return to an ordinary consciousness, one that is centered on the self and which does not perceive Divine Justice or the existence of God. By making a habit of doing Angel Recitation every chance we get, while taking a walk, for example, we stay connected. We maintain an Angelic level of Consciousness and that gradually helps us to read the signs more easily.

I would like to share with you some real life incidents that will help you read signs. First of all, I'm going to share with you a personal experience which concerns two symbols that we often come across: the army and the police. When we work with an Angel, Cosmic Intelligence shows us where we should improve. To do this, It uses whatever can be found in our immediate environment.

Recently I was invoking the Angel HAHEUIAH, and I was bearing in mind the idea of protection and the symbols related to it. These include the army and the police. There is a whole Celestial Army that exists to protect us. Remember that *all that is Up Above has its likeness on Earth, and all that is on Earth has its likeness Up Above.* Sometimes, however, the terrestrial army and police actions are distorted and not completely right yet. We can consider the army and the police as symbols of protection that will continue to have their place as long as distorted consciousness remains on Earth. Otherwise, evil would grow to such an extent that it would prevent the development of long-lasting good.

During this period, while I was meditating on Angel HAHEUIAH and protection and while I was connecting with the Celestial Army, I went to Rimouski, Canada, where my husband was teaching a dream workshop. A couple offered to accompany us there to help out. The man belonged to the Canadian Armed Forces, and he took turns driving with my husband. Their company was a beautiful sign for me. I had meditated so much on the Celestial Army and on protection, and here I was with a soldier driving the van. It was as if the protection from Up Above was materializing right down into our van. Once we had arrived at the hotel in Rimouski, a town we visit regularly, we saw a whole delegation of soldiers waiting for a general who was staying at the hotel. I had never seen that before. It was magic for me. And the final delightful sign was that the man accompanying us recognized a man among those waiting that he had known in Germany. His name was Colonel d'Amour. *Colonel Love.*

I was really moved. I asked him, "Is that a nickname you have for him?" "No, no, no," he replied. "That's his name. Colonel d'Amour. Colonel Love."

Just imagine! There I was meditating on the Celestial Army and I was being introduced to a Colonel Love. (laughter) I was so moved! I said to myself, "My God, how good You are!" It is wonderful. We experience mystical events through signs. It brought tears to my eyes and I was filled with gratitude.

That's the beauty of maintaining such levels of consciousness. We can constantly detect all the gifts that Cosmic Intelligence gives us. You are also given such gifts. But when we are too preoccupied and there's too much disturbance within ("Did I do this? Did I do that? Did I reach the material goals I set for myself?") we cannot perceive the signs that are sometimes very obvious but often very subtle. There comes a day when we continually read signs and guide our life by spiritualizing matter.

During this same period, while traveling along in the van and doing Angel Recitation with the Angel HAHEUIAH, we passed a lorry and I saw the name of the firm inscribed on it. It was called "Viking Fire Protection." This led me to better understand the notion of protection. When we are in these States of Consciousness, rather than simply reading horizontally as we usually do, we go deeper. I said to myself, "If the owner of that firm included the word 'Viking' in the name, there is no coincidence. That surely means that in another life he was a Viking or a warrior who set off fires." The Vikings often set fire to things. They were experimenting.

When we have committed criminal acts in one of our lives (we think, we feel, we commit an act) it is inscribed in our soul. That's the Law. Then comes another stage. Since we carry within us all we have ever done, then we attract people in the outside world who are going to subject us to the same lot we subjected others to. The owner of that fire protection company certainly saw his house destroyed by fire in other lives. He must have experienced all sorts of ordeals related to fire. And now, he is at the repair stage. We do not do a task, an activity, or a job by chance. Chance does not exist. Our work always corresponds to our inner needs. But even if that man is not necessarily aware of this, he is protecting. He is helping others not to be victims of fire. Given the Law of Resonance, he is protecting himself.

The job we do also reflects aptitudes and talents we developed in other lives. It is certain that this person has a lot of experience, and on both sides. He set things on fire and he was also set on fire himself. In his memories he carries a quantity of knowledge which allows him to understand the notion of fire protection much better than other people.

When we do Angel Recitation, we study life and we travel in our minds and in our spirit. We look at what's there, in front of us, and we aren't busy thinking, "How boring to be in the car. It's so long!" No, nothing bores us anymore. On the contrary, everything becomes interesting because we keep looking deeply and we maintain high levels of consciousness. We no longer live like a cow vacantly watching trains pass by. We overcome our animal nature. That's what it means to become an Angel. We reach high levels of understanding towards Creation.

Here is another incident that serves as an example of protection. It comes from a woman who told me her story. A few years ago, this woman lived in the country and she regularly had to drive a long way to work. Once, while driving, she saw a large animal that looked like an elephant cross the road. She was in Canada! (laughter) No elephants cross roads in Canada. All of a sudden, she realized that nothing of the sort had happened. She had had a vision. Coming home from work that evening, as it was getting dark, in exactly the same place as she'd had her vision, a moose came out onto the road and stopped just in front of her car, blinded by the headlights.

We can say this woman was protected. But even if the moose had crashed into her car, we could still say she had been protected, because everything is organized according to a person's evolution.

Why was she given the vision? No doubt she was open to receiving it. When we are driving, we can find ourselves in states of active meditation while still maintaining our vigilance. A sort of calm comes over us, whether we are driving in the country or in flowing traffic. This waking state is favorable to the opening of other dimensions, as if we were dreaming while still awake or while consciously sleep-walking between two parallel worlds. Through this vision, They, Up Above, wanted to tell her, "Stop all your worrying. As you can see, everything is planned." It was decreed that at twenty-nine minutes and thirty-nine seconds past eight o'clock, a moose would come out of the forest. There are guides who look after the animals so as to match them with events that help us perceive what it is we need to understand. And even if the event doesn't lead to a clear, precise understanding at the time, the experience may well serve our future understanding. Life manages to arrange experiences so well. One situation leads to another.

One day, we no longer have just a little vision from time to time. We live with intuitions, visions and dreams all the time. These are given to us at the right moment according to our evolution and to facilitate the accomplishment of our missions. That's why, when it is time to make an important decision, we should always consult Cosmic Intelligence to make sure our gestures are in accordance with the Divine Laws. This ensures that they don't conflict with what is ordained.

⊙

Everything Is Ordained

God gave us the capacity to make choices. So how can we understand the idea that everything is preordained? As I told you at the beginning, we all have destinies and life-plans that have been preordained. They are established according to our experiments in our past lives. That is an absolute fact. Everything is inscribed in our soul. Cosmic Intelligence develops a program that is personal to allow us to relive those experiences and to succeed in rectifying them. Everything is preordained but only the broad outlines.

It is important to understand that each human being has specific goals to attain. It is a specific goal and not another. Understanding this leads us to great compassion and understanding. Fanaticism has no place any more and we stop pushing others to make them advance more quickly. We know that even if a person is in a major distortion, he is also learning spiritually. He's learning from the distortion. The principle of Divine Justice applies to all of us. We reap what we sow, in this life or the next. That's the law. This notion, which is essential for spiritual balance, helps us to understand evil and to feel good with everybody.

In short, each person has goals that have been decreed in his life-plan. But the guides who supervise us are not constantly moving us around like puppets. We are not puppets. For these Great Intelligences we are a bit like small children. When a child is young, his parents watch over him. He isn't allowed to go out unaccompanied because he could hurt himself or get lost. He is allowed in certain parts of the house and, from time to time, his mother keeps an eye on him. However, he can do certain things. He has free will. We should view our relationship with the guides in the same light. But we are always supervised. In a certain way, we can even be made to act. If an event that is important for the accomplishment of our goals is about to take place in a particular location, Cosmic Intelligence can lead us there.

When we understand this, we work to acquire receptivity and spiritual listening. Our little intellect and our little personality stop ruling our life. In the spiritual world, things are what they are like down here on Earth. We learn to respect laws and hierarchies. The difference being that these Great Intelligences are Supreme Love and Wisdom. The more an initiate evolves, the more information he obtains through his dreams and meditations, and the more responsibility he is entrusted with. One day, we participate in Creation itself. Angel Work is so powerful.

Now I would like to tell you the story of an event which concerns the Law of Resonance and the inner integration of the complementary poles of masculinity and femininity. We saw that the Law of Resonance is based on the principle that we attract what we are. Sometimes, events turn up in our lives to show us our qualities and the results of our becoming more aware. These are pleasant events. But unpleasant events also show us aspects of ourselves. When we feel upset or disturbed by something, it is Their way, Up Above, of showing us hidden aspects of ourselves that are important to acknowledge.

Each woman has within herself an inner man, and each man has within himself an inner woman. The reading of signs and the understanding of the Law of Resonance help us detect and integrate the other principle hidden within.

Here's the story. A lady came to see me and she talked to me about the situation she was going through. It concerned the rather distorted aspect of coldness. There was a certain coldness in this woman, a sort of control that she needed to overcome. She told me that she lived in a semi-detached house and she spoke to me about the neighbors that lived next door. She looks after children and operates a daycare center. With a lovely smile, she told me, "I've got two angels and four rebels."

First of all, it is no coincidence that we have certain children rather than others. The two angels and the four rebels represent parts of herself. If one of the little rebels is a boy, she is being shown that her inner man is a bit rebellious.

If we understand the Law of Resonance we can use a situation like this one to adjust our teaching methods, our patience and our understanding. We have a talk with our little rebels. By educating the little rebel on the outside, we also communicate with our memories of rebelliousness. It is our intention that makes all the difference. This becomes of great interest as it helps us advance very rapidly on the path to Consciousness. It is an extraordinary path where we learn through concrete application.

When this woman said to me, "Sometimes I have to keep the children in check. I have to keep my eyes open." It was clear that sometimes her situation caused her problems, but we could also sense that she liked what she did. It wasn't that aspect of her work that bothered her. It was her neighbors. "My neighbors live really close and they are invasive," she told me. "They are retired and they have all the time in the world. They often want to chat with me, but I haven't time to talk to them. I understand that they need love but they are just far too invasive! I'm always under the impression I'm being spied on. They have been living there for two years and it's reached a point where I'm depressed."

With an ordinary conscience and without understanding, we might react by saying, "All the same, her neighbors are not so awful as all that. They may be a bit invasive but they aren't mean. Why is she depressed?" You'll see that this woman has reasons for being depressed. Up Above, They have opened up an inner department so she'll become aware of certain deep, hidden parts within herself. "Your neighbors are heaven-sent messengers," I told her. "They have come to help you evolve, just as they shall evolve thanks to you. You have Mutual Resonance."

At first, this cold and controlling woman seems to have nothing in common with her neighbors. They, on the contrary, are exuberant, invasive and begging for love. But we shall see they have a lot in common. Using symbolic language, we could say that her part of the semi-detached house represents her conscious aspect. It is what she knows about herself, including her controlling attitude. But through her neighbors who occupy the other part of the house, Up Above, They want to show her certain aspects that she is unaware of and that exist under the veil. They want to tell her, "Look within. You have memories crying out, 'Love me!'"

Diving into our unconscious memories leads to a destructuring of our personality. We become unsure of the usual, public behavior that makes us feel in control. If we haven't got Knowledge, if we haven't got the key to understand what is really going on, we avoid these memories because we know very well that visiting them will make us lose our footing. We push down these forgotten parts of ourselves, we don't deal with them and we don't want to talk about them. We continue to repress them. Thus, we become more rigid just to keep going.

"Use this situation," I added. "Your neighbors are a gift. It is wonderful! And a depression is very useful. A depression doesn't just happen by chance. It occurs because Up Above, They opened up a window and are saying, 'Now is the time. Look. There are parts of you that you must clean up. As long as you haven't cleaned them up, you are going to be depressed.'"

This is the reason why so many people who are committed to an initiatory path can suddenly find themselves in a deep depression. It is normal. When we understand what is happening to us and we change our approach, these states prove very useful and the depression doesn't last as long.

I gave her this advice: "From now on, rather than having a depressed attitude, imagine that your neighbors are parts of yourself asking you for love. Talk to them. By talking to them, you devote time to those parts you have repressed. Your neighbors will therefore become very useful to you. Even if you are very busy, it is worth it because whatever time you devote to these people, you will get it back a hundredfold. It is when we don't feel good that life is complicated. But the more we open up, the more time we find to organize our activities. Everything goes so much better. The choice is yours. If you refuse to do the work with your neighbors, those messengers sent to you from Heaven, you might as well sell your house and move. You certainly have the right to do so, and maybe you should when this period of apprenticeship is over. But if you haven't settled anything before you leave, you'll find yourself with the same problem elsewhere, but worse. And not necessarily in this life. It could be in another life. What scenario could you find yourself in if you don't rectify these aspects of yourself? You might find yourself with people living with you, not neighbors, with a cold, indifferent mother or father. It will be you, as a child, begging for love. You'll pull on your mother's skirt, 'Mummy, love me.' And you'll do all sorts of crazy things to get attention because your parents won't give you love. They'll be doing their best, but they won't be capable of giving you anything other than coldness." When we understand that, we find the motivation to settle all we are presented with so as not to project it onto other lives.

When we understand the Law of Resonance and the way these hidden and unconscious aspects behave, every situation in life becomes a real gift! In the case of this woman, for example, if she goes to talk to her neighbors, it is as though she were going to a workshop on how to get rid of coldness and how to warm up! Just imagine! Life is a succession of workshops and lectures, available to all, right here in front of us, in our daily life. These are personalized teachings provided to each one of us. It's mathematical.

When we know that coincidence doesn't exist, we understand the great dynamics of the Universe. Everything is mathematical. Cosmic Intelligence correlates neighbors, children and events to the millionth degree. God is perfect. He is flawless organization. He is a Living Super-Computer.

Here is another incident to illustrate that it is indeed from within that we receive protection. A woman who has worked a lot with Angel Recitation told me about a dream she had. In this dream, *she saw herself with a friend whom she doesn't know in real life. This friend told her, "I've had a pendant made and it's a present for Christiane." The dreamer replied, "I'd like to participate in this present too." The pendant was made of wood. A pair of snowshoes, a rocking-chair and a house were engraved on it.*

What was this woman being shown? All the characters in the dream, including me, represent parts of herself. I represent her spiritual part and in this teaching, as I am a woman, I symbolize her inner self. Through the dream, she was being told, "We are giving you a talisman." She was receiving a protective talisman.

Through symbolism we shall see where They wanted to lead her and what door was being opened in her. First of all, wood comes from trees. The tree is a great symbol of the link between Heaven and Earth. It's a symbol of Knowledge. Wood is also a symbol of construction. She was therefore being told, "You will gain access to greater Knowledge to edify and rebuild yourself." A pendant is a symbol of connection and identification. It symbolizes loyalty to whatever the medallion represents. Why a pair of snowshoes? We must always analyze according to concrete logic. What do we do with snowshoes? We go on the snow. Snow is frozen water and water represents a person's emotional side. So every time it is not sunny and bright, snow represents a form of solitude. The person feels lonely. And snowshoes are used to go to places that are hard to get to.

Thus, Up Above, They wanted to tell her, "From now on, you will be protected and you will seek to construct your spirituality and visit places far down in the depths of your unconsciousness."

The engraved rocking chair calls up a mother rocking her child. They were telling her, "When you have difficulties, We are going to mother you, console you and cuddle you. You'll be able to visit those faraway, unconscious zones more calmly and more confidently." As for the house, it said, "Yes, there will be storms, because you are penetrating more difficult zones. But you will have a shelter, a refuge where you can be calm and at rest."

After hearing me tell her dream a month later, this woman came and confided in me other, more recent dreams demonstrating that Up Above, They have opened other doors for her. She told me she found it easier to express herself than before, especially in front of people that once made her feel completely stilted. Through these dreams, she was being shown, "Now you can talk to them because you are calmer. You are more peaceful."

This dream leads me to talk to you about the talismans that we physically wear. As we have seen, a talisman is a symbol of protection and identification that represents a philosophy or teaching. Wearing a talisman, a person consciously or unconsciously states who he is and what philosophy or teaching he follows. He resonates with whatever the talisman symbolizes. It is therefore important to study what we wear. When the talisman symbolizes a teaching or something else that's positive, the wearer signals that he wishes to remember this in all those situations where he could be unfocused and a bit lost. Clothes, musical group logos, brand names, all convey a philosophy or a specific form of thought that has positive or negative consequences for the spirit of those who wear the symbol, as well as for those who look at it. I suggest you reflect on this sentence: *I am what I wear.*

The Angel HAHEUIAH resides in the Sephirah Binah, governed by Archangel TSAPHKIEL. It is the last Angel in the group residing in this Sephirah. All the Angels in this group lead us to rediscover original matter, or the Cosmic Womb.

The planet that governs this sphere is Saturn, which symbolizes exactly those qualities we mentioned when talking about Nelson Mandela. They include concentration, perseverance, discipline and a sense of duty. Without these qualities, we cannot go very far on a spiritual path. We absolutely must rediscover them in order to reach High levels of Love and Wisdom. One of the negative aspects of this planet is coldness or emotional indifference.

One of the Qualities of the Angel HAHEUIAH is that It *protects us against theft and murderers*. I'd like to tell you a little story that is quite interesting. It happened two years ago, between the 17th and the 22nd of July, while my husband and I were touring through Europe. It was the period of Angel HAHEUIAH's reign, according to the Angel Calendar no. 1, and both of us were invoking this Angel. There we were, with a friend, on the terrace of a restaurant. My husband had put his travel wallet on the table. It was one of those bags you attach around your waist. At one particular moment he felt a bit insecure, as if someone wanted to steal his bag.

He took note of his feelings and wondered, "Why am I afraid?" He had worked so hard on detaching himself from material things. "How come I'm afraid of having my bag stolen? What's going on?" He decided intuitively to put his hand on his bag. Imagine what happened next! A split second later, almost simultaneously, along came a man who stood there in front of us, completely still. He stood right beside me, his eyes fixed on the bag. It was as if he couldn't move, as if he was paralyzed. He stayed there a few seconds. And a few seconds is a long time in a situation like that.

What had happened? As we were working with the Angel HAHEUIAH, Cosmic Intelligence wanted to give us some information about protection, and my husband had intuitively perceived what was about to happen. But it all happened completely naturally. He hadn't noticed anything on a physical level. Obviously, the person wanted to steal the bag as discreetly as possible. He had intuitively anticipated what the man was intending to do. When he put his hand on the bag, the thief's timing was suddenly disturbed. The man stood there, in front of that travel wallet, as if a mysterious force had rooted him to the spot and was preventing him from doing what he had intended. Then he went on his way. The owner of the restaurant had seen it all and he came over to warn my husband. "Watch out," he said. "Don't leave your bag on the table. That man was here to steal it."

If it has been decreed that we shall be robbed, we shall be robbed. A thief will break into one particular house rather than another because the occupiers have a resonance with theft. Chance does not exist. Everything is orchestrated. A person who gets robbed is a person who has something to understand. Cosmic Intelligence lets the thief steal. He is even under the orders of Up Above.

If we aren't to be robbed, no one can rob us. The thief won't be able to get into the house or won't be able to take what he wants. If we are robbed, it is a gift. We say, "Thank you." We are getting a lesson and paying off karma. To understand the situation, you only have to analyze the inherent symbolism. For example, if we get our handbag stolen and it mainly contained our glasses, it means, "You haven't looked at things the right way in the past." We analyze what was stolen and what those objects represent. Thus, we can understand the message that we are being given, as in a dream. We also try to make a link with what we were experiencing at the time of the theft. Were we trying to hold something back? There is a multitude of interpretations. It can also be that Up Above, They are trying to tell us, "You stole in other lives. So now you are being repaid in kind." But to deepen the meaning of a particular theft, we have to push the analysis much further and find subtle aspects that need changing within ourselves. And we can even ask Up Above to receive a dream to understand better what happened.

We are now going to discuss two incidents that concern a more subtle aspect of theft: *energy theft*. The first account comes from a woman who told me a few of her dreams. While I was preparing this conference on the Angel HAHEUIAH, as if by magic, several people came to talk to me about dreams relating to theft. This woman told me that over a period of a few days, she dreamt three times that she was being robbed. In the first dream, *the four tires of her car were stolen*. In the second, *the whole car was stolen*. In the third, *the furniture she had put in storage was stolen*.

She explained why her furniture was in storage. "I have just sold my house," she said. "The place I've found is only available in three months' time. Meanwhile, I'm living at my daughter's. But it is not easy with my grandchildren. I don't really feel at ease there."

I listened to her and I said, "You think these dreams are showing you that your energy is being stolen, don't you? That's what you think?" I was mirroring her own thoughts. "You'll see what lesson They wanted to give you through those three dreams," I continued. "In the first dream, your tires were stolen. Tires and our car are important symbols. They show us how we conduct ourselves towards others and what type of behavior we have toward others in society. In the dream, you were shown that you had no more tires. The next day you probably didn't have much energy, did you? When we have no car, it's as if we had no inner vehicle to advance. Yes, it is true. Your energy was stolen. You were robbed, but not in the way you think. It was Beings, guides in the subtle dimensions, that took away your energy, and they had the right to do so. Up Above, They let those beings rob you because you had something you needed to understand. You had to modify some of the ways you think, feel and behave. As you didn't understand the lesson that day, They increased the dose, and they stole more energy from you. Your whole car was stolen. It must have been worse. And a few days later, as you still hadn't understood the sense of these dreams, your stored furniture was stolen."

Symbolically, furniture represents a person's sentimental structure. So I told her, "Through your third dream, you were being told, 'Sentimental poverty dwells in you.' Energy was taken away from you so as to make you change your feelings."

I asked her, "Don't you consider yourself blessed to have sold your house?"

"Yes," she replied.

"Don't you consider yourself blessed to have temporary lodging for three months?"

"Yes."

"Don't you consider yourself blessed to be put up by your daughter and to be with your grandchildren? No matter how they behave. They are doing their best. They are putting you up in their home."

"Yes."

"Don't you think there's a little ingratitude on your behalf? For three months your little habits are being disturbed. You are being placed just a little bit more in society, and that doesn't suit you at all. You harbor a certain type of thought and emotion and that's what you convey. Therefore, you got robbed in order to receive a lesson."

There she stood wide-eyed. She was beginning to see. The following month she came to the lecture. She heard me tell her dream and that made her very happy. "Now, I am so happy to be with my daughter," she said. "I feel so good with her. I am truly grateful for what you told me. I've understood something important."

You may say that if dreams are based on attitudes like that, there must be lots of them. Yes. It is true that energy thefts ordered by Up Above are going on all the time. It is like a bank taking back the loan granted to a client because he didn't fulfill his commitments.

Of course, people with an ordinary conscience don't have this kind of understanding. But as soon as we truly understand that we are here on Earth for the unique purpose of developing qualities and virtues, we realize that everything is orchestrated with this exact aim.

As we realize how we are robbed by our very own attitudes, we lose that old spiritual idea that we should protect ourselves from certain people or certain beings who could turn us into vampires. We know that if people or beings do this to us, they have the right to do so. They have been sent by Heaven. We understand that they are there to teach us and to make us change our behavior. Thus, fear disappears and receptivity can establish itself. We no longer need to avoid anything whatsoever. We can really go everywhere and feel fine and safe. But to reach this stage, we have to work on ourselves and change our behavior or attitude. When we feel aggressive, rebellious or sad tendencies surfacing, we take advantage of the situations to intensify our Angel Recitation and cleanse the memories that resonate with them. We call to mind the great principles and, one day, we acquire mastery and no one can rob us anymore. We become very rich while also benefiting from Providence's protection.

Here is another incident concerning theft. It brings out another, very interesting angle of the subject. A man who works with The Traditional Study of Angels told me this dream. He saw himself with a key that was engraved with the number 32, but it was twisted. When we do Angel Work, we can receive numbers which represent

Angels. Up Above, They know this will prompt us to go and look up which Angel corresponds to the number received. As Angel no. 32 VASARIAH is one of this man's Guardian Angels, the message was all the more important for him.

In the dream, he was trying in vain to start up his car with the twisted key. Suddenly, he found himself in a place absolutely full of safes belonging to other people. With his twisted key, he was able to open up all the safes. He was really surprised, but he didn't take anything. He left everything where it was. Then, he woke up. What did They wish to tell him? They wanted to tell him, "Be careful, you have within you a very powerful key. It bore his Angel's number. But sometimes you distort it. You have been given greater energy than normal, but you don't always use it in the right way."

This man has great charisma. He really knows how to talk to people and has great facility in expressing himself. So great is his charisma that he can get people to undertake any kind of project. Charisma is a powerful energy that radiates from a person. Politicians and many famous people have it, but they don't always use it very well.

Up Above, They wanted to warn this man. "Be careful," they were saying. "With the charisma that you've been given comes a whole set of responsibilities. You are capable of penetrating others deeply. Hence, if you are not correct, if you are twisted, you can extirpate their energy. Be very careful. Use your potential better. If you don't use it well in this life, you will find yourself energetically impoverished in your next life. You will seem transparent and no one will notice you because you'll no longer radiate at all." This man is very lucky to have been warned.

Another way to extort other people's energy is misplaced curiosity. When we are too curious about other people's lives, it is like rape. We steal their energy. There is a little exercise we can do for this. Whenever we pass by houses with lovely big windows that are lit up on the inside, we tend to just glance in out of curiosity. When we haven't got Knowledge, we may say it is natural. But we must train ourselves not to look. Eventually this practice is inscribed even in our dreams and in parallel worlds, and we no longer have this type of curiosity. As long as we maintain curiosity about other people's lives, we cannot be granted the Universal Passport which allows us to visit people in other worlds. We must be limited, because our spirit hasn't enough strength, concentration or conviction to respect the Divine Laws.

When I spoke to this man about curiosity, he told me, "It is so true that I am curious! When I see the inside of a house, if I could go right in, I would. I'm that curious." When I saw him again some time later, he said, "I tried that discipline. It is hard for me not to look. I have to hold my head." (Laughter).

Here is another example that shows how we can be afraid through lack of Knowledge. A woman confided in me an initiatory dream. In this dream, *she was lying on her bed beside her companion. All of a sudden she sat up and saw a large parasite hanging above her bed, right in front of her. She was really scared. She jumped out of bed and ran out of the room as fast as she could. Then, she collected her wits and began to say the "Our Father" and she regained enough courage to return to her bedroom. Back in the room, where the parasites had been, she saw a series of little red and black apples, each slightly burnt. Everything had changed. Still in her dream, she told a friend she doesn't actually know in real life what had just happened. After hearing the story, this person asked her, "Are you sure you surrounded yourself well with white light?"*

What did They, Up Above, want to tell this woman? The bedroom symbolizes a person's intimate parts. They wanted to speak to her about these parts and her anxiety related to her intimacy. The man at the dreamer's side represents her emissive part, or the part that manifests itself in her actions. Both her friend and herself represent her receptive part, or her inner world.

The parasites symbolize the dangerous intrusion of negative energies that muddy her intimacy and her spiritual vision. They wanted to show her how she could rectify her fears. The fact that she was able to go back into the room after saying the "Our Father" showed her the power of spirituality. She was being shown that by elevating her conscience, the situation was transformed, just like that. The parasite had disappeared and been replaced with slightly burnt apples.

This shows well that when we connect ourselves to God, it has the power to transform our fears and all things. And because she didn't have enough faith, we can see that the transformation was not complete. She still had the parasites inside her. She had the slightly burnt apples.

Since her friend, who is a part of herself, asked her if she had surrounded herself well with white light, this initiatory dream was an invitation for the woman to modify her concept of protection. Up Above, They wanted to tell her, "You don't understand the reason for evil very well."

In certain spiritual circles, we often hear, "If you are afraid that your car will be stolen, surround it with white light." Or, "Surround yourself with white light and you'll be protected. You'll see." That's fine. It is a beautiful concept. But it is only a first step. It is like saying to a child, "It's the stork that brings babies." The simple fact of surrounding ourselves or an object with white light allows us to connect with positive energy and that can instantaneously modify our level of consciousness. We feel better immediately. But the effect is only momentary, because our fears remain and resurface at the first opportunity. That memory which hasn't been reprogrammed is going to manifest itself again. Therefore, doing that is merely a stop-gap. We have to go back to the deep cause and cleanse the memories that give rise to these fears.

When we are afraid of being robbed, what does it mean? Either it's a warning that something is in the air, like the example of my husband on the terrace. In this case, it was an intuition. Otherwise, it is only fears and old difficulties that emerge from our memories. It is the fear of losing our possessions or all sorts of other fears that we have stored in this life, as well as in others, and that we project onto the outside and onto the situations we are going through. We are afraid of being robbed because we too have stolen other people's energy, often without realizing it. I suggest you meditate on this statement: *When you are afraid of others, it is yourself that you are afraid of.*

How can we acquire real protection? Say we are afraid of having our car or any other object stolen. Instead of telling ourselves, "I'll surround it with white light," we go right into the evil. We enter our own fear and we ask ourselves, "Why am I afraid?" We repeat these great principles: *Evil is educational, matter is temporary, reincarnation exists, the spirit is eternal, God is a Living Computer in which we all live, Divine Justice is absolute, etc.* and at the same time, we do our Angel Recitation with the Angel HAHEUIAH. We tell ourselves that there is something for us to understand and Cosmic Intelligence wants to show us what it is. Thus, in a very short time, we shall have dreams and experience situations relating to this in order to become more conscious. In this way, we learn to seize the nature of evil in order to transcend it. It no longer lives in our memories and, eventually, all our fears disappear.

During my conversation with this woman, I drew a parallel between the 'Our Father' she had recited in her dream and the Angel Recitation. I told her, "What you saw happen with the 'Our Father,' well, Angel Recitation has the same effect, except it touches a very precise department of your conscience. When we invoke the Name of an Angel, in fact, it is the Name of God that we invoke. For example, Angel HAHEUIAH means *God the Protector*. Of course we can continue to do the 'Our Father,' (it is a beautiful prayer) but when we do Angel Work, we enter in a State of Consciousness that represents God and it is so powerful to experiment. We get a clear image of the psychological aspect we need to change. Hence, we consciously participate in the activation of our program. Another example, if we invoke the Angel 9 HAZIEL, whose main quality is Universal Love, we'll have dreams and we'll experience concrete situations relating to Universal Love. The Angels are the keys of God's Consciousness."

"After reciting the 'Our Father', instead of seeing parasites and being afraid of them, you saw apples and they were damaged." I went on. "The fact that you have the power to transform means that your faith in God exists. It is there, but it is not powerful enough to really change your life and all your memories. You do not go deep enough when you pray and your concept of right and wrong is not quite right. One day, you will no longer fear evil. It will have become perfectly clear for you that evil is an educational process. It will then have become an illusion and will represent nothing more than a situation that needs rectifying. One day, the apples in your dreams won't be damaged because you'll have acquired more purity, understanding and stability." That's what Angel Recitation does.

One of Angel HAHEUIAH's qualities is *protection against murderers*. We may say, "Murderers don't concern me." We must remember that Angelic Qualities and Virtues have to be considered in terms of Consciousness. In this case, the idea of a murderer could apply to any virulent or aggressive words, because such words can kill. That may be shown to us through signs in our daily life and in our dreams.

Here is the experience of a woman who has been working with the Angels for some time now. She told me, "I've got to tell you something that happened to me. One day, I really didn't feel well. I arrived at work and I started talking to one of my colleagues who is a very critical person. She's a woman who's got a lot of problems with the masculine principle. She's always criticizing men. While talking, we went over a certain number of our colleagues in the firm and we criticized them one after the other. As I heard myself talk, I felt it wasn't right to criticize like that. I had done it in the past, when I wasn't conscious of this distortion in me. That day, however, I knew very well that it wasn't right. But I couldn't stop myself. It was stronger than me. At one particular moment, I even heard myself say, 'Don't you think we are being very critical?' My colleague replied, 'Yes, yes, a little.' But we went right on doing so, even more so than before. At the end of the conversation, I was completely exhausted. I felt diminished for having criticized like that. It was as if I had forgotten all the teachings."

She added, "But I accepted my fall. I didn't feel guilty. All the way home, right up until I fell asleep, I did my Angel Recitation." What dream was she sent during the night? *She was on a large battlefield during the time of Knights. There was water in a ditch and corpses as far as the eye could see. She had a sword in her hand and, at one particular moment, she thrust it into the water. Then, she laid it against her heart. She told me, "I felt the energy of my inner man, then I felt mine. All of a sudden, I knew that my man was me. It was really beautiful.* I woke up with this dream. The next day, I felt really good. I felt regenerated and my feeling of diminishment had disappeared."

What had They, Up Above, wished to tell her through this dream? She was shown what she had done. "Look at the damage you caused," They said. "Virulent, aggressive criticism kills. You created a battle-field within yourself." Because this woman's conscience is open, she was shown what she had done in the subtle dimensions. The sword, which is a great symbol of justice, was thrust into the water, symbol-izing emotions, and it is as if she was telling herself, "That's enough! Block evil! I've done enough damage." Thanks to this action, she was able to stop criticizing and destroying her entourage. She was able to unite emissivity (the sword) and love (her heart.)

Of course, this woman had a resonance with her colleague. When the latter was talking to her and criticizing, buried memories resur-faced, and she couldn't master them because there was a lesson she needed to receive. She added, "The next day, when I arrived at work, it was clear to me that all that had happened was a lovely wink and a nudge from Up Above, because my colleague wasn't there. She's rarely absent, but that day she wasn't there. I was glad because that gave me time to meditate right there at the scene of the crime and to continue my healing." It also gave her some respite to think about how she was going to behave in the presence of her colleague.

Often we hear, "I don't want to have anything to do with that person any more. He makes me fall. He brings out my bad sides. He's too negative." Whenever we say that, it means we don't understand the concept of evil. If a negative person has been put on our path we must, on the contrary, use this relationship. Of course it awakens resonances, but when we listen to that person, we are receptive and, at the same time, we do our Angel Recitation. Thus we cannot fall again. Each time we succeed in maintaining this state of not projecting onto others, we evolve on the path of wisdom. When we do this work 24 hours a day, we see incredible transformations in a very short time. If someone we had lost sight of for a number of years were to see us then, they wouldn't recognize us. The changes are enormous, because we purify ourselves 24 hours a day. The love, beatitude and light-heartedness that evolved beings radiate is extraordinary.

Now I would like to talk to you about symbols of protection that show up not only in our dreams, but also as signs in our daily lives. Let's first mention the army and the police, which are symbols of protection when there is conflict. Each time you hear a police siren, it is not a coincidence. Analyze what is going through your mind. Up Above, They may wish to tell you something or They may be watching over you. Even if the siren doesn't seem to concern you, you can analyze the thoughts you had at that moment, exactly as in a dream. When we hear a siren and we are scared, it means we have within ourselves something wrong. The siren sets off a signal in our unconscious. Thus, if they appear honest and upright, the army and the police are symbols of protection when there is conflict.

The grandfather and grandmother are other symbols of protection that are frequently used in dreams. The grandfather represents protection in our daytime actions, while the grandmother symbolizes inner, emotional protection. If an elderly person plays the role of a grandfather or grandmother in your reference library, even if he or she is not your grandfather or grandmother, and if he or she is an inspiring person for you, then he or she is a symbol of protection.

Where there is a question of protection, there is also a question of stability. If we aren't stable in our head, in our heart and in our body, we feel afraid and we are no longer protected. Belonging to the world of water, boats represent the level of stability in the emotional dimension. Thus, when we are shown a boat, we are being shown our present emotional stability and protection. Is there a big swell? Is there a storm? Are we capsizing?

The floor is also a symbol of stability. It particularly concerns the physical dimension. If we dream about a floor that is collapsing, it means, "Look. You are fragile for such and such a reason." In this case, we are being invited to correct certain attitudes so as to improve our stability in our actions.

We saw that some talismans are symbols of protection. Jewelry is too. If the piece of jewelry contains a stone, we must always analyze the stone, its color and characteristics, because every detail is important. For example, the color purple is the color of spiritual protection because it corresponds to the last chakra, or the crown. We can use this color in our meditations. We visualize the color purple and it really does us a lot of good. To stabilize this effect, however, it is the qualities and virtues pertaining to spiritual protection that we have to develop. We do that by cleansing our unconscious memories.

Raccoons are cute. We know that. They look like cute little dogs. But if we analyze their behavior, we realize that they are little thieves. They rob the trash cans and they steal food. If we dream about a naughty raccoon, it means, "Be careful. You seem nice and gentle but you've got a little instinctive energy that helps itself and takes other people's possessions or energy."

An animal's attitude in a dream, whether positive or negative, determines whether or not it represents a strength or a weakness. This also applies to a person. In real life, we analyze an event the same way we would in a dream. If a raccoon goes through our bins or steals our food, it is not a coincidence. There is something for us to learn. We have to say to ourselves, "What am I going through at the moment? How am I behaving?" We also need to remember that the symbol of an animal has two meanings. It represents the negative side, or the non-transcended animal side. It also symbolizes great positive forces.

A lady came up to me at the break and said, "I've been feeding raccoons for years whenever I go camping. Should I stop feeding them? One of them even came up and laid its head on my foot. It was so cute!"

"No, that's different. You tamed it. It didn't come to steal from you. We mustn't condemn raccoons."

"But it's the symbol of a thief."

"Each animal, even the most ferocious ones, always has a positive side," I explained. "If we manage to tame it, it's a sign that we have integrated its positive force within ourselves."

⊙

Angelic Help

We shall see that when a person receives spiritual help, it is because he has worked on himself. He has asked for help and his program corresponds to it. He receives Divine Grace. It is important to address our requests to the Highest Authorities, to God and to the Angels. When we ask the Angels for help, we call on Their Qualities and Virtues. And, when it is time, Up Above can help us, because They have an overall vision of our karmic program and our life-plan. The solution is sent on to spiritual guides, then to incarnate beings who, without knowing why, will do things that will help us.

Helping in the physical dimension is very good. Our ultimate aim is to become altruistic, fraternal and helpful towards each other. But the more we purify ourselves, the greater access we gain to the causal world. Eventually, we understand how the Universe works and God's Dynamics are revealed to us. We can even participate in these Dynamics through our dreams.

We saw that there are two types of dreams. At first, our dreams serve to cleanse our personal file. When we help someone or find ourselves in great difficulty in this type of dream, it indicates which parts of ourselves we need to work on, to transform, or which elements should inspire us.

The second type of dream we call participative because it allows us to work on the codification of a person's software or program.

It is only accessible to us, on a regular basis, from the moment we have attained a high degree of purity. In dreams of this type, we are authorized to participate in the dynamics of the Universe. We become a link in the whole chain of guides who live in the parallel worlds. It is real metaphysical work. This work also induces in us great humility, because through it we are brought to the realization that it is teamwork. When an incarnate being acquires the possibility of doing this work, he realizes that if he doesn't accomplish the given spiritual action, another guide will take over. This is because the program itself is preordained. The evolution goals set by Cosmic Intelligence must be reached.

The incarnate being who does this spiritual work through his dreams is a servant. He is an executor who participates in Divine Creation. He helps other people by going to visit them in parallel worlds. The symbolic language of participative dreams is the same as those concerning our personal purification.

When we help like this, we always see the results. The state of the person is shown to us, or else we meet him. We can follow the evolution that the spiritual work engendered. For the person who gives assistance, the assistance becomes an absolute reality.

We can help someone tie his shoelaces in the physical dimension. This assistance is as important as spiritual help, but this help remains limited to the physical dimension, although it does also touch on the affective dimension, since this help warms our heart. But if we see ourselves doing the same work in the spiritual dimension, as in a dream, for example, this gesture has a much greater significance. What significance? Shoes represent the social side of things, how a person behaves when he manifests himself. Is he at ease or does he feel embarrassed? If we help him tie his shoelaces, it means that we help him walk the path smoothly. How does this help our work? It is as if we modified a program in a computer. The Cosmic Computer will send that person greater energy potential, new ideas, social opportunities, etc. This will help him walk the path more easily. Spiritual guides living in the parallel worlds will accompany this person wherever he goes and will help him modify his way of behaving so that the new programming will take shape and materialize.

Through this slightly simplified explanation, we see how the Universe works. We see that when we help someone in the spiritual dimension, we participate in teamwork. It is totally impersonal work. We do not talk about it either. Most of the time, we don't even tell the person we helped. The greatest discretion is required.

This evening, I'm going to tell you about an experience my husband had. My husband does this kind of spiritual work every night. He helps people in his dreams. My husband and I have been authorized to share this experience for the purpose of teaching, to use it as an example to show you what lies ahead for all those who work with the Traditional Study of Angels.

It's the story of a family where the father and mother invoke the Angels daily. Their son lived far away while he was studying at university. When he came home, his life became extremely difficult. He had become a drug addict and he was battling with psychological problems and had suicidal tendencies.

His condition had really tested his family. Among other things, it had brought out real fears in his parents because of certain antecedents. The young man's paternal grandfather had committed suicide in the past. Of course, it was a family karmic problem that was resurfacing. The parents really worked very intensely, invoking and asking the Angels for help. And they didn't reject their son. They knew they all had something to learn from this situation.

One day, the son phoned my husband and asked him for help. He explained to him what he was going through. "My head is just exploding," he said. "I have ideas that are negative, aggressive and so destructive that I'm afraid of what they could lead to. I'm afraid of myself. What can I do?"

"The only person who can help you is God," my husband replied. "It's your spiritual path that can make all the difference. The evil isn't in your body. It's in your spirit."

Then, using a simple language this young man could understand, he talked to him about the psychology of the Angels. Later in the conversation, the young man told him,

"I've got an idea. I'd like to go to a monastery on a four-day retreat."

"That's a good idea," my husband told him. "If you feel called to do so, you should go."

At the end of the conversation, the young man seemed soothed. He told my husband, "I'm going to borrow my parents' copy of 'Book of Angels' and I'll read it during my retreat."

During this young man's retreat, my husband had a dream in which he met the father, the mother and the son. In the dream, *my husband was lying on a bed, meditating. The father arrived and asked him to help his son. My husband accepted. Another image followed. There, he saw the father sitting and worrying, but showing a certain dignity in his trial. Then, he saw the mother who was very disturbed, and the agitation was making her much too emissive. The son was also present, sitting there with clenched fists. His whole body was trembling. Then my husband got up and went over to a water basin and filled a glass with water. He handed the glass to the young man. After a few moments' hesitation, the young man accepted and he drank the glass of water. After that, my husband found himself in a kitchen. On the highest shelf there were speakers that were playing an extremely aggressive, almost demonic music. It was really powerful. My husband turned the volume down. It was quite hard for him to do so, but he managed.*

Let's analyze this first part of the dream. By taking and drinking the water, the young man was symbolically accepting emotional help and a way to purify himself. The kitchen represents an action in preparation, or the moment when new energies are being prepared. Through the symbol of the speakers, my husband was being shown what was going on in the young man's head because the speakers were on the highest shelf. Through the difficulty he had lowering the volume, he was being shown the intensity of what the young man was experiencing. It was something hellish and very strong. That's what was making his head spin and why his spirit had become almost demented.

In the same kitchen there was a spiritual guide who lives in the parallel worlds, representing many other guides who were going to make sure that this dream would materialize, in concrete terms. The whole family was going to be guided, including the father, the mother and the son. This way, a new dynamic could begin so that calm would be restored and the son could feel better.

Then followed another series of images where my husband was talking to the son. The son told him that he really had a lot of admiration for his father who had had a career in the Canadian

Armed Forces. Then, he saw the son beside an automatic beverage dispenser for athletes.

Thus, my husband was being shown the son's life in the near future. Through the symbol of the beverage dispenser, he was being shown that the young man wasn't going to take up a spiritual path. It wasn't time yet. As a first step, he was going to transform his aggression by doing sports. Fluids and water are linked to the emotions. Through the conversation in the dream, it was also being announced to my husband that the young man was going to follow in his father's footsteps. He was going to enlist in the Canadian Armed Forces.

A few days later, we learned that on his return from the monastery, the young man was transformed. His eyes were lit up. When my husband met him, he said nothing of what he had seen or of what had been done for him. He simply listened. The young man said, "It's amazing! Ideas aren't spinning around in my head any more. I've found a taste for life again."

This person had received Grace. And Grace is not given haphazardly. It is the result of a whole lot of work. The parents had worked a lot. The boy had also tried hard. Later, Destiny went to work. The young man applied to the army and was accepted as an officer in the Canadian Armed Forces.

This fine example allows us to see how the procedure of help from the guides works. The spiritual path is very difficult but we eventually manage to stop doubting the existence of subtle worlds. They remain with us permanently. Gradually, with the study of dreams and signs in our daily life, we realize that symbols serve as an interface between these worlds and the scenario of our own life. Eventually, our life becomes an excellent terrain for apprentices of wisdom. *Know yourself and you shall know the Universe.* This statement becomes the emblem of our wisdom.

Here is a final, true story. It's about a farming couple who also invokes the Angels daily. It was sowing time, and the man read the instructions on the new seed packet. It was recommended to sow a certain amount of seeds for a certain surface. It totaled 70 seeds for the surface he wished to sow. But, he was used to sowing 110 seeds for this surface. It bothered him because he was afraid that sowing the recommended number would yield a less abundant crop than usual.

He asked his wife what she thought. After hearing what was bothering her husband, she told him, "Well then, sow 72." He stood there surprised. He had been expecting her to suggest sowing 90, a figure midway between 70 and 110.

She said to him, "Yes. The 72 Angels!" "Yes!" he exclaimed. "The 72 Angels. But are you sure?" "Wait," she responded. "We shall ask for a sign."

She climbed up onto the tractor and turned on the radio, asking, "If it's really 72 seeds that we ought to sow, give me a sign through a song." Just imagine what she was sent! The minute she turned on the radio, Sarah McLachlan's song "Angel" was being played. "In the arms of Angels…" They were both in seventh heaven! The sign was magical.

There you have it. When we get used to reading signs, the day comes when we are no longer blinded by the material side of things. If we have doubts, we use everything at our disposal in the concrete world, or else we ask for a dream. We ask, "Is this the right direction?" We then wait for the signs with a receptive attitude. The answer will come one way or another. Once we have integrated this Knowledge, we realize that God really exists.

Angel 11 Lauviah
True Success

In a dream, *a woman saw her husband crouched inside a huge fireplace. The fire was out but intense heat radiated from the fireplace. Suddenly, she heard a man's voice say to her, "Your husband will go through fire," and shortly after, "And you, his partner, will meet the same fate."* Then, she woke up. The woman had this dream just as she was beginning to follow the teachings of the Angels. She had no idea of the extent of inner work this dream would set off both for herself and her husband.

To go through fire within symbolizes the death of old concepts and the birth of a new consciousness. Life had been preparing these two people to become initiates for a long time. This woman's husband is one of the founders of what had at one time been considered not only Canada's top construction company but also one of the most important of its kind in the world. An award-winner for its beautiful architectural work and official builder for The Montreal Universal and International Exhibition of 1967, this company built bridges, schools, churches, hospitals, and factories. It also built entire towns due, in part, to prefabricated houses, a totally innovative system at the time. At the head of the company were the Désourdy brothers. For 26 years, from 1950 to 1976, they encountered phenomenal success that they themselves have difficulty explaining. Certainly neither their modest origins nor the level of their education predestined these two brothers to head such an empire, estimated at one time to be worth more than 25 million dollars.

This evening, I would like to talk to you more specifically about Normand Désourdy who, along with his wife, follows the teachings of The Traditional Study of Angels and who was the subject of the dream I just mentioned. During his time of great fame and material success, when he rubbed shoulders with ministers and sheiks and when he received many earthly honors, Normand Désourdy was far from imagining that he had experienced but a pale reflection of true success. Today, he has opened his heart to share his story. In all simplicity, he invited me and my husband into his home. It was truly magical to see this man reveal his inner self as he explained how he arrived at his decision to live a spiritual life.

Before tasting Heavenly success, this man had to go through a long series of hardships. The first of these ordeals began in 1977. When his company sustained enormous losses in Saudi Arabia and he was forced into bankruptcy, Normand Désourdy lost his entire fortune. Today, thanks to the teachings of the Angels, the analysis of his dreams, and the interpretation of signs in his daily life, Normand Désourdy has managed to rebuild himself on the inside, thereby constructing a new kingdom. Later this evening, I will share his story with you in light of this teaching and all of its implied symbolism.

The theme of this evening's lecture is how to find *true success*. The Angel who can help us is Angel LAUVIAH bearer of number 11.

From early childhood on and during past lives, we accumulate a certain number of unconscious memories. We carry a lot of baggage. But, at first, it is better that these memories remain veiled. Then gradually as we grow, as we evolve and find our conscience anew, the veil is lifted. At that moment, we acquire the capacity to re-program these memories. This is what working with the Angels consists of. On the conscious level, we wonder, "Why am I not succeeding? Why am I so limited? And yet, I'm doing everything I should. I am kind and I work hard. Still things are not working out. What's going on?" Working with the Angels allows us to identify what, unbeknown to us, is going on, what is happening at the level of our unconscious memories.

Here is a true story that will help us understand how this works. It is the story of a woman who works with The Traditional Study of Angels. She told me about a dream that she received. *She saw herself in a huge cornfield in the presence of her father; the cobs were golden yellow, and there was also mint growing. All of a sudden, she entered a house and went downstairs. In the basement, to her surprise, she found a starving tramp. She began to feed him and to give him mint leaves.*

What did They wish to tell this woman? In this dream, all the characters are parts of her, including her father. By examining what each character represents and how they interact in the dream, we can obtain a detailed analysis of the person's situation on a psychological level. Corn is a great symbol. Its husk, whose form reminds us of a man's erect penis, represents the possibility of creating an abundance of material resources. It therefore symbolizes prosperity and material success. Through its nutritive qualities and its ability to be preserved for a long time, it symbolizes abundance and its golden yellow color represents confidence. The presence of a man in the dream—her father—represents the material world, the physical dimension, and the daytime. Therefore, the dream indicated to this woman that, on the surface, she enjoys abundance. Because we become accustomed to analyzing dreams with the logic of this world, what do mint leaves symbolize? How do we use mint leaves? Usually, we make herbal tea to stimulate the digestive system.

Since this woman went into a house and down to the basement, she was being shown what was behind the façade or the mask or what was hidden by the veil. The ground floor represents the conscious level; in other words, what we see and what we are conscious of. As for the basement, symbolically, it reveals subconscious elements that are closer to our consciousness than to our unconscious. Through the image of the tramp, she was being shown that despair and a tendency to give up dwelt within her. A symbol has so much power. It condenses hundreds, indeed thousands, of memories of situations we have experienced.

In the conscious world, this woman enjoys success at the professional level. Not too long ago she started a new job and lives a somewhat abundant material life. However, she is often nostalgic, lacks confidence in herself, and needs people's attention. The dream shows her where these attitudes come from. Since this woman has already started transforming her inner self, she has begun to feed this demanding part so that, one day, the tramp will also become rich. This means she will manage to reprogram all of the unconscious memories in which hopelessness is inscribed.

Even if a symbol only appears for a few seconds in a dream, it still represents much work that needs to be done and it can manifest itself in multiple forms over many lives. For example, if this woman does not rectify her memories and attitudes concerning the feeling of lack, she might actually become a tramp in another life. This is the magic of dreams. They are key messages sent to us from Up

Above. In a company, there may be two people who have the same salary, the same social status, and the same number of children. Concretely speaking, their situation is the same at the quantity level. When they hear rumours that there may be lay-offs, one of them remains confident, stable, and calm while the other panics. His stomach hurts and even he is surprised by his own reaction. He says to himself, "This is ridiculous! Why do I feel like this?" His confidence sinks very low.

As long as everything is fine at the concrete level or at the conscious level, as long as money is coming in and we have the means to live, our spirit focuses on the cornfield, so to speak, and we feel relatively good. But it only takes a rumor for the spirit to plunge into the unconscious and go straight to the memories that are marked with a feeling of lack. Terrible fears resurface. These reactions are uncontrollable so long as we have not cleaned up and reprogrammed these ancient memories. When we understand this, we truly want to cleanse these ancient memories that appear so clearly in our dreams.

Some people who have material success are ambitious and greedy. They never have enough and are ready to crush others to have even more. If we took a look into their unconscious—which is possible, by the way, when we have done our own inner work—if we approached one of these people, we would be able to sense the tramp that, in this case, would be aggressive and thieving. When we have acquired the spiritual power to visit the unconscious, our perception of reality changes considerably. We stop living an illusion and being attached to form.

Success comes from Up Above, even if it is achieved unfairly through cunning and ambition. Everything comes from Up Above. When confronted with success that hasn't been fairly earned, some people might ask, "But how could this success have come from God?" We must understand that we receive everything that we ask for. If we want material success, if we want to be rich and powerful, we shall obtain it, even if it takes three or four lives. Cosmic Intelligence tells us, "You want it? You shall have it. But you shall also have all that you are along with it." They let us experiment. A person can experience incredible success and then suddenly everything topples. Up Above, They take away his resources to allow him to visit the tramp and the other memories where he was forceful, where he wasn't fair, where he was proud of his success or where he was not grateful. Life is an experimentation of our consciousness. We experiment throughout all our different lives and evil helps us evolve. When we understand this, we feel compassion for those who lose their way. We do not pass judgment on them, no matter what they do. We know that one day, they will voluntarily decide to no longer do evil.

⊙

God as a Living Computer

In order to understand the Law of Synchronicity, let's imagine our Creator as an immense Living Computer in which each person lives, and where absolutely everything is recorded. This Great Intelligence always knows where we are in real time. If a satellite can localize a small object, imagine what this Great Intelligence can do. If I move my hand like this, the Cosmic Computer mathematically records the movement and situates it perfectly in space and time. This powerful image helps us to understand the nature of God. It also shows us that today's technology is a reflection of the Universe, although a very modest one.

Each person has a life plan that has been predetermined before birth. What determines this program? It is established according to what we have lived and asked or wished for in our past lives. Thus the broad outlines, the main goals of our present life, have been set. Guides also exist who permanently accompany us and help us to reach these goals.

Some people have great physical or psychological limitations that come from previous lives. Even if we have great limitations simply understanding their meaning, accepting them, and being on a self-help path allows us to improve our lives. A certain freedom is accessible to the spirit and, despite the physical limitations that persist in our present life, we are preparing our next life. If we do not make good use of the talents and resources we have been given in our life here on Earth, then, inevitably, we will have to face Divine Justice. It is a perfectly fair and rigorous Justice. The person who understands this and who accepts his own limitations, using them to help in the growth of his consciousness, manages, in only one life, to repair many lives. He starts up a process of Grace and blessings that will engender spiritual, intellectual, emotional, and material abundance.

A country also has a predetermined plan and each individual's program concurs with the plan of the country where he lives. If we stop to think about the great catastrophe that happened at the World Trade Center in New York, on September 11th, 2001, we understand that Heaven let this happen and that behind these events were reasons that concern evolution. Of course, evil was at its highest point but, even in such a case, it maintains its educational role. Because of this event, some people will become more fraternal and altruistic; they will develop nonattachment to material things. With the collapse of the Twin Towers, the symbol of a certain way of materializing was destroyed.

When we have a global vision of things, we can understand events on the individual as well as the collective level. And what we develop is not indifference but understanding. And where there is understanding, there can be pure compassion.

Let's have a look at the Qualities of Angel 11 LAUVIAH. *Victory, renown, celebrity, success.* Angel 11 LAUVIAH gives us access to renown. Public recognition is but a pale reflection of renown when its very essence is understood. We gain access to true renown when all parts of ourselves recognize our Divine nature. If we do not begin by recognizing our Divine nature and we seek fame externally, we will do all sorts of things to be acknowledged by our family, friends, partner and so on. This gives rise to karma and distortions.

Our social system places emphasis on personal fame, material success and prestige. This state of affairs results in essential and spiritual values being put aside. In the future, spiritual education and accessibility to the knowledge of symbolic language will bring about profound changes in our value system.

Angel 11 LAUVIAH is also the Angel of *confidence, enthusiasm and joy*. These qualities allow us to remain stable and to conquer our fears. It helps us create *businesses that are useful and profitable for humanity*. With this Angel, we get used to materializing in a just manner while respecting the Divine Laws. Some may say to me,

"Yes, but I don't know the Divine Laws." Knowledge of these Laws is given from the inside *via* the dreams we have and throughout our process of purification and spiritual evolution.

Can obtain anything from the greats of this world. Some people have great earthly power and are altruistic; they are the greats of this world. Angel 11 LAUVIAH is the field of consciousness in which *failure* is the result of a distortion. One day, there is no longer any failure in our lives. The idea of failure comes from a way of thinking, which we must rectify by learning to think in terms of quality rather than quantity. Each time our soul attempts to take a step towards greater consciousness, stumbles and gets up again, and each time our efforts do not lead to recognition, we say, "My intention was to develop my soul and that is what counts," instead of concluding that we have failed. Like scientists, we experiment. In a laboratory, if, after several attempts, a research scientist does not obtain the expected results, he talks not about failure but about experimenting. It is the same for us. If we learn, if we change an erroneous concept, if we integrate a more Divine way of thinking in our head, heart and body and, consequently we feel better, then we experience success.

When Angel LAUVIAH manifests Himself through distortions, we come into contact with *envy*. We become *jealous* of others and their successes, whatever they might be. When we remain on the level of pure form, we can always find someone to envy but when we move up into Divine Essence, we experience completeness. We no longer envy others because we know that every single person is on Earth to learn about good and evil. By doing our Angel Recitation with Angel LAUVIAH, all of the following distortions will appear in our dreams and in our daily lives: *envy, jealousy, ambition and greed.*

When we work with The Traditional Study of Angels, time as a symbol can be very useful. If we notice a certain time in our dreams and we look it up in Angel Calendar No. 3, we will see which Angel this time corresponds to. It gives us a clue as to the psychological aspect that is being shown in the dream, whether it be its quality or its distortion. We will see an example of this later.

I'd like to share with you an account that serves as a good illustration of the pathway to true success. It comes from a woman who is the mother of a young child. She told me that when she decided to go back to work, a close family friend offered to sell her his video shop at a very modest price. What's more, the shop was quite close to her home so the offer seemed very interesting indeed. As she always does before going to sleep, this woman asked, "Is it right for our evolution to buy this shop?"

She received an answer in a dream. *She saw herself in a dark and dismal video shop. It was empty and there weren't any videos in it.* You do not need great interpreting skills to know the answer to her question. She was being told, "If you get involved in this, it will result in emptiness. It will create sadness in your life."

The way we formulate our question and our reason for asking it are both very important when we ask for an answer. It is good and, also, very important to ask, as this woman did, "Is it right for my evolution?"

We may not get an answer or the one we get may not be as clear as this woman's was. It is meant to be this way.

Some people will then ask, "Why doesn't the answer come?" or "Why isn't it more clear?" If we are to go in a particular direction because it has been predetermined, the guides cannot give us an answer that will lead us to material success. If they did, they would not be doing us a favor. Up Above, They give us enigmas to make us think. Obviously, when in doubt, we refrain from doing anything; this is the Law of Wisdom. We continue our inner work and, eventually, we will obtain answers. Always ask and ask respectfully. This is the pathway to true success.

Here is another story that has a lot of magic and that also concerns true success. Some time ago, during a lecture on the Angels, a woman made a spontaneous offer to my husband. She offered to him the use of her voice for the musical productions he was working on, the fifth volume of a new album of Angel music. My husband said to her, "Send me a sample of your voice on a tape." Some time passed and, the day before going into the recording studio, he received the tape. The fact that my husband received the tape the night before the recording was in itself an important synchronicity as the woman did not know that he was going into the studio that particular week.

My husband listened to her voice and found her to be a great talent. All the same, he asked for permission in a meditation. It is not important to him that his actions succeed in the concrete dimension. What counts is that it is right, that the program–ours as well as others'–is respected. By behaving this way, he respects all the Laws of Nature. He received the go-ahead from Up Above and two days later he left a message on the woman's answering machine asking her to sing on the Angel's music. The woman related to us what happened.

My husband phoned at 9:17 a.m. Immediately after the message was recorded, her husband listened to it and, delighted, he went to tell his wife and woke her up out of a dream. What had she been dreaming about? *She was in a white van driven by my husband and I was in the back. She could feel my presence. Then, the van stopped at a gas station and she put in 56 dollars worth of gas. A clock indicated the time: 15:17. Then, the van drove off onto the freeway.*

When the woman phoned back my husband, she was very happy and she told him her dream, "I understand the general outlines of my dream but there is just a little something that intrigues me. You called me at 9:17 and, in my dream, the clock indicated 15:17. What does this mean?" My husband replied, "Your dream is very precise. The music you are going to be singing corresponds to Angel ARIEL, Angel number 46 and, in terms of hours, the regency period of this Angel is from 15:00 to 15:20. They even told you what music you were going to sing." She was moved and truly impressed to have received this revelation.

In the woman's dream, my husband and I represent parts of herself. It is in this category of dreams that such symbols appear. We represent spiritual symbols of this teaching. Since he is a man, my husband represents a situation that is going to manifest itself concretely, in the daytime. I symbolize an aspect of this woman that is taking place within. The white van represents her spiritual vehicle because white, the synthesis of all the colors, symbolizes spirituality. She was being told that she was about to begin a spiritual experience.

She was also being told that she was going to receive energy. Why do we put gas in our cars? To help us advance. What does 56 dollars signify? When we work with the Angels and we receive a number, we look up the corresponding Angel. Number 56 is Angel POYEL, Father Christmas of the Angels. He is the Angel of gifts. She was being told that she would receive a gift, both within and in the manifest world. The van headed for the freeway. Why do we use the freeway? To advance quickly. It is a symbol of easy access. She was being told that she would be very motivated and she would advance on her spiritual path.

This lady confided in us that a few years earlier she had dedicated her voice to God while praying and singing on the very same mountain in Europe where St Thomas received his Enlightenment. The Bible story of St Thomas tells us that, in order to believe, he constantly needed proof. Therefore, through this dream, this woman was being given quite the proof in order to encourage her on her path. She was given a taste of true success, of mystical magic.

I'd like to tell you another story that occurred while I was preparing the lecture on Angel 11 LAUVIAH. When I am preparing a lecture, I do my Angel Recitation with the Angel in question and I receive teachings *via* my dreams and the people I meet.

While I was out for a walk, I met a woman with whom I am acquainted. She was enthusiastic and happy because she had just received some good news: she had just been offered a job by a landscaper who was starting his own business. The more I listened to her, the happier I was for her because of how she loves gardening. During the night, even though I had not asked a question about this woman, I found myself in a dream in which I visited this woman's soul.

How do we know if the characters in a dream represent parts of ourselves or of the person whose soul we are visiting? Even though it is possible to visit another person's soul at the beginning of our spiritual path, the fact remains that in the majority of cases, the dream concerns us personally. It is part of us that is revealed. In the beginning, we have to cleanse our entire personal unconscious. This represents a lot of work. If our dream is a premonition concerning another person, Cosmic Intelligence will indicate this to us and the facts will be obvious. We will know. This is why, when in doubt, we must always refer back to ourselves. We do our Angel Recitation and this leads us to develop great humility. It is so easy for the human ego to get lost in spiritual pride.

In the dream, *I saw this woman with a set of educational cards on which was inscribed "Plant Elixir" and on the cards, there were illustrations of plants.* A plant elixir is therapeutic. Because plants represent feelings, I was being shown that this work was going to prove very good for the emotional side of her life and for other aspects of herself as well. Furthermore, *I was told, "Her job will be precarious,"* which indicated to me that this job would not be reliable.

When I woke up, I knew it was a teaching for me from Angel LAUVIAH. He was explaining to me that her experience with this work would be a good thing for her emotions but not for her finances. I knew from the symbols of the dreams that it was an important life experience for her because she had some emotional difficulties with her husband. Unless we receive a mission from Heaven to put in action, we must be wise enough to keep the information for our own understanding when we wake up with such a dream,. It's not easy to keep the information for ourselves. The first thing we want to do is pick up the phone and warn the person-especially when we know that that they need a salary to feed their children. We want to tell them, "Don't accept this job. Something negative will happen."

Once we have completely understood the principle of experimentation by taking a step back into our own lives, we can conceive of the same thing for others. These learning experiences are sometimes difficult but they are organized by Cosmic Intelligence. We should avoid obstructing whatever It has established unless we receive from Heaven a warning to transmit. Why then do we receive this kind of dream if we are not to reveal anything to the person concerned? Once we truly understand the concept of karma, we can receive these types of dreams to better understand and assist the person on their path of rectification. We have to remember that it is always a teaching for ourselves. The understanding of life plan and destiny is a long process that leads us to Angelic wisdom. Everything happens for a reason and sometimes, being human, we think that an ordeal is negative but in fact in the long run, it is always a positive experience that helps us integrate new qualities to become a better person.

Some time later, this woman called to tell me, "My boss hasn't paid me for quite some time. It's not that he is acting in bad faith. He can't get his customers to pay him." She added, "I had to change jobs because I needed money to pay the bills." Then, with a certain acceptance because she has done a lot of work on her inner self, she said, "If I don't get what I'm due, it's probably because I owe something to the Universe. He is not paying me but this work was a great relief for me. It gave me sometime to think about my life. Even if I do not get paid, I see this experience as a gift from Heaven."

This is what makes up our life on Earth: Up Above, They cause us to go through various apprenticeships. Once we realize this, we face up to our responsibilities in the material world but we understand what we have been given to experience. We have to be practical. We rectify what needs to be corrected, without fear and without reproof. And, thus, we move on to another learning experience. If we do not understand the Law of Resonance, then we simply collect more karma. If the woman had rebelled and become more critical and aggressive, if she had said, "I worked hard and he won't even pay me," then she would have not understood deeply the fact that this life lesson came from God. The apprenticeship itself is there to help us repair something unconscious and yet we rebel. This means we must go through other trials in accordance with whatever it is we ought to have improved. This is why the karmic chain continues until one day, we receive Knowledge. The Law of Resonance and the Law of Annoyance alone can be real treasures if we agree to use them.

Finally, after a certain amount of time, the woman's employer was able to pay her. She therefore received a comprehensive lesson.

Another method to achieve true success involves asking for signs. We have seen that we can ask for dreams and the same thing applies to signs. At first, we get used to asking for little things. Before making important decisions on the basis of signs, decisions that may lead to a change in our orientation or that have a long term impact on our lives, we must begin by acquiring Knowledge so as to be certain that we are acting in a spiritual manner. This is why it is suggested that we first practice asking only for decisions that have an immediate impact but are of no great importance in our lives.

☉

Reading Signs

Essentially, learning to read signs is learning a new language. This symbolic language has a very sacred aspect because each time we ask for a sign we are addressing God and His messengers. In fact, we gain access to *Skynet*. In a state of meditation, we should make our request with a sacred and respectful attitude. At first, in order to concentrate, it is good to meditate with eyes closed but, after a while, the symbol will present itself even when our eyes are open.

The symbolic language accompanies us all the time. At the beginning, when we are practicing, a symbol is sent to us in the form of an image, as in a dream, and we analyze it. If it is positive, we act; if it is otherwise, we wait. When we are not sure, we ask again. We meditate and do an in depth analysis of the action to be taken and of all its implications. When we get used to functioning like this, we receive very precise guidance indeed.

It is the intention that creates the sign. As for events, they are always there and, unless we are seeking significance, we will not extract meaning. Our spirit focuses on a question and our conscience acts like a personal computer connected to the great Cosmic Computer.

Signs reach us through a variety of means: a voice, a sound, a person talking in a shop, music playing on the radio, three words that we chance to overhear on television, etc. We are connected to the Angel station, to *Radio Angelica*. The guides know that while a sign has a particular meaning for one person, another will interpret it differently. The meaning also depends on what the person has in mind when he receives the sign. We understand the importance of the autonomy we acquire when we *read* in this way. When we follow this teaching, we have to think and meditate a lot, and, one day, spiritual autonomy becomes a daily reality.

When I was a novice, I used to say, "Well, I'm not going to disturb God and His guides for silly little things." Then, one day, I understood that if we had a business that we wanted to expand, we would go on the Internet. We go on Skynet. Everything is inscribed there. We can surf and find all the information we need for our evolution. It works quite well, especially if we are sincere and we ask in a sacred way whether it is right to do this or that. For example, we should not be wondering, "Am I going to make a lot of money?" or "Is this going to work out well?" Sometimes, too, we wish but, at first, we must not seek harmony. What is essential for an initiate is to aspire to being just.

We may receive a really positive symbol as a sign but when we decide to go ahead with our action, we realize that, instead, the result was an ordeal. We were sent towards karma. Even if we had not asked which direction to take, we would have gone towards this karma. We have a program inscribed within and we head towards experiences that are a part of it. But, with Knowledge, the difference is that we are no longer simply subjected to these experiences; we understand why we are going through them. This is truly an expansion of our conscience. It improves our life and, even if we still have a lot of difficulties and restrictions, we manage to perceive God's dynamic in Its entirety.

While learning to read signs, some people ask me, "What if I don't interpret correctly and I do things that aren't right?" It does not matter. We are practicing. We are experimenting. We interpret a sign, we act, and then we establish the correlation. "Ah! So that's what They wanted to tell me!" It is like going to school: we need to take the time that is necessary to learn. By gradually integrating symbolism through what we experience, we manage to penetrate the depths of the conscience and the unconscious and, from there, the Universe. Symbolic language is really a Universal language. It is possible to talk about one symbol for hours and hours. This is the extent to which it is complete.

Let's say that we are practicing reading signs and we have to call a friend. We ask, "Is it all right? Is it time to call her yet?" If we receive *the image of two bound hands,* this means, "No, it isn't time." *A white bird* means "Go ahead." *Toilets* suggest, "No, purify yourself first," or "No, she's purifying herself," and therefore we don't call. We analyze the symbol and, in this way, we train ourselves.

Reading signs is magical. One day, we live like children and we are permanently connected to the other dimension; we are continually tuned in. We no longer only live in the concrete world; we live in connection with our spirit. We know that it is the spirit that is responsible for making things materialize. This requires a long and difficult apprenticeship.

I'd like to share with you a funny story that happened to me when I started working with signs. A project was in the offing and the reply necessary for putting it into action was taking some time to come. I decided, "I'm going to ask." I settled myself comfortably on the sofa, in the half lotus position, I went within and asked my question but no image came. I waited patiently. All of a sudden, a voice replied and I will remember it for as long as I live. What did the voice say? It said, "*That's enough, you little pest!*"

What had happened? It was summertime, the window was open and a mother was speaking to her little girl. She was telling her that she was being a pest. Through this mother, Heaven was telling me, "You aren't asking properly. You are still asking because you want to succeed and you are afraid you won't." Of course, receiving such an answer demands a certain amount of humility and we work on this quality often when we work with the Angels. I was so happy with the answer. I opened my eyes and I burst out laughing because I thought They had a good sense of humor and They had succeeded very well in putting me in my place. This memory has engraved a lesson in my soul.

The Masculine and Feminine Principles

The Angels also help us locate our two principles. The masculine principle is emissivity and the feminine principle is receptivity. Using another symbol, we can say that man represents spirit and woman, matter. But both possess the two poles: every woman has an inner man and every man has an inner woman.

The attractions and repulsions we feel show us hidden aspects of ourselves and of our inner pole: our masculine pole if we are a woman or our feminine pole if we are a man.

Thus, we should always interpret symbols according to these two principles. In order to *read* resonance in everyday life, a woman must understand that the men she encounters—both those she is attracted to and those she rejects—show her aspects of her inner man. The same principle applies to a man with his inner woman.

When we begin to read in this manner, we learn on an ongoing basis and we perceive things in depth. The same applies when we analyze our dreams. If a man or a woman appears in the dream, he or she symbolizes the corresponding principle and the way it acts within us. If a couple appears, their behavior shows us how our two principles interact.

⊙

I'd like to tell you a dream that someone shared with me concerning both renown and the masculine and feminine principles.

The following are two symbols that often appear in the dreams of people from the province of Québec. They are symbols that represent people who are originally from Québec, Canada: René Angelil and Celine Dion. We are often asked to interpret dreams in which these two characters appear. It is possible to visit these people in a dream but, most of the time, they represent parts of the dreamer. What do René Angelil and Celine Dion represent? They symbolize great material success and widespread renown and because they come from the province of Québec, they are a great inspiration of material success for this part of Canada. Through these symbols many people are being shown inner aspects to work on or elements concerning our concept of material success that need to be rectified. And the success that is symbolized can be of any size, big or small.

This is the dream of a woman who told me, "I often dream about Celine Dion." She believed she was visiting her in her dream because she said, "What I see in the newspapers and on television very often corroborates with what I have dreamt." Here is her dream, "*René Angelil and Celine Dion were walking in front of me, in the snow. René Angelil was carrying Celine Dion's blue scarf and, at a particular moment, he dropped it and didn't bother to pick it up. His back was bent and he seemed tired and worn out. Celine picked up the scarf and turned to me and said, 'This is normal, so much rests on his shoulders, he has so many worries.' Then she went back to walking behind her husband.*"

This woman did not immediately ask me to interpret her dream. If I am not asked, I just listen. She went on to tell me about all sorts of things she was going through. Among other things, she said, "We've been wanting to sell our house for quite a while now but there have been problems. Sometimes the sale is on, then it's off. We had a potential buyer but he could only buy our house provided he sold his own. Not long ago, he called to tell us that he had taken down his 'For Sale' sign and that he was putting off buying our house until next spring." She added, "I know there are things I need to understand, but I have no expectations. I'm indifferent."

She continued talking then, eventually came back to her dream of Celine Dion and asked, "What, in fact, did that dream mean?" I explained to her the meaning of the symbols, "René Angelil and Celine Dion represent how both principles within you behave and interact in relation to material success, renown, and inner ambiance. I mention ambiance because these two people work in the music business. René Angelil symbolizes the way you manifest your concept of material success and the actions you perform. Celine Dion represents how you perceive and feel success from within. They were walking in front of you. This means that material success is what helps you advance. They were walking in the snow. Snow is frozen water. Water as a symbol always relates to emotions. The water is frozen therefore it leads to solitude. Unless the snow is bright and radiates a very positive atmosphere, it represents a feeling of solitude and coldness. We can see that the concept of success gives you a feeling of solitude and sadness. Your masculine principle is represented as being tired and demoralized. When you have good news on the outside, you are fine, but otherwise, you are demoralized and tired, just as you are at the moment."

What she added helped to clarify things, "Yes, but at least my inner principle was correct: Celine Dion didn't rebel. She supported her husband." I replied, "No, her attitude wasn't quite right. If They had wanted to show you that your inner attitude was correct, Celine would have helped her husband by giving him some manner of instruction. But, instead, she supported him. She thought it was normal that he be so tired and worn out because so much was riding on his shoulders. This means that you are trying to control your success even though it cannot be controlled. The message or the lesson given in your dream is that you ought to go within to cleanse your memories concerning material success. You should try to find the true concept of success. Think and materialize in a just fashion and find your motivation somewhere other than in exterior manifestations."

She agreed but, all the same, she did not recognize herself in this dream. A dream always manifests itself one way or another. I said to her, "I'll give you an example. Earlier, when you told me about the potential buyer who had taken down his 'For Sale' sign, you told me that you knew there was something you needed to understand. You said that you had no expectations and that you were indifferent. Behind your words, however, I felt something else. I felt that this situation really does bother you. Indifference is a distortion. Indifference is repression. We become indifferent when we are tired of seeing that things are not working out. Because we do not want to hear about it anymore, we push the subject down into our unconscious. At the slightest outside news, however, the sign is back up, we are happy, enthusiastic, and confident. We walk tall. Then, when the sign is taken down again, we go back to sagging shoulders and a feeling of unhappiness. We cannot seem to succeed. If our confidence, our enthusiasm, and our concept of success are based on external events, we will never enjoy stability. This is what They wanted to show you through this dream. Up Above, They can play around with your sign. They'll take it away, They'll put it back up and They'll take it away again. They are not doing this to play around with your emotions. They do it because They love you. They wish to help you find a different intention so that external events no longer lead you by the nose. They want you to lose this attitude of being happy only when you receive good news and being demoralized when events do not go the way you expect them to.

Some weeks later, I saw this woman again and, quite happily, she said to me, "Our potential buyer has put up his sign again. It's a good lesson for me." Later on, when I met her again, she told me he had taken it down. (laughter) She added, "That's when I realized there was still something I hadn't understood. It forced me to do a bit more cleansing." It does not matter if we see parts of ourselves that are not nice; what is important is that we notice them. It is important to notice when we are bothered, to become conscious of our state of mind, and to advance spiritually. This is the only way we can change the old memories of our soul. Otherwise, spiritual advancement will take a very long time and we will have to go through all sorts of ordeals before we acquire wisdom.

If it is indicated in a dream that material success will not happen, then it will not happen. This is an absolute truth. If limitations are inscribed in our life plan and if material success has not been planned for us, there is nothing we can do about it. Nothing, short of stealing, will make it happen. The entire earthly play exists so that we may experiment with different aspects of Consciousness.

Now, let's have a look at the position of Angel number 11 LAUVIAH in the Tree of Life. This Angel, which is governed by the Archangel RAZIEL, resides in the Sephirah called Hochmah. This is the Sephirah in which we find the Cherubims, those lovely chubby-cheeked babies that represent innocence or, in other words, great purity of Consciousness. The Angels that reside in Hochmah represent high levels of Wisdom and Love. When we attain these degrees of Consciousness, personal love no longer exists. There is only Unconditional Love. Very few people succeed in stabilizing these States of Consciousness.

The master planet of Angel 11 LAUVIAH is Uranus which, among other things, represents altruism and avant-garde ideas. Uranian energies are so powerful that they disintegrate anything that is not just. Through its secondary affinity with the Hesed Sephirah, Angel 11 LAUVIAH also has Jupiterian characteristics. Planet Jupiter symbolizes expansion and great power, resources, and prestige.

We can exteriorize this expansive energy in a selfish manner and direct it towards our own personal glory, our own renown, solely in relation to our own needs. They will let us do this. They will help us succeed and allow us to experiment with success. However, if we do not use success properly, eventually, we will have to experiment with the opposite: great limitations.

There comes a day when we are able to use this expansion in an Angelic way for humanitarian purposes and with altruistic intentions. Before we can get to this point, we have to experiment and, of course, in order to do this, we must understand evil. There comes a day when we have experimented so much with evil that we know how it works. Consequently, we voluntarily choose to no longer engage in it. The Jupiterian aspect of Angel 11 LAUVIAH gives us a grandiose vision of things. If our vision is altruistic and spiritual, this Angel bestows on us a grand scale vision at the Universal level. The Universe is so vast that the soul can expand its vision into the realization of great projects on Earth. If expansion in the physical dimension is part of our life plan, then we will have a lot of money and belongings and we will devote the surplus to helping others. This is a brief overview of this Angel's position in the Tree of Life.

I'd like to share a true story with you concerning one of the Qualities of Angel 11 LAUVIAH that illustrates quite well the powers of the Spirit. The quality is that of *confidence*. This summer, while I was preparing the lecture on this Angel, my husband, my daughter, and I went to look after our little one-year-old niece, Ariel. Her parents were away on vacation and we were staying in their house. That night, before falling asleep, I invoked Angel 11 LAUVIAH. In the middle of the night, I was awakened by a very loud noise directly in my ears. I heard the sound of footsteps on gravel. It was so loud that it was as though my ear were glued to the ground. I woke up, aware that someone was trying to steal something from the garage.

There is a freestanding garage in the yard next to the house and I knew we had left its door open. I got up and I looked out through the slightly open window. It was dark and I didn't see anything. All of a sudden, in a deep voice that I didn't recognize, I heard myself say, "Who's there?" I am incapable of reproducing this very impressive voice. I saw a young man scamper off. He came out of the garage, jumped over the fence and, taking to his heels, ran away.

I was sleeping upstairs beside the baby's room and my husband was sleeping in the basement. I went down to wake him and he went out to see if anything was missing. Nothing had been stolen. There was only a piece of cardboard that had been displaced and that had probably happened when the boy ran off. We calmly went back to bed. When I laid my head on the pillow, a thought came to mind, "Maybe, when someone tries to steal from a garage, he is definitely a beginner since there is not much worth stealing in a garage. Then, as a result of this experimentation, this young man will decide never to try something like this again." I fell asleep with this thought.

What happened to my hearing? Cosmic Intelligence turned up the volume: clairaudience. Thanks to clairaudience, I became aware of what was going on at a distance. They had turned up the volume. It was as if They had set up amplifiers in my ears so I could hear everything. But, imagine if my hearing had retained such a high volume. It was so loud that it would have been unbearable. Afterwards, They turned down the volume. (laughter)

As we can see, we are given powers only when it is necessary. The same applies to clairvoyance and clairsentience. At a given time, we receive what we need, when we need it. We must never ask for powers. We must only ask for qualities and virtues and, one day, They give us powers in their purest form. If we want to have powers because we want to show off or to be noticed by others and, if we do not stop asking, we shall end up getting what we ask for. Up Above, They will activate our perceptive capacities, but we will constantly see evil in others and we, in turn, will become evil. We will absorb these forces. We will attract many conflicting situations because we will have stolen the power instead of having done the work to deserve it. Because we will not yet have cleansed our unconscious, we will be filled with the resonance of wrongdoing and we will feel so badly that we will regret having asked for powers.

This, however, is all part of experimenting. We can certainly attempt the experience. There is no harm in it because we are experimenting. Then, once we have truly understood this concept, we will only ask for qualities and virtues and, naturally, in due course, the work we do with the Angels develops clairvoyance, clairaudience and clairsentience. If we allow Cosmic Intelligence to do so, It progressively opens up possibilities according to our rhythm of growth and our life plan, and, these, only as they become necessary.

Here is a story that will help us understand *enthusiasm*. Sometimes, we are so enthusiastic – to the point of overflowing – that it becomes a distortion and is no longer right. Excessive enthusiasm creates karma and results in misdeeds. Our eight-year-old daughter Kasara taught me this lesson while I was working with Angel 11 LAUVIAH. Our daughter is used to waking up very early. One evening, her father left her a little note that said, "If you have a dream, draw it for me when you wake up. I love you, Daddy." The next morning, Kasara had a drawing for us. She explained the dream she had had during the night.

Kasara had drawn a picture of herself and of a little black-haired girl that she did not know in reality but that she knew in her dream. Near the drawing of the little girl she wrote, "My name is Myriam." It was her friend Myriam. Kasara told us that, in her dream, *her friend made her laugh. She made her laugh so much that she dropped her glass of purple juice.*

She asked her father, "Tell me, Daddy, what does it mean?"

"Those two little girls are parts of you," he replied. "Since they are girls, they represent your inner world and your emotional side. Juice is a liquid and, as you know, water represents emotions. So, Up Above, They want to tell you, 'Today, you must be vigilant because your emotions are going to overflow. This is your program for the day.'"

This is the magic of dreams. They allow us to have a better educational approach with children and adults because dreams do manifest themselves. This is an absolute truth.

Her father told her, "Today, you are going to be very happy, but your emotions will overflow. The dream is warning you that there may be a few mishaps. It's no coincidence that the juice is purple as that is the color of spiritual power and protection. Be careful."

That day, though there were several little mishaps, Kasara was happy and full of enthusiasm. At one particular moment, her father said to her, "In a while, we are going to plant chive seeds." She was happy because she loves chives.

Every five minutes, she would ask her father, "Daddy, when are we going to plant the seeds?"

"Not right away, Kasara. It's not time yet. I'm busy at the moment. Just wait patiently, little angel."

She stopped coming around, yet she still paced up and down with the little packet of seeds in her hands. Her energy–her spiritual power–was growing. We could clearly feel this.

Earlier, I spoke of two principles: emissivity and receptivity. When we have desires, whether we express them or not, and when they are in our conscience, we can feel that our spirit is thinking about manifesting itself. This is what we call emissivity. In the case of our daughter, we could feel that her spirit was pushing to put her desire into action. For the moment, the surplus emissivity in this little eight-year-old girl had only very few consequences. But, if such an attitude manifests itself in an adult at a decisive moment in their life, this overflow of emissivity–this badly channeled spiritual force–could lead them to commit a misdeed that could prevent a project from succeeding.

After a moment, my husband said to Kasara, "All right! Now we can go plant the seeds." Well, when she went to find the packet, it wasn't there. She had misplaced it.

Her father asked her, "What is the sign, dear Kasara?"

"I was a bit excited, Daddy."

"That's ok. You see, your dream is manifesting itself. Your lost packet, that's the glass of juice that you dropped because you were so happy."

There exists an Angel to help us find what we have lost in the physical dimension as well as in the psychic and spiritual dimensions. It is Angel 69 ROCHEL. Of her own free will, Kasara began her Angel Recitation. She became very serious and began to pace while invoking Angel ROCHEL. She was so lovely to see. It is very important never to force a child or an adult to do this kind of inner work. It must come naturally. All of a sudden, she said, "That's it! I found it!" Where did she find it? Beside the toilet. Her father asked her, "What is the sign? The fact that you found the packet beside the toilet, what does this mean? The toilet is a symbol of purification. They wanted you to understand that you have to purify excessive vitality because too much enthusiasm leads to misdeeds."

She was so happy. They went off to the garden together to plant the little seeds. Kasara was so enthusiastic and in such a rush that she spilled the entire packet in the same spot. The chives, of course, did not grow very well. (laughter)

We can all recognize ourselves in this very simple example. When we have plans in the offing, we are happy and we are in a hurry because we want results. We push and we do not respect synchronicity. There are precise moments for doing things; everything is synchronized. But, when our desire for something is too strong and we push to get what we want, when we have too much emissivity and we can not seem to wait, it means that our spirit is somehow lacking. When our plans succeed on the outside, we believe that this will satisfy the emptiness we feel within and give us confidence or renown. But, such an attitude does not nourish our soul. It is the same as with food: you always have to begin all over again.

True success means a well-kept garden. If there is too much water, the symbol for emotions, the roots rot and our plans no longer have a solid base. If there is too much sun or fire, the symbols for will power, the plants burn and our plans are thwarted. If there is too much wind or, symbolically, if our mind is teeming with ideas, the ground dries up and we can no longer find the necessary resources to carry out our plans. Symbolism makes all of this easy to understand.

When we see someone who is successful and we are still attached to form, very often, we feel overcome by envy. It emerges from our unconscious like a gust of wind and it is unpleasant. Envy and jealousy lead to criticism and destruction. These are attitudes that must be transformed. Angel ROCHEL helps us cleanse the memories that are at the root of these attitudes.

The next dream concerns renown and success. Once again, Kasara had a dream. *She was at a ceremony where trophies were being presented. One of them was a child's bowl that had been won by a little boy and girl. Kasara was happy for them.*

Very often, parents who work with The Traditional Study of Angels see their children go through experiences related to the Angel they are invoking at that time. This is the case even if the child does not do the Angel Recitation. The adult's work has a direct impact on his child and those close to him.

Kasara's dream indicates that They were activating the field of consciousness that corresponds to success in her life program so that she could get used to seeing others succeed. Kasara was experiencing the vibration that I was invoking. In her dream, the children who were the recipients of the trophy, represented parts of herself. We can see the importance of learning to be happy for the success of others. The dream also highlights the fact that this attitude will come naturally to Kasara.

One day, we will no longer feel envy or jealousy We will no longer say in frustration, "He's successful and I'm not!" We will not allow such thoughts to come through. If, at a particular moment we feel envy, we do our Angel Recitation and we clean up our memories until this feeling has completely disappeared. Thus, with time, we obtain the perfect happiness to which we are all entitled.

We understand that it is by acquiring qualities and virtues that we learn to receive. We could be watching an Oscar winner or a movie star on television and truly be happy that they are successful. However, if we perceive a distortion with regard to this person and we still feel happy for them, there is a need for inner cleansing. We must always analyze and question what we are being presented with on television, at the movies, in music, and by family and friends. When we witness success, we should always ask ourselves, "Is it useful and advantageous for humanity? Is it right?" If we come to the conclusion that it is not, we refrain from criticizing but we evaluate according to spiritual criteria. We tell ourselves, "This person is experimenting. He is experimenting the distortion of celebrity and it is from Up Above that he is receiving all the resources that allow him to go through this experience." Knowledge allows us to understand that a life plan only applies for a certain period of time and that, sooner or later, we have to make amends for our errors. With this attitude, we feel admiration only for success that is right.

Most of the time, people believe that external success will nourish them because, in fact, they have not incorporated true success within themselves. When we watch television and when we are in certain people's company, it is good to ask ourselves, "How do I feel as far as their success is concerned?" Self-awareness alone will allow us to advance by leaps and bounds. When we voluntarily enter the field of Consciousness of Angel LAUVIAH, whatever requires cleansing concerning the illusion of success surfaces much more rapidly than if we had not invoked this Angel.

Going back to our childhood can sometimes help us understand our attitude towards renown. We may have had problems during our apprenticeship in our family if, for example, we had several brothers and sisters. When a new baby arrives in the home, we are particularly vulnerable. This thought came to me when we babysat our little one-year-old niece, Ariel. Our daughter, Kasara, was with us and, at one particular moment, my husband began to sing to the baby. He was carrying Ariel in his arms and singing with all his heart. Ariel was radiant. The connection between the two was beautiful and powerful.

Kasara was watching them and it was clear that she was preoccupied. This was a new experience for her. Her father is very perceptive and he immediately sensed her state of mind. He said to her, "You know, Kasara, I used to do exactly the same thing with you when you were small and you loved it! You reacted just like Ariel. You were radiant!"

When we speak, we set an intention with a particular objective that goes beyond the words themselves. In this case, the intention was, first of all, to help Kasara consider the baby as part of herself and, second, to encourage her to be happy that the baby was being sung to. The result was instantaneous: Kasara's preoccupation disappeared. Her dream in which she had been happy because of the success of others was being manifested. Having well anticipated Kasara's reaction, her father gently participated in activating a new ideological concept within her that will have beneficial repercussions for the rest of her life. Another child might have rejected it and remained stuck in an attitude of envy but, of course, Kasara was predisposed to receive this new concept favorably. In such cases, a long re-education process is foreseen.

If, in childhood, amidst brothers and sisters, we did not receive this kind of attention from our parents we may have developed a feeling of not being acknowledged. Thus, problems concerning renown set in and, subsequently, we bend over backwards to be acknowledged. Of course, if we experienced such lack in our childhood, it comes from previous lives.

The same thing can happen to a father upon the arrival of a newborn baby. The husband feels left out because all the attention is given to the baby. The wife can put forward an intention and say to the father, "This baby is the fruit of our love. It's a part of you that I'm rocking and feeding." The intention makes all the difference. With this approach, the recipient can, within a few seconds, change his state of consciousness. However, he must be accustomed to thinking in this manner. For some people, this requires that they spend a lot of time gaining self-insight.

When we feel a slight twinge of envy with regard to someone else's success, we might project a feeling of not being acknowledged, of creating scapegoats for ourselves, and of envying and criticizing the other person. Rather than go on in this manner, we interrupt the process. We admit to ourselves, "Yes, I envy him." This, of course, requires a lot of humility and work with Angel 11 LAUVIAH. We cleanse memories of experiences we had when we felt abandoned, left out, or unaccepted and we find renown within ourselves. The work we do with the Angels is very powerful.

I would now like to tell you the story of Normand Désourdy. I will not limit myself to the facts and events of his life. Thanks to symbolic language, we will delve quite deep. This exercise, wherein we will examine how a person's program comes into being, will help us better define the main thread of our own personal story.

Normand Désourdy is the youngest of a family of three. Hardly a year after his birth, his mother was diagnosed with Parkinson's disease. Therefore, his first feminine image was that of a sick woman who was bed or chair-ridden for 35 years. This woman became very pious. She was often seen praying with rosary beads between her fingers.

As for Normand's father, he was a farmer and a wood-seller. He was a man who lived up to his responsibilities. It is not easy having three children and an ill wife. He had a lot of willpower and he took on the responsibility of providing for his family. This man, therefore, was a powerful model for his son. The example that he set would later help Normand to overcome the ordeals of his own earthly life.

Let's examine the two parental models. Because we are not born into a family by chance, the Law of Resonance is applicable. We can say that the mother in the Désourdy family represents one of the main parts of Normand's inner woman. It is a part that is sick. Normand has always had extraordinarily good physical health but, in this instance, we are talking about an unconscious psychic illness. Why did Normand's mother get Parkinson's disease? If we go to the essence of this disease, we see that it concerns a disconnection of the nervous system. We can imagine that in another life, this woman lost herself in matter, that she disconnected herself on an energetic level and disconnected herself from the Spirit, from her Divine nature. Consequently, her life plan included great limitations. These limitations, however, were not there to punish her but to cause her to go within and to work on her spirituality. This is exactly what she did. She took responsibility for her karma. Simply by accepting her situation and by not rebelling against it, she remained pleasant and kind. She improved her life despite the burden of her physical limitations and she prepared her next life while inspiring her family and those near her.

This woman also represents the inner woman of Normand's father. On the inside, this man had great limitations. When we live with someone, we share certain psychological profiles and karma. This man was called Napoleon. We do not bear a name by chance; each name carries a vibration. What did the famous Napoleon do? He was quite the fighter and he killed for his own glory. He was experimenting. It is more than likely that he had been a warrior in another life and, because of this, he was given a program burdened with limitations. We only have to consider his wife's illness to understand this.

Nevertheless, he also took responsibility for his karma. When faced with great difficulties, some people, unable to cope, may compensate by developing serious addictions to alcohol and drugs. Napoleon Désourdy accepted his responsibilities and, like his wife, did the groundwork to make his next life easier.

We all have resonance with our parents. Their qualities inspire us and incite us to make choices geared to our personal evolution. We also resonate with their distortions and difficulties. Such resonance also helps us evolve. By cleaning up the personal and family parts of our unconscious, we succeed in transcending all the difficulties that marked our parents' lives. We no longer resonate with them, with the exception of the resonance that we have with their qualities and virtues. These contribute to the improvement of our soul.

We can already perceive the main theme of Normand Désourdy's life. From the age of 11, he began to do business with his brother Réal, who is three years his senior. They had a flourishing business selling blocks of ice. Until the age of 21, these two young men gave the money they earned to their father to help pay for the family's needs. Thus, Normand developed altruism, a distinguishing feature of his personality, which, since the opening of his conscience to spirituality, has not stopped blossoming.

What does an 'ice-business' symbolize? As I have already mentioned, chance or coincidence does not exist. The spirit is always attracted to an activity that corresponds to whatever it is the person has to develop within. The Universe is made of symbols. Earlier, we saw what ice symbolizes. Normand Désourdy had an enormous emotional potential lying dormant in his unconscious that was already beginning to manifest itself. This man had great possibilities.

At the age of 18, he began to do renovations with his older brother, Réal, and, for the first time, at age 21, he supervised the construction of a house.

The following year, he met an engineer for SNC, a consulting firm in engineering which, over the years, has become an important international firm. This man would greatly contribute to his success program. This man trusted Normand. He asked him to build a house for him in Montréal, Canada, near St. Joseph's Oratory. To satisfy the demands of his client, Normand had to do all sorts of things that he had never done before, such as building a roof in the shape of a diamond. He acquired the necessary documentation and, while studying and living in a little shed at the back of the house, he built the engineer's house. Successfully accomplishing such a project at the age of 22 gave him great credibility and opened the doors to public notoriety. This led to numerous contracts that his future firm would eventually carry out.

Normand, at the age of 23, had the necessary funds to become an equal business partner with his brother Réal, who was already in a good financial position. How did Normand manage to make so much money? He told us about his miraculous catch. He rented a boat and nets, hired some men, and came to an agreement with the buyers. His earnings were phenomenal. He had so many fish that he flooded the market. The likes of which had never been seen before. It was amazing! He cleared 2000 dollars in 15 days. This was after expenses and in 1950. Therefore, he had enough to set himself up in business.

In their new business, Réal was to look after the administration and Normand was responsible for everything related to building. The success of their business was so phenomenal that they themselves found it difficult to explain. Of course, they worked hard and were intelligent and innovative men, but many others who are just as gifted and who are very hard workers never obtain such results. These two brothers had a program directed by Cosmic Intelligence. The Désourdy brothers constructed buildings in numerous regions of Canada and introduced prefabricated houses to the market. This was a completely new concept at the time. They even built their own factory in which they employed 1500 workers and produced a house in only three hours.

Their renown spread abroad and, in 1975, they began to build in Saudi Arabia. Two years later, their destiny took a very different turn. Because of the jealousy of a competitor, they suffered heavy financial losses in that country and, from that moment, the entire business began to flounder. Normand Désourdy's program consisted of great material success but it was only to last up to a certain point in his life.

This person had been guided towards profitable partnerships and towards people who would open doors for him. Needless to say, it was not Normand Désourdy who created the great catch, but he was led to it because he was meant to succeed. Everything was remote-controlled by Cosmic Intelligence which was why his success came so easily. When we do not understand this and we experience personal success, ego gets the best of us and pride and vanity surface. We must learn to cultivate Knowledge by recalling spiritual experiences, our dreams, and the synchronicities that have marked our lives. One day, we are aware that everything comes from God and we never forget that.

It was written in Normand Désourdy's program that, in 1977, his destiny would take a turn for the worse and he would lose everything so that one day he could taste true success, Celestial Success. What is the significance of the fact that he went to work in Saudi Arabia? It is very likely that in another life, he lived in the Arab world and that he devoted himself to building on a large scale and to other commercial transactions. As for the unfair behavior of the competitor who caused his downfall, it shows that Normand had been a betrayer in another life. When we create injustice, it is written and, sooner or later, we bring it back to us. When we understand this, we pay our bills and we stop rebelling. We know that such an ordeal is our due.

Normand Désourdy lost a fortune of over 25 million dollars. When he told us about this, my husband asked him, "How did you feel at that moment?" "Ready to start over again, right away!" He replied.

His cousins lent him money and, once again, he started up in business with another innovative product: steel foundations. Foundations assure solidity and stability. Because of what he had just been through, Normand had seen his inner foundation falter. If we remember the aspects of his inner woman represented by his mother, we can easily imagine that he had unconscious parts to heal. He looked for something solid on the outside because, unconsciously, he was seeking inner solidity.

The new business went well but, a year and a half after its inception, the factory burnt down. Everything had to be rebuilt from scratch. His family advised him to go on a spiritual retreat. This domain was new to him but he took his family's advice and went to live at a spiritual centre in Europe. With great zeal, he began to build again, this time for the spiritual centre. Building began to acquire a new meaning for him. Through meditation, prayer, and self-insight, his thirst for material success gave way to a new aspiration: that of helping others.

After his stay in Europe, which lasted about a year, he returned to Canada. With his wife and one of his older sons he started up a business in framework. Framework represents structure. He needed to restructure himself from within and, more or less consciously, he chose work related to the development of his spirit. Two years later, business was going well. However, when he came home one evening, Normand received a terrible blow. On the table was a letter from his wife: she was leaving him for another man.

He was shattered. Normand told us, "Beyond the pain that I was feeling, my pride really took a blow." He left everything. His children were already grown up. He left the business and moved to another region so that he could live incognito. His name, which radiated an aura of success and glory, had become, in his eyes, synonymous with failure in every respect.

During this period, he even hesitated to pronounce his name, mentioning it only when it was absolutely necessary. He continued on his spiritual path and participated in meditations but, in hindsight, he realized that he was still wearing his mask. He gave the impression that he was fine and, even though he believed in reincarnation and the benefits of forgiveness, he harbored intense rancor towards his ex-wife who had abandoned him and towards the competitor who had caused his financial disaster. A great number of ill-digested experiences had accumulated deep within him. One day, he became acquainted with the teaching of the Angels and, at about the same time, he met his new wife. Since then, hand in hand, they walk the spiritual path while doing their Angel Recitation together.

As I described at the beginning of this lecture, Normand's new wife had a dream in which Cosmic Intelligence was announcing that both of them would go through fire. Normand also received a dream that foretold of great transformations. In this dream, he was not only told that he was going to die but was also taught the meaning of death. *He was lying on the floor and next to him were his luggage and an airplane in a vertical position. All of a sudden, a voice said to him, "No, no, no, it's not time yet."* He went through several stages. First he was quashed at the material level, then at the emotional level, and, now, it was at the spiritual level that he had to die.

Cosmic Intelligence was announcing great initiations at the level of his consciousness. Of course, profound structural changes would also manifest themselves on the outside, but not in physical death. This is why the airplane was in a vertical position. Luggage also represents a new departure, a form of death, because when we die, we take with us everything that is registered in our unconscious. This also represents new beginnings.

Normand has, in fact, gone through great initiations. He went to the heart of his unconscious memories and became wholly aware that his ex-wife had been a great initiator for him. The end of this relationship allowed him to take his life in a new direction and truly open up to spirituality. Ordeals are an integral part of the initiate's path. Normand Désourdy's unceasing quest for material success was interrupted in order that he gain access to self-knowledge. It was the beginning of the shedding of masks and illusions.

His inner work led him to cleanse the rancor he had accumulated and, one day, he received another dream that he asked us to interpret. *He was building a roof on stilts to allow a great sage to address the crowd without having to get his feet wet.* My husband said to him, "This dream announces a great change in you and increased understanding. The sage represents a part of you, and the roof–the superior part of a dwelling–symbolizes the head or the world of thoughts. The dream foretells changes in your way of thinking. Because of the new concepts that you are integrating, wisdom will incarnate within you and you will be able to manifest it concretely without getting your feet wet, without the sadness or excessive emotion that would confuse your spiritual vision. Your new wisdom will lead you much further than you have ever been. You will be aware of this. Your ideas will be clearer and more luminous."

After this dream, Normand became aware of many things. He was ready for a new stage of development. Following his accelerated evolution after the dream of the sage, Normand received another dream in which *his ex-wife received a new home that was golden yellow in color. It was a lovely house. He also saw Michel Jasmin, a well-known Québec television journalist.* In this dream, all the characters represented parts of him.

My husband asked him, "What does Michel Jasmin represent to you?"

"He's a person who experienced great success and who, after resolving serious problems, made a public comeback. He is now very successful once again."

The dream was announcing the same thing for Normand Désourdy. A journalist is someone who broadcasts on a large scale. Therefore, when we dream about a journalist, it means that we are no longer able to hide certain things that we had once concealed. We become more authentic. This allows us to share with others when the time is right. Normand had told us that, earlier on, he could not have let his story be known. He would have felt much too uncomfortable. Because of the tremendous inner work he has done, he now feels at ease sharing his experience publicly.

One day, we must all tell our story in detail to inspire our children, our friends, and other people close to us. We no longer need to hide or control anything to maintain our image and to pretend we are happy. There is no need to feel awkward. There comes a day when we are no longer ashamed of our past. We are able to talk about it and we no longer wish to erase it. We take responsibility for our life experience. Normand said to us, "The events of my life have been the cornerstone of my evolution. I certainly don't want to erase them. I have reconciled with my past."

In the dream in which his ex-wife receives a new home, the house was not meant for the woman he had known in real life but for part of his inner woman, the part that represents his past. He had brought back home the part of himself that had caused him so much sadness, heartbreak, and discouragement. He had reintegrated it with all its inherent potential because he had accepted it. This gave him increased confidence and great inner light. When we take the time for self-insight, it is possible for us to have dreams about any ex-partners we might have had. This is normal. These dreams do not necessarily announce that we will see them again or that we will return to live with them. They show us psychological aspects of ourselves that need to be remodeled so that, at a certain point, the distortions that our ex-spouses represent can be fully transcended. If a person happens on our path, it is because we have lessons to learn from this experience. One day, we must succeed in transcending everything.

To end this lovely story, I will tell you of the true success that Normand recently encountered. He was at the wedding of one of his sons and his ex-wife was also there. A tune was playing and Normand's new wife, from quite a distance, heard him say: "What lovely music! I'd love to dance." At about the same moment,

Normand's ex-wife, who was beside her, said: "Oh! I really love that music. I would so love to dance!" Normand's new wife said to her "Go on, go and invite him, he'd love to dance." They danced and it was truly beautiful.

When we have Knowledge, there is no more jealousy and no more fear. We can then help others. The new wife could have been worried and have said to herself, "Oh my goodness, what if he goes back to her?" and prevented the event from happening. But this woman is an initiate and she has Knowledge. Knowledge gives us a big heart and a lot of intelligence. Fear disappears with Knowledge and allows us to witness miracles.

Normand Désourdy has changed his life with The Traditional Study of Angels and with his new spouse. He falls asleep at night listening to Angel meditations. He, also, continues to use his great innovative talent for construction and is now building ecologically friendly homes. Every time he builds one, he knows that he is building within himself. He continues to respect the rules of construction but, first and foremost, what guides him is a great respect for Cosmic and Divine Laws which he seeks to apply every second of every day.

For Normand, the name *Désourdy* is no longer a beacon or a burden. He has found his identity within and he has acquired true renown. He now considers himself an initiate, a builder of the Eternal Kingdom.

Angel 19 Leuviah
Memories Of Past Lives

One day, while I was out for a walk with our seven-year-old daughter, Kasara, she looked at me and said, "I would so love to know about my past lives! Do you know about yours?"

"Yes," I replied. "I know about some of them."

"Could you tell me about them?"

"You know, Kasara, previous lives are personal. In general it isn't something that we talk about. And we don't ask for memories of past lives. We receive them."

"How do we receive them? How can I receive memories of my past lives?"

"We receive them in our dreams, and it is God Himself who decides and chooses the best moment. This moment is usually when we need certain information to gain access to Knowledge."

"But why doesn't He give them to us right away?"

"Imagine, Kasara, that among the people who are close to you, some might have hurt you in past lives, and others might have been hurt by you. It would be difficult to go on loving them if you knew everything. Once we have acquired wisdom and understanding, then we can know our former lives because even if these people have hurt us, we can continue to love them and even love them more."

She thought about this for a few minutes. She then said, "I understand. I understand that we need to do good deeds before we are given our past lives." In her own way, she was telling me that she understood. The subject was closed, until the next time.

There is a very special Angel who can help us find the memories of our past lives, but also our Memories with a capital M. This Angel allows us to rediscover our personal archives in the Great Universal

Library, where everything is registered. It is Angel LEUVIAH, who bears the number 19.

It is important to note that when we work with an Angel, we go from one extreme frame of mind to another. They are great Pedagogues. Up Above, we are made to experience new sensations, new to this life at least. Then, suddenly, we feel terribly anxious. We are confused. It's normal. If we don't understand these mood swings, we stop the process and say, "This is just too much!" We need to know that it's normal to feel shaken up. Cosmic Intelligence is telling us, "If you want to rediscover vibrations in their Purest Form within yourself, you have to cleanse your memories. There is no need to return to the places where you once lived. By invoking the Angel, you'll have the opportunity to see these experiences again and to cleanse them, because they'll appear to you in dreams or be presented to you in the form of situations similar to those you experienced previously."

A woman who had attended lectures several times, but without having fully understood Angel Work, told me, "One day, I was with my children and I felt a bit aggressive towards them. I wasn't being considerate enough. So I invoked an Angel. I said to Him, 'Come and help me so that I may be nicer to my children.' Then, the situation got worse. I felt an increase in my aggression to a point where I said things that I immediately regretted. I had to apologize to my children, who were rather young at the time. Afterwards, I spoke to the Angel and I told Him, 'I'm not talking to You anymore. You did the very opposite of what I asked.'"

Later, when she recounted this episode to a friend who had been attending lectures for a longer period of time, this woman said to her, "It's normal. Continue your Angel Recitation. Your unconscious aggression has to come out."

With time, we learn not to unload our aggression onto others. We keep it inside. "But that's repression," you'll say. "When we do that we repress our aggression and afterwards it becomes worse." No. With Angel Recitation, we learn to cleanse everything from the inside. We no longer seek a scapegoat. At the beginning of our spiritual path, we are not used to this, so anger and criticism automatically surge. That's when we immediately grab hold of what we were about to project on the outside, and our Work may begin. This is when it is very important to have understood the Law of Resonance.

Angel Work leads to a great opening into the dream dimension. As a result, our dreams become very intense and much more frequent. We have to know that the only means with which we may authenticate a past life is through the analysis of our dreams. In our dreams, there is no intermediary to intervene between our conscious and our unconscious states. The ordinary mind cannot get involved by inventing an experience based on an illusory past life of repressed desires.

While working with the Angels, we also learn to *read* signs. These are the simple events and little details that turn up in our everyday life. When we take the time to analyze them symbolically, they turn out to be important signposts, hence their name.

We shall see that reading signs is good for memory at all levels and this is a great way to rediscover lost memories. Scientists have established a relationship between memory and the interest we have in things. When we are interested in a subject and we like it, all our senses open up and this helps us concentrate and memorize whatever it is we are learning. This is exactly what our work with Angel LEUVIAH does for us. When we read signs, our interest remains constantly awake, because we know that the slightest detail may be loaded with importance and meaning for us. On the other hand, when we have little or no interest in a subject, our memory selects what it wants and moves on. This selection takes place both consciously and unconsciously.

Let's take a look at some of the Qualities of Angel 19 LEUVIAH.

Expansive Intelligence. When we work with Angel 19 LEUVIAH, when we meditate to His vibration, our intelligence grows because of the openings that are created. *Prodigious capacity for memorization, gateway to Memory, guardian of the Daath Archives.* This Angel opens the doors of Memory, the doors of the Archives in the hidden Sephirah, Daath, the Great Universal Library. The Orientals call this the Akashic Memory.

How do we gain access to Daath? We do it through our dreams and meditations. This is where our soul visits the parallel dimensions. As I mentioned when we were examining the Consciousness Diagram (Figure 1, page 5), we must go through several stages in order to have access to all of these dimensions. Before all else, we visit our own personal computer, because we must learn to know ourselves and purify our spirit. This is why no one can gain access to Daath without having received authorization. All information and knowledge is inscribed in the Great Universal Library and one who has not sufficiently evolved could use this Knowledge for the wrong purpose. We must have acquired great purity and great wisdom in order to respect the Cosmic Plan. A simple piece of information revealed at the wrong moment could have serious consequences for Universal Destiny. Our consciousness must evolve so that we can one day gain access to the Great Universal Library and the information that is necessary for our work here on Earth.

Thus, there is no need to get bogged down with tons of information. In our society, we place a lot of emphasis on memorization, horizontal memory, bookish memory. This allows us to accumulate only a minute amount of intellectual knowledge. With Angel 19 LEUVIAH, however, it's all about Memory with a capital M–the Memory of Daath.

Given this perspective, the idea that we lose our memory as we grow old disappears. When we are on a path of insight, the opposite occurs. Old age becomes synonymous with Memory. This functions in the computerized communication mode. When we need information we look for it without weighing ourselves down with a load of documents. It's like connecting to the Internet, but in this case we connect to the *Skynet*. If we need information, we meditate and there it is. We receive it. This is what happens when we have access to the Great Universal Library. Everything is written. Everything is inscribed in Daath.

When a person has purified his memories, he knows that when someone is angry or bitter, when someone complains or makes others feel guilty, he does so because he is unaware that he is being controlled by his unconscious memories, and because he does not understand the Laws. This is due to lack of Knowledge. The person who understands these Laws shows great generosity towards this person. He understands just how difficult it is to go through this, since he has gone through it himself. He has a lot of love for this person and does not make any judgments.

There is short-term memory and long-term memory. For instance, when we telephone someone for the first time, we have to read his number before dialing, and we only remember it for about 30 seconds. But if we use this number often, we end up keeping it in our long-term memory. The same is true when we take part in workshops and we hear about wonderful and truthful principles that move us. Within 30 seconds, we have already forgotten these principles. This is why Angel Recitation is crucial while cleansing the thousands upon thousands of old memories that burden our soul and keep us in a state of malfunction.

Intellectually, we understand this. But habits linked to unconscious memories get the better of us and automatically reassert themselves. So we have to continually repeat the Angel's name and keep doing so until all of the unconscious memories have been reprogrammed. There comes a day when not a single distortion remains. A person obtains the Universal Passport, which consists of Qualities, Virtues and Powers in their purest form. The rest is only information.

Everyone has the capacity to gain access to Daath. Here on Earth, however, very few have attained the High Distinction known as Enlightenment. It represents long and difficult work that is directed towards precise objectives and received through dreams on a daily basis. Only our dreams can show us the true level that we have reached in the integration process of Love and Divine Wisdom. We can be kind, altruistic, spiritual and stable, but we can still be in an unconscious state that is limited by distortions. If a person doesn't dream, it shows that he hasn't yet reached the initiation stage. Intensive Angel Recitation allows us to reintegrate this function of the spirit.

I'd like to open a door onto my own personal experiences and tell you about one of my past lives. I mentioned earlier that we don't normally discuss our past lives. Sharing one with you here, however, is an exception that serves the purpose of teaching. It will help you understand the remembrance of previous lives. I will explain to you how a memory of this particular past life was given to me.

During the summer of 1999, my husband and I left for Europe. It was June 22nd and we were in the period governed by Angel LEUVIAH, which takes place between June 22 and June 26. I was working intensively with Angel LEUVIAH and we had a very particular destination in mind: Gerona. It's a little town in Spain located near the French border. It is considered one of the cradles of practical Kabbalah and of the day-to-day study of Angels. As we discussed in the chapter on the Traditional Study of Angels, an entire community living in Gerona worked with the Angels during part of the Middle Ages.

Apart from the city of Gerona, we had no other precise destination. We simply let ourselves be guided. We were traveling in a camping-car, which had been very generously lent to us. We crossed Switzerland and France and, before reaching the Pyrenees, we spent the night in a wonderful forest.

In the middle of the night, I woke up in a sweat, struggling with deep anxiety. I had just received a dream of such intensity that its reality was still tangible. What was the dream about? I saw myself from behind, naked from the waist up. At one particular moment, a man came towards me with a red branding iron and marked my back with a fleur de lys. Then, there was a total blackout. The pain I felt was very intense. The blackout lasted a certain length of time (in dreams the idea of time is altered). Then, the pain went away and a man dressed in black, representing the Inquisition, presented me with a gold medal engraved with an Angel. The medal hung from a little gold chain. I probably don't need to tell you that when I woke up that morning I didn't feel very well.

We continued on our journey. As my husband drove, he suddenly did a U-turn. He is a very intuitive person. He said, "We're going to go there. I saw a signpost indicating 'Cathar Ruins.'" It was the ancient village of Montaillou! It is now in ruins with a few houses that are still inhabited. I had vaguely heard about the Cathars, but I had never really looked into the matter.

When we arrived at the top of the hill, near the ruins of the Montaillou Castle, I suddenly began sobbing. I was inconsolable. I felt a profound pain at the soul level and I couldn't stop crying. Then, I naturally made the connection between the tears and the dream. I invoked Angel LEUVIAH. I was breathing, crying and invoking, all at the same time. Finally, I regained my focus.

Then we went to the only shop in the village. There, we found leaflets on the Ariège Department. A lady told us the history of the Cathars. She said, "The Cathars were followers of Catharism, an esoteric Christian movement that greatly expanded and deeply influenced certain regions of France and Europe during the 13th and 14th centuries. The Cathars' aim was to create a society that was fair, fraternal, exempt of all luxury and tinged with love."

For more than a century (from 1209 to 1328), the Catharist movement became the target of persistent and extremely violent persecutions by the Inquisition and certain kings and noblemen of that time. When we think of the Cathars, we think of persecution. At one point, the shop assistant told us, "Before burning them at the stake, the Inquisitors branded them with a fleur de lys, the royal seal of the kings of France at that time." That took my breath away! I could feel my dream reverberating throughout my entire body. I was being told, "You were a Cathar in a previous life."

The Cathars inspired art, culture and quite a few initiate orders. Certain noblemen supported them financially. When we read the philosophy of the Cathars, it all seems very beautiful. The word *cathar* comes from the Greek *katteros*, which means *pure*. Moreover, they were called "the perfect ones." They dedicated themselves to purity and wished to detach themselves from material possessions. In reaction to the abuses of power and the accumulation of wealth, which prevailed among the privileged classes, they considered matter to be somewhat evil. They also thought of matter as an illusion and as a prison for the soul.

In light of this teaching, what did They wish to communicate to me through this dream? We are not given the memory of a past life without a reason. They wanted to tell me, "You have experienced persecution and we want to show you what awaits the person who transcends such levels of persecution." In my dream, this is why the representative of the Inquisition gave me a gold medal. It represents the Angelic States and a union with Heaven. This refers to the teachings that I am putting into practice. I was being told, "This transcendence leads a person to the highest levels." This revelation allowed me to break through another stage in the understanding of evil, but it also confirmed that we have to accept evil in order to be able to transcend it.

This dream also showed me that I still had some things to transcend at this level. Small ruins subsisted within me. I don't think that the Cathars knew the Kabbalistic Law of Resonance. Of course, they weren't the persecutors, they were the persecuted, but we attract what we are.

These Cathars must have been tough. They must have said to the rich, "Hey! You there! You're not making proper use of your power and your wealth." They were surely vindictive in their search for justice and earthly paradise.

With The Traditional Study of Angels, we come to such an understanding of evil that even what is distorted seems correct in our eyes. Needless to say, we don't approve of evil, but we do have a deep understanding of its nature. We understand that through evil, Up Above, They are helping us to experiment. They are saying, "Go on! A bit more! We're giving you even more energy so that you may experiment with power, so that you can learn to use it well."

When a person has sufficiently experimented, he may then wish to move on to another stage. He may realize that to limit himself to matter does nothing for him. When we understand this, we don't try to change others. We prefer to let them live their experiences. We understand them and we feel love for them. We transcend all puritanism.

It's not a coincidence that I was given the memory of this past life. It led me to better understand my own experience. In the beginning, when I started to speak publicly about spirituality, I had such stomach aches. What I felt, however, had nothing to do with the situation. My audience was composed of kind people. Everything went well, yet I remained terribly nervous. This situation lasted several months. I felt as though I were being led to the stake. Old unconscious memories were creating an association between spirituality and the stake. It was completely irrational. But whenever such an association is inscribed within us, reasoning with oneself isn't enough to get out of it. It got to the point where I told myself, "Up Above, They want me to understand something. So I'm going to take the plunge. I'm going to start teaching." But this truly required tremendous courage on my part.

I said to Them, Up Above, "Once I get through this stage, I'll stop giving lectures. I don't think teaching is for me. I've got the feeling that You have something else in mind for me."(laughter) We cleanse and cleanse and cleanse and, one day, our discomforts disappear. That's how we proceed with our memories. We have to revisit them often. This way, events and situations are organized. They provide opportunities for us to return to former places and activities. Thus, as we gradually cleanse our memories, unconscious and misguided associations disappear, one after the other.

This is true of all mental, emotional, and physical associations caused by fears and limitations. These associations are called interferences. When we listen to a person who is speaking, our unconscious memory records everything that he says and does, just as a video camera or tape recorder would do. Our conscious memory, on the other hand, is happy to record only certain elements, indicators, which could eventually serve as useful markers. Later, when the markers appear, something goes Click! This equals this. Eureka! Our unconscious memory brings out the whole repertory associated with it. All the feelings that were recorded spring to the surface, even if we don't know where they are coming from.

If I had been given this past-life memory 15 years ago, I would probably have told myself, "Oh dear! I was a martyr. The Cathars were perfect. I'm a victim of humanity. The world is terrible." If we don't understand the concept of Divine Justice and if we haven't integrated the Knowledge of good and evil, then we quickly rebel. This is one of the reasons why memories of previous lives are not given to us on demand. We are given them at a very precise moment, when our level of understanding and wisdom allows us to use them appropriately. If a person is not ready, he could attempt to live his life as he did in a remote past.

From our past lives, we bring with us a baggage of memories that are now part of our conscious and unconscious states. We must, however, move forward and use the experiences in our present life to evolve, because our daily experience is created in relation to this baggage. On the one hand, the recollection of certain elements of our past lives allows us to integrate the principle of reincarnation into our concept of the world. On the other, it lets us perceive our present-day strengths and weaknesses from a spiritual point of view.

I'm going to tell you a story concerning a personal experience of mine to show you how a sign can be as revealing as a past-life memory. While I was working with Angel 19 LEUVIAH in preparation for this lecture, I read a few medical texts about memory and the physical problems that are associated with it.

Amnesia, memory lapses and Alzheimer's disease are distortions of Angel LEUVIAH. While reading these texts, I learned that people who are lacking in potassium tend to have memory loss. That's very real. As I was reading, I happened to wonder, "Hmm, what food is potassium found in?" I went on to think about something else.

The following morning, I was shopping for groceries. When I reached the checkout counter, a woman approached. She had only one product in her hands: oranges. She looked at my bananas and said, "I've forgotten my bananas!" "Ah!" I said to myself. "She has forgotten." I immediately made the connection with Angel Leuviah. She added, "My husband loves bananas. He eats two or three a day. Apparently, they contain a lot of potassium."

Imagine! I looked at her wide-eyed. Heaven was communicating with me. Heaven always communicates with us. It speaks to us through those who cross our path. That's why it's important to keep our senses open in order to understand the signs, however subtle they might be.

I said to her, "Do you know that potassium is good for the memory?"

"Oh yes, that's right," she replied. "It's because he lacks potassium that the doctors advised my husband to eat bananas. And it's so true that he has no memory! Besides, he has just had two operations, one after the other. The anesthetics didn't make things any easier. They didn't help."

"Oh!" I said kindly and enthusiastically. "Put down your oranges and I'll keep them for you. The bananas are over there. Go on!"

Try to guess what she replied.

"No, no," she said to me. I was feeling deep inside that she did not really want her husband to heal. She had a masculine attitude of control as she spoke.

"Look," I insisted gently. "The cashier hasn't started yet, you've got time. Go on, put your oranges down. The bananas are just over there."

"No," she replied in a firmer tone of voice. "I'll get them later."

With this one observation, we can understand a lot about this woman, and without making any judgment, we can see the state of her masculine and feminine aspects. This woman is too emissive. On the energetic level, she takes up too much space and she lacks receptivity.

How can we interpret what happened? When this woman spoke of her husband, without knowing it, she was also talking about her own inner man. She revealed that he had lost Memory. Our inner man, the masculine principle, represents the spirit. A woman, the feminine principle, is symbolically related to matter. This woman was forgetting the spirit. She was forgetting to nourish her inner man with attention, love and devotion. Such an attitude leads to an eventual lack in potassium. And since she took up a lot of space with her strong personality, I'm sure her husband must have been one of those silent types who rarely speaks and tends to be introverted. This type of couple is typical.

From another point of view, if we consider this woman's exterior man, her husband, we understand that his inner woman is represented by this woman who forgot the bananas. Maybe he doesn't say much, but such an attitude is the perfect complement to his inner woman, whether he's conscious of it or not. As a result, he was losing his memory in a very real and concrete way, and we shall soon see why. This evening, through a number of examples, we shall discuss how memory loss is a compensatory phenomenon. When we forget the important values, life becomes so difficult that we lose our memory.

That day, I had been asking myself questions about memory and its sources, however subtle. I was being given answers to all of my questions. I was shown why a person ends up lacking in potassium. At the same time, I received a lesson on the marriage between the masculine and feminine principles. When we succeed in fusing these two poles within ourselves, it is an apotheosis. In fact, since our spirit is well balanced and is constantly working to maintain this essential balance, it always finds what it needs. One day we ask a question, and we receive an answer.

The way we act and how we treat others perfectly reflects what we, in turn, do to ourselves. Our attitudes and behavior are the result of what is inscribed in our cells and within the totality of our memories. The negligent attitude this lady has towards those around her shows up in her professional relationships, in her relationships with her children and friends, and in everything she does. In short, her behavior with regard to the bananas is only the tip of the iceberg.

At one particular moment when I was reading scientific and medical articles on the loss of memory and the loss of balance that is often associated with it, the telephone rang. The woman who was calling me, a woman I know well, was feeling very sad, even devastated. She told me that her husband had just been rushed to the hospital because he had completely lost his memory. I asked her, "Would you like us to go and see him?" "No," she replied. "I just wanted you to know. Please pray for us."

After I hung up, my husband and I decided to go and visit them. This woman's husband never complains, but that doesn't mean that he has sorted everything out. On the contrary, he still has a lot of repressed memories which haven't been cleansed. When I arrived in the emergency room, I took his hands and I told him that I loved him very much. This man doesn't usually show his emotions, but he started to cry. I told him, "Go on, keep crying. The source comes from the Angels." His wife told us that he had just had a heart attack.

Later, she told her husband, "I think you work too much." Imagine a man who is 72 years old and he still works 80 to 90 hours a week. His wife said to us, "I think that the shock he had is linked to the fact that the sale of our house has been finalized. I think he's too attached to the house." That night, I had a dream about this man. In the dream, *I could only see his right ear. It was all sewn up and he couldn't hear. Then, little by little, I could see that the stitches were coming apart and his ear was opening up.*

What was I being told through this dream? The ear is a symbol of receptivity and wisdom. The right side of the body represents action and the ability to put things into practice. I was therefore being shown that this man lacks wisdom when he works. He gets lost in matter, because of all sorts of insecurities, including financial ones. The ear, which was becoming unstitched and opening up, signified that this event was going to force him to listen more attentively and to feel better.

I also understood that this man's problems had deeper roots than it appeared. Of course he was attached to his house, but the sale had awoken certain deeply buried memories.

Quite a few years ago, this man had gone through a very painful divorce. It had involved the sale of the family home and plunged him into financial difficulties. Thus, the recent signing of the sales contract had set off an association related to that event, therefore causing repressed memories to resurface. That, along with the fact that he was already under a lot of pressure because he worked too much, was the last straw. Through this association, selling a house meant financial trouble, suffering, grief and separation. Of course, he was making an irrational association, because his present day situation was very different from the one at the time of his divorce. But the memory caused a disconnection. It was too much. We can see just how important it is to cleanse our old memories, to clean them up completely. If we don't do so, the difficulties reappear, because everything is recorded in our soul.

This man recovered very well. But a few days later, he phoned to tell us he'd had a little accident. He had been involved in a collision while driving his work truck. Nothing serious occurred, only material damage. At the time of the accident, he was coming out of a dental clinic, and the man who crashed into his truck was driving a new car, one that had been released on the market that very year. We analyze an accident exactly as we would part of a dream and by using the same symbolism. This accident was no coincidence. This man was being given a warning by Cosmic Intelligence. Fortunately, he came out of it unharmed.

Old memories are very powerful. They are like little voices whispering to us, "Go on then, work too hard and you'll be loved! Go on! Be ambitious. You can do it. You've recovered your health, haven't you? Go on." Without respite, our insecurities push us to work. They're stronger than we are.

This man hadn't waited long enough before going back to work. He had reassured his wife by telling her that he wouldn't work too much and that he would take breaks. She believed him, but we can't cheat with the Man Up Above! He knows everything about everything. We can imagine God saying, "We love this man very much. He has a lovely program. So, once more, I'm going to stop him just a little. I'm going to stop his truck because he hasn't understood the lesson quite well."

Through the symbol of the new car that crashed into the truck, we understand that God wanted to say to this man, "I gave you a new car to go forward and look how you behave!" Let me remind you that at the time of the accident, he had just had dental work done. In a dream, teeth represent the structure and the wisdom of our instinctive nature. This man was therefore in the middle of being restructured. We must learn to recognize and understand life's lessons. By creating all these events, God wanted to tell this man, "I repaired you. But once again you haven't been listening well. It's too early to start working again. Stop! Go within yourself a little. Listen to your inner voice. Take a day or two. I'm not asking you to give up work completely, but your intention must be one of better quality. When you work, you must not be led by insecurities. You must remember that what is important is to be a Heavenly worker. When you build, you are also building yourself, on the inside."

When we don't understand, we say, "I didn't need that on top of everything else!" We become bitter. All our distortions resurface, we are unhappy and we blame others. "Look at that reckless driver," we think. Even if the man who crashed into the truck was responsible for the accident, the fact remains that he was sent by Heaven. We should thank him. Of course, he too had something he needed to understand.

With this wonderful example of synchronicity we can see the entire line up of cause and effect. We realize that memory loss has deeply rooted causes. The veil between consciousness and unconsciousness (cf: Figure 1, p.5) means that we have to go through several stages to be able to gain access to all our dimensions. When we arrive here on Earth, our counter is put back to zero. I've often heard people say, just as Kasara wondered, "Why aren't we immediately given memories of our past lives? It would be so much easier. At least we'd know where we stand."

If you only knew just how much of a Divine Grace it is to have this veil. In some cases, if it were lifted for us, we'd quickly realize that simply correcting certain behaviors requires a hundred lives. Imagine! We'd be devastated. (laughter) We could no longer advance. We'd be completely discouraged. Just standing in line makes us grumble! The Creator has really done things well. We function with one goal at a time. I'm often asked, "Do you think I've completed the cycle?" (laughter). We may need lives upon lives in order to close one single cycle. The very fact of asking the question shows that we haven't finished the karma. When we arrive at the end of karma, a very explicit dream will show us that we have. Our changes in attitude and behavior will clearly bear witness to the fact.

⊙

Reincarnation and the Veil

When a soul arrives on Earth, it already has a program that has been preordained in its broad outlines. How is this program determined? It is determined by our past lives. At the beginning of its incarnation, the soul finds its counter put back to zero on the conscious level, but on the unconscious level the counter hasn't stopped working. The file containing the information on this soul and all of its memories is still there, except that consciousness no longer remembers anything. So much so, in fact, that a few weeks after its birth, the baby realizes for the first time that it is he, himself, who turns his own hand. This is a complete loss of consciousness, isn't it? He must relearn everything. This loss of consciousness is but a simple strategy, which aims at the integration of karma in our present life.

The program determines in which country the soul will incarnate. Why does a soul end up in Afghanistan when another arrives here? To live in one country rather than another has real implications. Our previous lives determine what it is, specifically, that we have to understand. Thus, we arrive in a country for which we have resonance and affinity.

We also arrive in a particular region. We can land in Shanghai, New York, in the region of Paris, in the canton of Geneva or anywhere else. Mentalities vary according to different regions. If, later on, we leave our native region the fact remains that it was no coincidence that we arrived there. It's the best region for us.

We also land in a particular family and, once again, it's the best family for us. Some people will say, "If you knew my family, you wouldn't say that!" (laughter) Yes, it is the best family. We have strong resonance with this family. But unless we have Knowledge, we don't know it.

Even if we understand that in past lives we did things that had considerable consequences, we mustn't feel guilty. Whatever we may have done, we did not do deliberately. We were ignorant. So, we rectify. We have to transcend and cleanse. Everything that bothers us about our parents, which are part of the family's unconsciousness, has to be transcended so that the day comes when nothing bothers us any more. When we have reached that point, we are flying! This is because the biggest pieces, the most difficult parts, are related to what happened in our family and in our personal life.

When we finally understand why we have landed in one place rather than another, everything becomes clear. In a dream, if we find ourselves in our childhood home, that means we are touching on past lives as well as our own childhood. This is because we arrive on Earth with all our baggage from previous lives. This baggage is inscribed and it influences and determines everything we do. The present and the past form an indivisible whole that prepares the future. At first, we don't need to know the details of these former lives, otherwise we'd have to study the Cathars, the Egyptians, etc. It suffices to know our father, mother, brothers and sisters. Through them, we know the psychological profile that They want us to work on in this life.

Finally, we reach the level of the individual. Here, all possibilities exist. In a family of ten children, one can be a criminal, another a saint. The first one fell into distortions and continued to cultivate them. The other one used his difficulties to grow. They brought out his potential, and he transcended his parents' distortions. All scenarios are possible and each one includes a great number of factors, all of which interact with one another. But everything has been calculated. God is a Living Computer.

In that case, our parents are really quite a gift! When we realize that, we thank them, no matter what kind of people they are or once were. We say, "Oh God, how well chosen they were for me! I couldn't have made a better choice."

Speaking of past lives, let's take a look at personal tastes. Why is it that we are attracted to Chinese Art, for example? Why do we furnish our flat with Chinese furniture when our parents never went to China and never even talked about China? Why is it that we are attracted to yoga rather than some other activity? We have resonance from past lives, but nothing allows us to assert for sure what context we lived in. For example, we cannot say, "I was Chinese." All of this is subjective. Only our dreams can confirm this sort of declaration. However, our personal tendencies can serve as indicators. We observe our tastes along with everything that bothers us, and this says a lot about our past lives. These indicators can lead us to understand some of our behavior and to define what most particularly influences us. In this respect, once again, we use symbolism, because everything has a meaning.

⊙

Why is the soul of a six-year-old child with heavy karmic baggage lighter than the soul of a sixty-five-year-old woman who, out of ignorance, hasn't done any soul searching? As I already mentioned, it is due to the child's consciousness counter having been put back to zero only six years ago. If the sixty-five-year-old woman doesn't understand the Law of Resonance, then she gets angry every time she senses injustice and she projects all her emotions on the outside, believing this to be normal. These are old memories resurfacing, but she doesn't do anything with them, because the level of evolution she has reached doesn't lead her to ask herself existential questions that forge the spiritual path. Her karma accumulates year after year, and that creates layers that pile up in her unconsciousness. Needless to say, she feels heavier and more bitter as the years go by.

What's more, from a certain age onwards, our personal experiences are sufficiently ample that interference is commonplace. We saw an example of interference when we examined the case of the man who suffered from a heart attack. Let's take the time to better define this key concept as it allows us to understand the nature and role of memory and the veil of forgetfulness. The following is an example of interference. A woman calls up her friend and says, "I must tell you what happened to me yesterday at the Granby festival." She goes on to tell her all that happened to her at the town festival. As for her friend, she doesn't hear a word that the woman is saying because she stopped listening on the word "Granby." She doesn't hear the rest.

She had interference with Granby. When she heard this name, the entire file containing her experiences in this town resurfaced. What happened to her in Granby? At the age of 10, she left her village because her family was moving to Granby. She stayed there until she was 15, but it was hell. Her father wouldn't let her go out and he repressed her in all sorts of other ways. She no longer had any friends. She never got over this experience in Granby. Now, when her excited friend calls her to say, "Wow! What a great festival!" she only has to pronounce the word "Granby" and all those disagreeable feelings resurface.

Here is another example of interference. A woman is experiencing a profound sadness. Her ex-husband left with a woman named Martina over 10 years ago. She still hasn't come to terms with this experience. She only has to hear the name "Martina" and all of the grief comes back.

Not only do interferences bring back what shocked or saddened us, but also what lightly affected us. If we don't like filling out forms, the mention of forms equates to inconvenience. In that case, someone has only to mention that forms need to be filled out and we automatically feel a slight interference. With the Angels, we work on everything that bothers us, including every interference. If we don't get down to doing the work of becoming conscious, we reach the age of 65 and all we hear is "Granby," "Martina," "Granby/Martina," "Martina/Granby," forms, "Martina/Martina." (laughter). Life becomes unbearable!

We really are well made. Up Above, They are so kind. They gave our body a compensation technique. What is this compensation? It is forgetfulness. We forget because life would be too difficult otherwise. We postpone becoming conscious and exploring emotions until later. This means that our unconsciousness becomes more and more loaded. This is why our society associates old age with forgetfulness and loss of memory. In serious cases, the problem is exacerbated and the compensation is Alzheimer's disease, which degenerates the nerve cells.

A nurse on duty with patients who have this disease told me that one day she asked a patient of hers who had a good sense of humor, "Do you remember what your blood pressure was yesterday?" The patient replied, "Oh no! I live in the present!" (laughter)

All spiritual teachings advise us to live in the present, but it's impossible to do so when there is continual interference. In this case, forgetfulness settles in. Before letting us know about our past lives, Up Above, They tell us, "First, you must settle everything that has to do with Granby and Martina, because if you go behind these personal experiences, which are only the front windows of your personal file, you'll find something else that comes from your former lives."

Behind a particular interference, we can usually find a large number of memories coming from previous lives. How do we reach them? Of course, if these experiences were painful or negative, the memory of them will bother us. So we do our Angel Recitation with Angel LEUVIAH and that allows us to cleanse them. With time, we penetrate this file more and more deeply. In this way, we cleanse instead of accumulate. We do a clean up, as in a house. Then, marvelous horizons are opened up and we return to our light-hearted feeling.

The little memory lapses in our everyday lives can be very useful. With Angel LEUVIAH, we learn to make forgetfulness our friend and, in return, it leads us to understand what Memory, with a capital M, really is. Here is an example of forgetfulness, one that we will analyze using the same symbolism as we would for a dream. I've forgotten my mittens. Forgetting my mittens is not of great importance, but we can receive quite a lesson from it, especially when the temperature is -40 Celsius! What do mittens represent? They represent warm hands. Hands represent the way we give and receive. If we forget our mittens in a dream, this means that there will be a lack of warmth in the way we give and receive. When we analyze this sign in our everyday life, the same symbolism applies. We ask ourselves, "What was I thinking about when I forgot my mittens? What am I going through at the moment? Am I bothered by something? What's my state of consciousness right now?"

These questions lead to the initiatory reflections that constitute active meditation. If another person forgets the same object in the same place, the meaning could be different. Up Above, They have a *forgetometer* (laughter). It measures the degree and nature of the disturbance. We can say, "I've forgotten my gloves and I can't find them anymore. That's unfortunate. I'll have to buy another pair." At that moment, financial insecurities arise. A memory lapse can activate a disturbance, and we are the only ones who can truly evaluate the degree of annoyance it creates, because no one can know what we are feeling better than ourselves. This is ongoing work that results in spiritual autonomy. It leads to the opening of our consciousness. Consciousness cannot be learned in books.

Here is another type of forgetfulness. This range of examples will help you analyze and identify your own lapses. We forget a half-full bottle of water in the car. It's winter and it's very cold. The next day, of course, the water is frozen. But the evening before, we hadn't felt like going to fetch it. This isn't just negligence. Water symbolizes emotions. By examining this little lapse in its own context we can unearth unconscious memories, which are at the root of some of our behavior.

If our memory lapses are recurrent, we should pay special attention to their meaning. Let's look at an example. We're at work and we always forget the same thing. We say to ourselves, "But I like this job! If these lapses continue, I could lose my job. But I didn't deliberately forget. What makes me forget? What's going on inside of me?"

Among our unconscious memories, a few of them may sabotage our happiness. In this particular case, each time we build something beautiful, we get the impression that certain forces interfere, forces that are telling us, "No, you have no right to happiness. You have no right to abundance or love." So we go to work on them. We do our Angel Recitation, we analyze these lapse and we remain focused on the symbol. This is how we can find elements that need to be rectified. If we take advantage of our lapses to cleanse the memories associated with them, we'll be able to improve our life and stabilize our happiness.

Here is an example of a positive memory lapse. Actually, all our memory lapses are positive, but this one has the advantage of showing that we sometimes forget for good reasons. A person is summoned to a meeting and she knows it will be an opportunity to meet one of her friends. She tells herself, "I've got a few things for her. I'll use this opportunity to give them to her." She arrives at the meeting and realizes, "Oh! I've forgotten these things." But then she finds out that her friend isn't coming because of a last minute obligation. She can say, "I had sensed she wouldn't be here." Indeed, everything is planned in the causal world, just as it was planned that this friend wouldn't come. Being as open as she is, she tuned in to this information, but not consciously. Before leaving her house, she didn't know that her friend wouldn't be at the meeting. She only realized it when faced with the fact. One day, we manage to pick up this subtle information consciously and regularly. The person is thinking, "No, my friend won't be there. I won't bring these things." Without any concrete indication, we can anticipate everything.

Here's a final kind of forgetfulness, and it's a lovely example. The week that I was working with Angel 19 Leuviah, I was meditating on the veil of forgetfulness. I was walking along, observing my feelings and, at one particular moment, I said to myself, "I must go and rent a video for my husband. I think there will be messages for him in the video." I followed up on my idea, which had presented itself as an inner feeling. There was no deep voice saying, "Christiane! Go and rent a video. Your husband needs it." (laughter) No, it was more subtle than that.

I entered the video shop. At one particular moment, I stopped in front of a cassette and I read the jacket. It seemed all right, but I was a little doubtful. When in doubt, I thought, refrain from action. So I put the cassette back and I used a method by which we ask to receive an answer in meditation. This is a method that gives us access to *Skynet*. We close our eyes and we ask for a symbol that we can then interpret exactly as we do with those that appear in dreams. We wait for a symbolic image to appear. Through intensive meditation, one day, when we ask for information to be used in the concrete world, images come easily. There is another important thing, however. To obtain the right answer, we must have no desires. Otherwise, interference corresponding to unsatisfied desires slips in and falsifies the answer. This is why it is essential to work on purity.

No personal need was pushing me to rent a video. Sometimes, we unconsciously rent a video because we are feeling down and seeking consolation, or we are bored and we need some action in our life. In order for this method to work, we must ask respectfully, dedicating our request to the good of our evolution. Whether we are guided here or there doesn't matter. We follow the message. If no image comes, we don't force things. We don't allow our intellect to say, "Give me an image." No! The image must surprise us because it hasn't been formed by our intellect. We aren't expecting it. It comes from the Cosmic Intelligence we have fused. It's as if we enter into God, because the symbol that was given to us, no matter how simple, is an answer calculated in relation to an unimaginable number of facts and parameters.

I asked for a symbol and I closed my eyes. No image presented itself. I said to myself, "Maybe You want to give me a sign through the people I'm going to meet," and so I walked around a bit. I observed. At one particular moment, I felt like closing my eyes again. I did and an image instantly appeared. It was a lighted torch in the dark, behind a huge veil. Suddenly, the veil was torn and light invaded the scene. I said to myself, "They want me to stay. I'm going to go back and find the cassette that I saw. It might be the right one."

I arrived at the display counter, but the box was no longer there. It was nowhere to be found. I had even forgotten the title and the color. I had a vague idea of what it was about, but I just couldn't find it. And then I felt a certain rigidity. It was subtle. The more we work on our inner selves, the more we feel the small changes at the energetic level. It was as if, Up Above, They wanted to make me forget. It's as if They were telling me, "Forget that one." I was happy! Also, because of the symbol of the torch, I knew I had to stay. There was something else for me, because the veil in front of the torch was the veil of forgetfulness. I had meditated intensely on the veil of forgetfulness, and Cosmic Intelligence wanted to teach me something about it. They wanted to show me how easy it is for Them, Up Above. They just push a little button and Bang! We forget! When we understand this, we let go and we are so happy to ask!

My inner dialogue continued. "They want something else for me," it said. "Otherwise They'd have given me another image." If They had wanted me to leave, They'd have given me a forbidden symbol, like the image of a cassette I didn't like or one of a light-bulb going out. For each situation, the range of possible symbols is endless. So I continued walking around the shop, conscious that the next step would be the one of the torch. All of a sudden, something went Snap! I put my hand on a cassette. I had no doubt whatsoever. It was the right one. No need to verify. It was a film about Nelson Mandela, the man who liberated South Africa from apartheid. My husband and I watched the film.

My husband had not told me his dreams that day. At the end of the film, he said to me, "I'm going to watch it again. Last night, I had dreams about civil disobedience, masses and crowds. This film is really giving me extraordinary and complementary information. Thank you for listening so well to your intuition." And he watched it again.

You see how it works. We ask and we continue to behave like everyone else. No one is aware of what is going on in our head, but our intention is different. And, in our meditative search, we always remember that what is important will materialize correctly. We get such joy from living like this! We feel continually guided by God. It's extraordinary!

One of the great Qualities of Angel LEUVIAH is *acceptance*. We accept everything that is presented to us, without guilt and without bitterness. But it is true that being and behaving like this requires a great deal of self-insight. When we have truly integrated acceptance, we become receptive. There is no longer a terrible racket going on within ourselves and we are constantly guided.

Speaking of dreams and videos, there is a film about dreams that I would like to recommend to you. It's called "Joseph: King of Dreams." It's an animated film that follows the same lines as "The Prince of Egypt." It is produced by Steven Spielberg's company DreamWorks and is just as suitable to children as it is to adults.

This film was inspired by the biblical story of Joseph, the man who interpreted the Pharaoh's dreams. One such dream involved seven fat cows and seven thin cows. In this film we are shown how Joseph made use of his dreams to guide him through his life, and where this adventure led him.

We have seen that we can receive elements of past lives in our dreams. Here's a little story. One morning while I was working with Angel LEUVIAH, our daughter Kasara told us her dream before going to school. In her dream, *she was wearing a sky-blue swimsuit of hers with stars on it. She was afraid of losing the stars. Then, a little boy who goes to the same school as her and who uses a lot of swear words, said to her, "Turn left." She said, "No! I have to turn right." A school monitor was also present.*

Suddenly she said to us, "*Then, I found myself in the Middle Ages.*" Being tuned in to former lives, I looked at my husband and, with a bit too much urgency perhaps, exclaimed, "Maybe it's a past life!" Kasara, inspired from Up Above, immediately answered, "No, it wasn't Middle Aged enough." (laughter) Once more, this little Star Child was teaching me something. She was reminding me that for a dream to reveal a memory of a former life, it mustn't contain any symbols that correspond to other eras. For example, when a dream concerns a life that took place in a certain era, its images can not contain characters or objects that couldn't have existed during that period, such as cars or watches. All the elements must be realistic.

In Kasara's dream, all the characters represented parts of herself, like the little boy, the school monitor, etc. She was being told that she ought to be vigilant because, during the course of that day, she could lose her stars. That is to say, she could lose her orientation, her lovely values and everything her good nature affected. For her, the Middle Ages simply signified ancient concepts and old habits resurfacing.

In a dream, if we find ourselves in a former era, it is possible that we are being shown elements of a past life. Quite often we find ourselves in the shoes of an individual of that era and we experience the event and all its intensity. For example, my being branded with the iron. However, and I must repeat this because it is important, if we see an object that is not from that era, such as a car in medieval times, it is certain that the dream is not of a former life.

We can also be shown ancient jewelry or other such symbols. This means that They, Up Above, are opening a window that gives us a view of the capacities we once had. They are telling us, "Look, if you change this attitude, you'll recover all of these resources."

Here is a dream in which one of the symbols indicated that old memories were going to be transformed. One day, a person dreamed *of a very old woman who was being told that They were going to change her teeth.* As we have seen previously, teeth represent the structure of our wisdom with regard to our instinctual nature. Since a woman in a dream generally symbolizes the inner world and emotions, the dream was announcing a profound, inner restructuring and a great cleansing of very old memories that would lead the dreamer to a new level of wisdom. In short, it was predicting a series of initiations. To have our teeth taken out corresponds to a profound destructuring of our instincts and basic needs. It also corresponds to a profound personality change. Upon waking, such a dream results in a substantial drop in energy and self-esteem.

When we know how to interpret our dreams, we understand what is happening to us. We aren't surprised and we are happy. We do our Angel Recitation. Even if we feel a lot less lovely than at other times, like the ugly duckling, and due to our having touched parts that are not very nice, we know that we have simply awakened an old memory. At the beginning of our spiritual path, there are so many changes that need to be carried out that we feel completely unstructured and our dreams seem to be a series of nightmares. It is very difficult. Then, gradually, one initiation at a time, dreams of this sort are interspersed with others which are ecstatic and marvelous. These bring us joy and understanding. What is paradoxical about being on a spiritual path is that our family and friends, who are not on this path, seem to be doing quite well, while we are feeling totally unstructured and even shattered. Know that their conscience minds do not have the same opening as yours and that a certain stability establishes itself little by little.

As you can see, we have at our disposal several indicators to help us discover if a dream concerns a past life or not. Other means are available and allow us to find out about these lives. A very popular one involves regression. This is experimentation.

Facts that we obtain through regressions are more or less accurate for two reasons. First, the inferior mind, or the ego, sometimes confuses the reading. Second, if Cosmic Intelligence judges that we are not ready to receive information about our past lives, It will not show us images from past lives, but rather images that are symbolically related to the inner work we must do. This happens much in the same way that It shows us images in our dreams.

We must not take fortune-tellers too seriously either. Very often they talk a lot of rubbish, and most of them are manipulated by lower astral entities that have this work to do. If it's practically impossible to get into the White House without permission, just imagine how well-guarded Cosmic Intelligence can be! Without permission, access is impossible.

I've heard all sorts of things about past lives. I know at least two people who claim to be the reincarnation of Judas. I've studied their behavior a little. They are people who don't understand the Law of Resonance. Every time they experience a situation which seems unfair to them, they feel betrayed. They are mortified, and they drag out their sadness. They tell themselves, "It's normal. I was Judas in another life." But there's something very unhealthy going on here. No inner work has been done.

The intellect and the ego can grab hold of past lives. A person who believes in reincarnation might tell himself, "I'm totally distorted. Since I'm so distorted, I may as well be famous." And he chooses Judas. (laughter) This can be carried out to great lengths. And so, They, Up Above, in the manner of the great Pedagogues, only give us what is necessary for our evolution.

Phobias can also come from previous lives. Burning and drowning are two examples of phobias. A person can be afraid of fire, or water, even if no event in his present life justifies such a fear. He asks himself, "Why is it that I am so afraid of fire? This is totally unreasonable. It doesn't make sense to be so afraid without reason." Through our dreams we can discover that in a past life we were a Viking and we set fire everywhere, for example. We understand that this turns against us in this life.

If we are afraid of water and we discover that we drowned in another life, it may be reassuring to say, "Well, I won't go into the water. I don't want to drown a second time." However, whether we go in or not won't change anything, because drowning signifies losing oneself in the world of emotions. As long as this issue has not been resolved, the source of the problem and the danger remains. Through self-insight, and assiduous cleansing of our emotions with Angel Recitation, we cleanse emotional problems and, one day, we are no longer afraid because we have stopped drowning in our emotions. We have gone to the essence of the problem.

Another reason why memories of previous lives are only slightly helpful is because certain fears are simply the result or materialization of a more essential problem. Once we understand this, and if we once again use the example of fear of fire, we recognize our incendiary spirit and we say to ourselves, "I'm going to work on my energy. It is too incendiary at times." You see, we can acquire a lot of understanding without the help of memories from the other side of the grave. We simply analyze our phobias by going to their source.

Here's a final example of a dream. A woman told me, "In my dream, *I saw myself with my husband in a van that he was driving. At one particular moment, there was a ravine and my stomach lurched. He was so close to the precipice that we were within a hair's breadth of toppling into it. I said to him, 'That was close!'*"

I interpreted her dream for her. I said, "At the moment you are going through things which are causing you such great fears and insecurities that they make you feel dizzy."

"That is so true! My husband and I have a small business. I'm in charge of the accounts. We have no employees and we often find ourselves on the edge of bankruptcy."

"Every time you get a bill, your stomach must lurch."

"Exactly!"

"Through this dream, you are being shown what you are actually going through," I continued. "Every time you enter a bill in your accounting system, all those feelings resurface. This is your fear of falling into the ravine. You do have financial insecurities but it goes much further than that."

"But why do I still have these insecurities? I've been working on them for years," she said. "I know they come from past lives."

"Insecurity can be the result of hundreds upon hundreds of old memories," I told her. "Use your work. Up Above, They see that you are committed to a spiritual path and that you wish to redis-cover your feeling of security. They know this. They are watching you. When They see you going about your day, They say, 'We really love this woman. Here, send down ten more bills!' They are telling you, 'Accept even bankruptcy.' If bankruptcy leads you to very high levels of consciousness, then it's very useful. It will teach you to put the Spirit first. Use each bill. Do your best. What's more, bills have numbers. Use the numbers of the corresponding Angels. Connect to an Angel every time your stomach lurches. Inhale and breathe in the Angel while you enter the bill. Little by little, through your work, you're going to cleanse your old insecurities which date back to Methuselah."

This made her happy. Her bills had become useful. These were karmic bills that she was paying.

To conclude this lecture, I'd like to leave you with the following thought. *If there is one thing we must never forget, it's that every-thing comes from God.*

Angel 15 Hariel
Living Without Addictions

Having been abstinent for a certain length of time, he still felt terribly anxious and torn by his addiction to alcohol. Whenever he felt desperate, he would pray to God. "Why do You let me suffer like this?" he would ask. "Why must I live in such agony? Why have You abandoned me, You, to whom I have prayed for so long?" That night, after several hours of agitation and intense inner combat, sobbing his heart out, he ended up falling asleep.

During the night, he received a dream. *He found himself at the beginning of the Creation of the world. All of a sudden, a cloud appeared. It was a beautiful, bright cloud that inspired in him a sense of purity and innocence. Wanting to touch it, he drew closer, but it disappeared. He searched for it everywhere. After a few minutes, it reappeared a little further. This time, he tried to get close enough so that he could catch it. It disappeared again. The same scenario repeated itself many times. Realizing that the cloud was inaccessible to him, he was overcome with sorrow. He felt emptiness. God Himself had abandoned him.*

Even if this dream was given to him more than 20 years ago, it remains fresh in his memory. This man asked me, "What does this dream mean?" He had been brought back to the beginning of Creation, when his own soul had been created and was in its original pure state. The beautiful bright cloud is a great symbol that is mentioned several times in the Bible and that represents one of the manifestations of the Creator.

Through this dream, God was telling this person, "*No, I haven't abandoned you. It is you who no longer feels My presence. You have done all sorts of experimenting, which has caused your fall and the loss of purity of your soul. You'd like to close the door on your past and regain this purity instantaneously, but it doesn't work that way. You cannot possess Me. You have to be inspired by Me and become like Me. Everything that you have done in past lives is inscribed in you.*

You must find every memory in which you committed unconscious and incorrect acts and you must transform them. Only you can do this work. I am with you, however, and one day you will no longer try to grasp Me on the outside. You will have integrated My Qualities and Virtues. You will have become the bright cloud because you will have found your original purity."

We are all dependent to some degree or another. In terms of conscience, we are a bit like babies. A completely pure soul, fresh and new, doesn't know evil. When a baby sees fire for the first time, he wants to touch it and he gets hurt. If we don't feed a baby, he dies. He is a very dependent being and he doesn't know what is good and what is bad for him. During the course of its lives, our soul evolves through all sorts of experimenting, both positive and negative. Eventually, it consciously and deliberately decides to no longer do evil because its experiments have led it to acquire wisdom. From this moment on, it becomes very rich. It repairs and detoxifies its consciousness. Then comes a day when it has transcended all evil, even the most pernicious and the most perverse. We can transform everything, absolutely everything. The evolved soul is a soul that decides, of its own will, to no longer do evil. Everyone will reach this stage one day.

Behind every form of addiction we find the same concept. It is a quest for purity. In the dream that we have just seen, it is this very quest that the cloud represents. A quest for the inaccessible and the unattainable is inscribed in the person's program and acts the way a computer program does. The person is on an everlasting quest. From time to time he has bursts of adrenalin. He thinks he has found love for someone or a mood that he has been seeking ever so long and with such fervor. After these moments of excitement have passed, however, and once he realizes that he hasn't got what he desires, everything becomes dull and uninteresting. It's as though he were telling himself, "Seek what is inaccessible. If this is accessible, it isn't interesting to you." The person therefore lives in constant frustration.

Some people with addictions are kind and devoted. Behind this kindness, however, enormous expectations are concealed. If he isn't fulfilled, the person is disappointed and becomes irritable, even aggressive. That's because his love is conditional. His addiction and expectations are even projected onto the Creator Himself.

The person says to Him, "I pray to You. I honor You so You had better take away my suffering and give me what I need. Otherwise, I will renounce You."

When we understand this concept, we tell ourselves, "Of course, I cannot eliminate my addictions overnight, and I understand that they are only the tip of the iceberg. If I feel the need for such a thing or such a person, I come back to myself and I cleanse the memories that are related to this need. I use my addiction to rectify whatever it is that disconnects me from my divinity." With such an attitude, we really do change. We remember that we are an in-finitesimal part of this Great Intelligence, wherein all beings are interconnected. Our inner divisions disappear and the program for the quest of the inaccessible disintegrates and everything becomes accessible because we merge with the Great Whole. This is how we live without addictions.

One day, we rediscover spiritual, emotional, and physical autonomy. We are not even dependent on God anymore. We merge with Him. We acquire great freedom on all levels, our receptivity increases and we experience an expansion within our soul. The path is very long, but we are here on Earth solely for this reason.

Today, we are going to talk about Angel HARIEL, bearer of number 15. This Angel helps liberate us from our addictions. First, let's take a look at His qualities.

Liberates from all forms of addictions. We have seen that behind every addiction the same problem exists. Through its symbolism, we shall also see that each addiction has, in essence, its own par-ticularities. *Liberates from paralysis, from anything that prevents action.* We shall see through real life experiences that when they are left uncontrolled, aggressive or critical thoughts can paralyze a person and take away his power to act.

Among the Qualities of Angel 15 HARIEL, we also find *Purification.* Among the human distortions, we find *puritanism.* There is a very fine line between the two. When we begin working with this Angel over a period of time, we sway between purification (the cleansing of vulgar behavior and addictions) and rigidity and puritanism, especially towards others. This pendulum action is normal when we don't have Knowledge.

Discovery of new methods, useful inventions. Dreams, daily signs, and meditation provide us with such precise guidance that once our addictions release their hold on our behavior, a world of discoveries opens up to us. The State of Consciousness of Angel 15 HARIEL helps us find new methods, first applicable to the work on our inner selves, but also applicable to exterior work, as inner progress always manifests itself on the outside. Thus, in both our professional and domestic work, new horizons will suddenly open up. We will have new practical ideas and a divine inspiration will help us find ways to make life easier and more harmonious. The addictions that inhabit our consciousness and unconsciousness are numerous. They affect all areas of our lives. Through the purification of unconscious memories brought about by the work with this Angel, all facets of our lives are transformed.

Procures great insight, awakens discernment. Our supreme goal as human beings is to one day succeed in mastering good and evil. This demands discernment and insight. Angel HARIEL has the capacity to reactivate these faculties.

Among the distortions related to the Angel HARIEL, we have *dry, hardened attitude* and *separatism*. This means a dry, dissecting intellect that takes away a person's capacity to love. Here is a very current and relevant distortion of this Angel: *willing to die to impose or defend an unnatural truth, terrorist.* On September 11th, 2001, the planet woke up to a new reality. We saw an extreme manifestation of this distortion. To better understand the global problem of terrorism, we shall scale it down to the individual, in light of the State of Consciousness of Angel HARIEL.

Sometimes we ask ourselves, "Why am I obsessed with this person? He's not kind and he's possessive and unfaithful." Or else, we are addicted to a thing, like cigarettes. We tell ourselves, "They discolor my teeth, they clog my lungs. Why do I keep on smoking?" When it comes to much of our erroneous behavior, we tell ourselves, "It doesn't make sense. It is so far from my real needs. Where does this come from?"

Addictions are only a consequence. They are only the tip of the iceberg of old memories that trouble us and often come from other lives. We don't even know that we have these memories in our personal computer. What we must do is purify them so that one day we may succeed in feeling good and in being free from all addictions.

Sometimes, we decide to put an end to an addiction. "It's over," we say. "From now on, it's abstinence." We shall see that this is only the first step. Later on, we realize, "Why is it that even though I've stopped, it still hurts right down to my very gut?"

Here's an example of this concept that applies to all forms of addiction. A man who was addicted to alcohol and who had abstained from drinking for several months told me that he often had the same dream. *He'd hear aggressive knocking at the door. When he'd go to open it, no one was there.* What was it that he needed to understand through this dream? First of all, Cosmic Intelligence was telling him, "It's very good to give up drinking. It's a good start," but Up Above, They wanted to show him that there were other stages to go through. The dream revealed to him the presence of dark, aggressive forces within him that were knocking on his inner door and that needed to be cleansed and purified.

When we receive a dream such as this one, we may feel aggressive during the day. When we haven't got Knowledge, we project our aggression onto others, we continue to act on the basis of our aggressive memories and we create additional karma. This is an absolute truth. For some people, it means constantly starting over again. They can't seem to find their way out of this cycle. The day we realize that the source of the problem is within, we stop projecting onto others. Then, when the negative and very powerful force arises, we do our Angel Recitation. We invoke the Angel, no matter where we are, and the memories are cleansed.

We have seen that our life program is predetermined before birth on the basis of our previous lives. Consequently, some people who suffered from addictions will manage to abstain for the rest of their lives. It will be difficult for them. It will imply rigidity and suffering, and abstinence is as far as they will go. Others will go to the root of the problem. Angel Work is truly a great detoxification of our consciousness. The man I have just spoken about had to cleanse the dark, aggressive forces that dwelt within him. This was part of his life-plan. A person who remains abstinent for the rest of his life but who doesn't cleanse the aggressive forces and the other dark forces that inhabit his soul risks relapsing into the same addiction, even in another life. That's because the source of the problem dwells in his unconsciousness.

Here is a story that shows to what extent the personal and the family unconsciousness are intimately connected. A woman who has been working with The Traditional Study of Angels for some time told me the following dream. *She was on a boat. Everything was calm, pleasant and harmonious. All of a sudden, she decided to take a break and went below into the hold. There, the atmosphere was totally different. A drinking party was underway and the intoxicated people were very vulgar. She was serving these drunkards little meat pastries on a tray.*

What was she being shown through this dream? Cosmic Intelligence was showing her part of her file, including memories of past experiences. She was being shown that in another life, among other addictions, she had had a problem with alcohol. In this life, she doesn't have this addiction. She is always sober, but she did land in a family where the father was an alcoholic. Because of this, her childhood was very difficult.

The fact that our father or mother has, or once had, alcohol-related problems is not a coincidence. We have a resonance with him or her. We mustn't, however, regard destiny from a punishment perspective. God doesn't say, "You did this. Now you are going to experience the other side of the coin." The dream was telling this woman, "You too did this in another life. It's inscribed in you. We are going to help you evolve." Having had an alcoholic father had, in fact, been positive in this woman's life. It allowed her to become conscious of this memory, which up until then had remained unconscious. Destiny is always positive.

Let's examine the symbols present in this dream. A boat goes on water. Water concerns the emotions. Therefore, the movement and position of the boat indicate the level of emotional stability. If the boat capsizes, this reveals an absence of mastery due to emotions. If, on the contrary, it is stable, a lovely emotional stability is being shown. Hence, the dream was telling the woman, "When you work on your inner self, you establish harmony and stability in your emotional life."

It is true that when we invoke the Angels, we can feel destabilized because we go down into the unconsciousness to do a cleansing. We go down gradually and, with every descent, we pick up a small piece of our unconsciousness and we bring it back to the surface of our consciousness, where we can cleanse it instead of projecting it onto others. Of course, this is long and arduous work and has its share of suffering, but we have no choice. If we don't do this consciously, concrete circumstances will continually bring us back to it, even in other lives. That is the Law. Justice applies to everyone. If you sow evil, you will reap evil.

In the dream, the woman had decided to take a break. This means that she was telling herself, "I'm so tired of being on this quest for enlightenment and being so disciplined and paying attention to everything. What if I allowed myself a little pleasure?" Taking a break, however, means relapsing into the old prototypes and resuscitating them. Since she went down into the hold, this means that she penetrated the unconsciousness. She went under the veil. There, she was shown unconscious parts of herself. I said to her, "You have the right to push the 'pause' button." Everyone has free will. The guides love us all the same whether we push our 'pause' button or not. This woman is on a self-help journey, and so her channels are open. Up Above, They were telling her, "Look what happens when you push the 'pause' button. You continue to nourish parts of your unconsciousness that you brought to the surface through your work. If you aren't careful, one day you'll become what you saw in the hold of the boat."

Pastry denotes a certain refinement, while meat represents the animal or instinctive side. This applies to an even greater degree as this woman is a vegetarian. Since she was serving little meat pastries, Up Above, They were telling her, "Instead of transforming these instinctual parts, you continue to feed them." When we nourish these parts, when we relapse into certain pleasures, we may feel a certain well-being. These forces do have a certain attraction, but such relief is only momentary and coming back to ourselves is even more difficult.

Some people know that they have no right to a break, not even for a few seconds. Who are these people? They are the people who have had problems with alcohol or other addictions. For this reason, they choose to abstain. They are, among others, members of groups such as AA. These services are of tremendous help and do essential work. These people know that it takes only the tiniest break, even one glass, to set off a relapse into hell and destroy their lives. The Sword of Damocles hangs constantly over their head.

An intermediate category includes people who, without having problems as serious as those I have just described, do have a burdened unconsciousness. This includes the woman who saw herself on a boat. These people behave normally. Their life is good or fairly good but some of their resources are taken away at a particular moment. They lose their job, go through a separation or lose whatever it was that artificially maintained their happiness. This exterior event causes their decline because they have an overloaded unconsciousness.

Our spirit is connected to all the memories of our past, including those of previous lives. This is why we see so many families that seem to function normally until, all of a sudden, the loss of a job or some other exterior event immediately gives rise to abject behavior. Since the unconsciousness was overloaded, the exterior event causes a disconnection within the person. Overnight, the person starts manifesting various levels of violence towards himself, his family and his friends.

In the last category, we find all the initiates who never take a break. Their work, lovingly done, is imprinted with a constant search for understanding. These beings do not have the Sword of Damocles hanging over them. In their case, we don't talk about breaks or work. The initiate simply continues to detoxify his consciousness. He seeks Hidden Wisdom and, at the slightest annoyance, he cleanses and transcends his memories. When an initiate has cleansed his personal and family unconsciousness, strong doses still await him in the collective unconsciousness. At this stage, however, his understanding is so vast that he maintains great stability. One day, the initiate must transcend all of the addictions and sufferings of humanity.

Initiates go through an intense apprenticeship during the night. In their dreams, they are exposed to extremely powerful situations that are sometimes very difficult. These are called initiations. Here, they are called upon to transcend evil. For them, a day will come when they no longer have resonance with evil and not a single one of their memories will resonate with distortions. At this stage, the person can truly be a benefactor. He feels good no matter where he is and no matter what is happening on the outside. His understanding raises him above good and evil.

The following is an example of the Law of Resonance. It touches on the addiction to gambling. It is the true story of a woman who confided in me. There is no such thing as coincidence. When I prepare a conference, I do my Angel Recitation with a particular Angel for several weeks. During this period, I receive information through my dreams and the people I meet. People confide in me about experiences they've been through and touch on the State of Consciousness of the Angel I'm working with.

Last month, a woman came to a lecture for the first time. She told me that she had had a problem with an addiction to gambling. For a few months now, she hadn't played thanks to a support group for people addicted to gambling. She was very grateful to this group, which had helped her a lot. She told me that these meetings had led her to see what she was really made of. If she hadn't had this addiction, she would never have realized who she was. There is something positive in every situation.

She explained to me how she had developed this addiction. At a certain point in her life, because her husband had been transferred, she had to move and leave all of her family behind. Her husband was often away at work. In his free time he went hunting. Consequently, she began to get bored. She told me, "I started by playing the slot machines and, little by little, I became hypnotized by gambling. I got hooked. After a while, I was forced to lie because my whole salary was being used up. I even took money out of the family account. Then, one day, I confessed everything to my husband. This is when I began to work on abstinence."

This woman told me about her childhood and about her mother who was possessive and stifling. Then she said, "I had a dream last night." She explained that in real life she had a grown-up daughter who wanted to have a baby. At the moment, however, she was unable to conceive. In her dream, *she was holding her daughter's baby in her arms. Her daughter begrudged her for monopolizing her baby, but she still didn't want to give it back to her.* We shall see what this dream means in a moment. First of all, let's try to understand what all forms of addiction, including gambling, have in common.

⊙

The Nature of Addictions

We are going to go through the most common addictions in order to understand their essence. Once we understand the essence, we understand everything.

Smoke belongs to the dimension of air and thoughts. When we are addicted to cigarettes, it means that we have something that needs to be rectified concerning our thoughts. Symbolically, smoke prevents us from being lucid because it confuses divine ideas. In a dream, if we see ourselves smoking, even if we don't actually smoke in real life, it signifies, "Be careful, your thoughts are a bit foggy." This is the essence of this addiction.

Alcohol is a liquid. Liquid, as we have already seen, symbolizes the world of emotions. The alcoholic has an emotional problem. Very often, people who consume too much alcohol have big hearts that overflow with emotion and they don't know what to do with this excess. Other people addicted to alcohol are situated at the other extreme. They have great inner rigidity because they are so inhibited. Their soul is overburdened with unconscious memories and they have to maintain suitable behavior in order to live in society. These are people who use alcohol to liberate themselves from their inhibitions. When inebriated, they can express themselves much more freely and they momentarily feel better.

What is the meaning of addiction to drugs? Behind this type of addiction is a person looking for an easy way to fulfill the need to be on a spiritual quest. Without knowing it, the person seeks to recreate within himself a state of being that resembles Angelic States of Consciousness, that is, a state of being without a single care or worry. He brings it about, however, through artificial means. With drugs, the person feels good for a short time only. On the other hand, with meditation and spiritual work, the Angelic States of Consciousness stabilize us and lead us to permanent well-being. The consumption of drugs touches on the world of the spirit and is symbolically linked to the element of fire.

As for gambling, we have only to ask ourselves, "What is the person who becomes addicted to gambling seeking?" He hopes to win a lot of money and he seeks to control his destiny. He even seeks to create it. Money is densified energy. In our society, it gives power.

In a dream, when we receive money and when the other symbols have a correct and beautiful significance, it means that Cosmic Intelligence is providing the person with resources. It is providing him with great potential to materialize. What happens when a person finds resources within himself? He regains the power to create and to manifest himself. He regains an expansive capacity to create.

Gambling is therefore a search for success and expansion. In cases where a person is suffocated or crushed by unconscious forces that dominate him, it is impossible for him to succeed. He doesn't have this divine power. Since he wants an immediate feeling of success, and if he hasn't taken the time for self-insight, he will seek success at the physical level. One day, with self-insight, this expansion comes from within. When this happens, we may also receive a lot of material and financial resources and use them altruistically.

We find the gambler's mentality in businessmen obsessed with profit. They do business as if they were playing roulette. Their attitude is that of a farmer seeking to harvest his fruits and vegetables without plowing or sowing, or without waiting for the growing period to be over. Farming is a wonderful and natural process. Spirituality functions in the same way. We must first travel a very long distance before harvesting, especially if we want to do things correctly.

Thus, we find in all of these forms of addiction a search for instantaneous beatitude or for an immediate feeling of expansion because the person does not have Knowledge. When we understand this, we no longer feel guilty or judgmental. We consider the addiction as a sickness of the soul. Toward the person who is addicted we behave as though we were going to see a patient at the hospital. We feel the same love and the same compassion for him as we would for a patient. We de-dramatize because we see a simple need to rectify unconscious memories in the addicted person.

Needless to say, addictions bring great suffering. One day, when our spiritual work has brought us the Knowledge to transcend the distortions, the guilt disappears. What happens is that we experimented with a distortion for a certain length of time and then we changed. We are given a new life in this lifetime. Of course, if our past addictions have caused other people problems, they can be expected to hold a grudge against us. We can ask for their forgiveness verbally or in thought only. If they won't accept an apology, we continue on our way and sow the seeds of new behavior and attitudes. One day, they allow us to erase our karma. It is true that, very often, if we have caused our close family and friends to suffer, only the proof of a real change spread over many years will succeed in erasing the errors committed in this lifetime. However, everything can be cleansed and everything can be changed. This is what is so important to understand.

If we think back to the woman whose mother had a very stifling attitude, we could say, "It's normal that she too has a stifling attitude. She gets it from her mother." That's true. There are no coincidences. We land in a family that bears the problem we have to work on. This person had a stifling attitude even before birth and she was shown this in her dream. This dream, incidentally, was not a premonition of her daughter's pregnancy. In her dream, all the characters were parts of herself, including the baby. This woman had this stifling, demanding and possessive character herself. Therefore, she was predisposed to gambling, which is an ardent desire to control destiny for personal gains.

If we go back to the dream about the cloud, where the addicted person was trying to grab hold of the inaccessible with concrete means due to those parts of himself that were disconnected, you'll understand my reply to this woman. "You complained that your husband was almost never at home," I said. "Considering what is inscribed in you and what you have just come to understand, if your husband had been with you all the time you'd have been really tired of having him around. You simply wouldn't have been interested in him anymore. His inaccessibility is the basis for your attachment to him." After thinking about this for a few moments, she said, "I think you're right."

We must always go back to our inner selves and, one day, we no longer project anything onto others. They are merely images, symbols that allow us to see what it is we shelter within ourselves. The people we meet and our close family and friends are all teachers. They show us what is inscribed within us.

We shall see that the Angels help us to better understand ourselves through the great Universal Laws. One of the Qualities of Angel 15 HARIEL is *Absolves one's conscience by simultaneously instilling Law and Knowledge.* In the name of the law, whether Divine or human, we sometimes become puritanical or a bit fanatical. This is because we apply the law literally without taking into consideration the person's level of evolution or degree of consciousness. When we respect the Divine Laws we gain access to Knowledge and we receive the Law in our heart. Without Love, Knowledge does not exist.

The next true story illustrates that everything in the Universe is perfectly calculated and that coincidence does not exist. This account comes from a man of law, a lawyer, who has been following the teaching of The Traditional Study of Angels for several years. You'll see that this example is simple and powerful at the same time. One Friday, this man, who lives in the Laurentians, was going to Montréal. He usually drives to the station and then continues on by train then by subway. That day, his daughter was just finishing her study week and they had arranged to do part of the journey back to the Laurentians together. They weren't supposed to catch the train at the same station but they had decided on the station, the train and the compartment that they would meet in.

Having arrived at the station, he wanted to buy a booklet of passenger tickets. He saw two automatic vending machines. He went to the one on the right that was free, but he realized that it didn't provide tickets for his destination. So he went to the other ticket machine.

In order to obtain your ticket, you have to read the instructions to find out the price, the itineraries and the operating instructions of the vending machine. In the line-up for the machine on the left, he found himself behind a woman with a little boy of about five or six years old. The train was about to arrive and the lady was reading the instructions, trying to understand how the system worked. Then the train arrived. The little boy jumped up and said, "Mommy, Mommy, quick! The train is going to leave. Hurry up, Mommy!" He held out his little hand for a ticket. The more time passed, the more the lady fiddled with the ticket machine and the more confused and flustered she became.

The man had stepped back a bit so as not to disturb her, but also to do inner work. He didn't want to lapse into impatience. This is a good example of apprenticeship that leads to true mastery, which we acquire through all of the tests They submit us to. What did he do to ensure that he wouldn't lapse into impatience? He started to do his Angel Recitation. He invoked the Angel related to patience: Angel 7 ACHAIAH. He went through the Laws that he had learnt through this teaching, all the while telling himself, "There's no such thing as coincidence. If this woman is here, it is God who has sent her. At the moment, I don't know why she's here, but I'll invoke. ACHAIAH, ACHAIAH, ACHAIAH. I am here on Earth to learn. I've got all the time in the world." He managed to keep his conscience elevated. What had to happen, however, did happen. The train left without them.

The lady turned around and she was upset. She was miserable. He looked at her and said, "It doesn't matter, madam. There'll be another train. Can I help you?" He proceeded to help her and she was able to buy her tickets. There was a short wait for the next train. He decided to go to the washroom. On his way there, he realized that there was a counter with an employee where he could have bought his booklet of tickets and he wouldn't have missed his train. He said to himself, "That was concealed from me. There must be a good reason." Suddenly he heard, "Daddy!" He turned around. It was his daughter calling him!

He said to her, "What are you doing here? This isn't where you were supposed to catch the train." "I changed my plans," she said. "I chose the same route that I took with you the other day. The city, the trains, it's all new to me. I felt more confident doing it this way."

That's why he had missed his train. When he saw her arrive, Divine thoughts arose in him. He said to me, "Everything that had just happened was going through my head. I kept saying to myself. 'My God!'" He was so happy not to have gotten impatient and not to have hassled the lady. He told me, "A few years ago, before being aware of this teaching, I would have done everything possible to speed things up. Believe me, I'd have gotten my ticket and I'd have caught that train. I would have asserted myself. That day, I remained stable. I maintained self-control."

This lawyer had understood one of the Divine Laws. Even in apparent disorganization, there is great organization. Through this situation, he had a mystical experience. His soul was exalted! This is the way in which the Laws are instilled in us through the events of our daily lives. We encounter these Laws, one after the other, and it changes the way we look at life and the way we live on Earth.

Through this experience, this man understood that even when things don't seem to be working out well, something better awaits. This is an idea that we've heard so often that it has become trite. Theoretically, it is beautiful. In our daily lives, however, and when events are forcing us to rush, it's not so easy to accept and to put into practice. Through daily tests, this is the way we one day manage to rediscover self-mastery and to stop feeding unconscious forces that make us impatient or aggressive.

When we no longer put matter first, everything changes. Needless to say, this requires a lot of work. If we continually apply the Divine Laws to our daily life, even with regard to events that might seem trite, when more important and difficult situations turn up, we will have done such a good job of incarnating these Laws that we will have achieved stability and self-mastery. First, however, we have to practice this technique on a daily basis. Angel Recitation is of tremendous help with this work.

Here is an example of an addiction that touches on the understanding of the masculine and feminine principles. A woman asked my husband to interpret a dream that she'd had a few days before. First of all, she said to him, "I have to tell you that I left my husband this morning." Then she told him her dream. *"I was kneeling in front of him. As for him, he was suffering from heart problems. In reality he has absolutely no heart problems. I wanted to help him but I was feeling hurt in my soul. What does this dream mean?"*

My husband asked her, "What does your husband represent to you?" "He's often told me that I am a being of love and that he doesn't deserve me," she said. "For this reason, he could no longer touch me. He had to leave me."

"That's a classic line," my husband told her. "Some people use it in order to leave the other person without any discussion or problems. In this dream, you were shown a part of your inner man and the program that is being activated within you. You are kneeling before him. Being on one's knees is a sign of subservience and profound dependency. This dream indicates that you are emotionally dependent. Heart problems also signal big emotional problems. We can see that you want to help this part of yourself, but the fact that you are on your knees shows that you are in admiration of it. When we are aware of someone's problem, we show understanding and compassion, but not admiration. If we admire, that means we approve of it and we nourish it. Therefore, the part of you that is sick cannot heal, because the schemas that are at the root of the problem are always being maintained."

The woman opened up a bit more and confided, "My husband has an extremely demanding and perverted sexuality. I decided that I no longer wanted to respond to this type of sexuality."

"Yes, but it's not a coincidence that you were with him," my husband said. "You have these aspects in yourself and this man was put on your path to show you distorted aspects of love and sexuality." "That makes sense," she said. "I've done several regressions and I have seen that, in other lives, I committed all sorts of sexual abuses."

It was important that this woman understand that if she didn't gain self-insight, three weeks later the sick and unconscious forces within her would resurface and lead her to feel that she was still in love with this man. This addictive part of her would lead her to say, "After all, it wasn't so bad." Or her lover could come back three weeks later with hidden intentions of a sexual nature and say to her, "Darling, I love you." She could then repeat the same pattern because, all this time, nothing would have been resolved.

It can be said that sex is a drug for some people. Sexuality between two people who love each other is a Divine act. One day, however, there remains no addiction in relation to this act. For some people, getting to that point implies much inner work. This necessitates a period of weaning much like that which is required of a person suffering from substance abuse.

Here is another example of emotional dependency that my husband witnessed. A woman told him, "I've just read the book 'The Cinderella Syndrome' and I've come to understand a number of things." In a certain way, she seemed to be identifying with Cinderella: a pure and gentle princess that everyone exploits. So my husband said to her, "Yes, it's true that Cinderella represents a part of you, but don't forget that the wicked stepmother and the two ugly sisters are also parts of you." So long as we haven't transcended these parts, they will remain.

In that lovely initiatory tale, what did Cinderella go through before becoming a princess? For years and years, she cleaned and cleaned. With what attitude? Without getting angry or aggressive towards the people who were mean to her. This is how, one day, we rediscover our Divine Origins. Without the slightest rebellion, we agree to transform evil until Cosmic Intelligence tells us, "That's enough. You have paid your karma." Whenever we feel mistreated, if we identify with the role of the victim, we cannot evolve. This prevents us from coming back to ourselves.

The day that we understand this principle and that we tell ourselves, "I did similar things in other lives, and I'm not angry with myself. It's all right," we take a step forward. From the moment we acquire the concept of eternity and of multiple lives, even if a lifetime seems long when it's marked with suffering and we know that we can repair everything, we activate a process of purification. At the end of such a process, a person no longer has resonance and begins to attract a different sort of person. This Law is absolute. I would now like to talk to you about the position of Angel HARIEL in the Tree of Life. This Angel resides in the Hochmah Sephirah, which is symbolically associated with the planet Uranus. Therefore, it has a Uranian type of influence, which is to say that it is marked, among other things, by altruism and rapid evolution. In other words, when we have integrated this State of Angelic Consciousness, we are inspired and we tend to serve humanitarian causes. Among the eight Angels who dwell in the Sphere of Hochmah, Angel HARIEL has Its own specificity, which we discover in the Sephirah called Hod. This one is under the influence of Mercury. This Sephirah is very close to earthly manifestation. Thus, Angel HARIEL is situated in the final elaboration of the Divine Plan, or the soul's program.

As a symbol, planet Mercury represents the intellect and the mind. In short, it represents everything that allows us to organize our life's scenario. Why is it that among certain people who preach great values such as love, purity and wisdom, we often find a great discrepancy between what they say and what they do? We observe their lives and we see that they are cold and puritanical. Instead of love, we find aggression and criticism. This discrepancy is due to an overburdened unconsciousness. Energies emerging from such people have to pass through so many memories and unconscious filters that they come out completely distorted. The result is a divided intellect that is full of rifts and imprinted with separatism. We find therein the following distortions related to the Angel 15 HARIEL: *Dry, hardened attitude, over-analytical mind, tendency toward excessive dissection* and *separatism*, that is to say, a mind that leaves no place for love.

This brings me to the following distortion, also related to this Angelic Energy: *willing to die to impose or defend an unnatural truth, terrorist.* On September 11, 2001, the day the twin towers of the World Trade Center in New York collapsed, we saw a manifestation of this distortion at its most extreme degree. How can we explain the worldwide phenomenon of fanaticism? To better understand this question, we will break it down to its individual level.

Shortly after this event, several people told me some of their dreams. In their own way, they corroborate what happened during the attacks. I'd like to tell you about one of these dreams. It was told to me by a woman who has been working with The Traditional Study of Angels for some time now. She had this dream on the 9th of September, two days before the attacks. *She found herself with two other people in a huge tower. All of a sudden, through the window, she saw an airplane in flames heading towards the tower. She was panic-stricken and asked the two people to leave. They did. Then the airplane crashed, not against the tower, but on the ground, creating an explosion and a lot of rubble.*

Why did They send this dream to this person? What does it mean? The events in the dream are a bit different from what actually happened. It is therefore not a premonition of the events of September 11. However, the link is obvious. Everything is inscribed in the parallel worlds, even before the actual manifestations.

Through this dream, Cosmic Intelligence had something to teach this lady. In this case, It was telling her, "The plane, the tower, and the people all symbolized parts of yourself. And what happened is also a part of you." Let's analyze the elements of the dream and their interaction. The commercial tower, with its exchanges and activities relating to work, is a symbol of materialism. An airplane flies in the air, the world of thoughts, and fire relates to the spirit. They wanted to tell her, "When you manifest in the material world, you have thoughts that destroy your life. They cause parts of you to collapse, as they do when you say to yourself, 'I've had enough of working here. It's too demanding. I'd much rather be elsewhere.'"

Sometimes, we criticize in silence. This creates a tornado of aggression that is intuitively or unconsciously felt by others. When we have Knowledge, when we read signs, and when we have acquired spiritual powers such as clairvoyance, clairaudience, and clairsentience, we instantly perceive and understand what the other person is going through. Since this woman has worked towards higher spirituality, she was being warned to pay attention to her thoughts. Even though she knew very well that the dream concerned her personally, when she saw the events on television, her conscience was truly marked by the extent of the damage. She became aware of the destruction she was imposing on herself. She said to herself, "This is what I do to myself when I maintain negative thoughts. I destroy my life and I paralyze my entire being."

This dream gave rise to a sudden and profound awakening of her consciousness. It allowed her to identify the cause of her discontent.

This dream was telling her, "You sometimes have little terrorists in your head. Be careful. It's destructive." Each time we feel frustrated and we have an aggressive or critical thought, we maintain little terrorists within ourselves. Collectively, we are nourishing a huge reservoir of negative and destructive thoughts. Certain people have a more concentrated version of this negative aspect, such as the fanatics and the extremists who planned these attacks. They channel the energies of this collective reservoir and manifest them through concrete action.

God allowed this to happen because there is always a lesson to be learned from a great ordeal. His point of view goes beyond good and evil. Terrorism has grown in order to help humanity change its way of thinking and to increase solidarity. It has grown to help man become more fraternal and less attached to the power of materialism. Of course, we must have a lot of compassion for the families affected, but we must also understand the message.

We have witnessed a confrontation between two extreme ideologies, that is, extreme materialism and extreme anti-materialism. Anti-materialists accuse materialists of exploiting women. They criticize them for the way they use women in bikinis to sell beer or chewing-gum, for example. As for materialists, they criticize anti-materialists for veiling women and for overshadowing them and crushing them. A woman symbolizes the force linked to the materialization of life. Considering the reasons behind the confrontation, we realize that neither the materialists nor the anti-materialists understand the correct use of matter.

When we hear authorities proclaiming that we must uproot evil and stop these people, we may agree with them. Specialists, including the police and the army, are necessary but their interventions have an effect in the world of consequences only. We live in a world of consequences for which we have to take responsibility. With the anti-terrorist intervention, we haven't yet reached the root of the evil. Since the problem is ideological, we need to intervene in the world of ideas. We must try to find out how extremists function. We must penetrate their soul and their unconscious.

What goes on in their head? Even if we arrest a few terrorists, hundreds of others will follow. This way of thinking has spread throughout the world. What are these people's accusations against the West? They accuse the West of abuse of power, bad use of resources and non-sharing. They are also very upset by all the waste that they see. This brings us back to the Law of disturbance. When something disturbs us, it is because we have it within ourselves. If we could get inside the head of these extremists, what would we see? We would see that they are saying, "Poor God, we must help Him. We must uproot evil."

In other lives, some extremists were probably rich people who abused their power and who enjoyed all sorts of vulgar pleasures. They could have lived in any country in the world, but one thing is for sure, they were abusive. Their attitude caused others to suffer and, in this life, their program is one that says, "That's enough! Stop." These people, however, don't have Knowledge. What they accuse others of doing they have within themselves, but they don't know it.

To better understand their attitude, we have only to think of how difficult it is, in the beginning, to start out on a spiritual path or decide to give up an addiction. It is so difficult. All of a sudden we become very intolerant of those who maintain the behavior we wish to eradicate in ourselves. Look at ex-smokers. When a person gives up smoking, he is the one who is most intolerant of other smokers. Why? When he sees others doing what he doesn't want to indulge in anymore, he feels a mixture of desire and rigidity. He is all mixed up. We all behave like this at first. We decide to give up our addictions on the physical level, but we have unconscious forces crying out within. When we say 'No' to these forces, we encounter a little terrorist within who wants to remake the world on the outside.

When a person starts out on a new path, he continually swings between the desire to relapse into his addiction and a rigid attitude. Later, if he continues on his quest for liberation, he'll find a fragile and artificial equilibrium that only becomes stable and natural when his distorted memories have been completely repaired.

Consequently we find ourselves facing an enormous social phenomenon of inner addiction. We won't be able to resolve this in one night or in one year. It will take a great change in the mentality of each and every individual. If each person knew the Law of disturbance, he'd say to himself, "What I see here is terrible. It's not right! I am upset by it! This means that I also have this in me. Before I can even think of eradicating evil on the outside, I have some cleaning-up to do within myself first."

Then comes the day when we have cleansed absolutely everything. Our reaction is no longer to want certain people at a distance because the resonance that we have with them causes us to feel bad in their presence. One day, a person can merge with everyone. Naturally, he understands the necessity to stop and re-educate people who commit extreme acts. In his conscience, however, he no longer has feelings of injustice, hatred or revenge. He has acquired understanding and compassion.

If we come back to the dream of the plane crash, we see that the message that They wanted to give this woman was, "Be careful! For the moment, your aggression is only in your head. You are rebelling, but these forces are true terrorists. If you don't cleanse them, this is what will happen." Sooner or later, a person who doesn't cleanse his thoughts will see them descend and manifest in the physical dimension. This is an absolute fact. In another life, he might even find himself in a war-torn country, surrounded by terrorist acts. Once we understand that thought is a creator, we acquire new motivation. We no longer talk about taking breaks.

This is what the Kabbalah, the Hidden Wisdom, provides. One day, we understand the way the Universe works and we have no negative resonance any longer. We see events taking place and we retain our self-mastery. There is no more panic. Panic no longer has a hold on us. Only then can we truly help others. This is not indifference. Quite the opposite, it is a lot of wisdom and love. When negative Cosmic Forces have been mobilized, we have to assume the consequences of their manifestation in the physical dimension. We must also remember that evil is educational.

Here is another testimony that touches on the issue of puritanism. You shall see just how well we are guided. This is about a man who follows the teaching of The Traditional Study of Angels and who is doing intense work to purify himself in order to rediscover his body of Glory.

He said to me, "One night, I had back pain in my spine. This pain, however, was at the energy level." When we do this much work on ourselves, we awaken the kundalini. The kundalini is the vital energy of all human beings. It strength rests at the base of the spine, and when this energy is awakened without spiritual consciousness having been acquired, it is used to satisfy all sorts of desires. In a person who is spiritually aware, it rises along the spine and nourishes the superior centers which, in turn, give a person great spiritual powers. Among these are clairvoyance, clairaudience and clairsentience. A healthy awakening of the kundalini requires a long period of purification. As we have already seen, if this powerful force is awakened too soon, that is to say, before the unconsciousness has been sufficiently purified, then it acts like a devouring fire that feeds our basic instincts.

This man felt that this energy was blocked in his spine and that this was the cause of his pain. That night, before going to sleep, he invoked an Angel with great intensity and They sent him a dream. *He was in a teaching hospital and he had a bucket for cleaning the floors. In the bucket there were amputated feet. These were feet that belonged to distant relatives that he didn't really know. He had a lighter in his hand and he set fire to the feet.*

The next day, someone phoned him to let him know that a distant uncle of his, an electrician he didn't really know, had been electrocuted and was in the hospital critically ill. We shall see the link between the electrician, the contents of his dream and his back. This person had an important lesson to learn.

In the dream, he was shown the reasons why this energy was blocked and couldn't rise. Why do we go to the hospital? To be cured. On the other hand, school is for learning and the bucket is for purification. This man had something to learn that would help him purify himself. Feet are a symbol of action and of the way we manifest in the outside world. In the dream, the man had a lighter. As in the dream of the plane crash, however, this was a destructive fire that he was holding. He was burning his distant relatives' feet. This means that his spirit was destructive. The distant relatives represented members of his inner family that he didn't yet know and with whom he hadn't merged.

This man thought and acted in a puritanical way, so much so that the dream was warning him, "Be careful. You still have prejudice and puritanism within you and you don't go back to yourself enough when you see certain things." He was projecting outwardly and judging others when he saw that their actions weren't just. He would say, "Look at him. What he's doing is not right." Rather than simply evaluating what he saw and then examining himself, which requires a certain amount of humility. He would criticize and make offensive remarks about others because he still had resonance with what he saw. Within himself, he had parts that he didn't really want to get to know. As we've seen, these were symbolized by distant relatives because when we visit these parts, what we see is not always very nice.

Why did this man receive news of his uncle the electrician? This event was a sign. We're going to analyze it as if it were part of a dream. The man told me that he didn't feel upset when he got the phone call. In this teaching, whether or not we feel upset constitutes a criterion. Normally, when we don't feel upset, it means that we no longer have resonance. Therefore, this man thought he had no resonance.

However, and although we may have the impression that we're not upset, hidden resonance exists just the same. For instance, extremists are upset by the evil they see, but they don't seem to be bothered by the unhappiness they inflict on their victims and their families. For this man, his uncle the electrician represented a part of himself that he didn't really know. Symbolically, electricity is what allows us stay connected, or plugged-in, to the Spirit and to

Divine Energy. He was being shown that his destructive spirit was disconnecting him. Hence, his sore back.

We go much further when we are attentive to the phenomenon of being bothered and when we immediately bring things back to ourselves. There are no more loopholes, but we do have Angel Recitation that allows us to cleanse our unconsciousness. We re-educate the inner forces that were ceaselessly knocking on our door and assailing us. We find peace. Therefore, we can open the door and merge with everyone, whatever they have done or are still doing.

⊙

Purification Symbols

I would now like to talk to you about the main purification symbols. These are taken from a very long list. Whether they appear in the concrete world, that is to say, as signs, or whether they appear in dreams, we interpret them in the same manner. One day, there is no difference.

With Angel HARIEL, the Angel of Purification, certain symbols return very often. Among these we have the toilet. When we work with the Angels, we find ourselves going to the toilet more often than usual, especially at the beginning. Up Above, They are telling us, "You want to attain these high dimensions? Then you have to purify certain negative states that still reside in you."

When the symbol is urine, a liquid, it signifies that we need to purify an emotional element. When we see excrement, it concerns the cleansing of elements of a material nature. To put it simply, the symbolism in purification dreams works as follows: we receive a dream in which we see ourselves going to the toilet and then follow a series of scenarios. The purpose of these dreams is to show us more precisely what it is that we are purifying. In this way, we acquire great spiritual autonomy because we receive our program from within.

We might see a washbasin where we are washing our hands. Hands represent the world of fabrication and the process of giving and receiving. This scene would mean, "Be careful. Purify your way of giving and receiving. Some of your actions are not just. Through a single image, and this is the beauty of dreams, all sorts of erroneous ways of behaving are shown to us. Then, all that is left to do is to establish the link with our life and to make the connection between our actions, emotions, thoughts and the messages received in our dreams.

The shower and the bath are other symbols of purification. We have seen that water symbolizes a person's emotional side. In general, it also symbolizes purification. Faced with a symbol, we simply ask the question, "What is this used for?" When we have a bath or a shower in real life, how do we feel afterwards? We feel good. At the level of the soul, such symbols signify that we shall feel better because a deep purification will have taken place.

Fire and the fireplace are also symbols of purification. When they appear in a dream, it means we are purifying at the spirit level. When we see a cleaning product, it means we are doing serious cleaning. We analyze the symbols one by one. When there are several, we identify the relationship they have with one another. Where do we find this product? What make is it? Is it in the living room? The living room represents the social aspect. We sit there to talk to others. So detergent in the living room signifies that we are purifying certain aspects of our social life. The kitchen represents preparation, and so on.

By proceeding in this fashion, we can identify what is really going on within ourselves. These symbols are very important and they recur frequently when we do our Angel Recitation. In actuality, whenever we have a problem with the washing machine or the washbasin, we interpret these signs using the same symbolism as if they appeared in a dream. There is no such thing as coincidence.

Here are some other examples. With a washing machine, we wash clothes. Clothes always represent our aura. Therefore, the washing machine represents the cleansing of the quality of our aura, that is to say, the way we release our qualities and distortions in the presence of others. Likewise, if we see dirty or torn clothing, it means that the radiation of certain aspects of our aura and our being needs to be corrected. With a dryer, we have the element of air. This concerns the world of thoughts. A dishwasher cleans dishes on which we receive our food. Thus, it symbolizes the purification of our receptivity to resources.

I'd like to share with you a story that relates to purification. It concerns quite an insidious and omnipresent form of addiction. The addiction to the desire to please, and not only vis-à-vis the opposite sex.

This account comes from a woman who works with The Traditional Study of Angels. Her husband is also inspired by this teaching. She told me that she was getting ready to go to Italy to accompany her husband on a business trip. They were also going to take the time to visit the country. She told me, "I made an appointment to see my hairdresser a few days before my departure. The night before the appointment, I received a dream." She told me her dream, "*I arrived at the hairdresser's and the atmosphere wasn't very pleasant. The hairdresser was very agitated. All of a sudden, I saw her kill her boyfriend.* I woke up at that point! I was very upset! I really didn't feel well after this dream."

After a dream like that, the person might say to herself, "Maybe I shouldn't go." This woman, however, kept her appointment. She would be traveling and she had already made the appointment. Essentially, she had to experience this dream in the concrete world. She explained to me how a few months before, in her search for more authenticity, she had decided to go back to her natural, light-brown color. She had been having her hair dyed blonde for the past 15 years, but this time, as she wanted to look her very best for the trip, she decided to postpone the change.

She told me, "I asked her for another blonde rinse. The result was awful. The roots of my hair were carrot-red and the tips were almost white. It was really ugly. I said to the hairdresser, 'You're not going to leave me like this, are you?' The hairdresser replied, 'I'm really sorry, but if I start all over again, the product is so strong that there won't be a hair left on your head.'" This lady went home very angry. Since she follows this teaching, however, and because of her dream, she couldn't stay angry for long. With an ordinary conscience, another person would have really been upset at the hairdresser. This woman, however, knew that through this experience she was receiving a lesson. She simply said to herself, "I should have cancelled the appointment. I was warned in my dream."

She meditated on the deeper reason for this misadventure. She said to herself, "I had taken steps towards being more natural, but I let myself be influenced by others. I didn't listen to my inner self."

She told me, "Even my husband tried to influence me by saying 'I've always known you with blonde hair. It suits you.' My friends did too. My desire to please won the day. I knew I had inner work to do concerning my appearance but not to that extent." (laughter)

I interpreted her dream for her. I told her, "In this dream, all the characters represent parts of yourself. Symbolically, a hairdresser touches the head and sets hair in place. She therefore represents the dimension of thought. She puts ideas back in the right place. She also represents seduction in the negative aspect. You had begun a process to become more natural and authentic. But the hairdresser killed her boyfriend. In a dream, a man represents action and manifestation. You were being shown that you were obstructing a process within yourself. You were killing it. Whenever we kill in a dream, it indicates that we are repressing something. And it will, of course, come back. One day, we no longer need to kill, symbolically speaking, because we have nothing left to kill. We have transcended evil."

This woman's dream showed her what was going on within herself. I said to her, "To help you better understand, ask yourself why a person dyes her hair. In a dream, when we see natural blonde hair, it's an important symbol. It's a sun symbol representing Divine manifestation. By dyeing your hair blonde you were seeking this sunny side. You felt dull on the inside because you still had parts that hadn't been cleansed yet."

She replied, "I have already settled part of this sun aspect. A few years ago, I was obsessed with the sun. I used to lie out in the sun for hours. When I was tanned people would tell me, 'You look like you're in top shape. You look really healthy.' When I was pale, however, people would say, 'Are you sick? Is something wrong?' This meant that I always felt healthy when I was tanned. Then, one day, the doctor discovered two melanomae. One was on my back and one on my breast. He told me, 'No more sun for you. If you expose your skin to the sun, you'll need high protection sunscreen.' I had no choice. Now, I'm no longer bothered by people's reaction to the pallor of my skin. I have come to terms with the sun aspect. As for the sunny side of my hair, that's a different story."

I told her, "You know, it's normal at first. When I was in my twenties, I already had white hair and so I dyed it. Then I did very intense inner work. My purpose was to rediscover the natural authenticity within. After a certain time, what I had done on the inside manifested itself on the outside. I was ready to stop dyeing my hair."

This example can be applied to many other aspects of our daily life. For instance, we may have tried to project a nice image of ourselves in the past, a spiritual image. We may have done things that seemed charitable but with intentions that weren't pure. One day, we decide to no longer do this. We resolve to change our mentality, but we don't change overnight. When we set off on a spiritual path, great forces confront each other within us and materialize in everyday situations. For a certain length of time, our behavior is awkward. Sometimes, it is more awkward than before due to the confrontation of these inner forces. It's normal. The day will come when all these forces will be aligned. At that moment, their materialization becomes beautiful, sun-filled and extraordinary. That takes time, and time is essential.

Here is a final true story that concerns spiritual dependency. A man told me of a dream he had received several years earlier. He explained to me that he'd had a problem with alcohol. He had been keeping this problem under control through abstinence for quite some time. In his dream, *just in front of him, he could see a man who was there to predict his future. Rather than talk to him, the man was suddenly transformed into a beautiful light. He approached the dreamer and touched his spine in three places. This resulted in noticeable energy. Then, he disappeared. The dreamer looked for him everywhere. At one particular moment he opened a door. It was dark but he could sense the presence of the being of light. He couldn't see him but he could sense him.*

This man said to me, "A short while after this dream, I met a woman who said she had all sorts of powers that came from the world beyond. She introduced me to a man she knew and who claimed to be the reincarnation of Mikael, the Archangel. So I told my dream to this man in order to have it interpreted." This Mikael, the archangel, told him, "The being of light was me. I am the one you saw in your dream."

I gave him a different interpretation of his dream. I told him, "In this dream, the person who was transformed into light was not Mr. Mikael the archangel. It was a part of you that is coming into being. You were being told, 'All that you have done is lovely. Sure, you fell by the wayside. You had alcohol-related problems but you have accomplished very fine work. Beautiful and great things await you.'"

Behind this being of light was a guide. Guides carry out trans-figurations in our dreams. Through the energy that this being had unblocked by touching the dreamer's back, the dreamer symboli-cally received an opening that would lead him to a spiritual quest. It was an awakening of the famous kundalini we talked about earlier. The unblocking took place in three spots: the head, the heart and the body. The man had been liberated at the level of his thoughts, at the level of his emotions and feelings and at the level of his actions. He had received an energy that would lead him to raise himself up.

Why did the dreamer search everywhere for the being of light? When we have had a taste of such energy, our quest inevitably be-gins. From that point on we look for it everywhere. In the dream, after opening a door, the dreamer felt the presence of the being despite the darkness. It was Their way of saying to him, "Before being able to wholly become this being of love and light, you must visit your dark areas. You must cleanse your unconscious parts. We are here, however, and We will accompany you."

It is no coincidence that, shortly after, the man met a woman claim-ing to have spiritual powers, along with the so-called Mikael, who claimed to be the incarnation of an Archangel symbolically repre-senting 1/10 of God in order to impress and manipulate people. These people have their place. If Cosmic Intelligence lets them do this, It has its reasons. Each person who comes into contact with these people has the opportunity to meet his own distortions and to work on them. That's what happened to this man. When we start out on a spiritual path, we may come into contact with all sorts of teachers. In this way we meet parts of ourselves. One day, we rediscover *insight* and *discernment,* two of the Qualities of Angel HARIEL. In the meantime, detours have their reasons for being. Thus, everything has its place.

The day will come when we no longer have spiritual dependency. We receive Knowledge directly through dreams, daily signs and all the people we meet. This is spiritual autonomy.

Angel 18 Caliel
The Children Of Truth

For about thirty years now, they have become more and more numerous. They are arriving. They have come to help us love the truth. Who are they? They are called Indigo children. They are also known as children of Aquarius, or children of the new Earth. We could also call them the children of truth because what is most important to them is to rediscover what is right.

In their quest for truth, they will have to learn a new language, that is, the language of symbols. This language will teach them to discover new realities through the analysis of their dreams and daily signs while helping them distinguish between true and false, between good and evil. They will then be able to live in harmony with their environment. These beings have come to build a new society based on altruism.

Not long ago, our daughter Kasara, my husband and I experienced one of these magical moments in the quest for truth. During the Christmas festivities, at a family reunion where we exchanged presents, Kasara discovered a price tag that had been left on one of her presents. When she saw the tag, she was surprised.

At that moment, she did not comment. When we got home, however, she went to see her father and said to him, "You have to explain something to me. I always thought that Santa Claus made his toys himself. Does he buy them at the store too? I saw a price tag on one of my presents."

"Come and sit down," he told her. "I'm going to tell you a bit more about Santa Claus. Santa Claus did, indeed, exist a long, long time ago. He was a man with a very generous heart who lived in the Scandinavian countries. He started to make wooden toys for children and, after a while, a lot of people went to help him make and distribute the toys. We told you that Santa Claus existed because, in a way, he does, and also because his story is so beautiful! Santa Claus is a bit like Jesus. He has become a symbol that helps people increase the kindness and generosity in their hearts. I believe in Santa Claus. Besides, just before Christmas, I saw him in one of my dreams, but as you know now, he represents generosity. So you can keep on believing in him because it is an energy that enters the hearts of people to make them good."

"But why wasn't I told the truth right away? I've been told a lie, haven't I?"

I told her, "Kasara, we told you part of the truth. You know that it's only been a few months since we explained to you, with the help of books, how babies are made. At the age of three or four, you wouldn't have understood this." "Ah," she said. "That's true."

She had just understood something. After a few seconds' reflection, she exclaimed, "Oh! I'm glad I know the truth."

Of course, for a while, her little friends at school had been saying, "The Santa Claus story isn't true. Santa Claus doesn't exist." To this, she would reply, "I believe my parents." Following this explanation, she was happy because everything made sense. The information was consistent.

If we do not give children the sort of explanations that validate the various energetic realities, the child starts his life with his most beautiful asset, that is, trust in his parents, and finds himself terribly disillusioned while fostering the feeling that adults lie to him. It is very important to validate various existing dimensions with children.

The theme for this evening's lecture is how to love the truth. You might say to me, "The truth is lovely indeed, but before reaching its essence, we see so many imperfections!" These imperfections are part of the truth. We do not, however, like these truths very much. There exists an Angel to help us love the truth. It is Angel CALIEL, who bears the number 18.

How do we acquire truth? What, for that matter, is truth?

We commonly use the word *truth* to speak about our personal reality. In this context, the term *reality* is more adequate. We each have our own realities and, as in Kasara's story with Santa Claus, we move from one reality to another. In our guidance on the initiatory path, Cosmic Intelligence uses the same process. We live with a certain reality until, suddenly, we notice a little tag, as Kasara did, and doubts surface. If we use them with the purpose of getting to know the truth, these doubts are positive because they lead us to perceive a new reality. We could have kept Kasara away from the concept of Santa Claus, but Santa Claus is everywhere during Christmas time and most children believe in him. If we had kept her away from this concept, she would have become too rational with the magic of Christmas and she would have been alone with this knowledge when she would have met other children. We've therefore chosen to create this sort of reality for her and to help her remain close to society.

During the course of our life, along with our previous lives, we move from one reality to another with the purpose of reaching the Essence, which is both truth and the manifestation of Qualities and Virtues in their purest form.

When we do our Angel Recitation with the Angelic Energies, we experience extreme frames of mind. This is normal. One day, we enjoy high states of consciousness. The next day, everything seems to swing to the other extreme. More specifically, Angel 18 CALIEL helps us feel just, truthful, and authentic. Then, all of a sudden, we are plagued by terrible doubts and feelings of injustice. It is not easy. It is like the tag on the gift that pushes us into another reality. Angel CALIEL breaks old concepts and old structures. He helps us to find new ones that are ever more supple. Then, one day, He leads us to the timeless and eternal structure. However, we have to unstructure in order to restructure. This is what we discover on our spiritual path.

The more we get used to this process, the easier it gets. In fact, Angel CALIEL helps us to love the truth and to love the process in which we integrate new realities. If we carry out this apprenticeship, one day we receive immediate answers to all of our questions. They give them to us through our dreams and daily signs. The great prophets such as Abraham, Moses, Jacob, Joseph, and Jesus were guided in this manner.

Let's have a look at the list of Qualities and Virtues of Angel CALIEL. When we work with this Angel, doubts may manifest themselves. Angel CALIEL brings them out so as to allow us to go further. We may have had a certain way of thinking when, suddenly, Oops! Doubts appear. (laughter) These are always positive and constructive doubts. By invoking Angel CALIEL, we seek to understand what They want to tell us through these doubts and events that force us to question our old ways of thinking or acting. Cosmic Intelligence wants to lead us further.

One of the principal qualities that Angel CALIEL confers on us is the *capacity to see through intentions.* Before we can guess other people's intentions, however, we must work on our own. Everything is based on intention. No matter what we do, what counts is how we do it and the intention with which we do it. Are we, for example, motivated by an intention based on qualities and virtues? Or is our action based on a desire to win or to succeed? This Angel is like a laser beam penetrating to the truth. He allows us to detect our unconscious lies making them stand out. As for the conscious lies, of course, we know what form these take.

Angel CALIEL can be symbolized by a sword because of His sharp, cutting edge. Psychologically, to slice through means to make a decision, or to render justice. Each time we decide to say yes or no, to turn left or right, to do or not do such and such a thing, we cut through doubt and make a decision. At that moment, we are in the State of Consciousness of Angel CALIEL. Actually, we cut through doubt and make decisions non-stop throughout the day. This is true no matter what our reality or degree of honesty. With Angel CALIEL, we learn to cut through with love and wisdom because whenever we cut through in the absence of these qualities, we hurt. The gestures we make and the words we speak can have serious consequences.

Whether we know Angel CALIEL or not, we find ourselves in His Qualities one minute and in the distortions related to this State of Consciousness the next. Whenever we are in His Qualities, we deepen our understanding of the various degrees of integrity and this put a light on our faults and weakness. Let's have a look at the distortions associated with Angel CALIEL.

If we look at *uses justice for the sole purpose of material gain*, we may say to ourselves, "That has nothing to do with me." However, every time we smooth the edges one way or another to acquire material goods, to please someone or to buy love, we manipulate justice. The gesture is corrupt. It is wrong and it is unjust. When we work with Angel CALIEL, He acts like a lie detector. We were living in a reality that seemed right to us. All of a sudden, however, we realize, "No! I was in the wrong." From that moment on, we cannot go back. A truth has been inseminated in us. It has entered our cells and we have to change. Thus, Angel 18 CALIEL triggers an important restructuring process. Truth is a natural process of change that compels us to transform our inner selves.

We have seen that Angel CALIEL confers upon us the capacity to discern intentions. This is also true for other people's intentions. It sometimes happens that, while speaking to someone, we think, "There's something not right here." We feel confused and mixed up. This means we have resonance with the person. In the opposite case, that is, when we have no resonance with him, we simply perceive his intention and our mind remains clear. We can then pass rightful judgment without criticizing the person.

The term *judgment* has become negative in our everyday language, but the ability to judge correctly is a quality. In fact, it is one of the Qualities of this Angel. We need judgment in order to evaluate situations and to make fair decisions. But if our judgment is one of criticism this means we have resonance with the person or situation in question.

I would like to share with you an example that touches on the Law of Resonance and the world of dreams. I was preparing this lecture on Angel CALIEL (there are no coincidences) when a man who dreams a lot and for whom Angel CALIEL is one of three Guardian Angels, told me, "I had just finished medical school and the time had come for me to decide in which town I'd set up my medical practice. So I asked for a dream. In my dream, *I was in Trois-Rivières, Canada, where I found a lovely place with windows. In reality, I knew the owner of this place but in my dream he wasn't exactly the same as in real life. He asked me for $300 a month for rent, which was very reasonable. Then he left and his wife arrived. She, however, asked me for $1,000 a month.*"

At first, this young doctor thought that his dream was motivating him to open a medical practice in Trois-Rivières. Later, he told me, "I found a large place, similar to the one in my dream. I already knew the owner, but he wasn't the man I'd seen in my dream. The rent was very high." He was a little confused and he wanted me to interpret his dream to help him clarify the situation. He was wondering, "Is this the place I should take? Was my dream a premonition?"

I said to him, "In your dream, the city of Trois-Rivières and each of the characters represent parts of you. You asked a question and you got an answer. However, you have to interpret this dream by going to its essence. What does the city of Trois-Rivières represent to you?"

"I did part of my medical studies there," he said.

"And the owner of the place?"

"When I lived in that city, I stayed in a small apartment that this man rented to me. His brother lived in the apartment next door. I went through hell there because this neighbor was a drug addict and he would make a lot of noise at night. He was so disruptive that I had to call the police. What's more, my studies were very intense and I had to be in top shape to be successful. It was very difficult."

"In that case, your dream doesn't indicate the place where you should open a medical practice at all, but rather what you need to change in your intention. This is why They used the town where you did your university studies as well as the owner of the flat you were living in at that time. You know that we do not have a particular neighbor by coincidence. You had resonance with him."

The resonance with the neighbor who was a drug addict was to be found elsewhere than in the physical dimension because this young doctor is healthy, he eats well and he does not take drugs. Where was this resonance to be found? I said to him, "They wanted to show you that you are addicted to work. When you said 'I had to be in top shape to be successful,' I saw that when you were studying you worked like a drug addict. And in your dream, They showed you why you worked, and still work, like an addict. The owner's wife who asked for such a high price had the wrong attitude and was not being completely honest. In dreams, men symbolize daytime and action, whereas women represent the inner, emotional side. You were being shown that by day, everything seems fine. Your way of doing things seems correct. On the inside, however, some parts of you never have enough. These are the memories you need to rectify. There are also lovely things in you, including the part that wants to help others. You did ask a question, however, and They are inciting you to change the memories that make you feel as though you constantly have to be in top shape. These are memories based on the need to succeed and to be acknowledged.

248

In your dream, They didn't give a direct reply to your question. Instead, They showed you what you have to rectify within yourself before starting your practice."

Why was he shown the city of Trois-Rivières? They wanted to tell him, "Remember what you went through and the attitude that you had while you were studying in this town. It is essential that you rectify this attitude because you are getting ready to go public. Otherwise, you can wish to help others all you like, but you'll be doing it with an energy that isn't just and you will attract additional karma. Because you are sincere, They are inviting you to rectify certain memories so as to allow you to be more generous and altruistic. Your dream clearly points out to you that despite all your good will as a young doctor, your main intention is to make a lot of money. The attitude of the two owners shows you what energy you will have towards your future patients."

He looked at me with big eyes! A light had just switched on. He had just had a revelation. It was correct, it was the truth and it was the first time that he saw the connection between his desire to succeed, what had happened in Trois-Rivières, and what he was preparing to do with his life. You see how revealing dreams can be. Whenever we ask a question while invoking Angel CALIEL, it is as if we were saying, "I want to know the truth in relation to this question." Cosmic Intelligence makes it Its duty to set the record straight. We may, of course, be in for a surprise.

I will tell you a story that relates to signs and to Angel Recitation with this Angel. One of our friends, a lawyer, has been working with the Angels for a number of years. At the beginning of this apprenticeship, while he was defending a client in court, he read the Qualities of Angel CALIEL and thought it would be very appropriate to invoke this Angel at this particular time, given His Quality of Justice. During the trial, when he did not have to think or to talk, he did his Angel Recitation with Angel CALIEL. You see that we can do our Angel Recitation anywhere, quite consciously and with our eyes wide open.

At a particular moment, while he was invoking the Angel, he was astounded to hear his client say things that he had kept secret in their private interviews. These facts were not in his favor. Quite the opposite, in fact. Once the hearing was over, he spoke to his client, man to man. He asked him, "Why did you hide these events from me?" His client was embarrassed. He did not know what had happened. He could not help himself. Angel CALIEL had struck a hard blow! The truth had come out, but not the way the lawyer had expected. (laughter) Since then, he has understood that what counts is not winning a case but rather to ardently wish that the truth prevail.

In the material world, we sometimes smooth the edges because it suits us. When we work with this teaching, however, the truth springs forth. The example we have just seen is a good illustration of the immediate impact of Angel Recitation. We invoke a particular Angel and events occur that are precisely related to this Angel. This is exactly what signs are. We see the link or the interaction that exists between our thoughts and the manifest world, that is, what is said and what is happening. Gradually, we become conscious of the nature of our relationship with the Divine world and the parallel worlds. We realize that we are always accompanied and guided and that we do not belong solely to material reality.

Of course, sometimes we lose our connection and we sink into matter. When we resume our Angel Recitation, however, we reconnect and we develop clairvoyance, clairsentience and clairaudience. These faculties allow us to make an in-depth reading of situations and of people. This is exactly what Angel CALIEL provides. He provides the *capacity to see through intentions.*

I'd like to tell you another true story that is very instructive. It touches on signs, symbolism, masculine and feminine principles, along with numerous other concepts that are defined in this teaching. I was invoking Angel CALIEL while preparing this lecture. During this time, I went to a store to buy a doormat.

Once there, I made my choice and a salesman came over. He rolled out the piece of carpet and I showed him the length that I needed. He measured and said, "That's 18 inches." I was, in fact, working with Angel number 18. In my mind, I said to myself, "Here comes a sign. Open your eyes and your ears. You're about to get a lesson from Angel CALIEL."

I remained very attentive. The salesman laid the carpet on the floor, unrolled it and, while cutting the mat with his special knife, he also cut the floor. He made a big mark on the floor. What do we do in such a situation? First of all, we observe our own reaction. We ask ourselves, "Am I disturbed by his action?" No. I'm not disturbed. Quite simply, I am observing the situation. I said to myself, "OK, I haven't any resonance. This means that They want to show me something about this man. I am being shown that he is very cutting, too cutting. His behavior damages his life and other people's lives. What he damaged was the floor, the foundation of his action."

With Angel CALIEL, I was focusing on the concept of the cut, or the cutting edge. The correct cut is the one carried out with love and wisdom. The salesman, who must have been close to sixty, went to the cash register and gave the mat to the young cashier and said to her, "It's 18 inches". She looked at him and asked, "OK, but how do I do this?" The length had been given to her in inches while the price was calculated by the meter. He replied sharply, "Well then, convert it." There again, his gesture and his manner of speaking were too cutting and his manner was harsh. She looked at him and replied with just as sharp a vibration and with a slightly arrogant tone, "I went to the school of meters, not to the school of inches."

The salesman was rather annoyed by her answer. Since he was in front of a client, however, he just came around from behind the counter and left. I continued my Angel Recitation with Angel CALIEL. I understood their reality and why they had such attitudes.

We can change our state of consciousness very rapidly. It can be instantaneous. I looked at the cashier. In the time that it took for the salesman to go around the counter, she softened and became like a little girl. Just in time for him to hear, she said, "That's why I have difficulty with inches."

In this example we can learn many lessons. These two people had quite a bit of resonance with one another. Both of them were too cutting. When a person is too cutting, it indicates a lack of some kind. For example, it may indicate a lack of self-confidence or an excess of rigidity. At school, in the French part of Canada (as in Europe), the young cashier had learned to calculate using the metric system. In North American building and renovation stores, however, the English measuring system is still in use. She has to adapt but she has not managed to do so. As for the older salesman, he too has a rigid attitude that prevents him from adapting to the metric system. These two people have quite a bit of resonance with one another. It is not a coincidence that they work together. They have a lot of things to learn from each other.

Let me explain that the French word for *inch* is *pouce*. It also means *thumb*. The young lady said that she did not go to the school of inches, or the school of *thumbs*. The thumb, like all the fingers of the hand, has a symbolic significance. It represents Universal Love. We cannot do anything without our thumb. If we want to hold something, we need our thumb. Also, we use our thumb on a daily basis for a certain purpose and through the symbolic analysis of this gesture we understand that the cutting edge of truth cannot be separated from love. We could spend a lifetime meditating on this gesture because it has so much meaning. What is it that we use our thumb for on a daily basis? We use our thumb to cut things. Without using our thumb, we cannot cut. But whenever we slice, dice, chop, cut, for example, when we cut a vegetable or a piece of fruit, we have to maintain the right balance and strength in the other fingers. We cannot apply too much force. Otherwise we risk cutting ourselves. We could meditate a long time on this simple gesture. It symbolizes the cutting edge of truth that must always be carried out with love.

The store is a half-hour's walk away and, on my way home, I meditated on what had happened between the salesman, the cashier and the symbolism of the thumb. This anecdote bears a very profound lesson. What is the moral behind it? In French, the pronunciation of the word *maître,* meaning *master,* and the word *mètre,* meaning *meter,* is exactly the same. We can derive an entire lesson from this pun. The lesson being that we must apply the rules of thumb before applying the rules of masters. (laughter) Now, every time I see my doormat, it reminds me of this State of Consciousness and it incites me to live with the love of truth. It is my little CALIEL. (laughter)

Let's have a look at where Angel CALIEL is situated in the Tree of Life. He resides in the sphere of consciousness called Binah. This Sephirah represents the dimension where the Spirit begins to take on a form and a structure. The energy there is very subtle and it is where we find original matter in its purest form. In order to rediscover this matter, we must do a great cleansing of the unconscious memories of this life as well as those of our previous lives. Gaining access to Binah means entering the combustion room and rediscovering original matter in its purest form.

The Sephirah Binah is associated with the planet Saturn, which represents perseverance, stability, a sense of duty and the capacity to concentrate, among other qualities. The eight Angels of Binah bathe in this saturnine atmosphere. Each one, however, preserves its own specificity, which is represented by an additional planet. Angel CALIEL's specificity is Saturn, which makes this Angel doubly saturnine. Thus, and because of Its great Quality of Concentration, Angel CALIEL is comparable to a laser beam that probes our inner depths.

I'd like to tell you about a very suggestive dream whose images allow us a better understanding of the saturnine aspect of Angel CALIEL. This is a dream that was told to me by a woman. In it, *she found herself in the backyard of her house where a very deep hole had been dug. Her dog, which she owns in real life, wanted to go down into the hole. She kept telling him, "No. You are not going into the hole." Then, a geologist arrived and, in the background, she saw the buildings of Laval University. The geologist descended into the depths of the hole and found a treasure.*

What was this woman being told? This dream is not one that describes what is going to happen the following day. Rather, it is an initiatory dream. It is therefore possible that its influence can stretch over several lives. They wished to tell this lady, "You are going to begin exploring your inner territories." Like all animals, the dog represents a person's needs and instinctual force. More specifically, and from its positive point of view, it symbolizes enthusiasm because a dog is generally playful and continually seeks affection. Thus, this woman was being told, "You have this instinctual force and lovely enthusiasm that give you the wish to explore your inner depths, but it is not enough. You cannot go down there with just your instinctual energy. You must explore more conscientiously." Then, she saw a specialist. A geologist represents knowledge of subterranean worlds. Therefore, he is the part of the dreamer that knows and works with the Angels. The fact that the geologist went down very deep into the earth and found a treasure indicated a deep and very fruitful exploration of her unconscious memories.

Angel CALIEL can also be compared to a diamond. Since coincidences do not exist, and while I was preparing this lecture, I came across an article on diamonds. Diamonds are in ever-greater demand on today's market, not so much for their function as jewelry as for their use in the manufacturing of microprocessors and certain mechanical tools. In fact, they are replacing silicon as a semi-conductor, because diamonds can bear temperatures and pressures superior to this metalloid. They are also used in fine layers on surfaces that need to be as sharp as possible. You can see that the diamond's cutting quality relates it to Angel CALIEL. Diamonds are produced by the natural heat and compression of carbon in the centre of the earth. Over long periods of time the carbon is submitted to pressures and temperatures so great that they reach the level of purity of a diamond. The diamond is a great symbol of purity.

Angel CALIEL allows us to probe our inner territories. Symbolically speaking, He allows us to explore, layer by layer, or level by level, the different kingdoms. First, we explore the animal kingdom. This, as we have seen, represents our vital and instinctual force. Next, we explore the vegetable kingdom, which is intimately associated to the world of water, or emotions. Finally, we explore the mineral kingdom, which represents very ancient memories, as well as our physical body. Thus, by cleansing our instinctual and emotional memories of all that is not just, one day the truth from Up Above is finally able to descend into our physical bodies. This means that we will manifest the truth and the Great Principles at every moment, in our every gesture, in every word and in all our deeds.

The lady who dreamt of the dog and of the geologist had never been to university. The presence of the geologist and the buildings of Laval University in a dream that is, you will remember, an initiatory dream, signifies that it is truly necessary to pursue advanced spiritual studies with the symbolic language of the physical plan in order to carry out this inner work. *All that exists here on Earth has its likeness Up Above, and all that exists Up Above has its likeness on Earth.* These advanced studies of our conscience, carried out daily in all simplicity, serve to probe our inner depths. Study material is provided within our own living book, as well as by people who are presented to us in our daily lives. Through these advanced studies, we can rediscover the diamond, that great symbol of purity that dwells within us all.

A few years ago, my relationship with the man who has become my husband was one of friendship. We were like brother and sister. We exchanged many ideas on the Kabbalah and on The Traditional Study of Angels. We then decided that we would work together to broadcast this teaching. We were far from imagining what the future had in store for us.

One day, we went to visit a site for Universe/City Mikaël with some friends. We traveled for approximately two and a half hours. That day, I felt something other than a simple exchange of energy between brother and sister. It felt more like a romantic energy. That evening, at home, I felt rather troubled, especially since this mission was very important to me, as it still is today. We had decided to work together and I certainly did not want romantic complications.

That evening, I chose to work with Angel CALIEL, even though it was not His regency period. Before going to sleep, I did an intensive Angel Recitation and I asked for guidance. I asked Angel CALIEL, "Please, give it to me straight. I am ready for anything. If I mustn't see him again because it's too troubling, then that's what I'll do."

That night, They sent me a dream. *A man in love arrived and he opened a door for me onto a great light. It was such an intense light! It was really quite powerful.* Up Above, They told themselves, "We are going to give it to her in a very precise way that will be nice and easy to interpret." That morning, after waking up with this dream, I called him and, of course, I did not tell him what I had felt in the car. Neither did I tell him what I had asked Angel CALIEL. (laughter) I simply told him my dream because I knew that he was very good at interpreting dreams. I asked him, "What do you think of that?"

He hesitated for a few seconds then he said to me, "I too had dreams about this subject a few months ago." Then he told me all the dreams and signs he had had about me. He admitted that he too had been very surprised, because we really did have a brother-sister relationship. We gave ourselves three days. We said, "We are going to think about it." Needless to say, I meditated intensively during those three days. I received other signs and other dreams. When the three days were up, he phoned me and at that very moment I was doing yoga, head down, in the pear posture. I got up a bit suddenly and, when I answered, I said, "I feel quite dizzy." Kaya understood with those words that my heart had been deeply touched. He said to me, "I think that's a sign. With what you've just said, you are giving me your answer." (laughter) It is true that I was giving him my answer, and I am very happy to have done so. Today, I have a deep understanding of the sacred concept of marriage. Without this union, I would have been limited on my spiritual path. In the past, I tended to have an Oriental view of spirituality. Now, even if I know that celibacy is a primordial and preparatory phase for some people, I also know that once we have found our inner man, or inner woman, we find our twin soul so as to go further. But I have to admit that if I had not had confirmation in my dreams, I would have stayed single.

The children of the new Earth will be guided in this way. They will ask Them, Up Above, if a particular person is the right one for them. However, when we ask, we must be ready to accept whatever answer we receive. We let go and we let ourselves be guided, even if we do not fully understand. It is this Angelic Voice that we are teaching our daughter Kasara to listen to. It tells us to wait for the person destined for us. Through the dream that I received, Angel CALIEL was telling me, "Whatever you do, do not close the door on love and light."

I'd like to tell you a story that shows us how to rediscover the great Spiritual Laws. It is the story of a man whose wife had been coming to lectures on The Traditional Study of Angels for two years, during which time he chose not to get involved. He would say to her, "Whatever you do, don't try to convince me about this stuff." He was receptive all the same. She used to talk to him about what she was experiencing and he would listen attentively. After two years, he noticed so many changes in his wife. She had become gentle, feminine, and had developed a lot of qualities. He became intrigued by The Traditional Study of Angels. He said to himself, "I'll go and see. I'll give it a try." He came and sat in on one of the lectures and the teaching really appealed to him.

To be attracted to a teaching, men, much more than women, need applicable situations and concrete results. First of all, women are more receptive than men and this is why there are generally a lot more women than men at spiritual workshops. At Universe/City Mikaël, however, a lot of men come to the lectures on The Traditional Study of Angels because this teaching leads us to understand these often abstract worlds through direct observation in our daily lives. In other words, the work we do with the Angels leads to immediate results. The teaching becomes concrete and does not remain simply theoretical. The Traditional Study of Angels leads us to truly marry spirit and matter, man and woman, day and night.

Here is what happened. Her husband was waiting to have his car washed at a car wash adjoining a gas station. The customers waiting for the same reason were so numerous that the queue had split in two to allow the drivers who only wanted gas to go through. This man found himself at the head of the second queue.

At one particular moment, a car slipped in sideways at the end of the first line up. This man got out of his car, knocked on the car window and explained that the line up did not end there and that he should get in line at the end of the second queue. The driver was a man accompanied by a woman who was probably his wife. He did not react. His wife, however, was furious. She started to swear (I won't repeat her words) and shouted at him, "Hey, you! Why don't you get back in your car?"

This man simply said, "OK. I'll let you have my place. I have lots of time. I'll go back and sit in my car." He was very surprised by his own reaction. Later, he told me, "Usually I would have gotten worked up. I would have answered aggressively. But in this instance, I was surprised that I was feeling so good." Shortly afterwards, the couple took their rightful place in line behind him. He watched the scene in his rear-view mirror. He could not get over it. Then, sometime after, the same scenario took place. This time, however, it was the people who had sworn at him who suffered exactly the same thing. Another driver arrived and pulled in front of them. We might have thought that they would have gotten into a rowdy discussion, but they did not react.

In just a few minutes, this man had seen a great Law being enforced. This Law, quoted in the Bible, says, "*What you do onto others will be done onto you.*" He had known how to put into practice another Angelic Law that could say, "*The Wise Man knows to await the hour of Justice.*" This law is absolute. We know it, but we do not apply it consciously. When we begin to apply these spiritual principles, they are very useful to us. Whether we are in a line up or anywhere else, we do our Angel Recitation. We maintain high levels of consciousness and we do not let ourselves get caught up in the aggression or distorted reality of others.

Up Above, They wanted to tell this man, "Look. Divine Justice is absolute. A wise man does not get angry. He knows how to wait." He does not, however, let himself be trampled on. He does what is right and sometimes he acts, as did this man, by telling the couple that what they were doing was not right. Confronted with their aggression, he himself kept the right attitude. He remained calm, went back and sat down. Suddenly, the couple went back to their rightful place and exactly the same thing happened to them. If the man had gotten angry, none of that would have happened. Two wrongs never make a right. Reacting wrongly only perpetuates conflict.

When we do something wrong or distorted, we do not always realize it. It does, however, come up again in the minutes, the days or the years that follow. It even comes up in another life. At the beginning of our spiritual path, even if we know the Law of Divine Justice, we do not necessarily see it being applied. Eventually, we continually see it being applied because we are taught this Law in dreams and through events. Eventually, we integrate it.

Integrating the concept of Divine Justice and of reincarnation as absolute truths necessarily leads to restructuring. This man, who is very sensitive, told me, "I can't get over it!" Unlike his wife, who had attended a lot of workshops before coming to these teachings, he had never done so. But he applied what he had learnt and it is amazing how fast he is learning. Now he has four or five dreams per night. His life has completely changed.

These Laws can all be applied and verified in our daily lives, but we so often live in stressful realities mired in matter that it is easy to pass them by and not notice them. The Laws from Up Above cannot be applied rigidly but they must be applied rigorously. *Whatever you do will be done onto you.*

Tonight, since we are dealing with Angel 18 CALIEL, The Angel of Divine Justice, I would like to share with you another account concerning earthly justice. Like all human beings, earthly justice is not perfect. It is going through an apprenticeship. One day, a woman who came to one of these lectures for the first time confided, "I think there's something I need to understand about justice. For six years now, I have had a case against a government agency. A judgment was rendered, but the other party has appealed. It's a real vendetta." This woman had tears in her eyes and she radiated very strong feelings. Clearly she was not happy.

She explained, "When the government carried out improvements to the waterworks in our street, my house was damaged. So I sued the government."

"Whenever we go through something related to justice," I told her, "the first thing to do is to analyze it symbolically. There is certainly something for you to understand."

"That's for sure. A medium even told me that I must have been a lawyer or a judge in another life. Besides, I work in the legal field."

"What do They want you to understand? The house symbolizes our own being and habitat. What caused the damage to your house relates to the improvement of the water system. Therefore, what damages your being relates to certain emotions that you need to purify in relation to social organization and public power. Up Above, They want to show you that you have memories that aren't correct and that touch on your emotions. What you are going through in your external life is not a coincidence. Through this accident to your house, you are being shown certain things that need changing within you."

When we are spiritual people, we do not seek litigation. But it is sometimes appropriate to use justice, because certain earthly deeds must be rectified. In such cases, it is important to always do so with qualities and virtues and a Celestial vision. Even if what we are going through seems very unfair, we must always maintain an attitude totally exempt of feelings of vengeance or anger. Our first intention must not be to win the case. Lawsuits are educational. If the other party has done something wrong, the situation must be rectified to help him grow. Whenever a person does something reprehensible and we do not say anything, he will go on doing it. He is living a reality that is his own but he is unconscious. He is in the wrong. We are going to help him, but we must do so with love. Whenever we go to court, we must always go there with the intention of helping the other person.

I saw the woman again a few weeks later. She told me, "I let go and there was a lovely result." The other party had called the lawyer and told him, "We don't agree with this judgment but we are stepping down." Without giving any other explanation, the government representative simply let the lawyer know that they would not be appealing. Our conversation had had an effect. This lady had laid down her arms and, Up Above, They wanted to give her this lovely lesson. "Look what happens when you let go," They said. "On the outside, everything falls into place. Everything comes from Up Above, no matter if the other party is completely distorted. This is a lesson for you." It is important to preserve a correct intention. If we become too vindictive or too aggressive, it is inscribed within us and we will have to live through the same process again, one way or another.

In the introduction, I spoke to you about the children of the new Earth. These beings are arriving with a new mentality in quest of Truth. We are going to see that Angel 18 CALIEL is an ideal Field of Consciousness that can help us understand these beings so that we may become like them.

Who are these children? What are their characteristics? Generally speaking, they have an intense and deep look in their eyes. As a symbol, eyes are related to truth and ears to wisdom. When we have eye problems, it means we are in the distortion of Angel CALIEL. There is something we do not want to see. This is not a rightful attitude.

Children of the new Earth are also very intense. Very often, parents and teachers have difficulty understanding them. When we do not understand these children, they sense it, often unconsciously, and they can have intense reactions. Their conscience is more open than most people's. Their reaction, which often bothers us, is in direct relation to what they experience. At present, this is generating excessive behavior in schools. Hence, the use of Ritalin. Instead of invoking an Angel and trying to understand these children, we give them Ritalin to calm them down.

What other particularity do these children have? They possess one of the greatest qualities Angel CALIEL can confer upon us. We saw it earlier. It is because of their great mediumship qualities, that is, clairvoyance, clairsentience and clairaudience, that they can perceive the intentions of others, whether consciously or unconsciously. Those who interact with them find themselves, without necessarily knowing it, in front of a subtle mirror that powerfully reflects hidden aspects of their soul.

I notice this with our daughter, Kasara. I am always impressed by it. Whenever she meets someone, she enters his energy and imitates him. She does not reflect his gestures or his manner of speaking, but what he is on an energetic level. She enters deep into certain aspects of the person and reproduces them. In the beginning, I was surprised by her sudden changes in attitude. Later, I understood the process. For instance, if she meets an overly rigid person, she changes her behavior and expresses this rigidity one way or another. A child is not yet fully conscious of what he is or of his powers. His personality is not yet established. Thus, he becomes the energy that is present and reproduces it in his own way. This is why so many teachers are finding their job difficult these days. Many of them suffer from burnouts or experience very difficult situations. The truth brought about by these children is very powerful.

These children are not perfect. They have their karma and their distortions. They, however, have come back from past lives that are imprinted with certain wisdom and they have very high ideals. They wish the truth and it is they who are going to change our society. We can compare each one to a little Jesus in the making, even though they are far from perfect. Jesus did not come to bring us peace. In the Bible, it is written that he came to bring the glaive, or the sword of Justice. Here, we find the symbol of Angel CALIEL: the glaive, the sword whose blade represents Justice. Therefore, it is the truth that these beings have come to bring us. Of course, they too are searching for who they are and so their intensity overwhelms us.

These children have come not only to destroy certain old concepts, but also certain family karma. When we observe the way some families function, we notice that they transmit karma from generation to generation.

These children of the new Earth have a very bright presence and are blessed with an abundance of intelligence of the heart. In general, they also have this lovely confidence in themselves and in life. Naturally they can fall and pick themselves up again, but they are like little kings and queens that we must try to understand. We have to guide them because their great energy tends toward extremes. If we do not orient them towards wisdom, they can become great manipulators. Whatever happens, they have a program and if they have to become great souls where high ideals predominate, they will be OK. Even if they experiment and test all sorts of things, these will not stick to them because they tend not to remain long in the distortion. When they are found to be at fault, of course they try to justify themselves (laughter) but they quickly admit to the distortion and they correct themselves if we incite them to do so. This is what we have to teach them and it is very important to do it because without Knowledge and high values, they can become future terrorists.

We can see that Angel CALIEL is of inestimable help in the understanding of the dynamics and the program of these children. Besides, our work with the Angels leads us to consciously develop the faculties of mediumship, wisdom, confidence and all the other particularities that these children have naturally.

I'd like to tell you a story that illustrates the mentality we develop with these children and with the work we do with the Angels. One day, Kasara came home from school. In all simplicity, she told us what her teacher had shared with them. The latter told her class that she was not happy because of what had happened to her the previous evening. She explained to them that her husband had wanted to borrow her car to go to Montreal, but she was afraid he would scratch it. She lent it to him all the same and he got back home safe and sound without a single scratch on the car. She told them that the following morning their neighbor knocked on the door to tell her that her car had been scratched. During the night, great gusts of wind had blown away her carport and it had scratched the paintwork and damaged the wipers. She said to her neighbor, "I am really not happy. This is the fourth time I have to bring my car to the garage to have it repaired."

Wide-eyed but without any criticism, Kasara said to us, "There was a sign there. But I couldn't explain it to her. She doesn't know about symbolism. She has to go through this. She has to accept it." She said this very naturally. Of course, Kasara does not yet have the capacity to interpret all these events in depth using symbolism, although it will not be long before she does. It was, nonetheless, very powerful when she spoke about the situation of her teacher.

Let's go through what this teacher experienced and analyze it using symbolism. This woman said she was afraid of her car being scratched. Whenever we are afraid of something, it means that we have it within ourselves. In order to read a sign properly, we have to interpret it according to the general context of the situation, just as we do for a dream. A car is what allows us to advance. It represents our behavior or the way we "drive" through life.

This lady's fear that someone would scratch her car indicates that she herself scratches with her own behavior. How? Through her prejudice. Prejudice scratches. The fact that the carport blew away in a gust of wind is no coincidence. In symbolism, the world of air represents thoughts. Up Above, They wanted to tell her, "You criticize too much. This creates turbulence in your thoughts. Your car is no longer protected." In symbolic or energetic terms, what does protection mean? Protection is our aura. For a person to be protected, the aura must be imprinted with qualities and virtues. This is the greatest protection there is. If this woman had been an initiate, she could have been warned of danger in a dream, or she could have had an intuition. It is possible to avoid all incidents if Cosmic Intelligence judges it necessary. Whenever we are critical or vindictive, however, and when our thoughts are spinning in our head, we lose our protection. At that moment, an ordeal becomes inscribed in our program. *We scratch and we get scratched.*

The windshield wiper was damaged. What is the purpose of a wiper? It allows us to see while we are driving when it is raining or snowing. It helps us avoid confusion. Water represents the world of emotions. Therefore, this woman was being shown that whenever she has thoughts that are not correct, it causes emotions to surface. Her vision becomes confused and blurred. Whenever we lose our clear-sightedness, we are no longer living in truth. We no longer see correctly. You see, because of the reading of signs, a little story as simple as this can lead us to understand a life-plan.

When we read signs, and if a person talks to us about something that happened to him, without even realizing it, he is talking to us from his inner depths. He is naked. This is why it is so important to interpret signs with love. Angel CALIEL gives us the ability to understand Divine Justice, but we must always proceed with love. Otherwise, the other person will be under the impression that we are spying on him and that we are lying in wait, as if in ambush, for the moment he stumbles. The task is quite a conscientious one. We will not succeed overnight, but there will come a time when the reality we can read concerning the other person will no longer change our opinion of him. We will love him the same as ever and we will grant him just as much consideration. The only difference will be that we will understand his reality.

Each person has a reality that is constructed on the basis of his experiences. The more we work with Angel CALIEL and the more we respect the reality of others, the more deeply we can accompany him and understand his reality, even in his distortions. We have quite a responsibility. The more we integrate Knowledge, the more incisive and deeply penetrating our sense of justice becomes.

Our responsibility even goes as far as refraining from talking about the Law of Resonance to people who are living in an ordinary consciousness and who have not been programmed to experience Knowledge in this life. No matter what their present reality may be, it is important that they go through this, even if they are completely within a distortion. They remain children of God.

Since we are talking about children of the new Earth, here is another example concerning a teacher, as many teachers come to the lectures on The Traditional Study of Angels. This woman is truly committed to cleansing and opening her unconsciousness. She came to me for an interpretation. She told me her dream. *From the outside of a house, she was looking through a window and she could see what was happening in one of the rooms. She could see very aggressive men and women with knives. Then, she saw a spider's web and a spider. All of a sudden, she heard an authoritarian voice say to her, "Don't go in there. If you do, you'll die." Then she fled over the snow on a sled.*

I asked her, "Did you feel anything or did you notice anything special that happened the next day?"

"Yes," she replied. "The following day, I was marking my students' dictations. I cried over them. There were on average 30 to 40 mistakes per copy. I also cried because I don't want the new school reform and neither do my students, by the way."

As you know, a new reform is being introduced in the public school system in Quebec, Canada.

I said to her, "Let's go back to your dream. What did They want to tell you through this dream? All the characters represent parts of you. There are as many men as there are women with knives. Both in your actions as well as in your emotional state, there is aggression, that is to say, too much sharpness. The spider and its web symbolize anxiety and the feeling of being imprisoned. Finally, when the voice of authority told you, 'Don't go there, you'll die,' you obeyed. You fled on your sled. In its negative aspect, snow represents solitude and coldness. The voice is that of a collection of old memories that are inciting you to run away rather than discover yourself. In a dream, when They speak of dying, it means that we have to be reborn to new states of consciousness. Therefore, new states of consciousness await you, but you flee them. In order to get to know them, you will have to face up to your inner aggression and your anxieties."

Then, I brought her back to the comments she made concerning school reform. I told her, "You told me that your students don't want this reform. Your students represent parts of you. You have students within you. You are being shown that your inner students are still making a lot of mistakes because this is just what our work consists of. It consists of correcting what is not right. Mistakes seem to upset you and you don't seem to accept them. It's as though there are too many of them for you. You still don't love truth enough. You feel the task is too much for you and you are giving yourself reasons to give up. You tell yourself, 'I can no longer do this job because this reform doesn't make any sense.' Angel CALIEL can help you to correct the message of this inner, authoritarian voice. It can ensure that it becomes right and that it stops inciting you to run away from the task of visiting your unconsciousness."

I added, "Personally, I've heard something different about the school reform from several teachers. Of course, this reform is far from perfect, but whenever we bring in changes, nothing is ever perfect immediately. One of the teachers, who talked to me about it, noted that a lot of emphasis is being put on the development of the students' competences. Following a conference on the reform, she said to the lecturer, 'If I've understood correctly, what you actually want to do is to develop the children's qualities and virtues.' She told me, 'They use the word *competence* instead of the terms *qualities* and *virtues*, but their goal is the same.'"

Thus, this other teacher who also works with the Angels applauds the present school reform. She left teaching for some time, taking several sabbatical years, not because she did not get along with the children, but because she did not get along with the other teachers. Now she is teaching part-time and, according to her, her students are her greatest teachers.

She told my husband and me, "Looking back, I realize that in my old reality I alternated between two extreme attitudes. At certain moments, I was imposing and I exerted my authority rigidly, as if I were saying, 'Hey! I'm the teacher.' At other moments, I tried to please the students."

Because she has changed her reality, she can no longer have this sort of behavior. She said to me, "I'm starting from scratch. When my former attitudes resurface and I feel distorted with my students, I take hold of myself. In any case, they reflect it back to me. I adapt.

It demands a lot of inner work, but I've never learned so much." For this woman, school has become an extraordinary place of application and of learning. She is relearning everything. When we give priority to qualities and virtues, and hold them as our one and only goal in life, everything changes.

This is a good example of humility and of the attitude that should be adopted with the children of the new Earth. We must both teach and be taught. If we are a parent, we must maintain this humility and say to ourselves, "Wait a minute. He's annoying me. He has just pushed one of my buttons. Yes! It's bothering me. I will come back to myself and calm down before exerting my authority. I will see more clearly. This way, I'll be able to discern whether I should intervene toward the child or whether he is simply reflecting my own faults." By doing this, we advance very rapidly. This is the new and forthcoming world. In fact, it is already here. We are now learning to live in this fashion and this is the way that prevails in more evolved worlds.

I'd like to tell you a final, true story. It deals with these children of the truth and it happened in a family where the father, the mother and the little boy work with the Angels. The mother was several months pregnant and she knew the baby was a girl. She was sent a dream. In it, *she felt stomach pains. Then, suddenly, she gave birth and she realized that she'd given birth to a beautiful little girl. The baby could talk and was teaching spirituality. She taught with great verve and enthusiasm. Then, the newborn's grandfather arrived and cut the umbilical cord. The father arrived also and the son was listening to the teachings.* The mother told me, "I don't know what she was saying, but I knew she was teaching spirituality."

This dream belongs to the category of dreams in which we visit the soul of another person. In this case, the soul that was going to be incarnated on Earth was manifesting itself and was showing its color. It's as if she were saying, "I have come for spirituality. That is my mission." Through the presence of the grandfather who cut the umbilical cord, she was being shown protection in daytime action. You can see that these children can present themselves in our dreams and already announce their program to us.

I have talked to you a lot about our daughter, Kasara. Today, I would like to invite her to come and tell you one of her dreams. Thank you, Kasara. Could you tell us your dream?

"Yes. *I am in a grocery store and a black cat is following me. Then, a little girl passes by. She takes the cat. I say to her, 'Watch out! It can bite.' Just then, the cat bites the little girl. Then, the cat jumps down and runs off and I chase after it, just a little way. Then, I come back. When the cat sees that I'm not running after it anymore, it comes back. It starts talking to me and says, 'I'd like to live with you.' I say, 'OK, but on one condition. You mustn't bite anybody any more. You must do poo-poo outside and you must listen to me.' Then, I woke up.*"

"It's a beautiful dream, Kasara! It is interesting and we are going to see what happened that day."

During the morning, we were getting ready to go out. We had been invited to spend the day with friends. At one particular moment, Kasara called out to her dad to ask him, "Could you help me choose my clothes?" He did. She was not completely satisfied with his choice and she begun sulking. He explained to her, "You know, it's cold today. These are the clothes that are suitable for you to wear." She put them on and went off into a corner to sulk. It really is not like her to sulk, because she is a very cheerful, enthusiastic little girl.

At one particular moment, her dad went over to her and, with a lovely smile, he said to her, "Kasara, your cat is biting you. Even if you aren't saying anything because, as you know, we can bite with our thoughts."

After a moment of surprise, she replied, "Daddy, it's stronger than me. I can't stop it."

"I understand," he said. "When we have a dream like that one, it's true that it isn't easy. I have had dreams like yours. I'll give you my trick. What do I do when this happens to me? I invoke an Angel. I repeat His name in my head. I breathe in the Angel's Name. You can use your Guardian Angel, Angel Menadel. You know Him well."

She gazed at him wide-eyed but made no comment. Later, I felt like giving her a little kiss. I found her in the bathroom. She was looking at herself in the mirror and talking to herself in a low voice. She had raised her little finger and was saying, "That's enough now! You are going to listen to me! You are in my head. That's enough!" (laughter) I withdrew. I could see that she was doing intensive inner work.

During the day, her bad mood went away. That evening, she told us that as soon as she would feel her bad mood resurface, she did her Angel Recitation with Angel Menadel. This, she said, was a lovely experience for her.

"What do you think, Kasara?"

"Oof! Angels! They work!" (laughter)

"Thank you. Thank you, dear initiate. Your sharing this with us helps us all a lot. Remember everyone, she is only seven years old."

Angel 23 Melahel
Medicine For The Soul

Where do we find the most pollution? In the earth, the air or in fire? The answer may surprise you. It is neither in the earth, nor in the water, nor in the air. It is in fire. To better understand this, we need to know that the four elements exist within the human being. Symbolically, earth corresponds to our physical body, water to our emotions, air to our thoughts, and fire to our spirit.

When a soul incarnates here on Earth, it arrives with baggage that contains both positive and negative experimentations from all of its different lives. It also arrives with a program that allows it to continue its apprenticeship in relation to good and evil and has as its eventual purpose their successful mastery. Working with the Angels accelerates our progress towards such mastery. This is called Enlightenment. This mastery, it must be noted, also gives us conscious access to our soul's program.

This evening we will study Angel MELAHEL, bearer of number 23. This Angel helps us depollute an unhealthy spirit that generates evil here on Earth. This Angel's action manifests itself at the individual level as well as at the collective level. It can be said that Angel MELAHEL is a soul Doctor, a Doctor for the conscience or a Doctor from Heaven. He helps us rediscover God's Universal Pharmacy. This Angel helps us diagnose our life and our conscience and gives us prescriptions. In other words, He prescribes behavior that will cleanse and make all of our dimensions healthy.

Here is a true story that someone told me. A doctor who is open to spirituality, and who works in a hospital, was seeing one of his patients. She was quite agitated when she arrived and she immediately recounted a dream that she had had. "Doctor," she said. "I dreamed that *there were two beige stains on my left ovary and I was told that they were cancerous.*" The doctor proceeded to do some tests but these revealed nothing abnormal. However, his patient was insistent. She said, "I know this dream is a premonition. You would have to pursue this and take X-rays." The doctor therefore took her to see a radiologist in that same hospital. He showed him his patient's file and waited while he studied it. Finally, the radiologist looked at him and said, "You haven't found anything. So why take an X-ray?"

The doctor asked his patient to explain to his colleague what her motivation was, which she did in great simplicity. She told him her dream. The radiologist gave a skeptic look that revealed what he thought of his colleague and as if to say, "You are wasting my time with this stuff." He took the X-ray just the same. A few days later, white as a sheet and quite agitated, he brought the X-ray to the doctor. When he arrived the doctor asked, "What's going on?" "The X-ray is showing two beige stains on the left ovary. But they are not malignant. They are benign."

This anecdote shows that we can have access to medical information above and beyond a simple diagnosis. We can also ask, "Why do I have to experience this illness?" In a case such as this one, the State of Consciousness of Angel MELAHEL will give us a Celestial diagnosis. Through a series of dreams and signs, He will show us erroneous behavior and parts of our being that are still anarchic, aggressive, or rebellious. He will also indicate the basis for such behavior, which, in fact, is a vast array of things left unsaid and an accumulation of repressed feelings. Angel MELAHEL will show us the true cause of the disease, which we must understand one day if we are to get better.

Angel MELAHEL does not only help to cure physical illness. He also treats whatever limits and restricts our soul. He cures us of everything that makes us suffer. Thus, the Angel Recitation with this Angel allows us to maintain high levels of consciousness while cleansing and healing our being of all its pain.

Here are a few comments on the Qualities of Angel MELAHEL, the main one being the *capacity to heal*. Among the 72 Angels, there are others who confer upon us this capacity to heal, but Angel MELAHEL touches on a very particular facet of healing, a facet that we can identify from His position in the Tree of Life. This Angel reactivates the intellect to allow us to diagnose and identify behavior and attitudes that create ill-being, soul sickness and, eventually, disease.

Knows the properties and virtues of medicinal plants. Sometimes, in herbal therapy, we talk of becoming a medicinal plant ourselves. What do we mean by this? Let's take an example by looking at the properties of burdock, one of several medicinal plants. One of the great therapeutic effects of this plant, which grows in heavy, badly drained soil, is this very capacity to drain. Burdock is a great depurative of the blood and skin. In other words, it cleanses. It is very useful in cases of eczema, psoriasis and acne because it helps eliminate toxins. It also decongests and cleanses the kidneys, the respiratory tracts and the sinuses. The Chinese have known about burdock for thousands of years. They use it, among other things, in cases of excess energy brought about by the presence of negative forces.

Where do these negative forces come from? They are generated by thoughts of criticism and by moods that pollute our spirit, like the sadness or anger that eventually affect our body. We shall see that our thoughts can be polluting. They act in a very powerful way on our body and on the whole of our being.

Certain herbalists and plant therapists accompany the plant throughout its lifecycle, from picking it to preparing it and, finally, to consuming it. If the person who does this chooses to work consciously, he enters the state of consciousness of the plant. For example, when he goes to pick burdock, he enters the state of consciousness of depollution, or of purging. The effect will be very strong. On the other hand, people who take the plant without being conscious of what they are doing simply because someone said, "Take this. It's good for you," will experience a far less powerful effect and, possibly, none at all. We can see how strong the influence of thought and mood is in the healing process.

In the introduction, we saw that pollution is found first and foremost in the dimension of fire or of the spirit, which is the inner domain. With a plant, there is an exterior element. By going deeper, however, and by meditating on its therapeutic virtues, we can gain access to great revelations.

Plants are truly our friends. Certain herbalists call them *the simple ones* because they are content to simply receive Heaven's beneficial effects. Let's have a look at camomile, a plant with a lot of therapeutic virtues. The more we stomp on this plant, the more it grows. What's more, it is said that taking a camomile elixir restores hope. Its little flowers are yellow, the color of confidence.

We bear the vegetable kingdom within ourselves. In other words, human beings possess all the virtues of plants and one day we must rediscover all of their therapeutic virtues. The vegetable kingdom, however, has a consciousness that is less open than that of a human being, so imagine what virtues a human being conceals! Even if a human being's intellect can help him attain very high levels of consciousness, it can also play great tricks on him. It can make him into one of the most destructive beings alive. Inspired by burdock and finding ourselves in a weighty environment where the atmosphere is heavy, we develop the opposite qualities. We transform the negative atmosphere by absorbing the evil and transmuting it.

The same goes for camomile. We can act or behave like this plant. Whenever it is trampled on, it does not complain by yelling, "Ouch! It's so hard! They're trampling me. All right then, I won't grow any more." (laughter) No. If we are inspired by camomile, others can stomp on us all they like but we will continue to grow. By imitating plants, we remain simple and open to a superior nature, to God and to the Great Cosmic Intelligence. In this way, we can continue to enjoy the therapeutic virtues of plants because we will have integrated them within ourselves.

Confronted with illness, we can adopt either of the following attitudes: fight it or welcome it. When we do not understand the true nature of illness, we tend to fight it. What is an illness? It is evil. In this teaching we learn never to fight evil. Evil is not to be fought. Evil serves Good and helps us understand the great principles, thereby allowing us to rectify our behavior and our erroneous concepts.

There are healing techniques based on positive affirmations. The person tells himself, "I want to get better and I'm going to get better." A person with a very strong will can heal himself using these techniques, but he incurs karma because he does not go to the root of the illness. He only wants concrete results. Up Above, They let him experiment with the strength of his willpower so that one day he can move on to other things. If this person has not understood the cause of the behavior that is the basis of his illness, it can come back again. It can come back in this life or in another, in the same form or in a different one.

On the other hand, if we welcome the illness instead of fighting it, we can ask Angel MELAHEL to help us diagnose the cause of it at the soul level. We ask, "Angel MELAHEL, help me diagnose the type of behavior that brought about this illness." Instead of focusing on physical healing, we concentrate first and foremost on healing our soul. Thus, we go directly to the source of the problem.

Of course, some of the suffering linked to illness is very intense. The person needs a reminder and the illness is there to make him understand that he must change his behavior while stimulating him toward a healing process.

One day, we no longer need this kind of stimulation. We are open, like the plants. We listen and we follow the guidance given. No matter what we experience, we continue to love and to emanate hope and love, whether or not the atmosphere is heavy and regardless of how often we get trampled on. This, however, requires substantial inner cleansing. Angel MELAHEL helps us through it.

In the spring, we do our spring-cleaning and we take depuratives. In the same way, we can use the Angelic State of Angel MELAHEL as a depurative for our conscience. This allows us to prepare for a new stage.

Let's continue to comment on the Qualities of this Angel, which include *pacifying and soothing, masters one's emotions* and *faith that anticipates Knowledge*. Angel MELAHEL confers a lot of calm upon us. We become very peaceful people. He also activates our intellect. A distorted intellect is one that criticizes and makes people aggressive towards others. When we find ourselves in a difficult emotional situation, we try to understand by asking Angel MELAHEL for a diagnosis and we remain in command of our own emotions.

Adapts to every situation. What a wonderful quality! The intellect has its little habits. Everything is fine and then, suddenly, something upsets its routine. Ah! Panic sets in. It is sometimes difficult for our intellect to adapt to new situations that are there to help us grow and advance. With this Angel, our intellect is ready for any situation. It is truly open to Guidance from Up Above. It continues to ponder, to discern, and to evaluate situations, but it does not panic because some of its habits need to be modified.

Healthy foods and crops. In this lecture on Angel MELAHEL, we will talk about several subjects concerning food. We will be doing Angelic dietetics, that is to say, we will discuss nourishment on the subtle levels. We will ask, "How does my soul nourish itself?" What we eat on the subtle level is very important. Because of the types of thoughts and emotions that dwell within us, we tend to lean towards a certain type of food on the concrete level. When we work with Angel MELAHEL, we are shown, in dreams as well as in our daily lives, whether our nourishment is natural or artificial. With this Angel, we also realize that we nourish others exactly the way we nourish ourselves.

Let's have a look at the distortions of the Angelic State of MELAHEL, which include *illness* and *disease*. Today we will see several examples of illness, including a contagious disease that affects animals. In each case, we will ask ourselves why these illnesses have to be experienced.

Difficulty improvising and expressing feelings. This distortion is the opposite of the Quality of adaptation that we saw earlier. We will talk about an experience that illustrates how Angel MELAHEL can generate a great inner release that can one day allow us to express all that we are. If we do not succeed in expressing ourselves, our energy is repressed. Once it is liberated, however, it does not always manifest itself in the most favorable manner.

Unhealthy thoughts and *a destructive and polluting mind.* This Angelic Energy cures destructive feelings and unhealthy thoughts and is useful in businesses where there is a lack of ethics. Today we shall see two examples of these distortions.

I'd like to talk to you about a dream that a man asked me to interpret. *He found himself opposite his two children, two boys who were about ten and eleven years old.* They were not his children in reality, because his boys are now grown-up. In the dream, however, he was told that they were his children. *At one particular moment, one of them caught fire and then the fire spread to the other boy. In a panic, the dreamer took a blanket, wrapped his two children in it and threw them onto the snow-covered ground. Then he saw a flame come out of his own forehead, and the fire that had reached his children went out. After that, he said to his two boys, "I wanted to protect you from the eternal fire."* He woke up.

As we have already seen, the characters in a dream all represent parts of ourselves. This is especially true in the first stages of our spiritual path. We examine what these characters represent to us. We analyze their personality and this allows us to interpret the message we have received.

In this dream, the children symbolized the dreamer's children. Children represent the way we are growing and learning. They are our potential achievements and our future. In this case, we could say that this man's children symbolize his concrete work since they were boys. Using them as characters, They wanted to tell this man, "Your future is starting to burn up. It is not the Eternal Fire that is present, but rather your destructive spirit. It is a part of yourself that is too extreme in its quest for truth and in the way it purifies itself. A great initiatory process has begun within you and you will have to learn to master the new spiritual forces that are being activated within you."

Of course, such a process can cause a person to feel troubled because he has stirred up old memories and set off a profound destructuring. It is not the Eternal Fire or God that burned this man's children in the dream. It is his destructive spirit that caused this situation. When he told his children that he wanted to protect them from Eternal Fire, he was misleading them. In reality, it was his own negative forces that were at work. These were emerging from his unconscious.

Every negative experience caused by our initiations, whether in our dreams or in our reality, comes from our own memories and our own experimentations with Eternal Fire. When we speak of God, imagine the Power of the Vibrations! As the little gods that we are, we must therefore learn to manifest and master these great Forces and Powers that dwell within us. We must, however, begin by learning. At the beginning of our path, it is perfectly normal to face such initiatory situations.

Under the influence of the fear caused by these trials, this man thought that God was responsible for his difficulties, but that was not the case. We ourselves create our trials and our misdeeds. They are part of the learning process. Through this dream he was being told, "You are putting the brakes on the greatest and most beautiful process that exists. You wish to stop your initiations because you believe that your trials come from God."

When we work with the Angels, we know that we can transcend the negative forces we have within. We know that we can rectify dozens of lives in one single life. It is therefore clear that, through this process, They set off extremely powerful forces. And it is indeed true that this can shake us up. I am warning you. The initiatory path is long and difficult. It is not accessible to everyone in his present lifetime.

Now, I would like to tell you the story of a lady who, along with her husband, has been working intensely with the Angels. This story, rich in meaning, illustrates what happens when we work with the Angels because it calls upon the Law of Resonance and it includes dreams and signs that we are going to interpret. For some months, this couple wanted to change their way of holidaying. They usually spent two weeks in a warm country during the wintertime.

When the time came to organize their holiday, they decided they would like to enroll in a self help course because they did not want to use this time to put their feet up and laze around, but rather to do intense inner work. The lady found out about certain courses. Then, They sent her a dream in which *she was told to go to Cuba*. However, to the couple's knowledge, there were no such courses offered in that country.

They went to Cuba and this lady told my husband and me what happened during their holidays. "Everything was fine," she said. "The hotel was lovely and the weather was hot. But there was one little drawback. We did get that course!" (laughter) What was this little disturbance? "Our hotel had three floors and our room was on the second floor," she explained. "Every morning at 6:39 a.m., I'd hear a bath running, followed by repetitive noises: *TIC-TIC-TIC-TIC-BRRR-BRRR-TIC-TIC-TIC-TIC*. Shortly afterwards, I'd hear the water flow down the pipes."

At one particular moment, when she looked up at the third floor balcony, the lady understood the morning scenario that bothered her so much. What was her neighbor doing? Every morning at precisely 6:39 a.m., she would run a bath, wash her underwear, take one garment, walk across the floor in her high heels, open the patio door, hang up the garment, return and fetch another. She would go back and forth several times.

Then, once her washing was done, she let the water out of the bath.

This ritual was annoying her. Her husband, however, was not annoyed in the least. As this woman follows the teachings of the Angels, she knows the Law of Resonance. She therefore did not want to deny that she was feeling annoyed. She felt like changing rooms and moving to the third floor. Before falling asleep, she asked, "Before changing rooms, I'd like to know why I am feeling annoyed. Is it a good idea to change rooms?"

That night, she was sent a dream. *She found herself in a hotel, in a Canadian city, where she takes courses on The Traditional Study of Angels. The lecture concerned work clothes. At one particular moment, she saw me change rooms. I was going to the Molson room and I said, "The entire hotel is undergoing renovations." There were little bits of debris on the floor and a volunteer was helping us vacuum it up. The room, which the workers were renovating, was very small but open. At one particular moment, the workers put up separating panels. Suddenly, the space became very narrow and cramped. The dreamer told the volunteer, "Stop vacuuming, we're leaving. We are changing rooms."* She woke up.

She understood that in the dream I represented her spiritual side, in relation with The Traditional Study of Angels. However, as she herself told me, changing rooms suited her just fine. She quickly equated that changing rooms means changing bedrooms. Without wasting any time, she went down to the reception desk with her husband. There did not seem to be any synchronicity, however. No room was available on the third floor. She went back to the reception desk to ask again the next day, and every day after that for two days. Finally, after a few days, and after she had forced things a bit, a room on the third floor became available. She said to me, "Ah! My second week was perfect. No more problems. So calm was it that, one night, my husband was awakened by the people in an adjacent room having intercourse, but I didn't hear a thing. This didn't disturb me at all." As far as she was concerned, the question was settled.

While she was telling me what she had experienced, at one point, she said, "At the moment I can't go for long walks because I sprained my ankle."

Then she added, "I consulted the list of situations at the end of your book. This list indicates which Angel to work with when we are going through certain problems or when we want to develop certain qualities. For a sprain, I saw that Angel MELAHEL, number 23, could be consulted."

"This is the very Angel that I am working with at the moment in preparation for next month's lecture." This is what happened.

Whenever I am preparing a lecture on an Angel, examples concerning that Angel are presented to me. It is so well synchronized!

She described how she got the sprain. "Back home from their holiday," she said, "when it was time to do the laundry, (laughter) I didn't feel like doing it right away. Even my husband was surprised because I'm a bit obsessive about the laundry, as he often tells me. The next day, I didn't feel like doing it either. He was surprised. He asked me, "Aren't you going to do the laundry?" "No," I said. "There's no rush.""

With the holidays over, this lady went back to work. She told me, "All of a sudden, right in the middle of the week, I felt an urge. I just had to go home and do the laundry from my holiday. My colleagues were surprised because usually I don't go home at lunchtime. They asked me, "Aren't you coming to lunch with us?""

"No. I have to go home and do my laundry."

"Is your laundry urgent?" (laughter)

She said to me, "Actually, I was in a hurry because I only had a certain length of time. I went off to do a few loads and towards the end of my lunch hour. I said to myself, 'I'll just do one last one before I go.'" While going down the stairs leading to the basement (*TIC-TIC-TIC-TIC-TIC*) she fell and sprained her ankle.

I asked her, "Do you see the link between this sprain and your holidays? Do you see any connection between your laundry and your hotel neighbor?"

"Well, no," she replied. "Not really."

Now that I am telling you the story, the events are linked together. When events occur where we ourselves are involved, it is not always easy to see the connection and to interpret the signs properly. That's OK. It is part of our apprenticeship. I said to her, "I'm going to give you a little Kabbalistic explanation. Let's go back to your neighbor and the Law of Resonance. You asked Them, Up Above, to give you a holiday program 'because I want a chance to do some inner cleansing.' They gave you first class conditions: the hotel, the beach, the sun and the whole set-up. But They also gave you a training experience, only a quarter of an hour every day, just enough time to do a bit of washing by hand."

This was the inner work that she had to do. While on holiday, she continued to do her Angel Recitation but did not quite understand the essence of what dwelled within her. I continued, "In your dream, the lecture I was giving was on work clothes. Up Above, therefore, They wanted to give you a job to do, that is, the laundry. They wanted to teach you a new method of washing, not with a new product or a new machine, but a method of washing yourself on the inside. Water touches the emotional side. Up Above, They wanted to help you depollute certain emotions that still dwell within you. Clothes represent the aura. They are beautiful if we express qualities and virtues, and they are torn and dirty whenever we are in a distortion. They wanted to show you a different way to purify yourself and to do your inner work. They wanted to lead you to new depths. You asked the Heavens, but despite your sincerity, you didn't immediately understand the task you were given."

That's OK. We must not be afraid and ask, "What if I don't interpret my dream or sign correctly?" If we are not meant to interpret it quite correctly, this has already been programmed. Such limits are part of our apprenticeship and they help us assimilate very profound lessons. We must dare to interpret. We do the best we can and, Up Above, They will continue to send us whatever we are in a position to receive.

This woman had asked in all sincerity, "Is it right to change rooms?" because she knew very well that when something bothers us, we must not ignore it. When we follow this teaching, we do not flee problems. She therefore asked Them to explain and to give her permission to change rooms. Since her request was spiritual, she received a spiritual symbol.

They wanted to tell her, "Look. Renovations in the hotel indicate work. They indicate improvements in the making. The hotel symbolizes the transitory aspect of a residence and of ourselves. You are in transition. You are renovating parts of yourself. These improvements are connected to the way you work spiritually and to the way you cleanse your aura."

In her dream, her spiritual aspect, which I represented, was moving into the Molson room. What is Molson? It is a brand of Canadian beer. Since beer is a liquid and therefore a symbol of emotions, They wanted to show this lady certain emotional aspects that needed to be changed. In this case, they were aspects surrounding emotional addictions.

The room, which was already small, became more and more cramped. The woman said to the volunteer, another symbol of her spiritual self, "Stop. We're leaving." This was a reflection of her way of reacting to what was going on within herself. Her situation was getting difficult and she decided to stop cleansing. This was a whole other dimension that she had not seen. She had interpreted her dream rather literally because it suited her to do so. She simply told herself, "My spiritual self is changing rooms. That means I can change bedrooms."

During the last week of the holiday, through the noise of the neighbors having intercourse, which, let me remind you, bothered her husband and not her, she was being shown that she did not have direct resonance with this particular incident. Her husband, on the other hand, represents her inner man while she represents his inner woman. Therefore, the two of them have a lesson to learn from both of the disturbances mentioned in this example.

This woman came to the lecture and heard me tell this story. I had already given her my interpretation, so it was nothing new. Right then and there, however, she realized a lot of things. She told me afterwards, "How true! My father used to drink beer and Molson was his brand. And of all the children, I'm the one who felt most upset that my father was an alcoholic."

What had They given her to work on during the holidays? They wanted to show her a different way to cleanse her inner depths. Because she did not get the message right away, and because she was sincere, They continued the lesson. Something was not right. Something was too rigid or too imprinted with discontent. Therefore, They presented her with another scenario. All of a sudden, in the office, old memories resurfaced. She said to herself, "I must go and do my laundry," even though it was not the right time to do it.

We interpret a sign the same way we analyze an element in a dream. The basement represents our unconsciousness and the ground floor symbolizes our consciousness. Therefore, They wanted to tell her, "Look. When you go down into your unconsciousness to cleanse your memories, you do not go about it in exactly the right way. You must modify your inner attitude."

In short, through her dream, she was being shown that she was in the process of purification but resisted when the going got tough.

With the sprain, she was being shown that her attitude would lead to difficulties for her.

During her childhood, if she had experienced difficulties due to alcohol, then she brought this karma from another life. People with alcohol addictions are people with very powerful emotional potential who have not learned to manage it properly. They treat their ill-being, or soul sickness, with exterior compensations that alleviate the inner suffering for a short lapse of time. You see, with simple resonance that lasts a quarter of an hour, we can discover important parts hidden within us. When we work with the Angels, seemingly trivial events that cause other people to say, "That example is too simple," can open up great depths of our unconsciousness. This is why the degree of resonance or disturbance is rarely proportional to the external event. An opening occurs that gives us a glimpse of memories that are not always very nice.

In the case of this lady, the fact that I appeared in her dream suited her just fine. It backed up her request to change rooms. Let me warn you, however. My husband and I can be used in your dreams to represent your spiritual self in relation to The Traditional Study of Angels, that is to say, we may appear luminous and full of love but we may also appear quite distorted. In this case, They are telling you, "Look at your inner attitude towards your spiritual life. You need to rectify this attitude."

When we are given a symbol that we feel is spiritual, it is very important to take it into account because what comes from Up Above descends into matter and touches all levels of our lives.

Like this lady, those who resist the process of inner cleansing and who really do aspire to purity in their hearts can develop an intense desire for external cleanliness. They create a mirror reflection of purity that will work for a short time. Of course, they soon become frustrated. The dog comes in and dirties the floor, the husband walks in with his boots, the children take out their toys and leave them lying around, and so on. The person does not get enough enjoyment from the cleanliness he has created and that his soul needs so much. The problem and true origin of his frustration is that he has invested all of his efforts on the outside only, while it is on the inside that he has to do the cleansing.

Cleanliness must, first and foremost, be found on the inside. Then, it can descend into the material world and we will no longer be upset when a child or anyone else moves things we have tidied up or dirties the floors. It will be easy for us to adapt. We will continue to show patience and love. We will understand the situation we are going through.

In this story, the situation in question was laundry, but the same idea applies in all sectors of life. In many cases, when we have not yet fully integrated this philosophy, we are in a rush to obtain the result in the physical world. Once we have obtained it, it becomes the subject of our affection or else it is defeated or destroyed. In both cases, we are destined for great frustration, which results in a spirit that pollutes our being and our soul.

I gave this woman the following advice: "From now on, when you do your laundry and you feel that these memories are resurfacing, memories that make you feel in a rush to have everything clean and to have the housework or the laundry done, try to become aware of your present thoughts and invoke Angel MELAHEL. Since They sent you the sprain as a sign, this Angel can help you understand a lot of things. Concentrate on putting another intention into your housework or your laundry. While you are invoking this Angel, say to yourself, 'It doesn't matter if what I'm cleaning is dirty again in five minutes. *Matter is temporal and educational.* This is an absolute Law. I'll take advantage of this opportunity to cleanse myself and to purify my emotions of all that caused my soul to be sick in the past, including my dirty and polluted waters.'"

Here is another very good example of how the Angels help us unite or fuse the masculine and feminine principles within us. Remember that the masculine principle is emissivity and the feminine principle is receptivity. In order to be able to read signs using the Law of Resonance, we must remember that, in simplified terms, a man has his inner woman and a woman has her inner man. We must try to associate our resonance to the principle being presented.

Someone asked me to interpret a dream. "I've just met a man," she said. "I asked Them if he was the right person for me." They sent her a dream. *She was standing in the street with her sister and, all of a sudden, she saw this man go into a funeral parlor.*

Since she could not interpret this dream, she asked in total sincerity for another dream. They sent her another one. *Once again, she was with her sister, who was taking her to a rendezvous with this man who had invited her for a coffee at the restaurant. She was being told that he was just passing through Québec City, where the dreamer's sister lives. When she finished her coffee, she asked the man to take her back to her sister's. He said, "No. You are staying here."*

She did not understand the meaning of the second dream. Unlike the first one, she had made a specific request so that They would open up a window on certain aspects of this man. Her sister represents part of herself and of her inner world. Since she appeared in both dreams, she is an important symbol. In any case, all symbols are important. We have to get used to understanding the essence of what people represent to us, in both their positive and negative aspects.

I asked her, "What does your sister represent to you?" "She has a great sense of direction," she said. "She never gets lost."

"Well then, in both these dreams, you were being shown that if you get involved with this man, you are going to lose yourself. In the first dream, the man went into a funeral parlor. He didn't go into a garden or a church. Why would someone go into a funeral parlor? To die or to say goodbye to the dead. They wanted to tell you, 'Let this relationship die.'"

Because she had not understood the first dream, in the second one, she was being told, "This man is just passing through." He had invited her to a restaurant. A restaurant represents socializing in a general rather than intimate sense. She was therefore being shown that their relationship or association was essentially on a social rather than intimate level. A restaurant is also a place where we receive food. It therefore represents physical resources, love and feelings, but again on a social level. What food did they share? They drank coffee. Coffee is a liquid. It therefore touches the emotional aspect of our being.

I said to this woman, "Coffee is a stimulant. In symbolic language, it indicates a tendency to force things and a desire to perform, that is to say, the desire to produce as much as possible in the material world, or the world of work. Therefore, in your attraction to this man, the material or financial side is central. They want to show you that within you, there is still financial insecurity and too much consideration for the material aspect. This is what stimulates you in this relationship. Then, when you want to find yourself again by returning to your sister's, home he says to you in a controlling manner, "No. You are staying here."

I asked her, "What do you feel for this man?" She said to me, "I find him very gentle, but it's true that something bothers me about him. He's a business man, and as you said about the dream, he's too attached to business."

Since her sister represents her capacity to find herself again, to make the right choices and to make good decisions, I added, "In both dreams, They are telling you, 'You are going to lose yourself if you take this relationship any further.'"

I added, "When you receive a reply to a request, you remain free to choose what suits you. You can therefore listen or not listen to the message. It won't change life Up Above. If you don't listen, it means you are going to experiment. On the other hand, if you do listen, if you follow your dreams, it is good. Just don't satisfy yourself by saying, 'They said no, so it's no.' Go further. Analyze what this man represents to you because he symbolizes part of your inner man. You were attracted to him. You were shown that you are still stimulated by an attachment to matter. Work on this part of yourself and do your Angel Recitation. If you don't, the next time you feel attracted to a man or one is attracted to you, it will be someone similar, someone who is too attached to matter. It might also be the complete opposite, that is, someone who rejects matter. Both these extreme manifestations have the same cause. They made you meet this man, even if you are now being asked to give him up. Use this encounter to understand aspects of your inner man."

Now let's have a look at where Angel MELAHEL is situated in the Tree of Life. He resides in the sphere called Binah. The Angels that dwell in this sphere bring us back to original matter. The spirit descends and takes on a structure, adopting the limits imposed by the laws of matter. In the dimension of the Sephirah Binah, however, the energies are still very subtle. This is why we speak of original matter.

As a symbol, the master planet of Angel MELAHEL is Saturn. Among other qualities, this planet represents perseverance, concentration and a sense of duty. The eight Angels residing in the Sephirah Binah lead us to the combustion room, or Eternal Fire, and to the powerful energy that burns everything that is not right within our being so as to enable us to reach original matter and rectify it. With these Angels, we can descend into absolutely every single one of our memories and reprogram them. The fact that Angel MELAHEL resides in the sphere of Binah means that His healing power acts on a very deep level.

The sphere in which the Angelic Energy MELAHEL expresses itself is the philosopher's dwelling of Hod, symbolized by the planet Mercury. It therefore relates to everything that touches the intellect. This Angel confers upon us many intellectual faculties, including a quick mind and the art of communication. He also provides us with the capacity to perceive our life-program with its borrowed scenario, that is to say, the way it manifests itself in our emotional and professional life and in other dimensions of our lives. All these qualities are those of a doctor of the soul. Angel MELAHEL helps us cleanse our memories at a very deep level, right down to the level of original matter. He bestows upon us the great faculty of discernment, which allows us to diagnose and identify erroneous behavior that needs to be modified.

I mentioned earlier that we would be talking about subtle nourishment and the profound significance of certain types of food. The following is the first example. This is the story of a man who began coming to the lectures about a year and a half ago. At that time, he came to see me at the break. He was working for a food company as a quality controller. What was the product for which he did quality control? Meat. He was the quality controller for meat.

This man continued to come to the lectures on a monthly basis and after two or three months he came back to see me at the break. He told me, "I've been fired. The atmosphere in the company was dreadful. It was an atmosphere of aggression. The problem dated from several months back. Finally, there was a conflict and I was fired."

Of course, this experience was difficult for him. He took a long sabbatical and used it to carry out intense inner work with the Angels. He came to understand a lot of things and he opened up to new dimensions, thanks in part to his dreams, which had become particularly frequent. After a year, he started looking for work. He did not really want to, but he knew how important it is to put all of our Knowledge and everything that we have received into practice. It is, in fact, part of this teaching. It is by applying what we have received that we can evaluate ourselves and see what is going on within us, especially at the unconscious level.

He was hired for a position that had been newly created. It once again involved quality control, but this time it was for fruit. Not just any fruit, however. He was hired to do the quality control for those little red berries that have such great therapeutic virtues: cranberries.

By returning to the workplace, he was putting himself in a position to evaluate how far he had come on the spiritual path since his dismissal. Another person might have said, "I've done a whole lot of work on myself and here I am right back in a similar situation." Of course, this man was still a quality controller. He was, however, able to note a distinct improvement. The atmosphere was better. His new job was going to give him a new life experience.

On the other hand, he was facing the same problems of communication. This man has difficulty expressing his feelings. We saw that *difficulty improvising and expressing feelings* is one of the human distortions associated to Angel MELAHEL. He therefore represses things. When he does express himself, his energy sometimes comes out in a rather rude and authoritarian manner. The challenge of working on certain thought patterns was proposed to him again, but the general context was more favorable. Thanks to his newly acquired consciousness and the new tools he had acquired, that is, the analysis of dreams, the Law of Resonance, and the reading of signs, everything was a bit easier for him.

At one particular moment, he came to talk to me about what he was going through. He told me, "Now I have a problem. My employers have discovered a large quantity of cranberries that had been forgotten in a freezer for two years." Of course, it had nothing to do with him as he had only been working there a short while. "But recently," he said, "a customer signed for a large order from the company and management wants me to slip in this forgotten batch. As the customer wants a particular size of packaging, the company has to repack the cranberries in another format. Management wants to take advantage of this to change the packaging date on the old cranberries."

He pointed out to me that the date inscribed on the packet is not the date on which they were picked but it is indeed the day the product is packed. This is the way it is done in a lot of companies. He said to me, "It's fraud. The date for that batch goes back two years and they want to put today's date." This man felt ill at ease with this fraudulent intention. He told me, "I've done that before when I was a meat controller. At that time, I wasn't alert and I didn't entirely understand the importance of doing the right thing. Now it seems that Heaven is serving me up the same dish. What should I do?"

We discussed the situation. I said to him, "In this teaching, we have great respect for others' reality and their rhythm of change. It is a teaching that invites us to marry spirit with matter, or to spiritualize matter. If we want to change everything too quickly, we cannot live in society. We have to withdraw and then we cannot have an effect on matter. On the other hand, if we commit an act ourselves, even if we've been told to do so by our boss, we have to answer for it and so we tote up karma for ourselves. We also have to answer for the human laws if the fraud is discovered. If we did it in the past when we weren't aware of the significance of our act, we still create karma, but to a lesser degree because of our ignorance."

I told him a story from my own personal experience. "I too was in this situation a few years ago," I said. "I was working in a Swiss bank and, several times, I was asked to do certain things and I invariably refused. This is where it is important to speak correctly, that is to say, without aggression and without wanting to put things right by using aggression. Each time, I refused very gently but very firmly. I'd say, 'Because of my principles, I can't do that.' They knew that what they were asking me to do wasn't right. Once I even replied, 'If you really insist on my doing this, I'll resign because I simply can't do it.'"

This man felt the same way. I added, "The role of a quality controller is not only to ensure physical quality. He must see to ethical quality as well." In the distortions of Angel MELAHEL, we saw *corrupt feelings and undertakings*. It is very important that the quality travel from Up Above to down below. I continued, "When you begin to take on such a position, of course, you must be ready for anything. It's a test. Because you have already committed an act that was wrong, you must assume responsibility for the karma. You are being put back in a situation in order to settle things. It is a great opportunity for the evolution of your soul. It's extraordinary. It's up to you to decide. But expect anything. We don't know what your Program is and what the result of your decision will be. You must be aware that this attitude could lead to dismissal."

Later, when I saw this man again, he told me, "The day that I went to see the accountant (it was the accountant who was organizing the whole thing) I was holding the Angel MELAHEL card in my hand and I was pacing up and down the corridor." This experience was difficult for him. He already finds it difficult to express himself, and now he had to go against the management's decision. He told me, "I was invoking Angel MELAHEL, doing my Angel Recitation and breathing in. This gave me the courage to go and speak to him. I expressed myself very well. The accountant said, 'I'll have to call the boss because he's on a trip.'"

The accountant came back and repeated what the boss had told him. "No," he had been told. "We are proceeding. We are putting today's date." This man continued to follow his ethical path. He sent a letter to his boss. It was a nice letter that said, "You are the boss and you decide. But I'd like to specify that I don't approve of this practice. I withdraw from this action."

He told me, "Whenever I would pass the accountant in the hallway, he wouldn't dare look at me. He'd fix his eyes to the floor. Nobody said a word to me about my message to the boss. I did, however, get a letter in which I was offered more responsibility and a salary increase!" He just couldn't get over this and a great big smile showed exactly how he felt. I said to him, "This is it. Heaven supports you. Whenever we do the right thing, we are upheld and supported by all of Heaven." In this particular incident, things went well but the boss's reaction could have been the exact opposite. That too would have been correct.

Let's learn from the example concerning this man to talk about the symbolism of professions. At first, this man controlled the quality of meat. Meat belongs to the animal kingdom. We saw that we have the vegetable kingdom within ourselves and also the animal kingdom that represents our needs, our vital energy and the laws of the jungle, or aggression. One day, we have to transcend our inner animal kingdom so as to preserve our vital energy in its purest state. On the first page of our personal history, however, our life centers around the satisfying of our needs. An animal has no altruistic conscience in the objective sense of the term. It is a consciousness that perceives and acts for its survival and for the survival of its kind.

It was no coincidence that this man had been led to this profession. Unbeknown to himself, he was controlling the quality of his animal kingdom. Because it was meat, and because the animals are dead, it goes without saying that the animality in his energy was still predominant. At the time, while not yet aware of it, he was doing this job because of his inner need to control the quality of his animal kingdom. The work he did on his inner self changed things and he found himself controlling the quality of fruit. Each fruit has a particular significance. A cranberry is red. This is the first color in the visible spectrum and in the rainbow. It represents willpower and matter. What's more, given its function as cleanser of the kidneys, the cranberry represents the purification of one's being. The new job was therefore announcing to this man that he was entering a new phase of great physical purification.

You see, we can understand the essential through symbolism. Each profession, each type of company we happen to work for, and the type of product we handle or transform, all of these facts are precious when it comes to analyzing how far our soul has come and which path it must take.

We saw that one of the distortions related to Angel 23 MELAHEL is *illness and disease.* These last few weeks there have been reports in the media on an important contagious disease called Foot and Mouth Disease. How can we understand this disease? I shall give you two types of explanations based on what the agricultural food experts say and a symbolic analysis that will help us understand the root cause of this disease.

Foot and Mouth Disease affect certain animals. It is called Foot and Mouth because these animals get ulcers in their mouths and between their hooves. Agricultural food experts attribute the occurrence and propagation of this disease to two relatively recent practices that have become widespread. The first is the recycling of dead animals to make cattle food. The animals eat their ilk. These domestic animals have always been herbivorous. In the past, nature took good care of things. When an animal died, it would decompose in the environment. With the recycling of meat in cattle food, the flesh of the animals that died from disease finds itself in the food chain of its species.

The second practice that has been exposed is the centralization of slaughtering. The animal is now transported from the farm to a gigantic slaughterhouse on a journey that can often cover long distances. Of course, an animal has a consciousness. It does not have a human consciousness, but it does have a certain consciousness.

Specialists attribute the propagation of the disease to the fact that animals from different origins are treated in the same building. Previously, when there were small slaughterhouses, livestock was treated separately. If a disease was detected, the animals affected could easily be separated from the healthy ones, thus contagion was avoided or at least limited. I read in a serious article on this subject that a hamburger can now contain meat from one hundred different animals.

These harmful practices are, of course, linked to the globalization of the world's markets. This is not necessarily a bad thing in itself. If the people who manage things do not have an evolved consciousness, it is their states of distorted consciousness that multiply. We then find ourselves with a globalization of distortions. However, it remains experimentation and we have to consider globalization as evolutionary in the long term.

Human beings have only just begun to open up their consciousness. One day, human beings will realize that orienting the world's diet towards the consumption of meat has knocked the Earth's biological clock out of order. Animals consume a great part of the cereal that is harvested and this contributes directly to the impoverishment of developing countries. For this reason, vegetarianism will be the food solution of future generations. Moreover, people will have understood that consuming animal flesh corresponds to eating the thoughts and emotions of animals. A vegetarian, by this very fact, becomes less aggressive and instinctual. We become what we eat.

Vegetarianism has other advantages. For example, it makes it easier to dream and to have out-of-body experiences. Meat requires at least forty-eight hours to be completely digested by our organism. Its consumption therefore limits the energy flow necessary for subtle experiences. This is why initiates opt for vegetarianism, or non-violent and intelligent food. If everyone were a vegetarian, there would be enough food to feed the world.

The attitudes that have caused the deregulation are due to a lack of consciousness. The lure of profit and the attachment to matter end up upsetting all of the natural cycles. The consequences are very real but also beneficial. Diseases such as Foot and Mouth Disease and Mad Cow Disease will gradually lead people to adopt a vegetarian diet. This is why we should not exclaim, "Oh my God!" and develop existential anguish. Such diseases are a purging implemented by Cosmic Intelligence to bring human beings to modify their consciousness.

In terms of consciousness, if a purging of the animal kingdom is taking place in the concrete world, it reflects the purging of this kingdom in humans. This is no coincidence. It is always the superior dimension in terms of consciousness that has an impact on the less evolved dimension. The purification of the animal parts of human consciousness consists in the purification of our needs, our sufferings, and our fears. Fear is an animal instinct. One day, when we have reached high levels, fear will no longer exist. Foot and Mouth Disease is a sign of the times that indicates a great purification at this level. This is an example of a diagnosis. If every human being got used to diagnosing in this way while doing the necessary spiritual work, things would change. We would be heading for a better world. But before we can hope to obtain mass changes, we have to begin by transforming ourselves. As more and more individuals change, the community as a whole will change naturally.

Let's continue with the topic of food. More specifically, let's discuss Angelic dietetics of the subtle worlds. In our dreams, we can be led to understand certain associations. For example, in one of my dreams where They revealed to me the behavior of someone I know, *I was shown this person coming towards me and asking me for chewing gum. I began to do an in-depth reading of this person. All of a sudden, I saw her with her hands cut off.* In dreams or in a negative scene, when a person is chewing gum, it means that he is ruminating, or brooding over the past. We can brood over the same subject for hours and hours.

A few days later, my husband, Kasara and I were in a room where I was going to be giving a lecture. On the edge of a table, Kasara found some red chewing gum. She asked me, "What does chewing gum symbolize?"

"If it's positive, like good, sugar-free chewing gum, it makes us think of fresh breath, or of something that promotes communication with others. Most of the time, however, when we see a person chewing gum in a dream, it's because he is chewing the same idea or worry over and over again. It's the same idea in the concrete world. Since this one was red, it concerns matter and willpower."

Kasara then went to another part of the room where there were a few volunteers. She told them she had found a piece of chewing gum and what this represented in symbolic language. At that moment, someone interrupted and asked, "But why matter?" I explained, "Because the chewing gum she found was red, a color that symbolizes matter, among other things."

I knew exactly why this person had asked that question. My dream concerned her. At the beginning of the day, she had received some news that brought on worries that she might lose her job. She was truly in the grips of deep insecurity. Throughout the day, we could feel this in her presence, even if she did not talk about it. This is an energy that we can feel. Through my dream, I had been told, "Look at what happens when a person broods. He loses his capacity to act. His hands are cut off. He can therefore no longer give or receive. He cannot even manifest himself any longer."

When we have a distortion or a problem, we think about it. That, however, is not the same as brooding. When we are in the process of thinking about something, we think in the light of the Great Laws. We say to ourselves, "OK. The Law of Resonance is at work. I have been given this sign. It is to help me avoid being too attached to matter and basing my feeling of security on it." We then do our Angel Recitation. If we plunge into insecurity and we brood over it, however, we cut ourselves off from any possibility of manifesting ourselves and finding hope again.

This is what constitutes working with the Angels of the Kabbalah. We receive very profound teachings through very simple elements. We are given a dream that tells us, "Look what this generates on the energy level." In the dream, we do not say anything. The following day, however, we can feel and recognize the energy of the dream. Then, we are given concrete confirmation of the dream, such as the discovery of some chewing gum under the table. All the elements are there and graciously provided by Heaven.

Thus we learn to penetrate great depths to better sense, feel and understand the nature of the Parallel Worlds. One day, we succeed in seeing through form and reading directly from those parallel worlds. An opening occurs. Of course, this cannot happen if we continually brood over the past without seeking to accept it as a page in our history. If a person is under the impression that he lacks something, it means that he is incomplete on the inside.

Here is a final account concerning food. A person told me her dream.

She was selling chocolate bars. All of a sudden, she noticed an insect on top of the shelf. She took the bar on which there was a mosquito and made sure there were no more mosquitoes on the other bars of chocolate. Then, she asked a young woman who was standing beside her, "Can I clean the chocolate with bleach?" to which the young woman answered, "That's out of the question! Here, cleaning with bleach is forbidden. We clean with soap and water."

Chocolate represents sweetness. Because they fly in the air, mosquitoes symbolize thoughts. Through this dream, They wanted to tell her, "Look. We have sent you sweetness. We are feeding you sweetness. There are, however, mosquitoes flying around. Certain types of thoughts arrive, and oops! They take away your gentleness and you want to use bleach." As this person is on a spiritual path, her first reaction was to take away the mosquito and clean everywhere it had been. Bleach, however, is a very strong and abrasive product. She was therefore told, "No bleach." Of course we may say, "Yes, but we have often heard that the Angels are powerful stuff!" At certain times, bleach is indispensable, symbolically speaking. We must, however, always purify ourselves with love, otherwise rigidity sets in. This is the essence of the message They wished to transmit to this woman through her dream.

When we cleanse our inner world, we can encounter zones that are unpleasant. Sometimes, they might even be extremely filthy. It is, however, extraordinary that we end up embracing even that.

What makes us want to use bleach? We do it because of pride, because when we touch on something that makes us exclaim, "Ugh! That's not nice," we undermine ourselves. We would like for everything to already be clean. We want to control the rhythm of the cleansing process. Therefore, pride and an excess of willpower is at the heart of the matter.

We can imagine that the beginning of an initiatory path is very powerful because we are cleansing lives upon lives. We may touch on burdened memories within us. We accept the evil we are shown, however, and we cleanse it. We say to ourselves, "This is what I've got to live through today. I won't try to reach the summit right away. I accept the program God has given me. He knows why I'm going through this, even if it's a terrible or difficult experience. I don't know everything about myself. I don't yet know my entire Program. I'm discovering it day by day."

Unless chocolate is made from natural ingredients, it is not a symbol of quality food. This is because it contains refined sugar. The more natural the food, the more it symbolizes quality. For instance, maple syrup and honey are quality sweeteners.

In general, if we are being shown chocolate in a dream, They are telling us, "We are gently stimulating you." Up Above, a Guide is stimulating us. When we dream of food, we can feel it right down into our physical body because the energy is coming down from the energy dimensions into the concrete level of matter. Thus, when we receive chocolate in a dream, it means, "We are regulating your emotional lack right now so that you won't get too depressed. You are going through a difficult phase at the moment. We are therefore sending you a little sweetness and energy to help you get through this."

We do an in-depth analysis of the symbolic significance of each type of food we are given in a dream, that is, those that nourish our soul as well as our body. The symbolic meaning can be positive or negative. It all depends on the type of food and whether it is good or bad for our health.

One day, a woman came up to me and said, "I was eating cat in my dream." In symbolic terms, a cat has good aspects. In this particular case, however, it represented the negative character of the animal, that is, its dualistic, hypocritical and overly independent aspects. She added, "Oh! I felt so bad the next day!" A particular inner part of hers had been touched upon. A hypocritical and dualistic part had been reactivated to give her the opportunity to rectify it.

It is very important to know what kind of nourishment we are absorbing in the subtle dimensions. Needless to say, in this teaching, we target what is the most natural. A healthy spirit aspires to the best food possible. In the concrete dimension, the best food is natural and organically grown. This also holds for the symbolism in dreams. In accordance with the Law that says everything comes from Up Above and descends to the physical level, however, if the person who eats only organic food has not done a spiritual cleansing and continually criticizes, all is wasted. His body becomes acidified and so we can no longer talk of a healthy body. The body may be healthy while the person is still young. Sooner or later, however, health problems will arise.

Of course, even if it is best to do so, it is not always possible to eat only organic food. We have to adapt to our environment because otherwise we become recluses and we cannot do anything. However, we can perform alchemy with our thoughts and our spirit. Everything first comes from the way we think and the kind of nourishment our thoughts and feelings absorb. Then, in a second phase, we nourish our body with more and more natural and healthy food. We must find a balance between the concrete possibilities and the ideal well-being.

Before moving on to another example, let's have a look at some major symbols.

⊙

The Interpretation of the Major Symbols: Elements, Colors, Characters and Other Symbols

In the beginning, the symbolic language that allows us to interpret dreams and signs may seem a bit vague. This is only because it is new. When we learn a new language, at first, we have to translate every word and make associations. Eventually, we succeed in thinking in the new language. In the same way, when we learn the language of symbols, we have to meditate daily in order to establish the connections between the symbols and their meaning. There comes a time, however, when interpretation is easy and natural.

The four elements, that is to say, fire, air, water and earth, play a key role in the structure of symbolic language. They define four main categories that can be associated with the majority of the other symbols. By becoming familiar with symbolic language, we realize that the Universe finds its perfect reflection in the human being. In fact, we realize that materialization is simply the creation of states of consciousness whose only goal is the development of qualities, virtues and powers in their purest form. Since the four elements are omnipresent in dreams and signs, we shall pay particular attention to their meaning. We shall then see how other symbols fit in.

Fire symbolizes the spirit or the soul. It represents Angelic Energies, the Primordial Creative Fire. Angels make us work in the world of fire so that the fruit of this work can materialize here on Earth. Thus, on the manifestation level, fire represents vital energy, or the abundance of energy contained within a person, along with will-power. The oven and the fireplace serve to contain fire. Therefore, when they are lit, they represent the alchemical process by which the energetic and spiritual transformation is accomplished. If the fire burns constructively, for example, by giving out a warm, comforting heat, it shows that our vital energy is harmonious. If, however, we see a fire raging through the environment, it indicates a destructive spirit, that is to say, a critical or aggressive energy.

Air symbolizes the world of thoughts. The movement of the wind, for example, represents our thoughts on a dynamic level. The same goes for airplanes, birds or mosquitoes. The nature and behavior of anything connected to the dimension of air gives us indications concerning our manner of thinking.

Water symbolizes feelings and emotions. For example, if we see a fish in a dream, its behavior shows us what we are experiencing on the emotional level. Likewise, the position or the movement of a boat shows us the level of our emotional stability. If we see troubled waters, the next day, we may experience unsettling or unpleasant emotions.

Earth represents our physical body and action in the physical world. All objects and all beings that are connected to the Earth, including animals, trains, houses, cars, chairs, tables, and the list goes on, represent, each in their own fashion, the way that we manifest ourselves and the stage of our apprenticeship at the physical level.

All combinations of the elements are possible. For example, the smoke of a cigarette is the combination of the elements of air and fire. In a dream, we may see ourselves, or someone else, smoking a cigarette, even if we have never smoked before. This means that They want to tell us, "Your thoughts are smoky. Your intellect is cloudy. The sun, which represents fire, or the spirit, cannot communicate with your heart and manifest itself through your actions."

Once we have interpreted the elements, we have to identify the other components of the dream, including objects and characters, with regard to their interaction with these elements. If our house is on fire, the meaning will be different than if our car is in flames.

Fire, air, water and earth form the context in which the scene takes place, while the other components fit in. Here is an example. What does a leaking roof mean? A roof symbolizes the intellect because it constitutes the top part of a house, just as our head is the top part of our body. If this appears in a dream, it means that They are showing us that there is something to be rectified or understood at the level of our intellect. Water, as we have just seen, represents the world of emotions. If we see a leaky roof, it therefore shows us that our emotions are confusing our thoughts. Unless we quickly rectify this situation, it may have a negative impact on our actions or on material aspects of our lives.

In a dream, everything is interconnected. A dream is like a sentence or an algebra equation and the symbols that appear in it are all interconnected. If we neglect to consider a symbol in our interpretation of a dream, it will be less precise, or even wrong. However, even if we have the impression that we have forgotten some details, what we remember is sufficient to carry out an analysis and to understand the message sent to us. In other words, we will still find enough matter for reflection on the behavior that we need to change or on the virtue that we are being invited to develop.

The same method of interpretation and the same symbolism applies to signs. A sign, however, only exists in relation to what we are thinking when it presents itself. It is a reply to a question that we have already asked. Our consciousness is in constant communication with the Divine. It is an integral part of the great Cosmic Computer and it directs us in our environment according to the contents of our thoughts. Despite appearances, earthly reality is just as virtual as dreams. The only difference, given the time required for the process of densification, is that physical manifestation occurs later. The forces we observe in our dreams and in the Parallel Worlds precede earthly manifestation.

Colors. Colors also play a fundamental role in the interpretation of dreams and signs. The symbolic meaning of a color can be positive or negative depending on what it emanates and what it evokes in each person. Thus, pure and bright colors are essentially positive symbols, while colors that evoke sadness, that is, dull, faded, grayish colors, or those that appear dirty, along with those that are aggressive or imposing, such as overly bright and fluorescent colors, are essentially negative symbols.

Upon becoming familiar with what follows, you will notice that the symbolism of colors is intimately related to the chakras.

From a positive symbolic point of view, the color white represents spirituality, purity, wisdom and Divine Power. In its negative aspect, it represents impurity, lack of wisdom, religious fanaticism and all forms of abuse of power in the name of spirituality. Generally speaking, the color black represents materiality and occult powers. From a negative point of view, it represents unconscious death, evil powers, a materialistic mind and unconsciousness in general. Of course, black also has a positive symbolic meaning, which is the hidden aspect of things in the name of wisdom, materiality (the spirit is hidden in matter) and occult powers that are used for pure or enlightened purposes.

From a positive point of view, the color gold represents Divine materialization. From the negative point of view, it symbolizes the desire for material possessions, avarice and pride. From the positive point of view, the color silver represents receptivity and internalization. From the negative point of view, it symbolizes lack of receptivity and black magic.

From a positive point of view, purple represents unity, spiritual understanding, fulfillment and the capacity to dream. In its negative aspect, it symbolizes uncertainty, the absence of a precise goal, separation, atheism and the rift between matter and spirituality. The color indigo represents clairvoyance, clairaudience, and clairsentience. In its negative aspect, it symbolizes the use of psychic powers for personal gain, the desire for material possessions, atheism and mental confusion.

From a positive point of view, blue symbolizes communication, sincerity and profound joy. In its negative aspect, it represents difficulty of expression, rough and vulgar language, a wily attitude and a deceiving mind. Green symbolizes love, affection, compassion and joy. In its negative aspect, it represents the feeling of not being loved, emotional insecurity and emotional dependence.

From a positive point of view, yellow represents authority, confidence, optimism, radiance and harmony. From a negative point of view, it symbolizes authoritarianism, rebellion, inner agitation, dissatisfaction, frustration, lack of self-esteem, repression, control and the desire to conquer. The positive symbolism of the color orange is purity, sexual transcendence, Divine pleasure and a love of life. Its negative symbolism represents a lack of refinement, an instinctual attitude, sexual addiction, vulgarity, sexual abuse and other problems related to sexuality.

From a positive point of view, red represents willpower, materialization, a profound link to Earth and its creatures, vital energy, stability, primordial confidence and creative action. From a negative point of view, this color symbolizes excess, anger, intimidation, a competitive spirit, excitement of the senses, lust, animality, violence, financial and material insecurity, exploitation and the lack of vital energy.

From a positive point of view, brown symbolizes matter and indicates a deep link with Earth. From a negative point of view, it represents a spirit that centers exclusively on matter. From a positive point of view, grey represents preparation for wisdom. From its negative point of view, it represents half-heartedness and confusion between good and evil.

We find the symbolism of combined colors by combining their respective symbolism. Turquoise, for instance, which is a mixture of blue and green, takes its positive symbolism from the synthesis of the positive aspects of blue, that is, communication, sincerity and profound joy, and green, which represents love, compassion and affection. Thus, this combined color represents warm-hearted, authentic, intuitive communication, or communication that comes from the heart. Likewise, turquoise gets its negative symbolism from the synthesis of the negative aspects of blue and green. Therefore, the negative aspect of turquoise will be communication centered on the satisfaction of personal and selfish expectations or desires.

Other symbols. We often encounter our father or our mother in dreams. Whether they are deceased or not, in most cases they constitute important archetypes. The father represents what happens in the daytime and how the dream will materialize in the physical dimension. The mother represents what happens during the night, that is to say, in our inner world. She is also associated with a person's emotional dimension. Her appearance in a dream gives us indications on the state of our inner world. This symbolism extends to the entire masculine-feminine theme. In other words, a man in a dream represents what happens in the daytime and in our actions, while a woman represents the inner world and emotions.

All the men that a woman encounters represent facets of her inner man, and all the women she encounters symbolize aspects of her personality. Likewise, all the women a man encounters represent facets of his inner woman, and all the men he comes into contact with symbolize aspects of his own personality.

If a boy appears in one of our dreams, even if he is not our own child, he symbolizes the apprenticeship that our inner child is going through in the world of exterior action. If a girl appears, she represents the apprenticeship that our inner child is going through in the inner world and the world of emotions. Children also symbolize our accomplishments and our potential evolution.

It is important to understand that all the characters in a dream serve to represent parts of ourselves, unless we are visiting someone else's soul. Even in such a case, the people presented still symbolize aspects of our soul. The study of symbolic language leads us to realize that everything that exists on the outside is also to be found within ourselves, and that a man and a woman have both a masculine and a feminine pole within themselves. Indeed, this is why we can be reborn in other lives as either a man or a woman.

When we see someone that we know in a dream, we have to ask ourselves what this person represents to us. The answer to this question reveals hidden traits of our personality and the person in question symbolizes specific facets of ourselves. If we do not know the person, we try to find the part of ourselves that he could represent. Hence, a doctor will symbolize our capacity to heal ourselves. If we dream about our own brother and he has a drinking problem, this indicates memories linked to emotional dependency. Since alcohol is a liquid, it is linked to emotions. This interpretation is valid even if we do not consume alcohol ourselves.

What is certain is that it is always possible to find the meaning of a character because when we receive a symbol, we invariably hold the key. We are the only person to hold this key and that will help us decode the dream. In our workshops, when a person talks to us about a character in a dream, we ask what his perception of that character is. In other words, we ask what that character represents to him or her so as to integrate this symbolism into the general meaning of the dream.

In order to properly interpret a dream, we must first analyze each symbol separately before any summary can be done.

In a dream, as in reality, everything exists first and foremost as a state of consciousness or as a psychological dynamic. This also applies to objects. For example, what does a chair represent? A chair allows us to rest. It puts us in a state of receptivity but it can also make us lazy. Therefore, rest and receptivity represent a positive symbol of the chair, while idleness represents a negative symbol of the same object.

Through meditation, we manage to discern the meaning of each symbol. With practice, it becomes easier and easier to interpret dreams and signs. For instance, when a chair appears and we know what it means. All we have to do now is determine whether it represents something positive or negative using the other components of the dream.

I would now like to tell you a dream that my husband was asked to interpret during a workshop on dreams. This example allows us to see, once again, the symbolism applied to ovens, plants and food. This is the dream of a woman who has been working with the Angels for some time now. *She could see herself in a room surrounded by plants. Then, I arrived and I whispered gently in her ear, "Put more water in your plants." Next, she was in a kitchen. My husband was there, all dressed in white. The kitchen was white and there was a black table in it. Two small children were sitting on a stove that was not lit. The children were unruly, and the dreamer felt annoyed with them. My husband saw that she felt annoyed by these two unruly children. At one particular moment, he opened the door on a freezer where he found a disproportionately large block of meat. Then he said to the woman, "I've been trying for eight lives now."*

My husband interpreted her dream. First of all, he said, "As you know, all the characters in this dream represent parts of you. Here, Christiane and I represent your two spiritual principles, that is, the inner and the outer principles of The Traditional Study of Angels. You've been given a diagnosis and you've been shown what you need to change in order to heal your soul. The first stage of your dream concerns water, or emotions, and love. This is the domain represented by plants. Therefore, your inner spiritual principle is telling you, 'Add more water and love when you do your inner work. Rigidity is drying up your life.'"

He continued, "The kitchen is a place where things are prepared for eating. Symbolically speaking, it is a place to renew our energies in the world of action. White, or the color of the kitchen and the clothing, represents spirituality. The table, on the other hand, was black. Black can symbolize a negative or unveiled characteristic, but it can also represent matter. As for the table itself, it is a symbol of realization and of sharing. Thus, They wanted to show you what limits your spiritual evolution."

My husband went on to explain, "The unruly children sitting on the stove also symbolize parts of you. They represent your inner children. Their spirit, represented by the oven, is stimulated not to listen. This indicates that you are not disciplined enough when you do your spiritual work."

Her spiritual principle in daytime action, symbolized by my husband, was opening the freezer door. This means that a door was being opened onto her unconsciousness. A freezer is used to preserve food for a long time. A refrigerator does the same, but not for as long a period of time as a freezer. Thus, she was being shown that she had an accumulation that had been there for eight lives, represented by the enormous block of meat. It concerned the animal kingdom, suffering, fear and aggression. This is what she needed to transform. This woman has been searching, but she has been going around in circles for eight lives, because her instinctual and animal side has not been transcended.

Since the block of food was frozen, it indicates that this lady is lacking in love. She is much too rigid in her way of being spiritual. Since this woman follows the teaching of the Angels, this dream is showing her that she needs to do her Angel Recitation much more assiduously, otherwise she will continue to stagnate for several more lives at the spiritual level. In the dream, my husband did not say to her, "You have been trying for eight lives." Instead, he said, "I have been trying for eight lives." As a man, he represents daytime and action. This means that despite her tremendous spiritual potential, this woman cannot seem to materialize her spirituality. Therefore, through this dream, They were telling this woman, "If you wish to one day reach the stage of incarnating your spirituality into matter, you must do your Angel Recitation much more assiduously and you must cleanse the memories linked to instincts."

This dream is a wonderful gift aimed at helping this woman. Without discipline and constancy in our spiritual work, it is impossible to attain Enlightenment because the path is long and difficult. It is important to remember this.

Angel MELAHEL relates to all activities that favor healing and well-being. In all the different types of treatment where the body is touched, whether it be osteopathy, chiropractic, massage, lymphatic draining or energy healing, what is of utmost importance? It is our intention. It is always our intention. Whenever a person touches another, he transmits all that he is, including the unconscious parts of which he is not aware.

I'd like to tell you a lovely story concerning massage. It is an account my husband received from a woman who has been working with the Angels for some time.

This woman had realized that she had a problem with touching and she was beginning to allow herself to think about it. Upon meeting her husband's family, she had noticed how easily these people embraced and hugged each other. In her own family, however, a family of eighteen children, people resisted or found it more difficult to show their affection in this way. For her, this difficulty was even more pronounced since she had been born when her mother was ill. For two months, she had had no physical contact with her mother. Needless to say, this had left its mark on her.

One day, she was having a bath and she said to herself, "I must change. I feel that it's time." She began intense meditation on touching, a problem she so ardently wished to heal, especially for her children whom she found difficult to hug and to hold. Despite the long, intense work that she had done in order to be able to show her affection through touch, she had not yet been able to do so.

This woman is a good mother and she usually sends her children off to sleep by singing them a lullaby. That evening, as she was singing them a song, she suddenly heard her 16-year-old teenager crying discreetly. She looked at her and asked, "Are you OK?" "Yes, yes. I'm OK," replied the young girl, a bit embarrassed.

She continued to sing. After a moment or two, however, she heard her daughter blow her nose. She checked once again and asked, "Are you sure you're OK?"

"Oh, mum," said the girl, bursting into tears. "You haven't sung that song for so long. The last time was when I was five years old. That day, you held me in your arms. I'd love you to hold me again."

"You remember that?" asked her mother with tears in her eyes.

Of course, she took her into her arms and kissed her. Her wish had been granted. There was a beautiful bond between her and her daughter. Just a few moments earlier, she had been in the bathtub, reaffirming her intention to change at a profound inner level. A miracle had just taken place.

We realize the importance of our intention. If we have resistance or blockage, we do the required inner work. We do not necessarily get the desired results immediately, but They set up all the conditions we need to help us get there. Often, a person's resistance comes from memories that date to other lives, as in the case of this woman who was born into a family that was not very affectionate and at a time when her mother was ill. The person is not conscious of the fact that in these memories lurk distortions that need to be cleansed.

Some people find it so easy to touch. For others, however, just thinking about it is as difficult as climbing a mountain. In most cases, a person that is upset flees, criticizes in silence and re-presses in exasperation. When we work with the Angels, we treat whatever it is that bothers us as important keys. When treated with Angel Recitation, these keys lead us to great openings of our consciousness.

Following this event, the woman had a dream. She dreamt that *she had seven babies, newborns that she was going to baptize in a lake.*

My husband told her, "This is truly a great dream. They want to tell you, 'Keep going. Stay on your path. You are seeing the results.' A baby represents a new project and a new birth, that is, the birth of your inner child who was deprived of love and of physical contact. The fact that there were seven children indicates a rebirth of all seven chakras."

This person will never be the same again. A great change has been announced for her because she dared. The fact that she was going to baptize the babies announces a Divine consecration of her inner child.

It is important to give our children massages. It creates a beautiful contact. When I am with Kasara in the evening, she knows she will get a massage. Sometimes we also tell her a story but she always gets a massage. I invoke an Angel while I am massaging her. She then falls asleep. It is so important to be touched lovingly in the evening. This is as true for adults as it is for children. The evening is an important time for the spirit. A person's unconsciousness registers all that he has been through during the day. Imagine how good it feels to fall asleep when we have received a massage. If we tell our child, "I don't have time," he interprets this as "I don't have time to love you."

However, if we have not received this kind of attention and affection ourselves, it is difficult to give it to others. So we do our best. One day, we rediscover this capacity. Everyone is able to do so, because everyone can cleanse his memories. Everyone can rediscover the capacity to touch, not only with our hands, but with our entire being, with all of our heart and with the whole dimension of the Creator. When we radiate unconditional love, it is God who touches through us.

In conclusion, I would like to relate to you two beautiful accounts that can inspire us to work with the Angels, to read daily signs and to interpret dreams. This, for some people, remains very abstract in the beginning.

Here is the first account told to my husband by a man. It is the continuation of the story of the farmer that is in our book "*How to Read Signs, Initiatory Psychology.*" I'll tell you about it, for those who don't know it. Then, I'll continue with what followed. A couple of years ago, in 1999, a farming couple had great financial success due to a very good harvest. They had a farm, but they didn't own all the land that they cultivated. Given the record profits, this couple, and the husband in particular, thought about buying a piece of land for the security it would provide, but also for the future of their children.

The wife asked a precise question, "Is it a good idea to buy this land?" She was sent a dream. *She saw a big tornado coming towards them. The family had just enough time to leave in a red vehicle.* In reality, this couple does not have a red vehicle. We saw that red represents matter and willpower. A tornado and wind belong to the world of air, or thoughts. These, as we know, can agitate a lot of things within us and can even destroy us. They have an impact on matter, represented by the color red.

As for the man, he asked for a sign. He is a man of great faith who loves to read the Bible. In a divinatory gesture, he opened the Bible asking, "Should we buy this land?" His eyes fell on the verse where Jesus asks the people who are with him to follow him. One of them refuses, saying, "I can't follow you because I have my land to take care of." Our man had his answer: "Do not buy the land."

Two years later, this lady told my husband what happened. She said, "It was good that we listened to my dream and to my husband's sign." What happened? These farmers were not the only ones to have had record profits in 1999. That year was a good year for all of the Québec farmers. But in 2000, the harvest was not so plentiful and the farmers had to absorb serious losses. Nearly everyone who had followed the current of expansion generated by good income found themselves in an extremely difficult, even insurmountable, situation. Naturally, anyone in their position would have said, "There is expansion, so let's invest." Our couple, however, had asked for Cosmic Guidance and was able to use the surplus from the previous year to absorb the debts caused by the bad harvest of the following year.

For most people, trusting messages received by way of dreams and signs seems to fly in the face of common sense. In the beginning, we think that these messages are abstract and offer no concrete use. One day, however, if we continue on the path of faith with patience and perseverance, They tell us, "You listened without really having concrete elements on which to base your decisions, and now look at what has happened." From then on, we maintain unshakeable faith. All sorts of events can occur yet we continue to let ourselves be guided by Up Above. We feel at peace because we know that this guidance is continually present. We know how to move forward and what to do at every moment, in accordance with our program.

The last account completes a story that I told you last month. Let me retell this story, particularly for those of you who were not there. This is about a couple who practices the teaching of the Angels and who were expecting a baby. The lady had a dream. *She felt some pain and, all of a sudden, she saw herself give birth to a beautiful little girl who was teaching spirituality. Then, her grandfather cut the umbilical cord. The husband and the nine-year-old son arrived and everyone was happy to be listening to the baby who was talking and teaching about spirituality.*

As I explained to her, through this dream, the soul was revealing its color. As a character in this dream, the baby was not there to represent a part of the mother (in one sense, however, it does represent her all the same.) Instead, it was announcing its mission, or the reason for its earthly incarnation. I had not told you what the father then experienced because it was not the time. Now I can tell you. Two months after his wife had announced her pregnancy, the father received a dream. *A doctor was telling him, "It will be a girl. She will weigh six pounds and ten ounces. She will measure 19 inches."*

He told me, "When I wrote down that dream, I was really excited. I couldn't get over it." He is a businessman who deals with statistics. He could not get over the fact that he had been given such precise facts. (laughter) At the appropriate moment, the mother went for an ultrasound and she was told that it was a little girl. This man, who has the mind of a statistician, did some calculations. "There is a fifty-percent chance of the baby being a girl," he thought. For the weight and height to be the same as in the dream, however, the chances were very slim. In conversations with his wife, he would sometimes ask her, "Do you think the dream will come true. Do you think she will weigh six pounds, ten ounces and measure 19 inches? That seems almost impossible to me. Why did They give me these figures?"

The mother gave birth on the 27th day of March. It was a lovely baby, a little girl named Elodie. When the time came to weigh her, the father was as tense as a violin string. The nurse said, "She weighs six pounds, ten ounces." Later he told me, "Oh! I was burning up! I felt so hot when I heard her weight. It was such a miracle! Luckily, they didn't measure her right away (laughter). I needed some time to take it all in. Then, I went back later. When they measured her, the nurse said, 'She measures 49 centimeters.' 'Yes,' I said. 'But what's that in inches?' Turning over her measuring tape, she said, 'That's 19 inches.'"

He told me, "Ah! When I heard that, I had goose bumps. I started shaking. I felt even hotter. I kept saying, 'How can this be?'" He's the one who does statistics, after all! Mathematically, what was the probability that the figures given would coincide with the dream? Often, my husband would say to him, "Everything is planned. God really does exist." Now, he understands what this means.

Not long ago, we met this man and his wife again. She told me, "To everyone who comes to visit, even if they don't at all believe in dreams and signs, my husband shows them his notebook of dreams and exclaims, 'Look! I wrote that on the 20th of August, seven months before the birth!' He still can't get over it."

Then, I asked her husband, "How did your son react to the news?"

"He's so happy," he said. "But he doesn't understand anything anymore. There's a part of him that just doesn't understand anything anymore."

Both the son's and the father's intellect, with its good old concepts, had been turned upside down. He added, "What has happened to me has truly led me to meet God for the first time. I am speechless."

"There you are," I said. "They have given you quite the gift." "Great proof that you'll never be able to forget," added my husband.

This is what the Kabbalah is all about. When we work with this teaching, we learn to receive information directly. We acquire spiritual autonomy because we receive our own proof in our inner world through our dreams. This is why Kabbalah means *The Hidden Wisdom* and *The Word Received*.

Angel 9 Haziel
Mystic Love

One day, a man knocked at the door of a dispensary in Africa. He knew the missionary nurse who was on duty. Since he had a lot of trust in her, he asked her for help. He was an African teacher who taught teenagers. He admitted to her that he had had an extra-marital affair with one of his students. She had become pregnant and recently died after giving birth. He asked her to take the baby in because his wife was very angry. Bringing the baby home to live with him was out of the question. The nurse accepted.

When the newborn arrived at the dispensary, he had no name. The African employees therefore called him Massida, which means *orphan* in their dialect. The missionary nurse pointed out that he was already stigmatized by being an orphan and they should not add to his burden by giving him this name. The employees replied, "It's our custom. That's what we do in our country."

Very soon, she noticed that little Massida was cross-eyed. Once again, the employees reacted by saying, "That's normal. Orphans are always cross-eyed."

When she touched the baby, she could sense that he was unhappy and sad. This upset her very much. She would think to herself, "I'd so love it if this little baby were happy, if he could laugh and if he had a different name." Some weeks later, she asked the employees once again to choose a new name for him, but the request was in vain. A kind of taboo and a feeling of fatalism hovered over this situation. Since the baby was an orphan, he had to remain one all of his life.

Then, one evening, she prayed. Specifically addressing the soul of Lorraine, the baby's deceased mother, she said to her, "This is your child. Help me find another name for him. I would so love it if he were happier." That night, she received a dream. *She saw herself in little Massida's room and she was walking up and down holding him in her arms. She was talking to him and laughing with him. Several times, she called him Patrick.*

In the morning, when she woke up and remembered the dream, she said to herself, "I'm certainly not going to tell the employees about my dream. I don't like that name." In the afternoon, however, as she was going through her report with the employees of the next shift, she found herself telling them her dream while mentally saying "No, no, no. Why am I telling my dream? I don't like that name."

As soon as she finished telling her dream, the employees rushed off and left her standing there. She wondered, "What's happening? Where are they going?" She followed them. They were all in little Massida's room, joyfully passing him around and calling him Patrick. It made no difference that she kept insisting, "No, no, no. Don't call him Patrick." The employees were not listening to her. She might as well have been talking to the wall. This truly gave her cause for reflection.

Some days later, she was looking at the baby and noticed that his eyes weren't crossed anymore! She also had the impression that he was more cheerful, as though he had regained a taste for life. She decided to call him Patrick as well.

Several months passed. One day, one of Lorraine's aunts (you'll remember that Lorraine is the baby's deceased mother) arrived at the dispensary to talk to the missionary nurse. She said to her, "I've just found Lorraine's notebook. On one of the pages, she wrote 'If it's a girl, she shall be called Cimwenwe,' which means *goodness* in their dialect. 'And if it's a boy, he shall be called Patrick.'" Like all the villagers, the aunt had heard about the nurse's dream. She was stunned that the missionary nurse had received the same name in her dream as the mother had chosen. She had mentioned this to all the employees at the dispensary before going to the nurse and giving her the information she had found.

While the aunt was talking to the nurse, the employees were listening at the office door. They rushed in as soon as the aunt left. Wide-eyed, they kept repeating, "Ciuta wali na Ngongono," or, "God is all powerful." They were truly impressed.

Some months passed and little Patrick was now over a year old. The missionary nurse had to leave Africa. She summoned Patrick's father to inform him of her departure. She told him, "It would be wonderful if Patrick could find a real family. Try and speak to your wife." That evening, before falling asleep, she prayed intently and asked a favor. "Dear God," she prayed, "please open this woman's heart. Help her to forgive so she can welcome little Patrick into her home."

The following morning, Patrick's father turned up at the dispensary with his wife. The nurse tenderly picked up little Patrick, brought him to the reception and placed him in the woman's arms. Oh! She was so surprised by the child's reaction! Little Patrick spontaneously put his arms around this woman's neck and clung to her, cheek to cheek and breast to breast. He wouldn't let go. Yet they had never met. It was so moving! Truly an eternal moment! As she observed this beautiful scene, she heard the employees murmuring behind her, "Don't let him see her. Otherwise, he won't want to stay with his adoptive mother."

She felt confident, however, because she had faith in the process. She walked around the teacher's wife to look at Patrick's face, but he continued to cling to this woman, as if there were no one else in the world. Through this powerful gesture, Patrick's soul was telling the nurse, "You can go in peace. I have found a new mother. You have accomplished your mission."

A miracle had happened. A very powerful force of love had touched the teacher's wife and had succeeded in absolving and dissolving all negativity, ill will and resentment, leaving room for the gift of forgiveness. At that moment, the missionary nurse truly recognized the expression *mystic love*, or, love that reveals the mysteries of God. *Ciuta wali na Ngongono*. The force of God's love is almighty.

This evening's theme is mystic love, that is, the love that reveals the mysteries of the Universe. This love is universal. It is a love that is so powerful it can transform anything. How can we regain this love in all its purity? An Angel can help us. It is Angel HAZIEL, the Angel who bears number 9. With this Angel, we touch the dimension of love at its highest levels, as well as in its strongest and purest vibrations.

By working with Angel 9 HAZIEL, we can find this love within ourselves. We repeat the Name of the Angel as often as possible, before going to sleep at night, for example, or during active meditation in the daytime. We repeat it while walking, driving and doing all sorts of tasks. We silently repeat, "HAZIEL, HAZIEL, HAZIEL." Thus, we connect with this totally pure Essence so that one day we ourselves may live within this Field of Consciousness and emanate its vibration.

Let's have a look at this Angel's Qualities, several of which are expressed in the story of little Patrick and the missionary nurse. *Universal Love* and *Divine Mercy*. Mercy is the capacity to forgive, no matter what has happened. *Gift of forgiveness, reconciliation, trust, sincerity, goodness that absolves all evil* and *powerful energy that transforms all negativity.* Little Patrick's story touched upon the goodness that absolves all evil when he wrapped his arms around his new mother. This was a very powerful moment. One day, we will no longer need outside events to trigger these high levels of consciousness. Within our energy we will constantly find this very powerful love, that is, a love that transforms everything on its path, within ourselves and on the outside.

Friendship, support, grace and favors from those in power. This support comes first and foremost from the invisible worlds, because the guides give their support to everyone. Whether we are in a loving state or in a negative one, they help us. In the first case, however, their help appears in lovely and harmonious events. In the latter, it comes to us through trials that are sometimes very difficult to bear. This is education through evil. It serves to break us so that one day we will be totally open and we will have eliminated all resentment. Sometimes, we think we have forgiven. Deep down, however, we haven't. The forgiveness is only superficial or intellectual, because even though we know we must forgive, inside us there remain a lot of distorted memories that prevent us from gaining access to those high levels of consciousness. With Angel Haziel, we receive support and favors from those in power and through the people we are led to meet here on Earth. In other words, this assistance also manifests itself in the concrete world.

Promise and *commitment*. Angel HAZIEL helps us to discern when to commit ourselves and how to do so wisely and with Knowledge. *Altruism* and *unselfishness*. This Angel puts us in contact with altruistic people and teaches us to give unselfishly. This is truly an Angel that teaches us to give. Our entire emissivity and the way that we give are touched upon so that, one day, we give unconditionally.

312

Childlike purity. This Angel is the cherub of all cherubs and has been represented by some artists as a lovely and chubby baby in order to illustrate the quality of purity in childhood. It also illustrates the confidence and the faith that allows us to receive everything.

Now, let's have a look at the distortions of this Angel. When we have not yet mastered the State of Consciousness of Angel HAZIEL, we end up in everything that concerns lack of love: *possessiveness, jealousy, passion* and *fear of loving and of being loved.* The list of by-products of the lack of love is rather long: *hatred, war, non-reconciliation, hypocritical* and *deceives others.* All conflicts in all situations where a person lacks integrity, or is unfaithful, are distortions of this Angel. *Manipulates to obtain the favors of those in power.* While we do indeed receive the support of those in power when we are in this Angelic state of consciousness, we also try to manipulate others for our own ends when we are in Its distortions.

At a conscious level, absolutely everyone seeks love. At the same time, however, love scares people! This fear is caused by unconscious and distorted memories. Sometimes, the quest for love is quality-oriented and sometimes it is distorted. However, the Angel Recitation with Angel Haziel allows us to visit these memories through our dreams and the conscious application of the Law of Resonance. This leads us to clearly see whether we are in Its qualities or in the distortions. Thus, as soon as we realize that we are leaning towards distortions, the memory is rectified simply by invoking the Angel.

As I said at the beginning, Angel HAZIEL is an Energy that teaches us to give. Quite often, people will come up to me and say, "I don't find it very difficult to give, but I find it so difficult to receive! When I have to receive, I become very awkward. How can I learn to receive?" I tell them that the first step is to learn to give. Then, receiving becomes very easy.

Why? How does this work? With the action of giving, we experience feelings and emotions. The act of giving is inscribed with all of our being. It's in our thoughts, emotions and way of giving. When we give, we think we are being generous. All of our unconscious impulses, however, are inscribed in our act of giving. Sometimes, when we give there is a desire to please behind our gesture. At that moment, our generous action is not unconditional but rather bears a desire to be loved and recognized. It also bears manipulation and all sorts of distorted impulses. We are not necessarily conscious of this, however.

What happens inside of us when someone wants to give us something or offer us a favor? Let's compare ourselves to a computer that has recorded all sorts of facts and associations on its hard drive. Faced with a gift, a large number of memories are called up in a split second. These are memories of situations where we gave as well as the way in which we gave. This content is brought up and projected onto the person who is giving us something or offering us a favor. What comes to mind? "Giving is manipulation, possessiveness and problems. I don't want this. Go away. I want none of it."

At the same time, another part of us does want to receive, because receiving is a Universal and Cosmic process. Therefore, when a person receives, his entire being is split. His mouth gets all twisted and he doesn't feel right. Sometimes, when we compliment certain people, they are incapable of simply accepting the compliment. They immediately return it with another one.

We say to ourselves, "Ok, now I understand. I know that my way of giving is inscribed within me. I'm therefore going to change my intentions." Of course, we do not become altruistic overnight. By working with this Angel, however, impulses that were unconscious and distorted appear in our dreams and we become more conscious of the way we give. We say to ourselves, "You are giving, but you've got something in the back of your mind. You want some time in exchange. You want to be looked after. Oh! No, no, no, no!" We therefore purify these memories by doing our Angel Recitation. We breathe in Angel HAZIEL and we say, "Oh Angel HAZIEL. Help me to give in a proper and altruistic manner. With Your powerful Force of Love, transform this distorted aspect that arises in me when I give".

Here is an example that will help us understand this mechanism. A lady told me that she always has a shower just before going to bed at night. She developed this habit because she noticed that whenever she had a shower at any other time of the day, she felt sleepy afterwards.

We condition ourselves all the time. That is the way we are. It is a natural process. In this lady's inner computer, certain memories say, "Shower means bedtime." Hence, she becomes sleepy. The same thing happens when love knocks on our door. Love means that all those memories linked to love, such as suffering, abandonment, rejection and sadness, emerge and come to mind. Naturally, we therefore do not want love. We are afraid to get involved because these are the associations that are inscribed within us. We tell ourselves, "Love hurts. I don't want it." At the same time, however, we do want love because without it, we die. Love is vital. This is why the simultaneous dynamic of attraction and repulsion is activated.

Through our work with the Angels, we rectify these memories one by one. This is a huge task that can take several lives. We must revisit all of the memories marked by the absence of love and where separation caused suffering and where we recorded feelings of abandonment, rejection, betrayal and pain. We are not alone, however. This is why we do our Angel Recitation. When we visit these zones of our being, we do not feel very good because we are aware of the lack of love. We therefore invoke an Angel and we cleanse just a small part at a time. Then, we cleanse another part and then another. By so doing, the day will come when, as the shower is linked to bedtime, the association will be made between love, blossoming, happiness, joy, bonding and well-being.

With hindsight, the missionary nurse who was part of little Patrick's story gained a much better understanding of what had happened. She follows the teaching of The Traditional Study of Angels and she understands that her call to Africa was not a coincidence. If we were to scrutinize her unconsciousness, we would certainly see that she had lived in Africa in her previous lives. In this lifetime, she had to complete the circle. She had an important rendezvous with Africa. No need to tell you (for you have surely realized it) that she helped change the destiny of little Patrick's soul. Imagine. She did this simply by helping to change his name.

A person's name is very powerful because it is symbolic. We need only take an everyday example to understand this. If a certain cereal were called *Abandon*, nobody would buy it. It would not matter if it were healthy, nutritious and delicious. No one would want to buy it or eat it. Symbolic associations are very powerful. With the name Massida, or orphan, the negative vibration penetrated even the boy's physical body.

However, this woman's gesture was not totally disinterested. It helped her disentangle one of her karmic knots. When we help another person, how do we know whether our gesture is totally altruistic or whether our soul seeks to disentangle itself from a karmic knot? If our gesture is a response to a personal desire and need, then it corresponds to karma. This is unlike the guides of the invisible world who help us, for example, while having no karma with us. They do it selflessly and altruistically because They have attained a superior level of evolution.

Let's analyze the behavior of this missionary nurse. First of all, the simple fact that she was upset by the baby's situation shows that she had resonance with what he was going through. Otherwise, the little one's suffering would not have been so upsetting to her. She would have felt compassion and understanding. She would have bonded with the baby without personally feeling any suffering. Her inner resistance at having received the name Patrick in her dream, along with her repeated reticence to his bearing this name, clearly reveals the resonance she had with this situation.

What was going on? This child showed her an inner part of herself that was orphaned. If we were to go into the unconscious depths of this woman, we would undoubtedly see that, in another life, she herself had abandoned a child. Everything that we do is inscribed within us. If it is distorted, then we will be led to relive it. There is also no doubt that this woman had also been abandoned. Over time, the ritualistic cleansing she carried out through her devotion and service allowed her to be released from this karma.

What are the reasons she put up so much resistance? Let me just draw your attention to the fact that we all tend to react like this when faced with karma. It is as though we indulge in our misery and in our difficulties. This tendency is due to certain forces that inhabit us and that we feed. We are engaged in a struggle between good and evil. We resist, but we are eventually freed. Thus, whether it was little Patrick or another soul that this woman had abandoned in another life is of no importance. These two beings had the same resonance and they were brought together because they had the same kind of problem to sort out at the same moment. When we understand this, we can only be filled with wonder at such precision!

I would now like to share with you an example that touches upon one of the by-products of the lack of love: *possessiveness.* A woman who has been studying this teaching for quite a while now was very happy to have her husband accompany her to one of the dream workshops. He had never been to one before. On this occasion, she asked my husband for the interpretation of a dream. In her dream, *she was at a big party that had been organized for her partner. All the members of his family and many other guests had been invited. She was surprised by the event, however, as if she hadn't been informed about the party. She found herself in the kitchen and, at one particular moment, she saw among the guests her partner's ex-wife. She was annoyed and she suddenly felt overcome with jealousy. She went down to the basement where she met her partner. She asked him, "Who invited HER?" "Your father," he replied.*

My husband asked her, "What does this woman represent to you?"

"Ah! A lot of problems. She interfered quite a bit at the beginning of our relationship."

As she answered, my husband could feel in her energy that there was a lack of love towards the ex-wife. He felt her insecurity and fear of losing her partner.

Then she admitted to this insecurity and added, "But this dream really surprises me because I never have jealousy fits. He's the one who is jealous all the time. He had a jealous fit just recently." "You see," replied my husband, "in your dream, you are being shown that you are the bearer of this jealousy and possessiveness. It is inscribed in your soul. Your partner is a reflection of your inner man. In this dream, everyone represents parts of you. It isn't the type of dream where you have visited the soul of your partner or his ex-wife. At the beginning, you were in the kitchen. The kitchen represents preparation, or the way we prepare an action. Then you saw that the ex-wife was there. That doesn't mean that she is coming back into your life. Rather, she simply represents a part of yourself. The two principles, male and female, are there to get closer and to celebrate. You were shown that you are the one who does the inviting and who creates interference."

In the dream the woman went down into the basement. The basement symbolizes the level that is situated just below the veil of the subconscious. It represents aspects of the subconscious, that is, elements of which we are not aware. Then, They informed her that it was her father who had invited the ex-wife. Since the father is a man, he denotes action, daytime and manifestation. They showed her that she is the one who invites these inner parts into the manifest world (inner parts, because the ex-wife is a woman.) This creates problems and keeps on destroying her happiness.

Following this interpretation, my husband said to her, "That doesn't excuse your partner's behavior. Of course, he will have to do a certain amount of work on himself. On the one hand, the fact remains that you attracted him. On the other, you don't commit yourself and give yourself wholly. When love comes knocking, it awakens memories. It's like the story of the shower: you associate love with suffering, difficulties, sadness, separation and abandonment. You therefore don't give yourself. Your energy is elusive. It's as if you have one foot in and one foot out the door, ready to leave. Even if you don't say anything, this is the message that your energy sends out. Your partner feels it and for the tiniest little thing and the slightest insecurity, he throws a fit of jealousy." This helped her understand many things.

When we experience disproportionate reactions in others, even without apparent reason, if we do not understand the process, that is to say, if we realize that we carry this problem within our soul and that we emit this scent, we can easily change partners while saying to ourselves, "There's no point in staying with him. He's too distorted." The problem, however, will come up again with another person. Or indeed, the same process can turn up in another form. Instead of suffering from our partner's possessiveness, we ourselves will be possessive and we will be the one to hang on, because we will have found an elusive and inaccessible partner.

To understand is a grace because it allows us to stop turning around in circles. We interrupt this karmic cycle. We come back to ourselves and we use our relationship to help with our ritualistic cleansing. Unless, of course, the relationship has been compromised by extreme difficulties such as physical or verbal violence. If this is not the case, however, then we ask Heaven, "Is it right for me to stay with this person?" When in doubt, we refrain from doing anything. We work on our inner man (or our inner woman) and we will receive guidance from Up Above. We also learn to give. We do not say, "I'm not sure if this is the man, or woman, of my life. So there's no point in giving myself totally." Commitment allows us to learn how to bond.

What is bonding or fusion? Fusion is not a naive love where we say, "I must always be available. I must devote myself entirely to him." That is not what it is. Fusion is only possible when we deal with resonance we have with the other person. First of all, we analyze everything that happens. According to such and such behavior of his, we become aware of resonance and we identify the distortion we bear within ourselves. Then, we rectify it. Since we understand what the other is going through, we do not begrudge him. Instead of reacting out of fear or aggression, we send him love and wisdom. Fusion acts like a circle of energy.

It is impossible to attain these high levels of mystic love if we do not have understanding. Besides, this Angel of Universal Love touches Wisdom and Knowledge. Without them, true Love is not possible because naive love only leads to frustration and, eventually, separation. A human being represses a lot of things. We can see that the relationship between a man and a woman is an extraordinary training ground. If we consider it thus, it will allow us to one day attain the highest summits of Universal Love.

Here's an anecdote that touches on signs and coincidences. While I was preparing this lesson on the HAZIEL State of Consciousness one evening, our daughter Kasara decided to watch a film we had on video cassette at home. It is a film that I highly recommend. It is very inspiring, as much for adults as for children. It is called "Kirikou and the Sorceress." It is an initiatory story that clearly shows that evil is educational and that we can transform it in order to arrive at a state of fusion within a marriage.

Kasara had decided to watch this film, but the cassette had not been rewound. While it was rewinding there happened to be a hockey game on television. She watched the players hitting each other. They were fighting. She shook her head and asked me, "Why are they fighting?" We could see thousands of spectators on the benches. She asked me, "Why are so many people watching?" Then she got up and began to mimic them. She said to me, "Look. It's as if I had a little ball that I throw to you, like this, then I'm being filmed and thousands of people are watching me. What's this all about?"

When she heard the click indicating that the cassette had finished rewinding, she rushed over. In her haste, she twisted the big toe on her right foot and she fell. She really hurt herself and was crying her heart out. I picked her up and consoled her. Then, we checked to see that nothing was broken or damaged.

After a moment, she got up. She was better. She was about to start her film when I said to her, "Kasara, before you begin, let's just talk a moment. You hurt your big toe. You know there is no such thing as coincidence. What do you think the sign is? What were you thinking about when you hurt your big toe?"

"Ah! I was going to turn on my film."

"What were you doing just before that?"

"Oh! The hockey players," she answered after thinking a while.

"That's it, of course. You're right. It's not right to hit each other, to hit others and to place so much importance on a little round puck. You can evaluate. 'It's right' or 'it's not right.' When you evaluate, however, there must always be love. Always. So when you were making your comments, your energy was a bit negative. That's why They gave you a sign. You fell and twisted your big toe. Big toes are like thumbs, they represent Divine Love and Divine Will. Just now, there was no Divine Love and you weren't doing the Divine Will. Clack! You hurt yourself. You were being shown that this sort of thought hurts."

She looked at me wide-eyed! I told her, "If you met a hockey player, he wouldn't feel good with you. He'd be ill at ease, even if you didn't say anything and only looked at him. His soul would know what you were thinking. Our soul knows what the other person thinks. He'd notice that you judge him and he wouldn't feel good."

"Yes, OK. I did that, but they weren't here. They were on TV."

"Ah! It doesn't work that way. We are all linked through our souls. You must practice evaluating while remaining in a loving state. You must also understand that everyone experiments and that they are all children of God, like you."

I went on, "You know, hockey players are people who have an enormous amount of energy and they don't always know what to do with it. For the moment, they don't know how to properly manifest it. There are specific places for this, where their aggression can be channeled in a well-organized way. This avoids it being projected onto their families and onto their children. This kind of game has its rightful place, Kasara. That's why God allows it. These people are experimenting."

She was all ears. I said to her, "Think of your little cousin Ariel. She's just a baby. Remember, a few months ago, she was discovering that she was the one who controlled her hands. When she was eating, Splatch! She'd throw her food on the floor and you'd say to her, 'No, Ariel. Don't do that. We don't throw food on the floor.' At that moment, you were full of love. You weren't criticizing when you spoke."

"Yes, but she's small. They're big."

"That's right. But you know it doesn't work that way. Don't look at it from the point of view of one life only and according to the person's age. You have to consider it over several lives and in terms of consciousness. You can look at the behavior of adults with the understanding that in their consciousness they are still little babies. Then you'll consider them the way you do Ariel. You'll know that it isn't right to throw food on the floor or to fight for a puck, but you'll still feel so much love!"

A totally different vision of things was being inscribed within her.

We began to watch the film and, suddenly, the phone rang. We paused the video player. The game reappeared on the screen. Kasara was watching the game and, from time to time, we would wink at each other and smile.

The telephone conversation lasted a while. When it was over, I said to Kasara, "God is certainly looking after you, isn't He? He wants you to understand."

"Ah yes, but it's not funny."

"Kasara," I said. "If you don't solve your problem with hockey players, what could happen in another life? Your dad, your husband, or even your little boy could be a hockey player."

"Oh! I'd better keep quiet."

"What I suggest you do is draw a picture in which you show love for hockey players. You can do your Angel Recitation with Angel HAZIEL because you were in the distortion related to this Angel. While you are drawing, invoke this Angel and ask the players for forgiveness. You can also send them love."

She did the drawing as I had suggested. In it, we see her sending love to the hockey players in the form of hearts. Drawing is a good way to teach children. When we write or draw, we actually think, feel and materialize these thoughts and emotions.

321

The next story concerns reconciliation and pardon. A woman who had come to our lecture for the first time asked me to interpret a dream. In this dream *she could see herself sitting on a sofa with her eyes closed.* In her dream, therefore, she was asleep. *She felt all sorts of negative energies invade her. She tried to pronounce the name of Jesus, but without success. Suddenly, her husband, who also had his eyes closed, came and sat beside her and told her, "It's these negative energies that have separated us. Let's make up." Then, still in her dream, she woke up. She opened her eyes and she was able to pronounce the name of Jesus.*

First of all, I asked her, "What does your husband represent to you?"

"Ah, some time ago, he left me for another woman," she said. "He left me with our two children. Then, I became friends with a woman in whom I confided a lot. This woman had had the same kind of problem. We supported each other and we confided a lot in one another. One day, she told me that she had met my husband and that he had confided in her. A few months later, however, I discovered that she had become my husband's mistress."

She continued, "I considered myself a spiritual person. When I would see the word *hate* (as we saw on the list of distortions related to Angel HAZIEL) I would see it as being far removed from me. I was sure that I'd never feel hatred. But I hated this woman. One day she turned up at my house and I actually chased her away."

What was she being told through this dream? Why had They sent her this dream? She was being shown that this betrayal and her suffering were there to awaken her to spirituality and to a greater, more universal love. This is why she was trying to pronounce the name of Jesus. Jesus attained the highest levels of Universal Love through suffering. That is what he symbolizes. This woman was suffering and, through this dream, They were telling her, "Your suffering is useful. Use it to grow and to attain high levels of Universal Love." In this dream, she visited her husband's soul, but at an unconscious level. He also represents a part of herself, that is, a part of her inner man.

Since the dreamer and her husband had their eyes closed in the dream, she was being told that there would not necessarily be reconciliation at the physical level. There would, however, be reconciliation at the inner level. A dream such as this one can manifest itself through the establishment of a good relationship with the ex-partner. However, when we interpret dreams we must not adopt a definitive interpretation. In this case, for example, we must not decide on the diagnosis of a non-return to their relationship. This dream could have shown only part of the trajectory that may lead this woman to a physical reconciliation with her husband. Of course, some dreams do indicate complete ruptures, but not this one. In this case, the woman should remain open to different possible scenarios while possessing enough mastery to be able to sacrifice her personal desires. The inner cleansing process required to attain such levels of consciousness is long and arduous. This is why it is impossible to receive ultra-precise information in our dreams until we have attained certain degrees of wisdom. Due to our personal desires, we tend to try to direct destiny in our favor.

In a dream, when we see someone who is sleeping, this indicates an ordinary consciousness, or one that is not awakened. What do we mean by a person with an awakened consciousness? A person who is in an ordinary consciousness imitates what he sees on the outside and learns by imitation. However, a person with an awakened consciousness learns from the inside. Of course, he uses interfaces and remains in contact with the outside, but he truly learns from the inside.

To reach these high summits of Universal Love, the person must have fused his masculine and feminine principles. He must have carried out an inner marriage. Here is a story that will illustrate this. A woman who follows this teaching told us one of her dreams. In her dream, *she was invited to the wedding of one of her friends. At the wedding, she danced a belly dance, that is, a kind of Arab dance. Then, her partner was chatting with her. All of a sudden, he asked her to marry him. This proposal scared her so much that she went off to find her four children and she ran away.*

When she woke up, she was surprised by this dream because she gets along well with her partner. Their relationship is stable and they have four children. I asked her, "Have you talked about marriage?"

"No," she said. "We don't talk about it."

This couple maintained a kind of taboo about marriage. Why did They give her this dream? In her dream, her partner represented her inner man and They wanted to show her that she had not completely bonded with him. She stimulated her partner, but she did not want to commit herself or completely bond with him. Since man represents the spirit, They also wanted to show her that she was afraid to bond or to fuse with the spirit. A person receiving such a dream might say, "Oh! I must get married immediately. I must solve my inner problem." That is not the aim of this type of dream. It simply indicates an opening through which They show us a certain number of memories that reveal why we are afraid of total commitment. Of course, it is not by getting married that we will solve the problems that go back to unconscious memories.

For decades now, it seems that couples blossom better outside the sacred bonds of marriage than within them. Why is this so? In the past, religion imposed marriage thereby stripping it of its profound and sacred sense. Imposition, of course, means rigidity and attachment to form. Therefore, marriage ended up evoking imprisonment, suffocation and the necessity to renounce to a part of ourselves. People therefore no longer wanted to get married and the old approach fell into disuse because it was not right.

However, marriage is back in fashion these days. More and more couples want to get married and be united by the sacred bonds of marriage. How does mystic love manifest itself in marriage? What is its place? First, we must understand one thing. For this love to form the basis of marriage, the person must begin with the goal of doing the necessary work to acquire qualities and virtues. Only then can he commit to marriage. Then, he will receive the authorization to such a commitment from Cosmic Intelligence. How will he receive it? On the inside, through a dream. Commitment will not be imposed on the outside as it was with the old mentality.

With this understanding, it is easier to comprehend the meaning of the expression *for better or for worse*. This phrase has been misunderstood because we had lost the profound sense of commitment. In this expression, to commit oneself for worse does not mean to put up with a violent spouse. Not at all. To commit oneself for worse means that when the other person experiences failure, loses his job, falls ill, has a problem with a child, or any other difficulty, the understanding of the Law of Resonance allows us to use these difficulties to grow. Our couple will serve an apprenticeship. Of course, with this attitude, such a commitment is truly evolutionary. The person edifies himself on the inside because he constantly rectifies inner parts of himself. He also edifies himself on the outside because he shows more stability, integrity and fidelity. The proof is clear.

As I indicated, understanding the Law of Resonance plays a key role for this type of couple. Let's see how. When two people meet, of course, they have many affinities or resonance related to qualities. They have just as many related to distortions, however. It is not because the person has received a dream giving permission to get married that everything is going to be perfect. He or she still has many distortions and therefore will have to adjust many times. However, with a marriage based on mystic love, instead of the couple's life being the worst of hells (obviously, nearness makes the distortions even more annoying), it can become exponentially more like paradise.

At first, as I have just said, each of the spouses still has a lot of distortions. However, the person who has Knowledge knows that when the other's behavior or attitude bothers or upsets him (of course, he knows that the other's attitude is not correct) he looks within and does the Angel Recitation. Thus, he cleanses his own distorted memories and waits until he is feeling better before talking things over with his spouse. Since his partner also knows these Laws (she also has Knowledge) they will talk about it at the right moment and with the right timing. In this way, their communication acquires and preserves a very high quality. That is the secret. Often, we know very well that we should communicate, but we do not seem to be able to do so. Therefore, when we understand these Laws, communication becomes easier and more effective.

It becomes easier to talk about our faults. Generally, as couples, we only want to talk about success and everything that is nice and rosy. We sweep the rest under the carpet. However, if we avoid talking about what bothers us, the pot finally boils over because we do not feel good inside. Then, when we start talking and we get angry, we quarrel. We need to realize that by understanding the Law of Resonance, talking about our faults is gratifying and very interesting. We are happy because we know that identifying them is part of the process. We know that to become an initiate we must be ready to see our own distortions. That's what it is to work with the Angels. First and foremost, Cosmic Intelligence says, "You want to touch (as in this case) Universal Love? Bravo! That's good. OK, but We are going to send you down into your unconscious memories where you can visit every instance of lack of love that has been recorded."

We know this process. We will therefore be happy to talk about our faults as well as our qualities. It will not make any difference. What's more, when two people work this way and recount their dreams, the relationship becomes of the utmost authenticity. When we tell someone our dream, we are naked. Already in the dream itself we are naked because the elements are not filtered. They emerge spontaneously from our unconsciousness. Sometimes we were not aware that we had this kind of problem. By talking about their dreams, both partners manage to say, "Ah! I understand. That's what I was feeling. I couldn't put my finger on it."

If the other person was upset, this understanding will give him some feedback that will allow him to discern the type of resonance in question. The person bares himself and it is in his best interest to do so. In fact, that is what he wants. It has become a priority for him. We have seen that the spiritual path of a couple requires that they desire to improve and become better, more altruistic people. Given this intention, the process that is put into action has a transforming and repairing nature for both spouses. We progress very quickly when we function in this manner. We rarely hear of mystic love within a couple, as if this dimension of love was reserved for the individual person working on his own spiritual evolution apart from any intimate relationship. We have seen that this work can be extraordinary in a couple. Of course, it is not easy and it requires adjustments, but it works.

When we work this way, we come to realize that every time we encounter a distortion that resonates within our couple, it is our inner man (or our inner woman if we are a man) who is the bearer of this distortion. This also allows us to understand multiple attractions to other people because we realize that they are manifestations of these divisions. When we are attracted to other people, rather than let these attractions manifest themselves on the outside, we breathe in the Angel and we come back to our spiritual goal of inner reunification.

In this type of marriage, instead of having the impression of losing a part of ourselves, as is the case with an ordinary consciousness, we know that we are recuperating various parts of our inner woman, or inner man, so as to reunify them. These parts were divided and scattered. With commitment, however, we find them within ourselves because love always comes from the inside. The outside is only a manifestation. The day will come when we will have transcended each of our inner divisions. We will be complete. This will then manifest itself on the outside. We can see that this type of couple is very evolutionary.

In an ordinary state of consciousness, the relationship usually starts with passion and very quickly degenerates into disagreement, or else it reaches a kind of status quo where love has lost all its poetry. On the other hand, with a spiritual consciousness, a couple's relationship begins with friendship that never ceases to progress. We often hear that people get bored in a marriage because the relationship stagnates and becomes tedious. With a spiritual couple, it is the complete opposite. The relationship is most stimulating and evolutionary because each person changes from day to day. At night, each one falls asleep in a certain state of consciousness. The next day, things are different. Each wakes up in a different state of consciousness because they both went to visit inner worlds through their own dreams. Many past lives are thus cleansed. The spouses change continuously. Since they share a common destiny, they do not feel as if they are on different wavelengths.

Here is a good example of this type of couple. One day, a woman who follows the teaching of the Angels told me about a dream she had had several months before. *She was in a restaurant with her sister. Her sister pointed out a man sitting at one of the tables and said, "There's your future spouse. You'll get married in February." She didn't know him and he wasn't looking at her. He remained in his corner.*

A few months went by. One day, she met a handsome man who, since meeting her, also follows the teachings of the Angels. She did not, however, remember her dream right away. It was only during their second meeting, while they were alone together, that she suddenly remembered the man in her dream. This man had the same haircut and physical appearance as the man in her dream. She said to me, "I blushed at the thought of it!" She blushed because she was so impressed. She added, "I didn't say anything. Of course, I felt quite shaken because there was a lovely friendship between us. As a woman, however, I didn't feel attracted to this man. Then time passed and I had another dream." In this dream, *she was told that she was going to move into the same type of house as the one owned by this man.* At that moment, she felt afraid. She knows that we must pay attention to dreams.

She came to talk to us. A few days before, my husband, who knew each of them very well, had seen them in a dream. He had visited their souls and *he had seen them go to a chapel in the East.* He knew that this was the announcement of a spiritual union.

When she talked to us about her dreams and her fear of commitment, my husband did not tell her about his dream. We can see many things in a dream when we visit others' souls. Most of the time, however, it is better not to talk to them about these things. It is better to let the other person experiment. He simply said to her, "When the energy passes through, if we don't know how to receive it, it won't pass again, or else we will have a very long wait before it comes back."

This encouraged her to begin a process of inner work. She chose an appropriate Angel and did her Angel Recitation to free herself from her fears because she knew that this message came from Up Above. Two days later, the handsome man knocked at her door. Standing on the doorstep, a bit embarrassed, he said, "I have something to ask you." She looked at him and simply said, "I know and the answer is yes." (laughter) He exclaimed, "And to think that I've been racking my brain trying to figure out how to ask you!" He was very happy.

They've been living together now for several years and this woman admitted to me, "As special as it was at the beginning–I felt attracted, but without emotion or passion–it's really become a relationship that is evolving." Often, at night, she addresses Them, Up Above, and says, "Thank you for sending me such a treasure." She pampers her partner and she cherishes him as he does her. They are so good together! It's amazing! Their relationship is growing and leading them to bond more and more. That's what evolutionary commitment is. We cannot commit ourselves 100% on an energy level as long as we shelter unconscious memories that have to be cleansed. Through experimentation and work on ourselves, this commitment deepens. Eventually, we attain inner fusion; then comes outer fusion. The two go together. *As it is Above so it is below, and as it is below so it is Above.*

As for him, this man confided in me, "If I had to replace this woman, I'd need several to find her equivalent because she's so complete." We can see that it is truly wonderful when we function like this. We can also see that if we wish to follow the path of mystic love, it is important to understand the fact that man and woman are truly complementary. Some traditions advocate celibacy in order to experience mystic love, but this is simply the first stage towards a concrete realization or exterior bonding or fusion.

Here is a story that touches on childhood purity that Angel HAZIEL helps us rediscover. One night, my husband received a dream. *Our daughter Kasara was standing in front of a washbasin where there was a rat. The rat wasn't nice. It was aggressive. She leaned over to touch it, but my husband said, "No, no, no! Don't touch it!"* He knew this dream concerned our daughter. It was not a dream that showed him parts of himself. He therefore waited to see how this dream would materialize. A dream always materializes one way or another because it symbolically describes the person's inner and/ or outer state of being.

The next day we were on tour. Usually Kasara helps us a lot. If we were to analyze this in depth, and we had to, that day we could feel that she was less committed than usual.

At one particular moment, I happened to be at the very back of the room and I heard what was going on at the other end. Kasara was getting the table ready with another one of our helpers. I heard the latter say to her, "No. The CDs must be put out in this order."

"No," answered Kasara. "It's this way. Not like that."

"I can assure you that it's like this."

"No, I'm telling you that my Dad showed me how to display them and it's like this."

The other person said nothing more. When my husband looked at the presentation table, he saw that the meditation CDs were not in the correct order and he told them. The other person turned towards our daughter and said to her, "I told you Kasara. I didn't insist because you were so adamant." Then, I took Kasara aside and gently said to her, "Kasara, you have to be careful. Look. You were too emissive just then. You were too bossy. You didn't leave her any space. What's more, she wasn't able to lay things out correctly. You saw that you weren't right. You have to watch out for that aspect." She understood.

During the following night, Kasara received a dream. *She was in a lecture hall and she could see that she didn't feel inclined to help. A lady disguised as a carrot came in* (laughter) *and she felt like going to the indoor fair.* When Kasara told us her dream she already had a pretty good idea of what it meant. It was sufficiently clear to her.

I immediately exclaimed, "Oh lucky you! You are so lucky!" She looked at me because she knew that her dream depicted distortions, that is, an attitude that was not right. I added, "Do you realize how lucky you are to receive this kind of information at eight years old? There are adults who won't receive any in their entire life. They'll have to wait for other lives to receive this kind of dream where they'll be clearly shown their intention. In this dream you were shown your real intention. You were also shown why you had this intention. The lady disguised as a carrot is part of your inner self since she was a woman. A carrot is a great symbol of emissivity. When distorted, the color orange represents pleasures that aren't correct. They were showing you that certain parts of yourself aren't being properly emissive. Disguises are wrong, aren't they?"

We then made the link with what had happened the day before. I said to her, "Remember how you spoke to the volunteer, Kasara. You were too bossy and emissive. You see, that's what you were shown in your dream. You were shown that that was the energy you had inside that made you feel like you didn't want to be of service. You would have preferred to go to the indoor fair."

Kasara was not conscious of this energy. As you can see, however, They reveal great things through dreams. At that moment, my husband remembered his dream with the rat and he was able to make the correlation with everything that had happened.

What does a rat symbolize? In a dream, an animal can have a positive or a negative meaning. To know which symbolism is intended, you just need to analyze the animal's behavior. In the dream, the rat was aggressive. It therefore indicated a distortion. Generally speaking, a rat lives in the sewer, eats rubbish and grabs anything and everything. It only thinks of itself. Thus, it symbolizes the opposite of generosity and altruism.

In the dream, my husband warned Kasara not to touch the animal. In other words, he had to interrupt the process in which she approached this type of energy. The dream therefore incited him to speak clearly and directly to her about service and the help we should give others. The reason is very simple: Kasara is still a child and now is the time when she has to learn the importance of being altruistic.

In the past, human beings went to extremes. We made children work too much and we were rigid and authoritarian with them. It was not right. Then, when these people became parents, they let their children do what they wanted. They were never asked to help out because the adults wanted to spare them what they had suffered. It is important to find the right balance and to teach children to participate in household tasks and to serve others.

One of the beautiful things about this teaching is that we can see actual tendencies in the World of Causes even before they take root in the concrete world. If the educators do not intervene while there is still time, eventually these underground energies start taking over, like weeds. Ten years later, the result will be a self-centered, egotistical and antisocial person. When we know that the path to happiness is an altruistic attitude, we give generously without expecting gratitude. This is the way to proper giving.

That same week, when she came home from school, Kasara gave her Dad a picture that she had drawn and signed *To Dad, with love*. In it, we could see stars, which represent her spiritual or psychic world. The love, however, had not yet descended into her body. It remained at a certain level. The drawing had a lot of scribbles that indicate a certain negative energy. Kasara never draws pictures like this. If we enter the energy of her drawing, we can feel what They, Up Above, showed my husband in his dream with the rat symbol. Her father told her about this dream and he told her how he interpreted it so she could really understand the aspects that are sometimes hidden and very subtle.

With children, we can use a teaching method that takes into account subtle worlds and the depths of our being. Sometimes, we say that a child loses his purity at six or seven years old. We blame other children, that is, those he socializes with and society in general. We are partly right, but this is only a consequence. For every child, the loss of purity or of Essence begins in the World of Causes–the invisible world–from whence negative energies are injected, that is, energies that the child has to learn to transform. These energies come from karma and they are reintegrated in a person according to his life-plan and what he has to learn on Earth. With an evolved person, the injection of negative energy will lead him to reinforce and direct his consciousness towards love and wisdom. With such a person, the negative energy is rapidly transcended. It does not engender any consequence or karma. Repeated progressively, this process leads to Enlightenment.

With The Traditional Study of Angels, we enter our distortions, that is, we stop fleeing them. Instead, we transform them. Once an initiate reaches the highest level of consciousness, he has managed to transcend the entire evil of humanity and he no longer has resonance. This key process is easily understood by observing how children behave during the multiple mutations of their consciousness. When we understand the Universal Laws, they become part of a wonderful teaching method to educate our children.

Mystic love is the fruit of a long process of spiritual cleansing.

Angel 17 Lauviah
Revelations

I recently met a woman who was torn between spirituality and the world of matter. At times, this uncertainty would plunge her into deep existential anguish. Her entire body hurt and her hands were often numb and lifeless. I listened to her with great compassion. Her account brought me back to the past when I, myself, started out on an initiatory path.

At that time, I thought I was pure. In my dreams, however, They would reveal the multiple seductive facets that made me who I was. I thought I was detached from matter. In my dreams, this detachment was shown to be a mere façade masking desires for power. I considered myself humble. In my dreams, I was shown that pumped-up pride lay camouflaged behind my supposedly generous gestures. I was sure I had been a good mother. In my dreams, however, I was told that I had been a controlling one at times. When I'd wake up, I would often sob my heart out, overcome with guilt and remorse.

Everything was collapsing around me. As I received these revelations, the image I had forged of myself crumbled bit by bit. One day, there was total emptiness. Yet I had asked Them, Up Above, to reveal the mysteries of the Universe to me. I did not understand anything anymore. I was lost, crushed under the weight of these revelations. Gradually, as time passed, I felt chronic fatigue set in. I was exhausted at times and uncomfortable while lying down or moving around. I felt strange and intense pain in my muscles, tendons and other parts of my body. These pains were more intense at night. Sometimes, I had a tingling sensation that moved from one point to another without any apparent reason. At other times, I had a burning sensation that moved up and down my spine and other parts of my body. Sometimes, my extremities were numb and lifeless. I found it difficult to express myself and certain smells and noises became unbearable to me. Only the sound of children playing outside brought me back to life while the rest of my existence had become lifeless. This seemed really strange to me because I had always been a very dynamic and optimistic woman.

After several years of intense inner struggle and a process of deep purification with the Angels (years in which I also touched on very high mystical states) I finally understood with all of my cells that these revelations had been gifts from our Creator and that they had brought me closer to Him. Gradually, I started enjoying life again. I then realized that all of my senses had sharpened. I had increased clairvoyance, clairaudience and clairsentience. My attitude towards my dreams had completely changed. I thanked God and his messengers, and I continue to thank Them. I was conscious of the value of what had been revealed to me about myself. Revelations of all sorts could now be multiplied. Hundreds of people tell me of experiences similar to mine. I listen to them with compassion. I am moved to the very depths of my soul because I understand their suffering. Like myself at that time, these people are experiencing the opening of their unconsciousness as the veil is lifted to give way to revelations.

This evening's theme is how to receive revelations. An Angel can help us with this. He is Angel LAUVIAH and he bears the number 17. This is the Angel of revelations *par excellence*.

Among the 72 Angels, there is another that bears the same Name. This Angel is also called LAUVIAH and is the subject of another chapter in this book. He bears a different number and has other Qualities, however. In the tradition, both are said to complete each other. Angel LAUVIAH, number 11 is the Angel of victory, expansion, enthusiasm and success. This is an Angel of the daytime and of action, while Angel LAUVIAH, number 17 is an Angel of the night. He works from the inside and helps us receive revelations through our dreams and daydreams.

One of Angel LAUVIAH's Qualities is that He *acts against torment and sadness*. Therefore, before being able to touch on this enthusiasm and this pure state of joy, we have to descend into the depths of our unconsciousness. We have to cleanse and transform everything that is at the root of this torment, that is, everything that lurks hidden in our unconsciousness and that forces us to seek compensation on the outside. One day, we confront all of these memories.

Each time we transgress a Divine Law, we generate torment or sadness, exactly as we do when we transgress an earthly law. Transgression inevitably leads to trouble.

When we work with the Angels, we can use numbers as signs and we can read their meaning. These numbers generally represent Angelic States of Consciousness. Some people who come to the lectures for the first time and who have no knowledge of initiatory science tell us, "It's very strange. For several weeks now, or even several months, every time I look at a clock, I always see the same number. I see 11:11. At other times, I always see 12:12 or 4:44." The number varies according to the person and the period of time but it keeps turning up again and again. At the beginning of our spiritual path, we also notice the occurrence of more and more coincidences.

At first, these coincidences have no precise meaning. Cosmic Intelligence simply wants to stimulate the person's consciousness in order to lead him to seek in-depth answers and to get him used to going behind the form, that is, behind the veil. Thus, we get used to penetrating the parallel dimensions. These coincidences lead us to develop our spiritual curiosity, that is, the curiosity of a child asking questions. This is the good kind of curiosity. These coincidences constitute the first door that opens a person up to a greater dimension, an opening through which he seeks to go deeper and deeper. This is the initiation of a process.

A number bears significance only from the moment a person establishes a link between what he sees and what he was thinking about at that moment. This link turns the number into a sign. The number takes on a particular significance. The same idea applies to everything that can be observed in our immediate surroundings. For instance, if a loud and sudden noise resounds in a room with a hundred people, it could have a different meaning for each one of those people. That meaning will, in turn, depend on what each person was thinking about when the noise occurred. One day, we begin to think in this manner. We begin to see and read events in depth. Then, once it has become a habit, we end up continually reading signs in our daily life. We are constantly connected. This, along with the interpretation of our dreams, leads us to develop great spiritual autonomy. A day comes when we no longer lose our Divine connection.

Let's have a look at the Qualities of Angel 17 LAUVIAH including *allows us to perceive the great mysteries of the Universe during the night* and *revelations in dreams, in daydreams*. Angel LAUVIAH helps us rediscover our propensity for dreaming if we have lost it. He also helps us to have a good understanding of what They want to tell us through our dreams. We have seen that before the mysteries of the Universe can be revealed to us, we must face a great number of obstructions within our unconscious memories. Thus, at first, They will reveal to us who we are and what we need to change. In the beginning, these revelations are very difficult to accept, but the day eventually comes when we manage to say, "More! More!" We do not want this revelatory process to stop because we know where it is leading us. It is truly a gift. At first, however, it does not seem that way.

One day, this process allows us to receive many different types of inspiration because Angel 17 LAUVIAH can give us the *gift for music, poetry, literature* and *transcendental philosophy*.

This Angel allows us to get to know the mechanisms of the psyche. The root of the word *psyche* comes from the Greek *psy*, meaning that which touches the soul. The psyche is also comparable to a mirror that we can incline whichever way we like. This concept of the psyche as a mirror is very old. So many aspects are veiled from us that when we have not integrated the ray represented by Angel LAUVIAH, that is, when we distort It, practically all of our perceptions are false. Hence *torments, depression, sadness, insomnia* and *hyperactivity*. These are all distortions related to this Angel.

I'd like to tell you a true story that shows how the psyche functions and how unconscious memories can falsify our perceptions. A lady told me that one morning in the boarding house where she lived, the cook had served strawberry jam and the woman sitting next to her asked, "Do you think this jam tastes like aspirin?" "No," she replied. "I think the jam is delicious."

Everyone at the table agreed. The woman who had perceived a taste of aspirin meditated on this. The following day, she understood why she had perceived this taste in the jam. She explained that when she was young, whenever she had a temperature, her mother would crush an aspirin and mix it in with strawberry jam so it would be easier for her to swallow. She added, "I didn't like this. But I had no choice. It was imposed upon me."

Through this simple example, we see that the spirit is powerful to the extent that it can alter our taste and materialize a taste different from the original one. We can see that unconscious memories can alter perceptions. In a situation like this one (in which we make an unpleasant association) we can react in two ways. With an ordinary consciousness, we say to ourselves, "If I taste aspirin every time I eat strawberry jam, then the solution is very simple. I just won't eat it anymore." The problem will therefore never be solved. On the other hand, with an awakened consciousness, we treat this same situation as a sign that is revealing certain parts of ourselves. In such cases, instead of avoiding the question, we meditate on it.

We often think that meditation asks that we empty our minds. However, emptying our minds is the final stage and we must never force ourselves to do so. When thoughts resurface, we simply deal with them. Often, they are but the tip of the iceberg, that is, the smallest visible part of a fairly big issue. By meditating, for example, this woman returned to her childhood and she took a step forward. We must not, however, stop there. We must take advantage of the opportunity to symbolically analyze the experience we had, as if it were a sign or a dream. That is the key.

I would now like to talk to you about a situation that a woman is going through which touches on certain distortions related to Angel 17 LAUVIAH, that is, *insomnia* and *anxiety*. This example also shows how we receive revelations concerning a person while he is talking to us, that is to say, the way in which we can perceive unconscious content that dwells within that person when we know how to read signs.

This lady was attending a lecture for the first time and she came to speak to me. First of all, she told me that her house had caught fire. There is no such thing as coincidence. When something happens in our life, we can always extract an inner meaning from it. Fire is linked to the spirit. It can refer to a positive, constructive and bright spirit, but it can also be a negative spirit that destroys. A negative spirit is like an incendiary person. He feeds on criticism and his thoughts go down into his emotions and manifest on the outside through aggression and destructive gestures.

I said to her, "There is something for you to understand in this. The materialization of an event always has its roots in the world of thoughts."

"Ah!" she remarked. "Our house did indeed catch fire just before my ex-husband and I separated. We had a lot of problems and there was a lot of agitation at the time. But it's my ex-husband who has always been afraid of fire."

Where do phobias and unreasonable fears come from? If we were to descend into this man's unconsciousness, we could probably see that he had suffered because of fires in other lives. Once again, however, we have to go further. Otherwise, we cultivate these fears and we justify them by saying, "It's normal that I'm afraid because I've already been through this." We must go to the root of the problem. We say to ourselves, "I had thoughts that weren't right. What were they?"

I commented to this lady, "Even if your ex-husband is the one who was afraid of fire, the fact remains that it is no coincidence that you were with this man. You have resonance with him." By examining the Consciousness Diagram, we have seen that our consciousness is only a tiny part of us. Within us, there is a mass of memories that are veiled and that attract specific events. Therefore, these events along with the people we associate with reveal what dwells within our unconsciousness. If we really want to understand what it is that we are going through, these contents are revealed to us. I therefore added, "In the causal world, what led to the fire is not only a part of your ex-husband, it is also a part of you. There are attitudes and ways of thinking that you need to rectify. If you do not change them, they will manifest themselves again, either in the same way or in another way."

She then told me about the difficulties she was experiencing at work. She said, "I've been working there for several years now, but my bosses, who are brother and sister, keep repeating the same thing over and over and I'm fed up listening to them. They're also aggressive and they criticize constantly."

What's more, this woman did not feel appreciated at work. I therefore said to her, "It's no coincidence that you are there. It's because you have resonance with them. Somewhere in your unconsciousness, similar memories lurk. Even if this idea is difficult to accept at first, if you learn to read at the vertical level, you'll see how much it will help you."

To show her how to do this, I asked her, "What does your boss keep repeating?"

"She often goes on about how her husband left with her credit card and spent everything, and that he never did any of the household chores and only wanted to be served."

"When a person talks about someone else, whether it is about what attracts him or what bothers him, he is actually talking about himself. A person always talks about himself, even when he is talking about others, unless he has transcended everything to do with the subject. In such cases, the vibration is quite different and the person generally does not talk about others. When your boss talks to you about her ex-husband, it is herself that she is talking about. You can analyze what she says exactly as if it were a dream she was telling you. The theft of credit cards indicates that certain parts of her steal and take other people's energy. In the beginning, it's normal to take other people's energy. We don't know how to receive energy because certain energy centers are blocked by all sorts of obstructions, such as criticism and aggression. We are therefore obliged to take energy from the outside or from others, since we cannot receive it directly. Also, when she says that her husband never wanted to do work around the house and only wanted to be served, she is also talking about herself. This shows that she still has self-centered aspects within her that do not want to look after others."

One day, we no longer hold such opinions. We are so happy to serve others, including our spouse. Of course, this exchange opened up new dimensions in her way of perceiving her boss.

I added, "As long as you feel upset by what your boss says, it shows that you are a bit like her. When she talks to you about these subjects, instead of getting stressed and repressing your feelings, take advantage of the situation and do your Angel Recitation. Silently repeat the Name of the Angel. No one can prevent you from doing this. Tell yourself, 'I am upset. This means that I also have these aspects somewhere within myself, even if they don't express themselves on the outside. By doing my Angel Recitation, blockages will be cleared.' Otherwise, you repress aggression and you silently criticize. Consequently, you nourish the same forces within yourself. At that moment, more karma becomes inscribed within you."

Let me share my trick with you. I'll tell you what I did for many years. Of all the Divine Laws, I worked at continually remembering four of them. These four Laws made up what I called my Angelic Memo.

During the entire period when I was remembering these Laws, I would talk to myself. We must not feel guilty. We must avoid saying, "Oh no! Why have I faltered again with the same person?" When we are on a spiritual path, we want to incarnate goodness, generosity and all the other beautiful qualities. When we fly off the handle, however, we don't feel right. We think we are ugly and we hit ourselves over the head, figuratively speaking. This is normal.

However, not maintaining perfect self-control is not necessarily a relapse. You have seen in the Consciousness Diagram (cf. page 5) the degree to which the reservoir of unconscious memories is vast. We touch upon multiple lives and, when dealing with someone, this person may incarnate a lot of distortions. We therefore work on one of them, then another, and then another. At a particular moment, the channel is opened to us. If They were to immediately open us up to all that we are, it would be so powerful that we would explode like a bomb. They proceed in the following way: They give us energy and They let us experiment all sorts of things that are more or less right. We feel fine doing this and we have ample energy. The day comes, however, when They open us up to our unconscious memories. Consequently, we proceed on a path of ritualistic cleansing and, at certain intervals, They say, "Great! He has gone through this stage. Let's take him a little further." The increase in the dose of evil or of distortions we are plunged into corresponds to a passage, that is, to a degree of initiation. To that effect, what strikes us as a relapse may only be the apprenticeship for a more difficult test.

I kept reminding myself of the four Laws that I had chosen. In the heat of the moment, when someone pushes our buttons with exactly the right intensity, we naturally forget everything. We get caught up in the power of the emotions that are resurfacing and the Law of Resonance. All those beautiful concepts go up in smoke. This is why I kept my Angelic Memo close at hand. At home, I stuck it up all over the place, wherever I would spend most of my time, such as the fridge door. It served to inscribe these Laws deep within me.

⊙

My Angelic Memo

The first Law concerns Justice. I would say to myself, "Christiane, don't forget. You are upset. What that person is doing right now is not right. Remember: *Divine Justice is absolute.* We reap what we sow. The guides will take care of that person. It is an absolute certainty." I would also say to myself, "It's not time for you to intervene so as to see justice done. You don't feel good, you aren't focused and you are angry. If you talk to him now, you'll simply be accumulating more karma. If you have to talk to him, it must be done gently, without any feeling of revenge. Breathe in and meditate."

Keep in mind that we need to be careful when we say that the guides will take care of them, because we must remember that when something bothers us it is because we have within us the attitude that the other person manifests. In the beginning, it is difficult to come back to ourselves because the forces that rise to the surface when resonance is awakened are very powerful. Thus, as soon as we have left it to the Creator to judge the other person, we concentrate on what is going on within ourselves and we call to mind the *Law of Resonance*, which is the second Law in my Angelic Memo.

I kept repeating to myself, "You have this problem. You are simply paying off your karma. You are growing." It is not necessary to have done advanced studies in psychology to detect what bothers us in other people's attitude and behavior. When we feel that something is bothering us, we come back to ourselves. Thus, we discover certain parts of our unconsciousness. By doing our Angel Recitation, we are in the process of cleansing these memories. In this way, we break the chain of karma, which we would otherwise continue to accumulate.

When we feel good with someone, it is easy to feel that we are part of the Great Whole and say, "You are me and I am you." In fact, these are words we often hear in so-called spiritual circles. It is not so easy to say that others are parts of us, however, when we are bothered by something they did. That is a big step to take! If we cannot manage to do this, it means that we are not yet committed to the initiatory path. When we come back to ourselves, as soon as we feel upset, the force that emerges from our unconsciousness no longer has any outlet. Since we cannot get angry any more, this force cannot pour out and procure momentary well-being. It remains within us and we are obliged to confront it. Of course, it makes quite a fuss on the inside. This, however, is definitely not repression. It's OK because repression is not right. What is happening is that we are becoming conscious that we are an integral part of everything. We do our Angel Recitation, we ask the Angel to help us, we breathe in and we cleanse. At one particular moment, calm is restored and we can sense that a blockage has been cleared. We have come through a stage. It is a victory. Of course, we have to repeat this process often because cleansing the unconsciousness is a long undertaking. One day, however, we are so used to doing it that it becomes automatic.

Here is the third Law: *evil is educational.* Evil has its place. It is there to help us grow. It strengthens and stimulates us. If certain events did not happen in our lives to shake us up a bit, we would stay in our cozy little routine and keep on cultivating incorrect attitudes and behavior. Hence, what at first may seem to be an unfortunate event can be considered a blessing. Understanding that evil serves good helps us face up to situations no matter what they are.

I would also repeat the fourth Law. I would say to myself, "Christiane, remember that *matter is temporal.*" For all sorts of reasons that usually stem from our need to be acknowledged and loved, we attach importance to concrete results. We believe they will procure prestige, admiration and power. Our actions are based on results. I used to tell myself, "Matter is temporal, but the quality you are developing is eternal."

I repeated these four Laws for years. Gradually, they sprang to mind faster and faster when I needed them to keep my self-control. They would calm me down and help me refocus and get on with my inner work. When we do this, our vibration level rises and, at a particular moment, as if by miracle, the clouds part and we see clearly. Everything becomes easier to assimilate and the situation in question straightens itself out. This is absolutely certain and we realize it when we have applied this procedure a certain number of times. These Laws (representing the fundamental basis of the first degree of Enlightenment) are eventually inscribed in our hearts and in all of our cells. Needless to say, we must practice before they can be inscribed.

Here is a very simple analogy that reminds us of the importance of repetition and perseverance. It also shows us that when we are on a spiritual path, a certain amount of discipline is indispensable. In Canada, cars are driven on the right. When we get into our car we don't say, "Hold on a minute! What side do I drive on, right or left?" No. We get into the car and we drive on the right. It is inscribed in us.

If we live for a few years in a country where they drive on the left, we inscribe within us memories of driving on the left. When we return to Canada, we have to be very vigilant in the beginning. We have to constantly ask ourselves which side to drive on because we have some memories of driving on the right and others of driving on the left. We get all mixed up. Even after several years, we can have a moment of weakness and find ourselves driving on the left. This can cause accidents. Well, the same thing applies to our consciousness. Numerous memories have accumulated that make us lapse into our former distorted attitudes and behavior. Even if we have done a lot of inner work, we can slip up and lose our self-control and our mastery. This is why we must be vigilant and constantly remind ourselves of the Great Laws that allow us to keep this self-mastery.

I will continue with the example of the lady to show you how the job we do can reveal inner needs that are in accordance with our life-plan. In other words, we are not in a job by coincidence.

The lady said to me, "I didn't choose this job or these bosses. I was unemployed and I ended up in this place. I had no choice. I've endured this situation for several years now."

"Ah!" I replied. "If we've ended up in a workplace or profession, that is to say, one that we haven't consciously chosen, that doesn't change the fact that our work on the outside shows us what we need to develop and inscribe within us. When birds migrate, they are guided by their instinct, which leads them to follow certain trajectories that are determined by electro-magnetic fields. The same applies to us. We have a program and we are guided towards certain places and certain people. We think we choose, but we do not. It is, among other things, the karmic dimensions of our program that take us to where we are. Consequently, we find ourselves exactly where we should be."

Therefore, as we begin to awaken and to understand this process, we say to ourselves, "I am here and I don't feel like being here. I really don't feel good here, but it's part of my program. I understand that I have to inscribe this kind of activity within myself." We see the usefulness of our work. Even if it represents a karmic element, our life becomes pleasant because we have acquired an understanding of what we are going through.

What did this lady do for a living? She sewed canvasses for the manufacturing of carports. When we analyze a job, we use the same symbolism as we do in dreams. We examine it in as much depth. First of all, when we sew, we put pieces together, that is, we reunite parts. On the inside, therefore, sewing represents the need to unify our different personalities. We have seen that in our unconsciousness there are different types of memories that create as many different personalities. When we sew a garment (garments are linked to the aura) it indicates a need to unify our personality. This lady sewed canvasses for car shelters. A car, like any other vehicle, symbolizes our manner of behaving towards others in society. This woman's job therefore concerned the protection of personal behavior in society. Thus, this woman is assembling parts of herself which, when sewn back together, will ensure her inner protection. For that to happen, however, she must stop behaving with others the way she does at the moment.

There is positive and negative protection, and the negative one must be worked on. What is negative protection? Negative protection consists in isolating ourselves when we do not feel good with others. We close ourselves up and build a shell. By closing ourselves up, however, we end up isolating ourselves from the Great Whole, that is, from the Creator Himself.

I said to this woman, "Since your work consists in sewing, you often do repetitive gestures. You can therefore take advantage of the fact that you have a lot of time to do your Angel Recitation. You have great availability to work on your inner self. By using the Law of Resonance while sewing, you can say to yourself, 'Ah! This disturbs me. But instead of closing myself off, I accept the idea that I too have this aspect within me. It's opening up the wound and it bothers me!' This way, you will be working on your inner protection."

Towards the end of our conversation, this lady told me that she suffered from a phobia that had taken hold of her. She was afraid she would become aggressive, burst out and lose her self-control. This really worried her and caused her sleepless nights. I said to her, "This phobia you've told me about reveals resonance you have with your ex-husband. For him, it is expressed through a fear of fire. It concerns memories of aggression. The same applies to your bosses whom you said were aggressive. You have memories concerning this subject that need to be cleansed. When you spoke about them, in truth it is your own aggression that you were talking about. That's all right. One day, we learn to read in this manner. Everything we repress and keep in our unconsciousness ends up creating a heavy load of emotional problems that can burst at any moment. When the veil of the unconscious is lifted, the valve that normally keeps this load under control suddenly becomes ineffective. Thus we are obliged to take care of these memories. Those who do not will end up bursting. This manifests itself right down to the physical level and might even translate into a criminal act." This lady was happy. These explanations were true revelations for her.

Furthermore, she said, "I read a book about white magic where it explained that we could help others with this technique. I thought I'd like to do that." It seemed simple to her. "That evening, before going to sleep, I asked if it was a good idea for me to do white magic to help others. That night, I had a dream. *I was on a beach that was crawling with insects. There were insects everywhere. There was even an empty bottle that was filling up with insects.* When I woke up the next morning, I realized that I had had my answer. The dream was clear, 'No white magic! Deal with your own insects first before dealing with those of other people.'" (laughter)

I congratulated this woman. I said to her, "Well done, madam! I congratulate you on your spiritual honesty and on your integrity. Some people think they are doing white magic. Unbeknownst to them, however, what they are doing is injecting it with desires for personal power. It then becomes black magic. Truly, you have spared your soul some serious karma." Magic is experimentation and, from this point of view, it is not dramatic. It does, however, create karma that has to be cleansed. We can help others, that is, we should be altruistic, but before practicing white magic we first need to do a lot of cleansing within.

Before leaving, this woman told me another dream that, as you will see, is very revealing. She said, "Just before my husband and I separated, at which time I wasn't getting along with him any more, They sent me a dream." *A woman was climbing a set of stairs. At the top, settled in a dog's basket was a skinny man who seemed to be coming home from the war. The woman was indifferent. She didn't even look at him. Then she fell down the stairs and broke into smithereens.*

What does this dream mean? I told her, "All the characters in the dream represent parts of yourself. In relation to the ground floor, the top of the stairs symbolizes the future. Together they represent the causal world and what is yet to come. This dream has two parts. Let's have a look at the first one. The man symbolizes the world of action and manifestation. The fact that he is skinny and seems to be coming home from the war indicates a lack of resources and of love. He has been through conflicts and aggression and that has emptied him of all his energy. He's in a dog basket. This shows that a part of you felt that it was being treated like a dog. In the second part of the dream, the woman, who represents the inner world, is indifferent. She sees nothing and remains cold. You were being told that your shell or your indifference would soon be broken. What would remain would be the feeling of not having been treated well, or of having been crushed. The content of a dream always manifests itself. Whether we like it or not and whether we take it into consideration or not, it describes the program that's been prepared for us."

That is exactly what this woman felt when she was with her employers. She had had this dream some time before and it was already materializing. We can see that she retired under a shell of indifference. She had hardened herself so as to lessen the pain caused by resonance others awoke in her.

Revelations occur in this manner. We develop certain attitudes and behavior as compensation. At a particular moment, however, They break our shell and we must visit everything that has been bothering us. Such situations can lead to depression, especially if we do not understand the process. Therefore, we are happy to have dreams like this one. They are so liberating. They are beautiful dreams.

How can such a dream manifest itself? It is good to have dreams and to interpret them correctly, but we should always try to detect their manifestation in our daily life. A dream like this one can manifest itself several times throughout the day and during the weeks and months that follow. The lady we have just talked about could work for years on the content of this dream. In reality, she could encounter a very confident and well-spoken man. Unconsciously, however, she would touch on that part of herself that was lying in the dog basket and she would feel crushed. Whether the man was correct or not, she would compare herself to him by thinking, "I don't have such ease," and she would feel diminished. Two minutes later, another man might arrive who was clumsy and poor looking, and she would adopt a completely indifferent, even disdainful, attitude towards him.

Of course, we are not aware of such attitudes and behavior (this woman is a lovely person) because they happen at the energy level. In the example we have just seen, this woman's behavior would have seemed correct from the outside. She would not have said anything hurtful to the poor man. We could, however, have felt her disdain at the energy level. In the beginning, we do not perceive these subtleties because they are mixed in with coarser perceptions.

When we receive a dream that calls our attention to certain distortions, we can target this specific ray and when the situation turns up, we can perceive our inner reactions with greater ease. At that moment, we say to ourselves, "No! This comes from me. This has nothing to do with that man. Clean up this part." By making a habit of observing ourselves and reacting this way, we can eventually receive anything and understand our environment all the time.

We can see the richness and beauty of such dreams. They are great gifts. Up Above, of course, They are very kind. From time to time, They send us dreams full of light and They say, "Look. You have evolved." These lovely dreams are easy to accept, but we have to be able to receive all kinds of dreams and maintain a humble attitude, even when faced with dreams that are not very gratifying. This way, we progress very rapidly. Up Above, They say to themselves, "She doesn't need too much balm or encouragement. Let's go!" and They do not skimp on the mirror effect messages and we are happy. It is as if we were taking part in a continual workshop where the teaching is completely personalized, because the information is constantly communicated to us directly and from the inside. This is what we call spiritual autonomy.

I will now talk to you about another situation that concerns revelations and shows us that the workplace is an ideal location to receive revelations and to develop qualities and virtues. This situation was experienced by a man who has been following the teachings of The Traditional Study of Angels for a number of years and who often confides in my husband and asks him to interpret some of his dreams. He works for a multinational company and he manages financial portfolios worth millions of dollars. At one particular moment, he told my husband, "I'm tired of working with certain people. I have to work on important projects and this sometimes leads me to work with businessmen who are really full of themselves." He felt torn between his spiritual philosophy and what he had to go through in his workplace.

My husband told him, "You know that the Law of Resonance also applies in your case. As long as you are uncomfortable with the pride that these businessmen display, it means that this aspect is still present somewhere in your unconscious memories. One day, you'll be able to love those people and consider them as little children boasting about the great toys they have. That's exactly what they're doing. Until then, you should use the work that you do for this company to cleanse your memories. That is why you feel this discomfort."

Later, this man told my husband about one of his dreams wherein They revealed the progress he had made on his spiritual path. *He found himself in Mexico, at the top of a mountain, with businessmen. As he was coming down the mountain, about halfway down, he suddenly felt something prick him in the chest. It was a thistle. When he tried to take it out, he tore his skin but he didn't see any blood. At one particular moment, he found himself with the thistle in his hand. Inside his chest, at the level of his heart, there was a living eye.*

My husband said to him, "That's a lovely dream. It's an important dream. They are showing you that, during your descent into matter, there is an opening. There is a spiritualization of matter. From now on you will be able to see with your heart's eye. You'll be less bothered by the distortions of the businessmen because you have done such a considerable amount of work on yourself." Ah! The man was happy! He was all smiles when he said, "That's how I had interpreted it myself."

Let's analyze this dream. Considering what this man is going through at work, the fact that he found himself in Mexico (he lives in Canada) with businessmen indicates that he was being brought back to an-cient memories related to his way of doing business. He discovered a thistle in his chest. He could have been given a completely different symbol of pain, but the thistle has a particular significance. First of all, it belongs to the vegetable kingdom, which is symbolically linked to feelings. This symbolism is reinforced by the fact that the thistle was situated close to his heart. Furthermore, the thistle has therapeutic qualities. Among its other virtues, it stimulates the secretion of bile and is very effective in cases of liver poisoning.

With his dream, this man was able to understand the deep-rooted cause of a serious case of food poisoning he had had a few years before. When we do an in-depth analysis of an intoxication of this kind, we may say, "Well, I ate such and such food and that's the cause of it." This dream, however, showed him the deep-rooted cause of the intoxication, that is, the collection of resonance he had with businessmen who did not use their power correctly. This man has a very spiritual program, so They wanted to incite him to change certain behavior and attitudes that were still unconscious within him. Through the symbol of the thistle, we can see once more that evil, or that which hurts, can have therapeutic value and can help us grow. The dissonance this man felt at work led him to a spiritual cleansing and to the adoption of an attitude that came from the heart.

These realizations led him to receive another dream that to him turned out to be a very surprising revelation. *He was walking on university grounds when, all of a sudden, he realized that everybody was looking at him. He looked down at himself and saw that he was wearing a baby's diaper.* (laughter) *"Ah," he said to himself. "That doesn't make any sense." He felt embarrassed.* Imagine. It's as if I were in a diaper right here in front of you. Wouldn't that be something?

Why was he given this dream? In a dream, even if we have never been to one, a university symbolizes advanced studies at the con-sciousness level. He was being told, "Where advanced studies at the consciousness level are concerned, you are just a little baby. You are still in diapers. You are only at the very beginning." All the people who were looking at him represented parts of him. He could have been given a different dream where the people found it completely normal to see him walking around in a diaper. What difference would that have made? The dream's characters, including the dreamer, are conscious that he is wearing a diaper. This shows a higher degree of spiritual evolution because it shows that this man knows what level he has reached. This man has great professional responsibilities and he has been to university, therefore he enjoys great social prestige. In this dream, however, he was being told, "Where advanced studies at the consciousness level are concerned, you are just a little baby."

What purpose does this kind of dream serve? It serves the purpose of teaching us humility. That is the key. If we wish to receive revelations we must develop humility. It is an absolute fact. For this reason, when They begin to open our consciousness and reveal to us who we are, every image we had forged of ourselves, such as our belief that we were generous and had all sorts of qualities, turns out to be completely false. We realize, "No. That's not what I'm like. Nor am I like that." In the beginning, faced with these revelations, we are truly shaken. We feel broken at the mental, emotional and even physical levels. We do, however, end up reconstructing ourselves. In the meantime, we accept the fact that we are as we are and this makes us very happy! Humility is truly the pathway to revelations. Many traditions declare it so, but we must experience it for ourselves.

This man has great charisma and a nice simplicity. He is truly a lovely being. He receives revelations in his dreams and he uses them in real life. For example, at one particular moment, he decided to change the recruitment procedure in his firm (from time to time, he has to recruit personnel). He told the employment agencies involved that, from that moment on, he wanted them to make the first selection among the applicants after which he would meet the candidates they had selected. His idea was to wait near the end of the procedure before consulting their curriculum vitae, just before making the final decision.

In short, he no longer wanted to make decisions based on CVs. Of course, he would continue to give the agencies the list of the specific tasks and competences required. From that moment on, however, they would have to check whether the candidates fulfilled these criteria. The agencies and the candidates were disconcerted. This way of proceeding is most unusual, especially when hiring executives.

Why did this man want to modify the hiring procedure in such a way? It is because he realized that when he read the CV first, he approached the candidate with certain preconceived ideas. The analytical approach limits our perception by creating a set image. Moreover, he had acquired confidence in an intuitive and non-analytical approach, which is one of the Qualities of Angel 17 LAUVIAH. He believed this new way of proceeding would help him further develop his intuition and his faculty for getting a sense of the person through subtle perception, that is, by feeling the vibration behind the words and the concrete presentation. In any case, this method did not prevent him from studying the CVs later.

Of course, non-analytical methods of getting to know others are not new. Many studies on human resources, for example, deal with this subject. This is good and these studies have their use, but the fact remains that the depth with which we can perceive another person depends on the level of knowledge we have of ourselves. In other words, it is impossible for us to understand someone in depth if we have not done this work within ourselves because the image we will form of him will be distorted by our own unconscious memories. In a conversation, the other person will say something to us, and this will touch on an unconscious memory. To use the former example, we will think that the other person has put aspirin in the strawberry jam. We will be mixed up and our perception will be confused, but it is we who will have added the aspirin. Therefore, only part of our perception will be correct and the other part will be distorted. This is how perception works. Of course, in the beginning, we cannot perceive clearly and thus we cannot be correct in our estimation of the other person. We can, however, learn to say to ourselves, "Ah! I felt that. In my dream, I was shown this and that, and certain memories resurfaced within me. In this way, we learn to get to know ourselves through others."

We unravel our own karmic knots and, one day, we have no more resonance owing to distortions and we succeed in understanding others. In a way, we become neutral. From then on, if we say to ourselves, "Yes. Okay. This is jam but there's aspirin in it," it will be because the jam really does contain aspirin. We have to go through a long process of inner work to reach such a level of perceptive precision. This requires that we refine our inner work. It involves turning our consciousness into gold.

As I have told you, this man felt torn between his spiritual philosophy and his professional work. You have seen the reasons behind this. For some time, he wondered if he should leave or keep this job. He talked about it to my husband who advised him to simply ask for a dream. This man dreams a lot and his dreams are very precise. "Ask Them to make it clear," my husband said. "Ask Them to say, 'Okay. Now it's time to leave. You've finished your apprenticeship in this firm.' But you must be committed to following orders and not react by saying, 'Okay, but I had a promotion coming up and this and that. And what am I to live on if I leave this job?' Our relationship with Them, Up Above, does not work this way." When we ask for guidance through our dreams, we must get used to working without a safety net.

When we start living like this, many horizons are opened up to us. At first, we experiment with questions that are not very important. Gradually, we base decisions of greater and greater consequence on the guidance from Up Above. One day, taking direction from dreams and signs becomes a way of life. We develop total trust in Divine Intelligence.

This man was relieved and, for the moment, he knows that there are still experiences he must live through in this company. He no longer keeps one foot in the door and the other out, tortured by ambivalence. He has accepted his program and, when the time comes, he will move on to something else.

I would now like to share with you an account that illustrates how our two principles work. We must always remember that we have two principles within us: the masculine and the feminine.

This account comes from a woman who came to ask me to interpret a dream. Her appearance is natural and very conservative. I'd even go so far as to say that her appearance reveals a slight touch of austerity. She said to me, "I had a dream. *I was in the house where I was born and where I spent my childhood. At one particular moment, I heard a noise outside. I went into the kitchen and I looked out the window to see what was going on outside. I saw a cow sitting on the ground quietly chewing grass. All of a sudden, a bull arrived and it was full of vitality. It looked very dapper. It started nudging the cow with its muzzle, lifting up its hooves and frolicking about flirtatiously. Ah! The bull was happy! The cow looked at him and said, 'Go away! Leave me alone!' Then she went on chewing her grass, swinging her jaws left and right. The bull went away. After a while, he came back just as frisky as ever. He began to nuzzle the cow again. The cow got*

annoyed. She looked at him and said, 'Go away, frisky! Stop bother-
ing me.' The bull went away and the cow continued chewing her cud.
After a while, he came back and, this time, he puffed out his chest
and began to sing like a tenor. (laughter) *I was surprised.* I woke
up." (laughter)

This woman was contemplating the idea of having a companion
and when she received this dream, she wondered, "Are They telling
me that it will be the Don Juan of the choir? Oh no! Please, not
him! Not the fancy pants in the choir!" (laughter) She also thought,
"Maybe They are announcing the arrival of a man whose sign is
the Taurus," because she dabbles a bit in astrology.

I told her, "You weren't being told that it was the Don Juan of the
choir nor a man whose sign is the Taurus. In this dream, the tenor
and the cow represent parts of you." Oh! She was surprised! She
recognized herself a bit in the cow, (laughter) but not at all in the
bull. She briefly spoke to me about her life and how she had always
been quite shy with men.

I interpreted the dream for her. I told her, "In this dream, you
were brought back to the place of your childhood. This means
that memories of your primary forces are being called upon. You
were in the kitchen. A kitchen symbolizes preparation for action,
that is, what is going on and how we prepare ourselves. This dream
shows you how you prepare yourself for manifestation. Why were
animals used as symbols? That's to point out to you that you have
work to do on unconscious memories related to your vital energy.
The bull has quite a sexual and materializing energy. It's powerful
and frisky. It stimulates the other person. You also have parts of
your vital energy that reject it and say, 'Go away' and that rumi-
nate over things. In everyday language, when we say, 'Stop chewing
over things, stop ruminating,' we mean, 'Stop brooding over your
troubles.' The cow was chewing grass. Grass, like all plants, symbolizes feelings. Green represents love. So you have unconscious
memories that lead you to brood about questions concerning love.
That does not make you happy."

This lovely woman stared at me wide-eyed and said, "Ah! Now
I understand my life better." In the past, she had observed that a
certain number of men courted her but they were men that other
women lusted after and these were women that she personally felt
were very seductive. When these men approached her, she would

either flee them or else become very shy. Following these explanations, she had a better understanding of her reaction to the men who were attracted to her.

I went on, "This is why you didn't recognize yourself in the bull that was trying to excite the cow." On the outside, this woman did not at all appear seductive. Her appearance was very conservative and there was nothing that led us to believe she could harbor tantalizing parts within her. The cow she had been shown could represent memories of wounds related to break-ups or to being abandoned. As these memories are painful, the person resists facing them. This creates a certain duality in the person's energy. All at once, the person stimulates and rejects the other person. This was quite a revelation for this woman.

When I saw her again some time later, she told me, "Now I recognize my bull." In other words, whenever this energy or perfume is released, she senses it. You can see the beauty of such revelations. In actuality, these attitudes are not at all obvious. They sometimes manifest themselves in a completely opposite way, as in the case of this apparently conservative and austere woman, for example. How can we become conscious of what dwells within us? We realize that these dreams are, in fact, true revelations and precious gifts. With a dream such as this one, this woman's life could change completely. Needless to say, she will have to do a certain amount of work to purify her memories.

⊙

Fibromyalgia, Chronic Fatigue and Depression

This evening I would like to share with you a revelation about one of the illnesses of the 21st Century. For the moment, it is very badly defined by medical institutions and cannot be detected by X-rays or by biological examinations. It has not been classified yet. It is therefore referred to as a syndrome.

What is this illness? It is fibromyalgia. What are the symptoms? The list is long: chronic fatigue that can lead to total exhaustion, intense pain in the tendons, muscles, and other points of the body (sometimes felt as either tingling sensations moving from one point to another or as burning sensations along the spine that get worse during the night,) occasional difficulty when speaking or expressing oneself, insomnia and anxiety that can lead to depression, intolerance to certain odors and noises and, finally, numbing of the extremities that is sometimes accompanied by cramps.

Do these symptoms sound familiar? They are the same as those I outlined in my introduction. I suffered from such symptoms years ago, at the beginning of my initiatory path. If, at that time, I had consulted a doctor who was not open to spirituality, he could have diagnosed me as suffering from fibromyalgia, although at the time this was not recognized as an illness.

As is the case with depression, chronic fatigue and burnouts, doctors feel helpless when faced with the problem of fibromyalgia and most prescribe anti-depressants. When we know that the use of these substances is limited to freezing the pain and postponing real treatment, we do indeed question it. In Canada, more than 700 million dollars are spent every year on anti-depressants. This represents one-hundred dollars per family per year. We know that in just five years, the number of prescriptions for anti-depressants increased from 2 to 5 million for a population of 30 million in Canada. Can you imagine the number of prescriptions in the USA and elsewhere in the world? Some doctors even go so far as to prescribe these substances as soon as a patient goes through bereavement, a separation, or the loss of a job. This phenomenon, which has become a real problem for our society, bears serious consequences.

As I was telling you, I suffered from fibromyalgia for a certain length of time. My husband also went through the same types of pain and anxiety, along with other difficulties. Thank God, we got over it because we work with The Traditional Study of Angels and we never once thought of taking anti-depressants. We searched for the deep-rooted cause of this ill-being and we discovered that it was basically a reaction to the opening of the unconsciousness. The person is immersed in his memories, many of which are painful. It is not easy because our spirit resists. What we call fibromyalgia is, in fact, a problem at the level of the soul. Seen from this point of view, it is not an illness.

One day, instead of saying, "I'm ill," we will simply say, "I'm entering initiation." It will make all the difference. For years we enjoy great vitality, we experiment and everything is fine. Suddenly, without knowing why, some people are plunged into their unconscious memories. They find themselves on the threshold of revelations. Fibromyalgia is the person's reaction to this sudden plunge into the unconsciousness. The person feels terribly misunderstood because, on the outside, he appears to be like everyone else. Nothing has changed except the fact that an event such as bereavement, termination of employment or a separation often precedes the diagnosis. Such an event only serves as a trigger. Specialists attribute the cause of fibromyalgia to an insufficient secretion of the neurotransmitters responsible for the modulation of pain. In other words, the hypothalamus would no longer be doing its work.

The Traditional Study of Angels provides the person suffering from this condition with an explanation and a method. An extraordinary goal reveals itself: that of retracing our Celestial Origin and regaining our purity of consciousness and Love in its purest state. One day, nothing bothers us and we live in compassion because we understand other people's suffering. We have been through it ourselves. At that moment, the physical suffering linked to fibromyalgia disappears. This also applies to chronic fatigue, burnouts, premenstrual and menopausal problems. This is a great message of hope. Over the years to come, a great opening of the unconsciousness of a large part of society will occur. Many will experience what has been described this evening. Man has a program and when the time comes for him to visit his unconsciousness, he has no choice. He cannot even do his former compensatory activities any more because he does not have the strength.

Chronic fatigue exists for the very reason that it brings the person totally back to himself. On the outside, everything is blocked. However, even if the body is virtually paralyzed, the spirit can continue to travel. Thus, with this great opening of his unconsciousness, it is easier for the person to visit old memories imprinted with poverty, violence and all sorts of other distortions. He is then submitted to great tension. This is why he feels so shaken and destructured. It is also why his body becomes practically dysfunctional.

Here is a real-life case that provides a good illustration of this situation. A woman who had been diagnosed as having fibromyalgia wanted to get better. She wanted to know which Angel to work with for this purpose. She received the following dream: *She was at the hospital to meet a surgeon she had made an appointment with and who was to operate on her stomach. She was in the waiting room with the number 19 in her hand. When her number was announced, she didn't hear it and she missed her turn. Another woman took her place.*

After a while, she realized what had happened and she went to speak to the nurses. They only listened to her with half an ear. They weren't paying attention. She insisted, "Yes, but I took the day off today. I have to go back to work tomorrow. If I don't, what will my boss say?" The nurses simply told her, "The surgeon is not available."

What did They want to tell this lady? All of the characters in the dream represent parts of her. She was being shown how she could improve the way she was healing herself. Since she was going for a stomach operation, a transformation at the emotional level was being announced. She had number 19 in her hands. Angel number 19 LEUVIAH leads us to visit our previous lives. This Angel is the specialist of past lives. Therefore, They wanted to tell her, "Your problem is actually related to memories of past lives. You must cleanse these memories."

In the hospital waiting room, either she was not listening when her number was called out, or it was simply skipped. A lack of attention or forgetting something is never insignificant. They wanted to show this woman that, within herself, she had unconscious forces that prevented her from doing what was necessary to get better because her entire being knew that if she started the process of healing, it would not be easy. Consequently some parts were holding back.

The female nurses (symbols of the inner world) were not paying attention. Therefore, they represent parts of her that do not devote all of the necessary energy to getting better. The fact that the surgeon was not available means that this lady is not yet ready to actively go to the heart of the problem which, as we have seen, is linked to memories of past lives, that is, karma to be paid and purification that needs to be carried out. This is what constitutes an initiatory path. Since she said, "I have to go back to work tomorrow. If I don't, what will my boss say?" we can see that she granted more importance to her job than to her healing.

This dream shows that she should act. How? By taking more time for herself to meditate on what she has repressed and on certain emotional shocks she has had. This should be done while repeating the four Laws I spoke to you about and doing her Angel Recitation. This descent into her unconsciousness will allow her to transcend her memories and rediscover her true nature, which is the very meaning of life on Earth.

I'd like to end with the interpretation of a dream wherein They revealed to a young woman that she was about to enter initiation. This lovely young woman, attending a lecture for the first time, came up to talk to me at the end. With shining eyes, she said, "While listening to the lecture, I understood a dream that I had four years ago, when I was 19 years old. *I found myself in a kitchen and my brother, whom I trust completely, was perched high up on a stepladder. He was cleaning out the pantry. At one particular moment, he handed me an enormous Bible. When I opened it, I saw demons come out. There were so many of them. They didn't stop emerging. Ah! I was so afraid! I ran out. Then I found myself in my bed and I saw the image of a friend that I also trust. She told me, 'Pray. Ask for help. It begins with M.' I said to myself, 'M. M for Mamaca.'* Then I woke up."

I asked her, "May I ask what Mamaca means to you?" "Ah!" she replied. "It's the name of a blues-rock singer that I used to listen to four years ago but that I don't listen to anymore. Lately, I went into a chapel and I saw a painting entitled *Mikaël, the Archangel, He who overcomes demons* and I understood that the letter *M* in my dream was for Mikaël. Shortly afterwards, I saw the name *Universe/City Mikaël* on your poster. I came and, indeed, you spoke on this subject.

That evening we had talked about the Apocalypse, which means revelation, and of the understanding of good and evil. Through this dream, this young woman was being shown that she was going to experience an opening of her unconsciousness which would give her access to the Knowledge of good and evil. This path is the path of all the great Sages including Abraham, Moses, Jesus and several others whose names have been forgotten throughout History. They all went through it. They transcended the evil of humanity and acquired mastery. They were able to receive the Divine Revelations, that is, the Hidden Secrets.

LIST OF SITUATIONS AND COMMON PROBLEMS
AND THE ANGELS TO INVOKE

A

Abandonment, Feeling of	9 HAZIEL, 56 POYEL
Abundance	30 OMAEL, 43 VEULIAH, 48 MIHAEL
Accidents	28 SEHEIAH, 42 MIKAEL
Accompanying the dying	70 JABAMIAH, 72 MUMIAH
Accusations	11 LAUVIAH, 32 VASARIAH, 18 CALIEL
Acne	30 OMAEL, 66 MANAKEL, 68 HABUHIAH
Adultery	13 IEZALEL, 16 HEKAMIAH
Advertising	59 HARAHEL
Affinity, friendship	61 UMABEL
Aggression	33 YEHUIAH, 44 YELAHIAH, 71 HAIAIEL
Agoraphobia	12 HAHAIAH
Agriculture	8 CAHETEL, 30 OMAEL, 31 LECABEL
Alcoholism	15 HARIEL, 33 YEHUIAH, 40 IEIAZEL
Altruism	9 HAZIEL, 11 LAUVIAH, 14 MEBAHEL, 65 DAMABIAH
Ambassador	16 HEKAMIAH, 26 HAAIAH, 42 MIKAEL
Amnesia	19 LEUVIAH
Anxiety, anguish	12 HAHAIAH, 17 LAUVIAH
Architecture	3 SITAEL
Arthritis	66 MANAKEL, 68 HABUHIAH
Astrology	61 UMABEL, 51 HAHASIAH
Audacity	1 VEHUIAH, 44 YELAHIAH, 71 HAIAIEL
Authoritarianism	33 YEHUIAH, 34 LEHAHIAH, 39 REHAEL
Awakening	45 SEALIAH

B

Back	1 VEHUIAH, 3 SITAEL, 19 LEUVIAH, 45 SEALIAH
Bacteria	30 OMAEL, 68 HABUHIAH
Beatitude, bliss	49 VEHUEL, 54 NITHAEL
Beauty	6 LELAHEL, 54 NITHAEL
Beginning, help to begin	1 VEHUIAH, 19 LEUVIAH, 45 SEALIAH
Betrayal	4 ELEMIAH, 13 IEZALEL, 16 HEKAMIAH
Birth	30 OMAEL
Birth, giving birth	8 CAHETEL, 30 OMAEL, 72 MUMIAH
Bleeding	65 DAMABIAH, 23 MELAHEL, 68 HABUHIAH

Fatigue	64 MEHIEL, 72 MUMIAH
Fear	12 HAHAIAH
Feet	1 VEHUIAH, 27 YERATHEL
Femininity	9 HAZIEL, 48 MIHAEL, 54 NITHAEL
Fertility	30 OMAEL, 48 MIHAEL
Fever	23 MELAHEL, 45 SEALIAH, 68 HABUHIAH
Fidelity	13 IEZALEL, 16 HEKAMIAH, 35 CHAVAKHIAH
Floods	8 CAHETEL, 65 DAMABIAH
Force and strength	44 YELAHIAH, 52 IMAMIAH, 71 HAIAIEL
Forgetfulness	19 LEUVIAH, 69 ROCHEL
Forgiveness	9 HAZIEL, 10 ALADIAH
Frankness	16 HEKAMIAH, 18 CALIEL
Fraternizing	61 UMABEL
Freedom	27 YERATHEL, 29 REIYEL
Friendship	61 UMABEL

G

Gardening	23 MELAHEL, 30 OMAEL, 68 HABUHIAH
Generosity	56 POYEL, 22 YEIAYEL
Gentleness	56 POYEL
Germs	30 OMAEL, 68 HABUHIAH
Goodness	9 HAZIEL, 56 POYEL, 65 DAMABIAH
Grace	10 ALADIAH
Guilt, Feelings of	32 VASARIAH
Gums	68 HABUHIAH
Gynecology	30 OMAEL

H

Hemorrhage	65 DAMABIAH
Hemorrhoids	68 HABUHIAH
Hallucinations	12 HAHAIAH, 17 LAUVIAH
Hands	3 SITAEL, 63 ANAUEL
Healing	6 LELAHEL, 10 ALADIAH, 23 MELAHEL, 68 HABUHIAH
Heart	45 SEALIAH
Hernias	33 YEHUIAH, 39 REHAEL, 45 SEALIAH
Herpes	20 PAHALIAH, 30 OMAEL, 68 HABUHIAH
Hips	3 SITAEL, 28 SEHEIAH
Homeland, Return to one's	24 HAHEUIAH, 35 CHAVAKHIAH, 36 MENADEL, 69 ROCHEL

Homeopathy	23 MELAHEL
Honesty	18 CALIEL, 32 VASARIAH
House/Home, Blessing of	8 CAHETEL, 12 HAHAIAH, 25 NITH-HAIAH
Humility	56 POYEL, 65 DAMABIAH
Humor	56 POYEL
Hurricanes	8 CAHETEL, 45 SEALIAH

I

Ignorance	21 NELKHAEL, 62 IAHHEL
Illnesses (in general)	23 MELAHEL, 51 HAHASIAH, 68 HABUHIAH
Illusions	12 HAHAIAH, 17 LAUVIAH, 25 NITH-HAIAH
Impatience	7 ACHAIAH
Impotence	20 PAHALIAH, 33 YEHUIAH, 48 MIHAEL
Improvisation	50 DANIEL, 64 MEHIEL
Indiscretion	26 HAAIAH
Infection	23 MELAHEL, 68 HABUHIAH
Inflammation	23 MELAHEL, 68 HABUHIAH
Inheritance	35 CHAVAKHIAH, 69 ROCHEL
Insomnia	12 HAHAIAH, 17 LAUVIAH
Instruction	21 NELKHAEL, 42 MIKAEL, 62 IAHHEL
Intelligence	19 LEUVIAH, 31 LECABEL, 58 YEIALEL, 59 HARAHEL
Intestines	15 HARIEL, 70 JABAMIAH, 72 MUMIAH
Intoxication	23 MELAHEL
Inventions	31 LECABEL, 63 ANAUEL

J

Jealousy	11 LAUVIAH, 13 IEZALEL, 16 HEKAMIAH, 48 MIHAEL
Joy	11 LAUVIAH
Judgment	18 CALIEL, 32 VASARIAH
Jurors, juries	18 CALIEL, 32 VASARIAH
Justice	18 CALIEL, 32 VASARIAH

K

Karma, Helps solve	10 ALADIAH, 44 YELAHIAH, 52 IMAMIAH
Kidney stones	15 HARIEL, 68 HABUHIAH, 70 JABAMIAH
Kidneys	15 HARIEL
Kindness	9 HAZIEL, 56 POYEL, 65 DAMABIAH
Knees	39 REHAEL

Knowledge   21 NELKHAEL, 62 IAHHEL

L
**Languages, Learning and
speaking**   5 MAHASIAH
Laughter   56 POYEL
Laws, Respect of   18 CALIEL, 20 PAHALIAH, 32 VASARIAH,
                                 42 MIKAEL

Laziness   1 VEHUIAH, 45 SEALIAH
Learning   21 NELKHAEL
Legs   1 VEHUIAH, 27 YERATHEL
Liberation   29 REIYEL
Liberty   27 YERATHEL, 29 REIYEL
Light   6 LELAHEL, 27 YERATHEL
Lightning   11 LAUVIAH, 28 SEHEIAH
Links   26 HAAIAH, 35 CHAVAKHIAH
Links, Reinforcing   26 HAAIAH, 35 CHAVAKHIAH, 61 UMABEL
Litigation   18 CALIEL, 32 VASARIAH
Liver   70 JABAMIAH
Longevity   28 SEHEIAH
Loyalty   13 IEZALEL, 16 HEKAMIAH, 35 CHAVAKHIAH
Lucidity   55 MEBAHIAH, 57 NEMAMIAH, 58 YEIALEL
Lumbar vertebrae   3 SITAEL, 20 PAHALIAH
Lust   20 PAHALIAH, 43 VEULIAH, 62 IAHHEL
Lymphatic drainage   15 HARIEL, 23 MELAHEL, 65 DAMABIAH

M
Magic   25 NITH-HAIAH, 38 HAAMIAH
Magnanimity   22 YEIAYEL, 32 VASARIAH, 63 ANAUEL
Malevolence   9 HAZIEL, 66 MANAKEL
Marriage   2 JELIEL, 48 MIHAEL, 62 IAHHEL
Martyrs   41 HAHAHEL
Materialization   8 CAHETEL, 30 OMAEL
Mediation   2 JELIEL
Medicine   51 HAHASIAH
Memory   19 LEUVIAH, 32 VASARIAH
Memory, Lapses of   19 LEUVIAH, 69 ROCHEL
Meningitis   60 MITZRAEL
Menstruation   15 HARIEL, 65 DAMABIAH
Mercy   9 HAZIEL

Mind, mental problems	58 YEIALEL, 59 HARAHEL, 60 MITZRAEL
Mission, Sense of	41 HAHAHEL
Modesty	32 VASARIAH, 56 POYEL
Mother	9 HAZIEL, 61 UMABEL, 70 JABAMIAH
Mouth	50 DANIEL
Mucous membranes	68 HABUHIAH
Multiplication	30 OMAEL
Muscles	45 SEALIAH
Music	40 IEIAZEL, 50 DANIEL, 59 HARAHEL
Mystical experiences	55 MEBAHIAH

N

Nape of the neck	68 HABUHIAH
Negotiating	26 HAAIAH, 63 ANAUEL
Nervousness, nervous tension, excitability	1 VEHUIAH, 60 MITZRAEL
Nutrition	23 MELAHEL

O

Obedience	34 LEHAHIAH
Obesity	10 ALADIAH, 68 HABUHIAH
Objects (lost)	69 ROCHEL
Obscurity	6 LELAHEL, 25 NITH-HAIAH
Omniscience	21 NELKHAEL
Operations (surgical)	51 HAHASIAH
Optimism	11 LAUVIAH, 45 SEALIAH, 56 POYEL
Orator	50 DANIEL, 53 NANAEL, 56 POYEL
Order	20 PAHALIAH, 34 LEHAHIAH, 42 MIKAEL
Organization	31 LECABEL, 42 MIKAEL, 63 ANAUEL

P

Paralysis	28 SEHEIAH
Parasite	23 MELAHEL, 30 OMAEL, 68 HABUHIAH
Pardon	9 HAZIEL, 10 ALADIAH
Parents	26 HAAIAH, 35 CHAVAKHIAH
Patience	7 ACHAIAH
Peace	28 SEHEIAH, 63 ANAUEL, 66 MANAKEL
Perspicacity	47 ASALIAH
Pessimism	1 VEHUIAH, 17 LAUVIAH, 45 SEALIAH

Phobia	12 HAHAIAH
Plants	23 MELAHEL, 30 OMAEL
Poisoning	23 MELAHEL
Politics	26 HAAIAH, 42 MIKAEL
Pollution	8 CAHETEL, 23 MELAHEL
Possessiveness	9 HAZIEL, 48 MIHAEL
Precision	31 LECABEL
Pregnancy	8 CAHETEL, 30 OMAEL, 48 MIHAEL
Preparation (on all levels)	3 SITAEL, 38 HAAMIAH, 63 ANAUEL
Pride	11 LAUVIAH, 56 POYEL
Printing	7 ACHAIAH, 40 IEIAZEL, 64 MEHIEL
Prisoners	24 HAHEUIAH, 36 MENADEL, 52 IMAMIAH, 57 NEMAMIAH
Professions	31 LECABEL, 36 MENADEL
Programmers	7 ACHAIAH, 58 YEIALEL, 64 MEHIEL
Prosperity	43 VEULIAH, 56 POYEL
Prostate	20 PAHALIAH, 39 REHAEL
Protection	24 HAHEUIAH
Prudence	28 SEHEIAH
Psychiatry	39 REHAEL, 60 MITZRAEL
Psychology	60 MITZRAEL
Publicity	59 HARAHEL
Purity	65 DAMABIAH

Q
Quarrels	26 HAAIAH, 35 CHAVAKHIAH

R
Rancor, resentment	9 HAZIEL
Rebel	33 YEHUIAH, 34 LEHAHIAH
Rebirth	72 MUMIAH
Reconciliation	9 HAZIEL, 35 CHAVAKHIAH
Recording	7 ACHAIAH, 64 MEHIEL
Rectify	5 MAHASIAH, 60 MITZRAEL
Refuge, Finding	12 HAHAIAH, 25 NITH-HAIAH
Reincarnation	19 LEUVIAH, 52 IMAMIAH, 72 MUMIAH
Reparation	4 ELEMIAH, 60 MITZRAEL
Restitution	69 ROCHEL
Return to one's homeland	35 CHAVAKHIAH, 36 MENADEL, 69 ROCHEL
Rheumatism	3 SITAEL

Riches (on all levels)	43 VEULIAH, 56 POYEL
Rituals, Sense of	38 HAAMIAH

S

Sadness	17 LAUVIAH
Scenario	64 MEHIEL
Schizophrenia	60 MITZRAEL
Sciatica	27 YERATHEL, 28 SEHEIAH
Sexuality	2 JELIEL, 20 PAHALIAH, 48 MIHAEL, 62 IAHHEL
Shipwreck	65 DAMABIAH
Short-sightedness	58 YEIALEL
Shyness	56 POYEL
Singing	40 IEIAZEL, 50 DANIEL, 53 NANAEL
Sinusitis	58 YEIALEL, 60 MITZRAEL, 68 HABUHIAH
Skin	23 MELAHEL, 65 DAMABIAH, 68 HABUHIAH
Slavery	22 YEIAYEL, 33 YEHUIAH, 39 REHAEL, 36 MENADEL
Sleep	12 HAHAIAH, 17 LAUVIAH
Spitefulness	9 HAZIEL, 66 MANAKEL
Spleen	23 MELAHEL, 68 HABUHIAH
Sprain	1 VEHUIAH, 3 SITAEL, 23 MELAHEL, 45 SEALIAH
Stability	66 MANAKEL
Stimulation	45 SEALIAH
Stomach	70 JABAMIAH
Strength	44 YELAHIAH, 52 IMAMIAH, 71 HAIAIEL
Stuttering	50 DANIEL, 56 POYEL
Succession	35 CHAVAKHIAH, 69 ROCHEL
Suicides	72 MUMIAH
Support	40 IEIAZEL, 56 POYEL
Surgery	51 HAHASIAH

T

Talents	31 LECABEL
Teaching	21 NELKHAEL, 42 MIKAEL, 47 ASALIAH
Teeth	3 SITAEL
Television	7 ACHAIAH, 59 HARAHEL, 64 MEHIEL
Temptations	10 ALADIAH, 66 MANAKEL
Tenacity	1 VEHUIAH, 45 SEALIAH
Throat	50 DANIEL

TABLE OF CONTENTS

Acknowledgements
We would like to thank all the volunteers who have helped us and who participate in spreading the teachings of The Traditional Study of Angels around the world.

To reach us:
Universe/City Mikaël gives conferences on The Traditional Study of Angels, workshops on dream interpretation, Angelica yoga classes and summer camps. People·interested in organizing activities in their areas or in joining the team of volunteers is invited to contact us at:

uɴiveɾse/ciᴛʏ Mikɑël
Non-profit organization
Publishing House
51-53, Saint-Antoine Street
Sainte-Agathe-des-Monts, QC
Canada J8C 2C4

Administrator: Jean Morissette, Lawyer

Telephone: 514-351-7272
Business and Administration: 819-321-0072
Fax: 819-351-5272
Email: publishing@ucm.ca
Website: www.ucm.ca

Universe/City Mikaël is a non-profit organization with no affiliation to a religious group or movement. Its teachings are universal and are open to all.

universe/city mikaël (ucm) publishing
www.ucm.ca

SOON AVAILABLE WITH UCM PUBLISHING:

THE BOOK OF ANGELS
Dreams – Signs – Meditation
The Healing of Memories
Kaya and Christiane Muller
ISBN: 978-2-923097-59-6

HOW TO READ SIGNS
Initiatic Psychology
Kaya and Christiane Muller
ISBN: 978-2-923097-61-9

THE 72 ANGEL CARDS
Dreams – Signs – Meditation
Kaya and Christiane Muller
ISBN: 978-2-923097-60-2

DREAMS AND SYMBOLS
The Materialization of Life
Kaya
ISBN: 978-2-923097-57-2

DREAMS AND SYMBOLS
Secrets and Revelations
Kaya
ISBN: 978-2-923097-62-6

ANGELICA YOGA
Introduction
Kaya and Christiane Muller
ISBN: 978-2-923097-63-3

ANGELICA YOGA
Volume 1
Dr. François Bouchard and Denise Fredette
ISBN: 978-2-923097-64-0

ANGELICA YOGA
Volume 2
Dr. François Bouchard and Denise Fredette
ISBN: 978-2-923097-58-9

THE SPIRITUAL JOURNAL
OF A NINE-YEAR-OLD CHILD
True Stories
Kasara
ISBN: 978-2-923097-66-4

IN THE COUNTRY OF THE BLUE SKY
by Gabriell, Kaya and Christiane Muller
ISBN: 978-2-923097-65-7

ANGELICA MEDITATION (Vol. 1 to 12)
Christiane Muller

CD Vol. 1	(Angels 72 to 67)	ISBN: 978-2-923097-68-8
CD Vol. 2	(Angels 66 to 61)	ISBN: 978-2-923097-69-5
CD Vol. 3	(Angels 60 to 55)	ISBN: 978-2-923097-70-1
CD Vol. 4	(Angels 54 to 49)	ISBN: 978-2-923097-71-8
CD Vol. 5	(Angels 48 to 43)	ISBN: 978-2-923097-72-5
CD Vol. 6	(Angels 42 to 37)	ISBN: 978-2-923097-73-2
CD Vol. 7	(Angels 36 to 31)	ISBN: 978-2-923097-74-9
CD Vol. 8	(Angels 30 to 25)	ISBN: 978-2-923097-75-6
CD Vol. 9	(Angels 24 to 19)	ISBN: 978-2-923097-76-3
CD Vol. 10	(Angels 18 to 13)	ISBN: 978-2-923097-77-0
CD Vol. 11	(Angels 12 to 7)	ISBN: 978-2-923097-78-7
CD Vol. 12	(Angels 6 to 1)	ISBN: 978-2-923097-79-4

ANGELICA MUSICA (Vol. 1 to 12)
Instrumental Music by André Leclair and Kaya

CD Vol. 1	(Angels 72 to 67)	ISBN: 978-2-923097-80-0
CD Vol. 2	(Angels 66 to 61)	ISBN: 978-2-923097-81-7
CD Vol. 3	(Angels 60 to 55)	ISBN: 978-2-923097-82-4
CD Vol. 4	(Angels 54 to 49)	ISBN: 978-2-923097-83-1
CD Vol. 5	(Angels 48 to 43)	ISBN: 978-2-923097-84-8
CD Vol. 6	(Angels 42 to 37)	ISBN: 978-2-923097-85-5
CD Vol. 7	(Angels 36 to 31)	ISBN: 978-2-923097-86-2
CD Vol. 8	(Angels 30 to 25)	ISBN: 978-2-923097-87-9
CD Vol. 9	(Angels 24 to 19)	ISBN: 978-2-923097-88-6
CD Vol. 10	(Angels 18 to 13)	ISBN: 978-2-923097-89-3
CD Vol. 11	(Angels 12 to 7)	ISBN: 978-2-923097-90-9
CD Vol. 12	(Angels 6 to 1)	ISBN: 978-2-923097-91-6

Notes

_____

_____

_____

_____

_____

_____

_____

_____

_____

_____

_____

_____

_____

_____

_____

_____

_____

_____

_____

_____